About the Cover Image

***Literacy*, by Diego Rivera, Fresco Detail, ca. 1928** This painting from the mid-1920s by the famous Mexican artist Diego Rivera depicts the distribution of books to children, women, and workers as one of the major achievements of the Mexican Revolution (1910–1920). It is part of a large collection of Rivera's murals in Mexico City, which celebrate all things Mexican and especially the revolution. In the aftermath of Mexico's revolution, literacy grew from just 15 percent in 1910 to 37 percent in 1940 and to over 90 percent by 2000. In this respect, the Mexican Revolution resembled other major upheavals of the twentieth century, including the Russian, Chinese, Cuban, and Vietnamese revolutions, all of which emphasized literacy and education as a means of overcoming what they saw as the cultural backwardness and inequalities of the past. Mexico's history also paralleled global patterns in which literacy rates rose dramatically, reaching 85 percent in 2014. *Literacy*, by Diego Rivera (1886–1957), detail from the Ministry of Education frescoes (1923–1928), Mexico City, Mexico, 20th century/ De Agostini Picture Library/M. Seemuller/Bridgeman Images. © 2018 Banco de México Diego Rivera Frida Kahlo Museums Trust, Mexico, D.F./Artists Rights Society (ARS), New York

THE CONTEMPORARY WORLD

In addition, whenever an instructor assigns the **LaunchPad e-book** (which can be bundled for free with the print book), students have at their disposal all the resources of the comprehensive print text (*Ways of the World: A Brief Global History with Sources*), including its special features and its primary and secondary sources. But they also gain access to **LearningCurve**, an online adaptive learning tool that helps students actively rehearse what they have read and foster a deeper understanding and retention of the material. With this adaptive quizzing, students accumulate points toward a target score as they go, giving the interaction a game-like feel. Feedback for incorrect responses explains why the answer is incorrect and directs students back to the text to review before they attempt to answer the question again. The end result is a better understanding of the key elements of the text. Instructors who actively assign LearningCurve report that their students come to class prepared for discussion and their students enjoy using it. In addition, LearningCurve's reporting feature allows instructors to quickly diagnose which concepts students are struggling with so they can adjust lectures and activities accordingly.

Further opportunities for active learning are available with the special online activities accompanying *Thinking through Sources for Ways of the World* in LaunchPad. When required by instructors, the wrap-around pedagogy that accompanies the sources virtually ensures active learning. LaunchPad is thus a rich asset for instructors who want to support students in all settings, from traditional lectures to "flipped" classrooms.

For instructors who need a mobile and accessible option for delivering adaptive quizzing with the narrative alone, Macmillan's new **Achieve Read & Practice** e-book platform offers an exceptionally easy-to-use and affordable option. This simple product pairs the Value Edition with the power of LearningCurve's quizzing, all in a format that is mobile-friendly, allowing students to complete their assignments on the bus or in the library.

Another aspect of the book important for the promotion of active learning involves the stimulation of curiosity. A **contemporary vignette** opens each chapter with a story that links the past and the present to show the continuing resonance of history in the lives of contemporary people. Chapter 6, for example, begins by describing the inauguration in 2010 of Bolivian president Evo Morales at an impressive ceremony at Tiwanaku, the center of an ancient Andean empire, thus emphasizing the continuing cultural significance of this ancient civilization in contemporary Bolivian culture. At the end of each chapter, a short **Reflections** section raises provocative, sometimes quasi-philosophical, questions about the craft of the historian and the unfolding of the human story. We believe that these brief essays can motivate our students' curiosity, stimulate their own pondering, and provide grist for the mill of vigorous class discussions.

A further technique for encouraging active learning lies in the provision of frequent contextual markers. Student readers need to know where they are going and where they have been. Thus Part-opening **Big Picture essays** preview what follows in the subsequent chapters, while a **chapter outline** suggests what is coming in each chapter. **Snapshot boxes** present succinct glimpses of particular themes, regions, or time periods, adding some trees to the forest of world history. A **list of terms** at the end of each chapter invites students to check their grasp of the material. As usual with books published by Bedford/St. Martin's, a **rich map program** provides striking visual markers that enhance the narrative.

What Else Is New in the Fourth Edition?

In this new edition, *Ways of the World* continues to change, most notably in a **revision of Part 6**, which deals with the past century. Previously the several chapters of that Part were organized regionally and in terms deriving from the cold war: the Western capitalist world, the communist world, and the third world of developing countries. But with the cold war now more than a quarter of a century in the past, it seemed appropriate to reorganize our treatment of the past century in more global terms. We have done so by distinguishing between major events or milestones and longer-term historical processes. Thus the first two chapters of Part 6, Chapters 20 and 21, focus on milestone events such as the world wars, revolutions, the cold war, decolonization, the demise of communism, and much more. With these "milestones" of the past century in mind, Chapters 22 and 23 turn to the larger and perhaps even more consequential processes occurring beneath the surface of major public events. Chapter 22 treats the enormous acceleration of technological innovation as a decisive driver of a deeply interconnected world economy and of pervasive social change. Chapter 23 then turns the spotlight on the explosive growth of human numbers, on the movement of many people to cities and to new lives abroad, and on the cultural transformations that accompanied modern life during the past century. The chapter—and the book—conclude by examining the enormous and continuing impact of human activity on the entire biosphere, which represents by far the most significant long-term process of this new era and the most critical challenge of the next century.

Another new element in this fourth edition is a section titled **Controversies,** intended to highlight the debates that accompany so many historical inquiries. These Controversies, which appear in one chapter of each Part of the book, explore debates about key historical issues: when history begins; the origins of major religious traditions; the nature of empires; the idea of the Atlantic world; why the Industrial Revolution began in Europe; and the concept of globalization. We believe these brief essays will counteract any remaining notion of a textbook as an authoritative, encyclopedia-like tome to be assimilated, while conveying an understanding of World History as a frequently contested conversation.

Promoting Active Learning

As all instructors know, students can often "do the assignment" or read the required chapter and yet have little understanding of it when they come to class. The problem, frequently, is passive studying—a quick once-over, perhaps some highlighting of the text—but little sustained involvement with the material. A central pedagogical problem in all teaching is how to encourage more active, engaged styles of learning. We want to enable students to manipulate the information of the book, using its ideas and data to answer questions, to make comparisons, to draw conclusions, to criticize assumptions, and to infer implications that are not explicitly disclosed in the text itself.

Ways of the World seeks to promote active learning in various ways. Most obviously, the primary and secondary sources in the companion reader *Thinking through Sources for Ways of the World* (also available on LaunchPad) invite students to engage actively with documents and images alike, assisted by abundant questions to guide that engagement.

time, some of their essential features — cities, states, patriarchy, and class inequality, for example — have long endured.

A third "C" involves frequent **comparison**, bringing several regions or cultures into our field of vision at the same time. It means constantly asking "what's the difference?" Thus this book makes comparisons between the Agricultural Revolution in the Eastern and Western hemispheres; between the beginnings of Buddhism and the early history of Christianity and Islam; between the Russian and Chinese revolutions; and between feminism in the Global North and the Global South. These and many more comparisons frequently punctuate our account of the global past.

The final "C" emphasizes **connections**, networks of communication and exchange that increasingly shaped the character of the societies that participated in them. In our account of the human story, world history is less about what happened within particular civilizations or cultures than about the processes and outcomes of their meetings with one another. Cross-cultural encounters then become one of the major motors of historical transformation. Examples include the clash of the ancient Greeks and the Persians; the long-distance commercial networks that linked the Afro-Eurasian world; the numerous cross-cultural interactions spawned by the spread of Islam; the trans-hemispheric Columbian exchange of the early modern era; and the more recent growth of a thoroughly entangled global economy.

These emphases have remained at the heart of *Ways of the World* since its initial publication in 2008. But the book has also changed, grown, and matured. Originally a brief account of the global past by a single author, Robert Strayer, it has acquired a fine co-author in Eric Nelson from Missouri State University.

Further changes in the book have derived from new scholarship in the rapidly expanding field of World History. Thus we have increasingly integrated issues of gender, the environment, and technology into this account of the human journey. Coverage of particular areas of the world, such as Southeast Asia, Latin America, and Pacific Oceania, has likewise been strengthened. This fourth edition in particular has completely reimagined our treatment of the past century in a more global fashion, moving beyond the cold war framework of earlier editions. And over time the book has more often highlighted individual people and particular events, which sometimes get lost in the broad sweep of world history. Finally, *Ways of the World* has acquired a very substantial electronic and online presence with an impressive array of innovative pedagogical and learning aids.

These changes remind us that textbooks are not fixed and finished compilations of what happened in the past. Rather, such books develop as they respond to new technologies, to new historical research, and to the evolving political, social, and economic conditions of the contemporary world. As authors, we are acutely aware of how much debate and controversy lie behind many of the issues that are explored in *Ways of the World*. This book, then, is a snapshot of our current understanding of World History, shaped by the particular time (the early twenty-first century) and place (the United States) in which it was composed. Such a book written fifty years ago, or in contemporary China, Nigeria, Iran, or Brazil, or in the mid-twenty-first century, would surely be very different. Thus *Ways of the World* can and should be criticized, assessed, and argued with, not simply accepted as a definitive account of the global past.

Preface
About *Ways of the World*

The Value Edition of *Ways of the World* is an intentionally brief global history of the human experience that focuses on the big pictures of world history, using examples selectively rather than cluttering the narrative with endless details. It repeatedly highlights issues of change, of comparison, and of connection among culturally different peoples throughout the narrative.

The main title of the book, *Ways of the World*, evokes three dimensions of its distinctive character and outlook, all of them based on our experience as teachers and scholars. The first is **diversity** or **variation**, for the "ways of the world," or the ways of being human in the world, have been many and constantly changing. This book seeks to embrace the global experience of humankind, both in its common features and in its vast diversity, while noticing the changing location of particular centers of innovation and wider influence.

Second, the title *Ways of the World* invokes major **panoramas**, **patterns**, or **pathways** in world history rather than a highly detailed narrative, which can often overwhelm students. Thus, most chapters are organized in terms of broad global or transregional themes, illustrated by a limited number of specific examples.

A third implication of the book's title lies in a certain **reflective quality** that appears in the Big Picture essays that introduce each Part, in the Reflections section at the end of each chapter, and periodically in the narrative itself. This dimension of the book offers many opportunities for pondering larger questions about how historians operate, about the dilemmas they face in reconstructing the human journey, and about the relationship of the past to the present.

These elements of *Ways of the World* find expression repeatedly in what we call the **four Cs** of world history: context, change, comparison, and connection. The first "C," **context**, refers to the larger frameworks within which particular historical figures, events, societies, and civilizations take shape. In our telling of the human past, context is central, for in world history nothing stands alone. Like Russian nesting dolls, every story finds a place in some more inclusive narrative. European empires in the Americas, for example, take on new meaning when they are understood as part of a global process of imperial expansion that included the expansion of the Inca, Russian, Chinese, and Ottoman empires at the same time.

The second "C," large-scale **change**, both within and especially across major regions of the world, represents another prominent emphasis in *Ways of the World*. Examples include the peopling of the planet, the emergence of "civilization," the linking of Eastern and Western hemispheres in the wake of Columbus's voyages, the Industrial Revolution, and many other significant changes during the course of human history. The flip side of change, of course, is continuity, implying a focus on what persists over long periods of time. And so *Ways of the World* seeks to juxtapose these contrasting elements of human experience. While civilizations have changed dramatically over

For Evelyn Rhiannon with love

FOR BEDFORD/ST. MARTIN'S

Vice President, Editorial, Macmillan Learning Humanities: Edwin Hill
Program Director for History: Michael Rosenberg
Senior Program Manager for History: William J. Lombardo
History Marketing Manager: Melissa Rodriguez
Director of Content Development, Humanities: Jane Knetzger
Senior Developmental Editor: Heidi L. Hood
Senior Content Project Manager: Christina M. Horn
Workflow Project Supervisor: Joe Ford
Production Supervisor: Robin Besofsky
Senior Media Project Manager: Michelle Camisa
Media Editor: Tess Fletcher
Editorial Assistant: Stephanie Sosa
Copy Editor: Susan Zorn
Indexer: Leoni Z. McVey
Editorial Services: Lumina Datamatics, Inc.
Composition: Lumina Datamatics, Inc.
Cartographer: Mapping Specialists, Ltd.
Photo Editor: Christine Buese
Photo Researcher: Bruce Carson
Permissions Editor: Eve Lehmann
Design Director, Content Management: Diana Blume
Text Design: Lisa Buckley
Cover Design: William Boardman
Printing and Binding: King Printing Co., Inc.
Cover Image: top, Panel, third quarter of the 15th century (silk cut & uncut voided velvet, brocaded with gold-metallic wefts), Italian School (15th century)/Museum of Fine Arts, Boston, Massachusetts, USA/Gift of Philip Lehman in memory of his wife, Carrie L. Lehman/Bridgeman Images; bottom, *Literacy*, by Diego Rivera (1886–1957), detail from the Ministry of Education frescoes (1923–1928), Mexico City. Mexico, 20th century/De Agostini Picture Library/M. Seemuller/Bridgeman Images/© 2018 Banco de México Diego Rivera Frida Kahlo Museums Trust, Mexico, D.F./Artists Rights Society (ARS), New York

Manufactured in the United States of America.
8   9   24   23   22

For information, write: Macmillan Learning Curriculum Solutions, 14903 Pilot Drive, Plymouth, MI 48170   (macmillanlearning.com)

ISBN 978-1-319-31185-8

ACKNOWLEDGMENTS

Text acknowledgments and copyrights appear at the back of the book on page 705, which constitutes an extension of the copyright page. Art acknowledgments and copyrights appear on the same page as the art selections they cover.

VALUE EDITION

Ways of the World
A Brief Global History

for North Carolina A&T State University
Fourth Edition

Volume 2: Since the Fifteenth Century

Robert W. Strayer
The College at Brockport:
State University of New York

Eric W. Nelson
Missouri State University

macmillan learning
curriculum solutions

bedford/st.martin's • hayden-mcnell • w.h.freeman • worth publishers

Ways of the World

VALUE EDITION

Teaching History in the Digital Age

Because the teaching of history is changing rapidly, we have created online interactive complements for *Ways of the World* via Macmillan's premier learning platform, **LaunchPad**, an intuitive and interactive e-book and course space. Free when packaged with the print book or available at a low price when used on its own, LaunchPad grants students and instructors access to a wealth of online tools and resources built specifically for this text to enhance reading comprehension and promote in-depth study. LaunchPad's course space and interactive e-book are ready to use "as is," or they can be edited and customized with your own material and assigned right away.

Developed with extensive feedback from history instructors and students, LaunchPad for *Ways of the World* includes the complete narrative and special features of the comprehensive edition plus the companion reader, *Thinking through Sources for Ways of the World*, and **LearningCurve**, an adaptive learning tool designed to get students to read before they come to class. With **an expanded set of source-based questions in the test bank and in LearningCurve**, instructors now have more ways to test students on their understanding of the narrative in the book as well as sources. The addition of the **new Bedford Document Collections modules in LaunchPad** means instructors have a flexible repository of discovery-oriented primary source projects to assign. This makes LaunchPad for *Ways of the World* a one-stop shop for working with sources and thinking critically in a multitude of modes.

LaunchPad also includes additional **primary source online activities** for each chapter of the *Thinking through Sources* companion reader. These activities supply a distinctive and sophisticated pedagogy of self-grading exercises that help students not only understand the sources but also think critically about them. More specifically, a short **quiz after each source** offers students the opportunity to check their understanding of materials that often derive from quite distant times and places. Some questions focus on audience, purpose, point of view, limitations, or context, while others challenge students to draw conclusions about the source or to compare one source with another. And a **Draw Conclusions from the Evidence activity** challenges students to assess whether a specific piece of evidence drawn from the sources supports or challenges a stated conclusion. Collectively these assignments create an active learning environment where reading with a purpose is reinforced by immediate feedback and support. This feedback for each rejoinder creates an active learning environment where students are rewarded for reaching the correct answer through their own process of investigation.

More broadly, in this interactive learning environment, students will enhance their ability to build arguments and to practice historical reasoning. Thus, this LaunchPad pedagogy does for skill development what LearningCurve does for content mastery and reading comprehension.

LaunchPad also provides a simple, user-friendly platform for individual instructors to add their own voice, materials, and assignments to the text, guiding their students' learning outside of the traditional classroom setting. Available with training and support, LaunchPad can help take history teaching and learning into a new era.

For instructors who need a mobile and accessible option for delivering adaptive quizzing with the narrative alone, Macmillan's new **Achieve Read & Practice** e-book platform offers an exceptionally easy-to-use and affordable option. This simple product pairs the Value Edition with the power of LearningCurve's quizzing, all in a format that students can use wherever they go. Available for the first time with this edition, Achieve Read & Practice's interactive e-book, adaptive quizzing, and gradebook are built with an intuitive interface that can be read on mobile devices and are fully accessible and available at an affordable price.

To learn more about the benefits of LearningCurve, LaunchPad, Achieve Read & Practice, and the different versions to package with these digital tools, see the Versions and Supplements section on page xvii.

"It Takes a Village"

In any enterprise of significance, "it takes a village," as they say. Bringing *Ways of the World* to life in this new edition, it seems, has occupied the energies of several villages. Among the privileges and delights of writing and revising this book has been the opportunity to interact with our fellow villagers.

We are grateful to the community of fellow historians who contributed their expertise to this revision. For this edition, they include Andreas Agocs, University of the Pacific; Tonio Andrade, Emory University; Monty Armstrong, Cerritos High School; Melanie Bailey, Piedmont Virginia Community College; Djene Bajalan, Missouri State University; Anthony Barbieri-Low, University of California, Santa Barbara; Christine Bond, Edmond Memorial High School; Mike Burns, Concordia International School, Hanoi; Elizabeth Campbell, Daemen College; Theodore Cohen, Lindenwood University; Bradley Davis, Eastern Connecticut State University; Denis Gainty, Georgia State University; Duane Galloway, Rowan-Cabarrus Community College; Jay Harmon, Houston Christian High School; Michael Hunt, University of North Carolina at Chapel Hill; Ane Lintvedt, McDonogh School; Aran MacKinnon, Georgia College and State University; Harold Marcuse, University of California, Santa Barbara; Merritt McKinney, Volunteer State Community College; Erin O'Donnell, East Stroudsburg University; Sarah Panzer, Missouri State University; Charmayne Patterson, Clark Atlanta University; Dean Pavlakis, Carroll College; Chris Peek, Bellaire High School; Tracie Provost, Middle Georgia State University; Masako Racel, Kennesaw State University; and Eddie Supratman, Arkansas State University-Beebe.

We also offer our gratitude to reviewers of earlier editions: Maria S. Arbelaez, University of Nebraska–Omaha; Veronica L. Bale, Mira Costa College; Christopher Bellitto, Kean University; Monica Bord-Lamberty, Northwood High School; Stanley Burstein, California State University–Los Angeles; Ralph Croizier, University of Victoria; Gregory Cushman, the University of Kansas; Edward Dandrow, University of Central Florida; Peter L. de Rosa, Bridgewater State University; Carter Findley, Ohio State University; Amy Forss, Metropolitan Community College; Denis Gainty, Georgia State University; Steven A. Glazer, Graceland University; Sue Gronewald, Kean University; Andrew Hamilton, Viterbo University; J. Laurence Hare, University of Arkansas; Michael Hinckley, Northern Kentucky University; Bram Hubbell, Friends Seminary; Ronald Huch, Eastern Kentucky University; Elizabeth Hyde, Kean University; Mark Lentz, University of Louisiana–Lafayette; Kate McGrath, Central Connecticut State University; C. Brid Nicholson, Kean University; Donna Patch, Westside High School; Jonathan T. Reynolds, Northern Kentucky University; James Sabathne, Hononegah High School; Christopher Sleeper, Mira Costa College; Ira Spar, Ramapo College and Metropolitan Museum of Art; Kristen Strobel, Lexington High School;

Michael Vann, Sacramento State University; Peter Winn, Tufts University; and Judith Zinsser, Miami University of Ohio.

The fine people at Bedford/St. Martin's (Macmillan Learning) have provided a second community sustaining this enterprise and the one most directly responsible for the book's fourth edition. It would be difficult for any author to imagine a more supportive and professional publishing team. Our chief point of contact with the Bedford village has been Heidi Hood, our development editor. She has coordinated the immensely complex task of assembling a new edition of the book and has done so with great professional care, with timely responses to our many queries, and with sensitivity to the needs and feelings of authors, even when she found it necessary to decline our suggestions.

Others on the team have also exhibited that lovely combination of personal kindness and professional competence that is so characteristic of the Bedford way. Editorial director Edwin Hill, program director Michael Rosenberg, and program manager William Lombardo have kept an eye on the project amid many duties. Christina Horn, our content project manager, managed the process of turning a manuscript into a published book and did so with both grace and efficiency. Editorial assistant Stephanie Sosa has efficiently and thoughtfully directed the revision of the *Thinking through Sources* companion reader and handled countless other project details. Operating behind the scenes in the Bedford village, a series of highly competent and always supportive people have shepherded this revised edition along its way. Photo researcher Bruce Carson identified and acquired the many images that grace this new edition of *Ways of the World* and did so with a keen eye and courtesy. Copy editor Susan Zorn polished the prose and sorted out our many inconsistent usages with a seasoned and perceptive eye. Melissa Rodriguez has overseen the marketing process, while Bedford's sales representatives have reintroduced the book to the academic world. Media editor Tess Fletcher supervised the development of supplements and media products to support the book, and William Boardman ably coordinated research for the lovely covers that mark *Ways of the World*. Eve Lehmann conducted the always-difficult negotiations surrounding permissions with more equanimity than we could have imagined.

A final and much smaller community sustained this project and its authors. It is that most intimate of villages that we know as a marriage. Sharing that village with me (Robert Strayer) is my wife, Suzanne Sturn. It is her work to bring ideas and people to life onstage, even as I try to do so between these covers. She knows how I feel about her love and support, and no one else needs to. And across the street, I (Eric Nelson) would also like to thank two other residents of this village: my wife, Alice Victoria, and our little girl, Evelyn Rhiannon, to whom this new edition is dedicated. Without their patience and support, I could not have become part of such an interesting journey.

To all of our fellow villagers, we offer deep thanks for an immensely rewarding experience. We are grateful beyond measure.

Robert Strayer, La Selva Beach, California
Eric Nelson, Springfield, Missouri

Versions and Supplements

Adopters of *Ways of the World* and their students have access to abundant print and digital resources and tools, the acclaimed *Bedford Series in History and Culture* volumes, and much more. The LaunchPad course space for *Ways of the World* provides access to the narrative as well as a wealth of primary sources and other features, along with assignment and assessment opportunities at the ready. Achieve Read & Practice supplies adaptive quizzing and our mobile, accessible Value Edition e-book in one easy-to-use, affordable product. See below for more information, visit the book's catalog site at **macmillanlearning.com**, or contact your local Bedford/St. Martin's sales representative.

Get the Right Version for Your Class

To accommodate different course lengths and course budgets, *Ways of the World* is available in several different versions and formats to best suit your course needs. The comprehensive *Ways of the World* includes a full-color art program and a robust set of features. Offered now for the first time, *Ways of the World*, Value Edition offers a trade-sized two-color option with the full narrative and selected art and maps at a steep discount. The Value Edition is also offered at the lowest price point in loose-leaf format, and these versions are available as e-books. To get the best values of all, package a new print book with LaunchPad or Achieve Read & Practice at no additional charge to get the best each format offers. LaunchPad users get a print version for easy portability with an interactive e-book for the full-feature text and course space, along with LearningCurve and loads of additional assignment and assessment options; Achieve Read & Practice users get a print version with a mobile, interactive Value Edition e-book plus LearningCurve adaptive quizzing in one exceptionally affordable, easy-to-use product.

- **Combined Volume** (Chapters 1–23): available in paperback, Value, loose-leaf, and e-book formats and in LaunchPad and Achieve Read & Practice
- **Volume 1: To the Fifteenth Century** (Chapters 1–12): available in paperback, Value, loose-leaf, and e-book formats and in LaunchPad and Achieve Read & Practice
- **Volume 2: Since the Fifteenth Century** (Chapters 12–23): available in paperback, Value, loose-leaf, and e-book formats and in LaunchPad and Achieve Read & Practice

As noted below, any of these volumes can be packaged with additional titles for a discount. To get ISBNs for discount packages, visit **macmillanlearning.com** or contact your Bedford/St. Martin's representative.

Assign LaunchPad—an Assessment-Ready Interactive E-book and Course Space

Available for discount purchase on its own or for packaging with new books at no additional charge, LaunchPad is a breakthrough solution for history courses. Intuitive and easy to use for students and instructors alike, LaunchPad is ready to use as is and can be edited, customized with your own material, and assigned quickly. LaunchPad for *Ways of the World* includes Bedford/St. Martin's high-quality content all in one place, including the full interactive e-book and the companion reader *Thinking through Sources for Ways of the World*, plus LearningCurve adaptive quizzing, guided reading activities designed to help students read actively for key concepts, auto-graded quizzes for each primary source, and chapter summative quizzes. Through a wealth of formative and summative assessments, including the adaptive learning program of LearningCurve (see the full description ahead), students gain confidence and get into their reading before class. Through the Bedford Document Collections for World History (see full description ahead), embedded within LaunchPad, instructors get a flexible set of primary source projects ready to assign. These features, plus additional primary source documents, video sources and tools for making video assignments, map activities, flashcards, and customizable test banks, make LaunchPad an invaluable asset for any instructor.

LaunchPad easily integrates with course management systems, and with fast ways to build assignments, rearrange chapters, and add new pages, sections, or links, it lets teachers build the courses they want to teach and hold students accountable. For more information, visit **launchpadworks.com**, or to arrange a demo, contact us at **historymktg@macmillan.com**.

Assign LearningCurve So Your Students Come to Class Prepared

Students using LaunchPad or Achieve Read & Practice receive access to LearningCurve for *Ways of the World*. Assigning LearningCurve in place of reading quizzes is easy for instructors, and the reporting features help instructors track overall class trends and spot topics that are giving students trouble so they can adjust their lectures and class activities. This online learning tool is popular with students because it was designed to help them rehearse content at their own pace in a nonthreatening, game-like environment. The feedback for wrong answers provides instructional coaching and sends students back to the book for review. Students answer as many questions as necessary to reach a target score, with repeated chances to revisit material they haven't mastered. When LearningCurve is assigned, students come to class better prepared.

▲ Achieve READ & PRACTICE Assign Achieve Read & Practice So Your Students Can Read and Study Wherever They Go

Available for discount purchase on its own or for packaging with new books at no additional charge, Achieve Read & Practice is Bedford/St. Martin's most affordable digital solution for history courses. Intuitive and easy to use for students and instructors alike, Achieve Read & Practice is ready to use as is and can be assigned quickly. Achieve Read & Practice for *Ways of the World* includes the Value Edition interactive e-book, LearningCurve formative quizzing, assignment tools, and a gradebook. All this is built with an intuitive interface that can be read on mobile devices and is fully accessible and available at a discounted price so anyone can use it. Instructors can set due dates for reading assignments and LearningCurve quizzes in just a few clicks, making it a simple and affordable way to engage students with the narrative and hold students accountable for course reading so they will come to class better prepared. For more information, visit **macmillanlearning.com/ReadandPractice**, or to arrange a demo, contact us at **historymktg@macmillan.com**.

▷ iClicker **iClicker, Active Learning Simplified**

iClicker offers simple, flexible tools to help you give students a voice and facilitate active learning in the classroom. Students can participate with the devices they already bring to class using our iClicker Reef mobile apps (which work with smartphones, tablets, or laptops) or iClicker remotes. We've now integrated iClicker with Macmillan's LaunchPad to make it easier than ever to synchronize grades and promote engagement—both in and out of class. iClicker Reef access cards can also be packaged with LaunchPad or your textbook at a significant savings for your students. To learn more, talk to your Macmillan Learning representative or visit us at **www.iclicker.com**.

Take Advantage of Instructor Resources

Bedford/St. Martin's has developed a rich array of teaching resources for this book and for this course. They range from lecture and presentation materials and assessment tools to course management options. Most can be found in LaunchPad or can be downloaded or ordered at **macmillanlearning.com**.

Bedford Coursepack for Blackboard, Canvas, Brightspace by D2L, or Moodle. We can help you integrate our rich content into your course management system. Registered instructors can download coursepacks that include our popular free resources and book-specific content for *Ways of the World*. Visit **macmillanlearning .com** to find your version or download your coursepack.

Instructor's Resource Manual. The instructor's manual offers both experienced and first-time instructors tools for presenting textbook material in engaging ways. It includes content learning objectives, annotated chapter outlines, and strategies for teaching with the textbook, plus suggestions on how to get the most out of LearningCurve and a survival guide for first-time teaching assistants.

Guide to Changing Editions. Designed to facilitate an instructor's transition from the previous edition of *Ways of the World* to this new edition, this guide presents an overview of major changes as well as of changes in each chapter.

Online Test Bank. The test bank includes a mix of fresh, carefully crafted multiple-choice, matching, short-answer, and essay questions for each chapter. Many of the multiple-choice questions feature a map, an image, or a primary source excerpt as the prompt. All questions appear in Microsoft Word format and in easy-to-use test bank software that allows instructors to add, edit, re-sequence, filter by question type or learning objective, and print questions and answers. Instructors can also export questions into a variety of course management systems.

The Bedford Lecture Kit: **Lecture Outlines, Maps, and Images.** Look good and save time with *The Bedford Lecture Kit.* These presentation materials include fully customizable multimedia presentations built around chapter outlines that are embedded with maps, figures, and images from the textbook and are supplemented by more detailed instructor notes on key points and concepts.

Print, Digital, and Custom Options for More Choice and Value

For information on free packages and discounts up to 50%, visit **macmillanlearning .com**, or contact your local Bedford/St. Martin's sales representative.

NEW *Thinking through Sources for Ways of the World,* **Fourth Edition.** Designed to accompany *Ways of the World,* each chapter of this reader contains approximately five to eight written and visual primary sources organized around a particular theme, issue, or question. Each of these projects is followed by a related **Historians' Viewpoints** secondary source feature that pairs two brief excerpts from historians who comment on some aspect of the topics covered in the primary sources. *Thinking through Sources for Ways of the World* provides a broad selection of over 140 primary source documents and images as well as editorial apparatus to help students understand the sources. This companion reader is an exceptional value for students and offers plenty of assignment options for instructors. Available free when packaged with the print text and included in the LaunchPad e-book with auto-graded quizzes for each source. In LaunchPad each chapter of the reader includes special primary source online activities—self-graded exercises that challenge students to assess whether a specific piece of evidence drawn from the sources supports or challenges a conclusion related to a guiding question. Also available on its own as a downloadable e-book.

NEW Bedford Select for History. Create the ideal textbook for your course with only the chapters you need. Starting from one of our Value Edition history texts, you can rearrange chapters, delete unnecessary chapters, select chapters of primary sources from *Thinking through Sources for Ways of the World* and add document projects from the Bedford Document Collections, or choose to improve your students' historical thinking skills with the Bedford Tutorials for History. In addition, you can add your own original content to create just the book you're looking for. With Bedford Select, students pay only for material that will be assigned in the course, and nothing more. Order your textbook every semester, or modify from one term to the next. It is easy to build your customized textbook, without compromising the quality and affordability you've come to expect from Bedford/St. Martin's.

NEW The Bedford Document Collections for World History. Found in the LaunchPad for *Ways of the World* and available to customize the print text, this collection provides a flexible repository of discovery-oriented primary source projects ready to assign. Each curated project—written by a historian about a favorite topic—poses a historical question and guides students through analysis of the sources. Examples include "The Silk Road: Travel and Trade in Pre-Modern Inner Asia," "The Spread of Christianity in the Sixteenth and Early Seventeenth Centuries," "The Singapore Mutiny of 1915: Understanding World War I from a Global Perspective," and "Living through Perestroika: The Soviet Union in Upheaval, 1985–1991." For more information, visit macmillanlearning.com.

NEW The Bedford Document Collections for World History Print Modules. Choose one or two document projects from the collection (see above) and add them in print to a Bedford/St. Martin's title, or select several to be bound together in a custom reader created specifically for your course. Either way, the modules are affordably priced. For more information, contact your Bedford/St. Martin's representative.

NEW Bedford Tutorials for History. Designed to customize textbooks with resources relevant to individual courses, this collection of brief units, each 16 pages long and loaded with examples, guides students through basic skills such as using historical evidence effectively, working with primary sources, taking effective notes, avoiding plagiarism and citing sources, and more. Up to two tutorials can be added to a Bedford/St. Martin's history survey title at no additional charge, freeing you to spend your class time focusing on content and interpretation. For more information, visit **macmillanlearning.com/historytutorials**.

The Bedford Series in History and Culture. More than 100 titles in this highly praised series combine first-rate scholarship, historical narrative, and important primary documents for undergraduate courses. Each book is brief, inexpensive, and focused on a specific topic or period. Recent titles in the series include *Apartheid in South Africa: A Brief History with Documents* by David M. Gordon; *Politics and Society in Japan's Meiji Restoration: A Brief History with Documents* by Anne Walthall and M. William Steele; and *The Congo Free State and the New Imperialism: A Brief History with Documents* by Kevin Grant. For a complete list of titles, visit **macmillanlearning.com**. Package discounts are available.

Rand McNally Atlas of World History. This collection of almost 70 full-color maps illustrates the eras and civilizations in world history from the emergence of human societies to the present. Free when packaged.

The Bedford Glossary for World History. This handy supplement for the survey course gives students historically contextualized definitions for hundreds of terms— from *abolitionism* to *Zoroastrianism*— that they will encounter in lectures, reading, and exams. Free when packaged.

Trade Books. Titles published by sister companies Hill and Wang; Farrar, Straus and Giroux; Henry Holt and Company; St. Martin's Press; Picador; and Palgrave Macmillan are available at a 50% discount when packaged with Bedford/St. Martin's textbooks. For more information, visit **macmillanlearning.com/tradeup**.

A Pocket Guide to Writing in History. Updated to reflect changes made in the 2017 *Chicago Manual of Style* revision, this portable and affordable reference tool by Mary Lynn Rampolla provides reading, writing, and research advice useful to students in all history courses. Concise yet comprehensive advice on approaching typical history assignments, developing critical reading skills, writing effective history papers, conducting research, using and documenting sources, and avoiding plagiarism—enhanced with practical tips and examples throughout—has made this slim reference a best seller. Package discounts are available.

A Student's Guide to History. This complete guide to success in any history course provides the practical help students need to be successful. In addition to introducing students to the nature of the discipline, author Jules Benjamin teaches a wide range of skills, from preparing for exams to approaching common writing assignments, and explains the research and documentation process with plentiful examples. Package discounts are available.

Brief Contents

Note: This custom edition of *Ways of the World*, Value Edition, Volume 2, Fourth Edition for North Carolina A&T State University omits Chapters 12, 13, 14, and 15, which are not covered by your instructors.

Contents

Note: This custom edition of *Ways of the World*, Value Edition, Volume 2, Fourth Edition for North Carolina A&T State University omits Chapters 12, 13, 14, and 15, which are not covered by your instructors.

CHAPTER 17

Revolutions of Industrialization, 1750–1900 483

CHAPTER 18

Colonial Encounters in Asia, Africa, and Oceania, 1750–1950 512

CHAPTER 19

Empires in Collision: Europe, the Middle East, and East Asia, 1800–1900   543

PART 6

The Long Twentieth Century, 1900–present   568

CHAPTER 20

Milestones of the Past Century: War and Revolution, 1900–1950   571

CHAPTER 21

Milestones of the Past Century: A Changing Global Landscape, 1950–present   603

CHAPTER 22

Global Processes: Technology, Economy, and Society, 1900–present   635

Maps, Figures, and Tables

Prologue
From Cosmic History to Human History

History books in general, and world history textbooks in particular, share something in common with those Russian nested dolls in which a series of carved figures fit inside one another. In much the same fashion, all historical accounts take place within some larger context, as stories within stories unfold. Individual biographies and histories of local communities, particularly modern ones, occur within the context of one nation or another. Nations often find a place in some more encompassing civilization, such as the Islamic world or the West, or in a regional or continental context such as Southeast Asia, Latin America, or Africa. And those civilizational or regional histories in turn take on richer meaning when they are understood within the even broader story of world history, which embraces humankind as a whole.

In recent decades, some world historians have begun to situate that remarkable story of the human journey in the much larger framework of both cosmic and planetary history, an approach that has come to be called "big history." It is really the "history of everything" from the big bang to the present, and it extends over the enormous, almost unimaginable timescale of some 13.8 billion years, the current rough estimate of the age of the universe.[1]

The History of the Universe

To make this vast expanse of time even remotely comprehensible, some scholars have depicted the history of the cosmos as if it were a single calendar year (see Snapshot). On that cosmic calendar, most of the action took place in the first few milliseconds of January 1. As astronomers, physicists, and chemists tell it, the universe that we know began in an eruption of inconceivable power and heat. Out of that explosion of creation emerged matter, energy, gravity, electromagnetism, and the "strong" and "weak" forces that govern the behavior of atomic nuclei. As gravity pulled the rapidly expanding cosmic gases into increasingly dense masses, stars formed, with the first ones lighting up around 1 to 2 billion years after the big bang, or the end of January to mid-February on the cosmic calendar.

Hundreds of billions of stars followed, each with its own history, though following common patterns. They emerge, flourish for a time, and then collapse and die. In their final stages, they sometimes generate supernovae, black holes, and pulsars—phenomena at least as fantastic as the most exotic of earlier creation stories. Within the stars, enormous nuclear reactions gave rise to the elements that are reflected in the periodic table known to all students of chemistry. Over eons, these stars came together in galaxies, such as our own Milky Way, which probably emerged in March or early April, and in even larger structures called groups, clusters, and superclusters. Adding to the strangeness of our picture of the cosmos is the recent and controversial notion that perhaps 90 percent or more of the total mass of the universe is invisible to us, consisting of a mysterious and mathematically predicted substance known to scholars only as "dark matter."

SNAPSHOT	THE HISTORY OF THE UNIVERSE AS A COSMIC CALENDAR	
Big bang	January 1	13.7 billion years ago
Stars and galaxies begin to form	End of January / mid-February	12 billion years ago
Milky Way galaxy forms	March / early April	10 billion years ago
Origin of the solar system	September 9	4.7 billion years ago
Formation of the earth	September 15	4.5 billion years ago
Earliest life on earth	Late September / early October	4 billion years ago
Oxygen forms on earth	December 1	1.3 billion years ago
First worms	December 16	658 million years ago
First fish, first vertebrates	December 19	534 million years ago
First reptiles, first trees	December 23	370 million years ago
Age of dinosaurs	December 24–28	66 to 240 million years ago
First human-like creatures	December 31 (late evening)	2.7 million years ago
First agriculture	December 31: 11:59:35	12,000 years ago
Birth of the Buddha / Greek civilization	December 31: 11:59:55	2,500 years ago
Birth of Jesus	December 31: 11:59:56	2,000 years ago

Adapted from Carl Sagan, *The Dragons of Eden* (New York: Random House, 1977), 13–17.

The contemplation of cosmic history has prompted profound religious or philosophical questions about the meaning of human life. For some, it has engendered a sense of great insignificance in the face of cosmic vastness. In disputing the earth- and human-centered view of the cosmos, long held by the Catholic Church, the eighteenth-century French thinker Voltaire wrote: "This little globe, nothing more than a point, rolls in space like so many other globes; we are lost in this immensity."[2] Nonetheless, human consciousness and our awareness of the mystery of this immeasurable universe render us unique and generate for many people feelings of awe, gratitude, and humility that are almost religious. As tiny but knowing observers of this majestic cosmos, we have found ourselves living in a grander home than ever we knew before.

The History of a Planet

For most of us, one star, our own sun, is far more important than all the others, despite its quite ordinary standing among the billions of stars in the universe and its somewhat remote location on the outer edge of the Milky Way galaxy. Circling that star is a series of planets, formed of leftover materials from the sun's birth. One of those planets, the third from the sun and the fifth largest, is home to all of us. Human history — our history — takes place not only on the earth but also as part of the planet's history.

That history began with the emergence of the entire solar system about two-thirds of the way through the history of the universe, some 4.7 billion years ago, or early September on the cosmic calendar. Geologists have learned a great deal about the history of the earth: the formation of its rocks and atmosphere; the movement of its continents; the collision of the tectonic plates that make up its crust; and the constant changes of its landscape as mountains formed, volcanoes erupted, and erosion transformed the surface of the planet. All of this has been happening for more than 4 billion years and continues still.

The most remarkable feature of the earth's history—and so far as we know unrepeated elsewhere—was the emergence of life from the chemical soup of the early planet. It happened rather quickly, only about 600 million years after the earth itself took shape, or late September on the cosmic calendar. Then for some 3 billion years, life remained at the level of microscopic single-celled organisms. According to biologists, the many species of larger multicelled creatures—all of the flowers, shrubs, and trees as well as all of the animals of land, sea, and air—have evolved in an explosive proliferation of life-forms over the past 600 million years, or since mid-December on the cosmic calendar. The history of life on earth has, however, been periodically punctuated by massive die-offs, at least five of them, in which very large numbers of animal or plant species have perished. The most widespread of these "extinction events," known to scholars as the Permian mass extinction, occurred around 250 million years ago and eliminated some 96 percent of living species on the planet. That catastrophic diminution of life-forms on the earth has been associated with massive volcanic eruptions, the release of huge quantities of carbon dioxide and methane into the atmosphere, and a degree of global warming that came close to extinguishing all life on the planet. Much later, around 66 million years ago, another such extinction event decimated about 75 percent of plant and animal species, including what was left of the dinosaurs. Most scientists now believe that it was caused primarily by the impact of a huge asteroid that landed near the Yucatán Peninsula off the coast of southern Mexico, generating enormous earthquakes, tsunamis, fireballs, and a cloud of toxic dust and debris. Many scholars believe we are currently in the midst of a sixth extinction event, driven, like the others, by major climate change, but which, unlike the others, is the product of human actions.

So life on earth has been and remains both fragile and resilient. Within these conditions, every species has had a history as its members struggled to find resources, cope with changing environments, and deal with competitors. Egocentric creatures that we are, however, human beings have usually focused their history books and history courses entirely on a single species—our own, *Homo sapiens*, humankind. On the cosmic calendar, *Homo sapiens* is an upstart primate whose entire history occurred in the last few minutes of December 31. Almost all of what we normally study in history courses—agriculture, writing, civilizations, empires, industrialization—took place in the very last minute of that cosmic year. The entire history of the United States occurred in the last second.

Yet during that very brief time, humankind has had a career more remarkable and arguably more consequential for the planet than any other species. At the heart of human uniqueness lies our amazing capacity for accumulating knowledge and skills. Other animals learn, of course, but for the most part they learn the same things over and over again. Twenty-first-century chimpanzees in the wild master much the same set of skills as their ancestors did a million years ago. But the exceptional communication abilities provided by human language allow us to learn from one another, to express that learning in abstract symbols, and then to pass it on, cumulatively, to future generations. Thus we have moved from stone axes to lasers, from spears to nuclear weapons, from "talking drums" to the Internet, from grass huts to the pyramids of Egypt, the Taj Mahal of India, and the skyscrapers of modern cities.

This extraordinary ability has translated into a human impact on the earth that is unprecedented among all living species.[3] Human populations have multiplied far more extensively and have come to occupy a far greater range of environments than has any other large animal. Through our ingenious technologies, we have appropriated for ourselves, according to recent calculations, some 25 to 40 percent of the solar energy that enters the food chain. We have recently gained access to the stored solar energy of coal, gas, and oil, all of which have been many millions of years in the making, and we have the capacity to deplete these resources in a few hundred or a few thousand years. Other forms of life have felt the impact of human activity, as numerous extinct or threatened species testify. Human beings have even affected the atmosphere and the oceans as carbon dioxide and other emissions of the industrial age have warmed the climate of the planet in ways that broadly resemble the conditions that triggered earlier extinction events. Thus human history has been, and remains, of great significance, not for ourselves alone, but also for the earth itself and for the many other living creatures with which we share it.

The History of the Human Species . . . in a Single Paragraph

The history of our species has occurred during roughly the last 200,000–300,000 years, conventionally divided into three major phases, based on the kind of technology that was most widely practiced. The enormously long Paleolithic age, with its gathering and hunting way of life, accounts for 95 percent or more of the time that humans have occupied the planet. People utilizing a stone-age Paleolithic technology initially settled every major landmass on the earth and constructed the first human societies. Then beginning about 12,000 years ago with the first Agricultural Revolution, the domestication of plants and animals increasingly became the primary means of sustaining human life and societies. In giving rise to agricultural villages and chiefdoms, to pastoral communities depending on their herds of animals, and to state- and city-based civilizations, this agrarian way of life changed virtually everything and fundamentally reshaped human societies and their relationship to the natural order. Finally, around 1750 a quite sudden spurt in the rate of technological change, which we know as the Industrial Revolution, began to take hold. That vast increase in productivity, wealth, and human control over nature once again transformed almost every aspect of human life and gave rise to new kinds of societies that we call "modern."

Here then, in a single paragraph, is the history of humankind—the Paleolithic era, the agricultural era, and, most recently and briefly, the modern industrial era. Clearly this is a big picture perspective, based on the notion that the human species as a whole has a history that transcends any of its particular and distinctive cultures. That perspective—known variously as planetary, global, or world history—has become increasingly prominent among those who study the past. Why should this be so?

Why World History?

Not long ago—in the mid-twentieth century, for example—virtually all college-level history courses were organized in terms of particular civilizations or nations. In the United States, courses such as Western Civilization or some version of American History served to introduce students to the study of the past. Since then, however, a set of profound changes has pushed much of the historical profession in a different direction.

The world wars of the twentieth century, revealing as they did the horrendous consequences of unchecked nationalism, persuaded some historians that a broader view of the past might contribute to a sense of global citizenship. Economic and cultural globalization has highlighted both the interdependence of the world's peoples and their very unequal positions within that world. Moreover, we are aware as never before that our problems—whether they involve economic well-being, global warming, disease, or terrorism—respect no national boundaries. To many thoughtful people, a global present seemed to call for a global past. Furthermore, as colonial empires shrank and new nations asserted themselves on the world stage, these peoples also insisted that their histories be accorded equivalent treatment with those of Europe and North America. An explosion of new knowledge about the histories of Asia, Africa, and pre-Columbian America erupted from the research of scholars around the world. All of this has generated a "world history movement," reflected in college and high school curricula, in numerous conferences and specialized studies, and in a proliferation of textbooks, of which this is one.

This world history movement has attempted to create a global understanding of the human past that highlights broad patterns cutting across particular civilizations and countries, while acknowledging in an inclusive fashion the distinctive histories of its many peoples. This is, to put it mildly, a tall order. How is it possible to encompass within a single book or course the separate stories of the world's various peoples? Surely it must be something more than just recounting the history of one civilization or culture after another. How can we distill a common history of humankind as a whole from the distinct trajectories of particular peoples? Because no world history book or course can cover everything, what criteria should we use for deciding what to include and what to leave out? Such questions have ensured no end of controversy among students, teachers, and scholars of world history, making it one of the most exciting fields of historical inquiry.

Context, Change, Comparison, and Connection: The Four Cs of World History

Despite much debate and argument, most scholars and teachers of world history would probably agree on four major emphases of this remarkable field of study. The first lies in the observation that in world history, nothing stands alone. Every event, every historical figure, every culture, society, or civilization gains significance from its inclusion in some larger framework. This means that **context** is central to world history and that contextual thinking is the essential skill that world history teaches. And so we ask the same question about every particular occurrence: where does it fit in the larger scheme of things?

A second common theme in world history involves **change** over time. Most often, it is the "big picture" changes—those that affect large segments of humankind—that are of greatest interest. How did the transition from a gathering and hunting economy to one based on agriculture take place? How did cities, empires, and civilizations take shape in various parts of the world? What impact did the growing prominence of Europe have on the rest of the world in recent centuries? A focus on change provides an antidote to a persistent tendency of human thinking that historians call "essential-ism." A more common term is "stereotyping." It refers to our inclination to define particular groups of people with an unchanging or essential set of characteristics. Women are nurturing; peasants are conservative; Americans are aggressive; Hindus are religious. Serious students of history soon become aware that every significant category of people contains endless divisions and conflicts and that those human communities are constantly in flux. Peasants may often accept the status quo, except of course when they rebel, as they frequently have. Americans have experienced periods of isolation-ism and withdrawal from the world as well as times of aggressive engagement with it. Things change.

But some things persist, even if they also change. We should not allow an emphasis on change to blind us to the continuities of human experience. A recognizably Chinese state has operated for more than 2,000 years. Slavery and patriarchy persisted as human institutions for thousands of years until they were challenged in recent centuries, and in various forms they exist still. The teachings of Buddhism, Christianity, and Islam have endured for centuries, though with endless variations and transformations.

A third element that operates constantly in world history books and courses is that of **comparison**. Whatever else it may be, world history is a comparative discipline, seeking to identify similarities and differences in the experience of the world's peoples. What is the difference between the development of agriculture in the Middle East and in Mesoamerica? Was the experience of women largely the same in all patriarchal societies? Why did the Industrial Revolution and a modern way of life evolve first in Western Europe rather than somewhere else? What distinguished the French, Russian, and Chinese revolutions from one another? Describing and, if possible, explaining such similarities and differences are among the major tasks of world history. Comparison has proven an effective tool in efforts to counteract Eurocentrism, the notion that Europeans or people of European descent have long been the primary movers and shakers of the historical process. That notion arose in recent centuries when Europeans were in fact the major source of innovation in the world and did for a time exercise something close to world domination. But comparative world history sets this recent European prominence in a global and historical context, helping us to sort out what was distinctive about the development of Europe and what similarities it bore to other major regions of the world. Puncturing the pretensions of Eurocentrism has been high on the agenda of world history.

A fourth emphasis within world history, and in this book, involves the interactions, encounters, and **connections** among different and often distant peoples. Focusing on cross-cultural connections—whether those of conflict or more peaceful exchange—represents an effort to counteract a habit of thinking about particular peoples, states, or cultures as self-contained or isolated communities. Despite the historical emergence of many separate and distinct societies, none of them developed alone. Each was embed-ded in a network of relationships with both near and more distant peoples.

Moreover, these cross-cultural connections did not begin with Columbus. The Chinese, for example, interacted continuously with the nomadic peoples on their northern border; generated technologies that diffused across all of Eurasia; transmit-ted elements of their culture to Japan, Korea, and Vietnam; and assimilated a foreign religious tradition, Buddhism, that had originated in India. Though clearly distinctive, China was not a self-contained or isolated civilization. Thus world history remains always alert to the networks, webs, and encounters in which particular civilizations or peoples were enmeshed.

Context, change, comparison, and connection — all of them operating on a global scale — represent various ways of bringing some coherence to the multiple and complex stories of world history. They will recur repeatedly in the pages that follow.

A final observation about this account of world history: *Ways of the World*, like all other world history textbooks, is radically unbalanced in terms of coverage. Chapter 1, for example, takes on some 95 percent of the human story, well over 200,000 years of our history. By contrast, the last century alone occupies four entire chapters. In fact, the six major sections of the book deal with progressively shorter time periods, in progressively greater detail. This imbalance owes much to the relative scarcity of information about earlier periods of our history. But it also reflects a certain "present mindedness," for we look to history, always, to make sense of our current needs and circumstances. And in doing so, we often assume that more recent events have a greater significance for our own lives in the here and now than those that occurred in more distant times. Whether you agree with this assumption or not, you will have occasion to ponder it as you consider the many and various "ways of the world" that have emerged in the course of the human journey and as you contemplate their relevance for your own journey.

PART 5
The European Moment in World History 1750–1900

The Big Picture

European Centrality and the Problem of Eurocentrism

During the century and a half between 1750 and 1900, sometimes referred to as the "long nineteenth century," two new and related phenomena held center stage in the global history of humankind and represent the major themes of the four chapters that follow. The first of these, explored in Chapters 16 and 17, was the creation of a new kind of human society, commonly called "modern," emerging from the intersection of the Scientific, French, and Industrial Revolutions, all of which took shape initially in Western Europe. The second theme of this long nineteenth century, which is addressed in Chapters 18 and 19, was the growing ability of these modern societies to exercise enormous power and influence over the rest of humankind through their empires, economic penetration, military intervention, diplomatic pressure, and missionary activity.

These developments marked a major turning point in world history in several ways. Western Europeans and their North American offspring now assumed a new and far more prominent role in the world than ever before. Furthermore, this "European moment" in world history established a new phase of human connectedness or entanglement that later generations labeled as "globalization." Finally, Europeans were also leading a human intervention in the natural order of unprecedented dimensions, largely the product of industrialization. Thus the long nineteenth century represents the starting point of the Anthropocene era, or the "age of man," a concept that points to the many ways in which humankind itself has become an active agent of change in the physical and biological evolution of the planet. It marks an epic transformation in the relationship of humanity to the earth, equivalent perhaps to the early stages of the Agricultural Revolution.

Europe's global centrality during the nineteenth century generated understandings of both geography and history that centered the entire human story on Europe. Thus flat maps placed Europe at the center of the world, while dividing Asia in half. Europe was granted continental status, even though it was more accurately only the western peninsula of Asia, much as India was its southern peninsula. Other regions of the world, such as the Far East or the Near (Middle) East, were defined in terms of their distance from Europe. History textbooks often portrayed people of European extraction at the center of human progress. Other peoples and civilizations, by contrast, were long believed to be static or stagnant, thus largely lacking any real history. Most Europeans assumed that these "backward" peoples and regions must either imitate the Western model or face further decline and possible extinction. Until the mid-twentieth century, such ideas went largely unchallenged in the Western world.

The rise of the academic discipline of world history in the decades following World War II represented a sharp challenge to such Eurocentric understandings of the human past. But in dealing with recent centuries, historians have confronted a distinct problem: how to avoid Eurocentrism when dealing with a phase of world history in which Europeans were in fact central.

At least five responses to this dilemma are reflected in the chapters that follow. First, the "European moment" has been recent and perhaps brief. Other peoples too had times of "cultural flowering" that granted them a period of primacy or influence—for example, the Arabs (600–1000), Chinese (1000–1500), Mongols (1200–1350), and Incas and Aztecs (fifteenth century)—but all of these were limited to particular regions of Afro-Eurasia or the Americas.[1] Even though the European moment operated on a genuinely global scale, Western peoples enjoyed their worldwide primacy for two centuries at most. The events of the late twentieth and early twenty-first centuries—the dissolution of colonial empires, the rise of India and especially China, and the assertion of Islam—suggest the end, or at least the erosion, of the age of European predominance.

Second, we need to remember that the rise of Europe occurred within an international context. It was the withdrawal of the Chinese naval fleet that allowed Europeans to enter the Indian Ocean in the sixteenth century, while Native Americans' lack of immunity to European diseases and their own divisions and conflicts greatly assisted the European takeover of the Western Hemisphere. The Industrial Revolution, explored in Chapter 17, benefited from New World resources and markets and from the stimulus of superior Asian textile and pottery production. Chapters 18 and 19 make clear that European control of other regions everywhere depended on the cooperation of local elites. Europeans, like everyone else, were embedded in a web of relationships that shaped their own histories.

A third reminder is that the rise of Europe to a position of global dominance was not an easy or automatic process. Frequently it occurred in the face of ferocious resistance and rebellion, which often required Europeans to modify their policies and practices. The so-called Indian mutiny in mid-nineteenth-century South Asia, a massive uprising against British colonial rule, did not end British control, but it substantially transformed the character of the colonial experience. Even when Europeans exercised political power, they could not do precisely as they pleased. Empire, formal and informal alike, was always in some ways a negotiated arrangement.

Fourth, peoples the world over made active use of Europeans and European ideas for their own purposes, seeking to gain advantage over local rivals or to benefit themselves in light of new conditions. During the Haitian Revolution, examined in Chapter 16, enslaved Africans made use of radical French ideas about "the rights of man" in ways that most Europeans never intended. Later in Southeast Asia, a number of highland minority groups, long oppressed by the dominant lowland Vietnamese, viewed the French invaders as liberators and assisted in their takeover of Vietnam. Recognizing that Asian and African peoples remained active agents, pursuing their own interests even in oppressive conditions, is another way of countering residual Eurocentrism.

Moreover, what was borrowed from Europe was always adapted to local circumstances. Thus Japanese or Russian industrial development did not wholly follow the pattern of England's Industrial Revolution. The Christianity that took root in the Americas or later in Africa evolved in culturally distinctive ways. Ideas of nationalism, born in Europe, were used to oppose European imperialism throughout Asia and Africa. The most interesting stories of modern world history are not simply those of European triumph or the imposition of Western ideas and practices but those of encounters, though highly unequal, among culturally different peoples.

Finally, despite Europeans' unprecedented prominence on the world stage, they were not the only game in town, nor were they the sole preoccupation of Asian, African, and Middle Eastern peoples. While China confronted Western aggression in the nineteenth century, it was also absorbing a huge population increase and experiencing massive peasant rebellions that grew out of distinctly Chinese conditions. Furthermore, cultural influence moved in many directions as European and American intellectuals began to absorb the spiritual traditions of India and as Japanese art became highly fashionable in the West.

None of this diminishes the significance of the European moment in world history, but it sets that moment in a larger context of continuing patterns of historical development and of interaction and exchange with other peoples.

16

Atlantic Revolutions, Global Echoes

1750–1900

THE HAITIAN EARTHQUAKE OF JANUARY 2010 NOT ONLY DEVASTATED an already impoverished country but also reawakened issues deriving from that country's revolution against slavery and French colonial rule, which finally succeeded in 1804. Twenty-one years after its independence, the French government demanded from Haiti a payment of 150 million gold francs in compensation for the loss of its richest colony and its "property" in slaves. With French warships hovering offshore, Haitian authorities agreed. To make the heavy payments, even after they were somewhat reduced, Haiti took out major loans from French, German, and North American banks. Repaying those loans, finally accomplished only in 1947, represented a huge drain on the country's budget. In 2010, with the country in ruins, an international petition signed by over 100 prominent people called on the French government to repay some $17 billion, effectively returning the "independence debt" extorted from Haiti 185 years earlier. While the

French government dismissed those claims, the issue provided a reminder of the continuing echoes of events from an earlier age of revolution.

The Haitian Revolution was part of and linked to a much larger set of upheavals that shook both sides of the Atlantic world between 1775 and 1825. Haitians had drawn inspiration from the earlier North American and French revolutions, even as their successful overthrow of French rule helped shape the Latin American independence struggles that followed. These four closely related upheavals reflect the new connections among Europe, Africa, North America, and South America that took shape in the wake of Columbus's voyages and the subsequent European conquests. Together, they launched a new chapter in the history of the Atlantic world, while the echoes of those revolutions reverberated in the larger world.

Atlantic Revolutions in a Global Context

Writing to a friend in 1772, before any of the Atlantic revolutions had occurred, the French intellectual Voltaire asked, "My dear philosopher, doesn't this appear to you to be the century of revolutions?"[1] He was certainly on target, and not only for Europe. From the early eighteenth century to the mid-nineteenth, many parts of the world witnessed political and social upheaval, leading some historians to think in terms of a "world crisis" or "converging revolutions." By the 1730s, the Safavid dynasty that had ruled Persia (now Iran) for several centuries had completely collapsed, even as the powerful Mughal Empire governing India also fragmented. About the same time, the Wahhabi movement in Arabia seriously threatened the Ottoman Empire, and its religious ideals informed major political upheavals in Central Asia and elsewhere (see "Expansion and Renewal in the Islamic World" in Chapter 15). The Russian Empire under Catherine the Great experienced a series of peasant uprisings, most notably one led by the Cossack commander Pugachev in 1773–1774 that briefly proclaimed the end of serfdom before that rebellion was crushed. China too in the late eighteenth and early nineteenth centuries hosted a number of popular though unsuccessful rebellions, a prelude perhaps to the huge Taiping revolution of 1850–1864. Beginning in the early nineteenth century, a new wave of Islamic revolutions shook West Africa, while in southern Africa a series of wars and migrations known as the *mfecane* (the breaking or crushing) involved widespread and violent disruptions as well as the creation of new states and societies.

Thus the Atlantic revolutions in North America, France, Haiti, and Latin America took place within a larger global framework. Like many of the other upheavals, they too occurred in the context of expensive wars, weakening states, and destabilizing processes of commercialization. But compared to upheavals elsewhere, the Atlantic revolutions were distinctive in various ways. The costly wars that strained European imperial states—Britain, France, and Spain in particular—were global rather than regional. In the so-called Seven Years' War (1754–1763), Britain and France joined battle in North America, the Caribbean, West Africa, and South Asia. The expenses of those conflicts prompted the British to levy additional taxes on their North American colonies and the French monarchy to seek new revenue from its landowners. These actions contributed to the launching of the North American and French revolutions, respectively.

Furthermore, the Atlantic revolutions were distinctive in that they were closely connected to one another. The American revolutionary leader Thomas Jefferson was the U.S. ambassador to France on the eve of the French Revolution, providing advice and encouragement to French reformers and revolutionaries. Simón Bolívar, a leading figure in Spanish American struggles for independence, twice visited Haiti, where he received military aid from the first black government in the Americas.

Beyond such direct connections, the various Atlantic revolutionaries shared a set of common ideas, as the Atlantic basin became a world of intellectual and cultural exchange. The ideas that animated the Atlantic revolutions derived from the European Enlightenment and were shared across the ocean in newspapers, books, and pamphlets. At the heart of these ideas was the radical notion that human political and social arrangements could be engineered, and improved, by human action. Thus conventional and long-established ways of living and thinking — the divine right of kings, state control of trade, aristocratic privilege, the authority of a single church — were no longer sacrosanct and came under repeated attack. New ideas of liberty, equality, free trade, religious tolerance, republicanism, and human rationality were in the air. Politically, the core notion was "popular sovereignty," which meant that the authority to govern derived from the people rather than from God or from established tradition. As the Englishman John Locke (1632–1704) had argued, the "social contract" between ruler and ruled should last only as long as it served the people well. In short, it was both possible and desirable to start over in the construction of human communities. In the late eighteenth and early nineteenth centuries, these ideas were largely limited to the Atlantic world. While all of the Atlantic revolutions involved the elimination of monarchs, at least temporarily, across Asia and the Middle East such republican political systems (those operating with elected representatives of the people rather than a monarch) were virtually inconceivable until much later. There the only solution to a bad monarch was a new and better one.

In the world of the Atlantic revolutions, ideas born of the Enlightenment generated endless controversy. Were liberty and equality compatible? What kind of government — unitary and centralized or federal and decentralized — best ensured freedom? And how far should liberty be extended? Except in Haiti, the chief beneficiaries of these revolutions were propertied white men of the "middling classes." Although women, slaves, Native Americans, and men without property did not gain much from these revolutions, the ideas that accompanied those upheavals gave them ammunition for the future. Because their overall thrust was to extend political rights further than ever before, these Atlantic movements have often been referred to as "democratic revolutions."

A final distinctive feature of the Atlantic revolutions lies in their immense global impact, extending well beyond the Atlantic world. The armies of revolutionary France, for example, invaded Egypt, Germany, Poland, and Russia, carrying seeds of change. The ideals that animated these Atlantic revolutions inspired efforts in many countries to abolish slavery, to extend the right to vote, to develop constitutions, and to secure greater equality for women. Nationalism, perhaps the most potent ideology of the modern era, was nurtured in the Atlantic revolutions and shaped much of nineteenth- and twentieth-century world history. The ideas of human equality articulated in these revolutions later found expression in feminist, socialist, and communist movements. The Universal Declaration of Human Rights, adopted by the

United Nations in 1948, echoed and amplified those principles while providing the basis for any number of subsequent protests against oppression, tyranny, and deprivation. In 1989, a number of Chinese students, fleeing the suppression of a democracy movement in their own country, marched at the head of a huge parade in Paris, celebrating the bicentennial of the French Revolution. And in 2011, the Middle Eastern uprisings known as the Arab Spring initially prompted numerous comparisons with the French Revolution. The Atlantic revolutions had a long reach.

Comparing Atlantic Revolutions

Despite their common political vocabulary and a broadly democratic character, the Atlantic revolutions differed substantially from one another. They were triggered by different circumstances, expressed quite different social and political tensions, and varied considerably in their outcomes. Liberty, noted Simón Bolívar, "is a succulent morsel, but one difficult to digest."[2] "Digesting liberty" occurred in quite distinct ways in the various sites of the Atlantic revolutions.

The North American Revolution, 1775–1787

Every schoolchild in the United States learns early that the **American Revolution** was a struggle for independence from oppressive British rule. That struggle was launched with the Declaration of Independence in 1776, resulted in an unlikely military victory by 1781, and generated a federal constitution in 1787, joining thirteen formerly separate colonies into a new nation (see Map 16.1). It was the first in a series of upheavals that rocked the Atlantic world and beyond in the century that followed. But was it a genuine revolution? What, precisely, did it change?

By effecting a break with Britain, the American Revolution marked a decisive political change, but in other ways it was, strangely enough, a conservative movement because it originated in an effort to preserve the existing liberties of the colonies rather than to create new ones. For much of the seventeenth and eighteenth centuries, the British colonies in North America enjoyed a considerable degree of local autonomy, as the British government was embroiled in its own internal conflicts and various European wars. Furthermore, Britain's West Indian colonies seemed more profitable and of greater significance than those of North America. In these circumstances, local elected assemblies in North America, dominated by the wealthier property-owning settlers, achieved something close to self-government. Colonists came to regard such autonomy as a birthright and part of their English heritage. Thus, until the mid-eighteenth century, almost no one in the colonies thought of breaking away from England because participation in the British Empire provided many advantages—protection in war, access to British markets, and confirmation of the settlers' identity as "Englishmen"—and few drawbacks.

There were, however, real differences between Englishmen in England and those in the North American colonies. Within the colonies, English settlers had developed societies described by a leading historian as "the most radical in the contemporary Western world." Certainly class distinctions were real and visible, and a small class of wealthy "gentlemen"—the Adamses, Washingtons, Jeffersons, and Hancocks—wore powdered wigs, imitated the latest European styles, were prominent in political life,

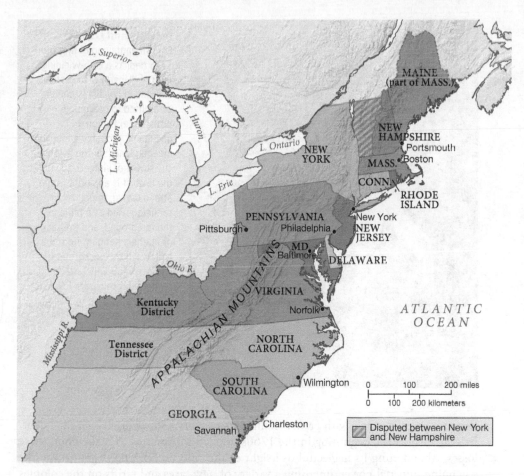

MAP 16.1   The United States after the American Revolution
The union of the thirteen British colonies in North America created the embryonic United States, shown here in 1788. Over the past two centuries and more of anticolonial struggles, it was the only example of separate colonies joining together after independence to form a larger and enduring nation.

and were generally accorded deference by ordinary people. But the ready availability of land following the dispossession of Native Americans, the scarcity of people, and the absence of both a titled nobility and a single established church meant that social life was far more open than in Europe. No legal distinctions differentiated clergy, aristocracy, and commoners, as they did in France. All free men enjoyed the same status before the law, a situation that excluded black slaves and, in some ways, white women as well. These conditions made for less poverty, more economic opportunity, fewer social differences, and easier relationships among the classes than in Europe. The famous economist Adam Smith observed that British colonists were "republican in their manners . . . and their government" well before their independence from England.[3]

Thus the American Revolution grew not from social tensions within the colonies, but from a rather sudden and unexpected effort by the British government to tighten its control over the colonies and to extract more revenue from them. As

Patriots and Loyalists This English engraving dating from 1775 depicts a club-wielding mob of "Liberty Men" forcing a Virginian loyalist [someone committed to continued British rule] to sign a document, probably endorsing independence for the colonies. The threat of violence toward the loyalist is apparent in the armed crowd, the barrel of tar being used as a table in the foreground, and the sack of feathers hanging from the gallows in the background. Patriots frequently tarred and feathered recalcitrant loyalists during the lead-up to the American Revolution.

Britain's global struggle with France drained its treasury and ran up its national debt, British authorities, beginning in the 1760s, looked to America to make good these losses. Abandoning its neglectful oversight of the colonies, Britain began to act like a genuine imperial power, imposing a variety of new taxes and tariffs on the colonies without their consent, for they were not represented in the British Parliament. Many of the colonists were infuriated, because such measures challenged their economic interests, their established traditions of local autonomy, and their identity as true Englishmen. Armed with the ideas of the Enlightenment—popular sovereignty, natural rights, the consent of the governed—they went to war, and by 1781 they had prevailed, with considerable aid from the French, who were only too pleased to harm the interests of their British rivals.

What was revolutionary about the American experience was not so much the revolution itself but the kind of society that had already emerged within the colonies. Independence from Britain was not accompanied by any wholesale social transformation. Rather, the revolution accelerated the established democratic tendencies of the colonial societies. Political authority remained largely in the hands of the existing elites who had led the revolution, although property requirements for voting were lowered and more white men of modest means, such as small farmers and urban artisans, were elected to state legislatures.

This widening of political participation gradually eroded the power of traditional gentlemen, but no women or people of color shared in these gains. Land was not seized from its owners, except in the case of pro-British loyalists who had fled the country. Although slavery was gradually abolished in the northern states, where it counted for little, it remained firmly entrenched in the southern states, where it counted for much. Chief Justice John Marshall later gave voice to this conservative understanding of the American Revolution: "All contracts and rights, respecting property, remained unchanged by the Revolution."[4] In the century that followed independence, the United States did become the world's most democratic country, but this development was less the direct product of the revolution and more the gradual working out in a reformist fashion of earlier practices and the principles of equality announced in the Declaration of Independence.

Nonetheless, many American patriots felt passionately that they were creating "a new order for the ages." James Madison in the *Federalist Papers* made the point clearly: "We pursued a new and more noble course . . . and accomplished a revolution that has no parallel in the annals of human society." Supporters abroad agreed. On the eve of the French Revolution, a Paris newspaper proclaimed that the United States was "the hope and model of the human race."[5] In both cases, they were referring primarily to the political ideas and practices of the new country. The American Revolution, after all, initiated the political dismantling of Europe's New World empires. The "right to revolution," proclaimed in the Declaration of Independence and made effective only in a great struggle, inspired revolutionaries and nationalists from Simón Bolívar in nineteenth-century Latin America to Ho Chi Minh in twentieth-century Vietnam. Moreover, the new U.S. Constitution—with its Bill of Rights, checks and balances, separation of church and state, and federalism—was one of the first sustained efforts to put the political ideas of the Enlightenment into practice. That document, and the ideas that it embraced, echoed repeatedly in the political upheavals of the century that followed.

The French Revolution, 1789–1815

Act Two in the drama of the Atlantic revolutions took place in France, beginning in 1789, although it was closely connected to Act One in North America. Thousands of French soldiers had provided assistance to the American colonists and now returned home full of republican enthusiasm. Thomas Jefferson, the U.S. ambassador in Paris, reported that France "has been awakened by our revolution."[6] More immediately, the French government, which had generously aided the Americans in an effort to undermine its British rivals, was teetering on the brink of bankruptcy and had long sought reforms that would modernize the tax system and make it more equitable. In a desperate effort to raise taxes against the opposition of the privileged classes, the French king, Louis XVI, had called into session an ancient representative body, the Estates General. It consisted of male representatives of the three "estates," or legal orders, of prerevolutionary France: the clergy, the nobility, and the commoners. The first two estates comprised about 2 percent of the population, and the Third Estate included everyone else. When that body convened in 1789, representatives of the Third Estate soon organized themselves as the National Assembly, claiming the sole authority to make laws for the country. A few weeks later, they forthrightly claimed in the **Declaration of the Rights of Man and Citizen** that "men are born and remain free and equal in rights," and this declaration later became the preamble of the 1791 French Constitution. These actions, unprecedented and illegal in the *ancien régime* (the old regime), launched the **French Revolution** and radicalized many of the participants in the National Assembly.

The French Revolution was quite different from its North American predecessor. Whereas the American Revolution expressed the tensions of a colonial relationship with a distant imperial power, the French insurrection was driven by sharp conflicts within French society. Members of the titled nobility — privileged, prestigious, and wealthy — resented and resisted the monarchy's efforts to subject them to new taxes. Educated middle-class men such as doctors, lawyers, lower-level officials, and merchants were growing in numbers and sometimes in wealth and were offended by the remaining privileges of the aristocracy, from which they were excluded. Ordinary urban men and women, many of whose incomes had declined for a generation, were hit particularly hard in the late 1780s by the rapidly rising price of bread and widespread unemployment. Peasants in the countryside, though largely free of serfdom, were subject to hated dues imposed by their landlords, taxes from the state, obligations to the Church, and the requirement to work without pay on public roads. As Enlightenment ideas penetrated French society, more and more people, mostly in the Third Estate but also including some priests and nobles, found a language with which to articulate these grievances. The famous French writer Jean-Jacques Rousseau had told them that it was "manifestly contrary to the law of nature . . . that a handful of people should gorge themselves with superfluities while the hungry multitude goes in want of necessities."[7]

These social conflicts gave the French Revolution, especially during its first five years, a much more violent, far-reaching, and radical character than its American counterpart. It was a profound social upheaval, more comparable to the revolutions of Russia and China in the twentieth century than to the earlier American Revolution. Initial efforts to establish a constitutional monarchy and promote harmony among the classes gave way to more radical measures, as internal resistance and foreign opposition produced a fear that the revolution might be overturned. In the process, urban crowds organized insurrections. Some peasants attacked the residences of their lords, burning the documents that recorded their dues and payments. The National Assembly decreed the end of all legal privileges and eliminated what remained of feudalism in France. Even slavery was abolished, albeit briefly. Church lands were sold to raise revenue, and priests were put under government authority.

In 1793, King Louis XVI and his queen, Marie Antoinette, were executed, an act of regicide that shocked traditionalists all across Europe and marked a new stage in revolutionary violence. What followed was the Terror of 1793–1794. Under the leadership of Maximilien **Robespierre** (ROHBS-pee-air) and his Committee of Public Safety, tens of thousands deemed enemies of the revolution lost their lives on the guillotine. Shortly thereafter, Robespierre himself was arrested and guillotined, accused of leading France into tyranny and dictatorship. "The revolution," remarked one of its victims, "was devouring its own children."

Accompanying attacks on the old order were efforts to create a wholly new society, symbolized by a new calendar with the Year 1 in 1792, marking a fresh start for France. Unlike the Americans, who sought to restore or build on earlier freedoms, French revolutionaries perceived themselves to be starting from scratch and looked to the future. For the first time in its history, the country became a republic and briefly passed universal male suffrage, although it was never implemented. The old administrative system was rationalized into eighty-three territorial departments, each with a new name. As revolutionary France prepared for war against its threatened and threatening neighbors, it created the world's largest army, with some 800,000 men,

The Execution of Robespierre The beheading of the radical leader Robespierre, who had himself brought thousands of others to the guillotine, marked a decisive turning point in the unfolding of the French Revolution and the end of its most violent phase. (Musée de la Ville de Paris, Musée Carnavalet, Paris, France/Bridgeman Images)

and all adult males were required to serve. Led by officers from the middle and even lower classes, this was an army of citizens representing the nation.

In terms of gender roles, the French Revolution did not create a new society, but it did raise the question of female political equality far more explicitly than the American Revolution had done. Partly this was because French women were active in the major events of the revolution. In July 1789, they took part in the famous storming of the Bastille, a large fortress, prison, and armory that had come to symbolize the oppressive old regime. In October of that year, some 7,000 Parisian women, desperate about the shortage of bread, marched on the palace at Versailles, stormed through the royal apartments searching for the despised Queen Marie Antoinette, and forced the royal family to return with them to Paris.

Backed by a few male supporters, women also made serious political demands. They signed petitions detailing their complaints: lack of education, male competition in female trades, the prevalence of prostitution, the rapidly rising price of bread and soap. One petition, reflecting the intersection of class and gender, referred to women as the "Third Estate of the Third Estate." Another demanded the right to bear arms in defense of the revolution. Over sixty women's clubs were established throughout the country. A small group called the Cercle Social (Social Circle) campaigned for women's rights, noting that "the laws favor men at the expense of women, because everywhere power is in your hands."[8] The French playwright and journalist Olympe de Gouges appropriated the language of the Declaration of Rights to insist that "woman is born free and lives equal to man in her rights."

But the assertion of French women in the early years of the revolution seemed wildly inappropriate and threatening to most men, uniting conservatives and revolutionaries alike in defense of male privileges. And so in late 1793, the country's all-male legislative body voted to ban all women's clubs. "Women are ill-suited for elevated thoughts and serious meditation," declared one of the male representatives. "A woman should not leave her family to meddle in affairs of government." Here was a conception of gender that defined masculinity in terms of exercising political power. Women who aspired to do so were, in the words of one revolutionary orator, "denatured *viragos*" (unnatural domineering women), in short, not really women at all.[9] Thus French revolutionaries were distinctly unwilling to offer any political rights to women, even though they had eliminated class restrictions, at least in theory; granted religious freedom to Jews and Protestants; and abolished slavery. Nonetheless, according to a leading historian, "the French Revolution, more than any other event of its time, opened up the question of women's rights for consideration" and thus laid the foundations for modern feminism.[10]

If not in terms of gender, the immediate impact of the revolution was felt in many other ways. Streets got new names; monuments to the royal family were destroyed; titles vanished; people referred to one another as "citizen so-and-so." Real politics in the public sphere emerged for the first time as many people joined political clubs, took part in marches and demonstrations, served on local committees, and ran for public office. Ordinary men and women, who had identified primarily with their local communities, now began to think of themselves as belonging to a nation. The state replaced the Catholic Church as the place for registering births, marriages, and deaths, and revolutionary festivals substituted for church holidays.

More radical revolutionary leaders deliberately sought to convey a sense of new beginnings and endless possibilities. At a Festival of Unity held in 1793 to mark the first anniversary of the end of monarchy, participants burned the crowns and scepters of the royal family in a huge bonfire while releasing a cloud of 3,000 white doves. The Cathedral of Notre Dame was temporarily turned into the Temple of Reason, while a "Hymn to Liberty" combined traditional church music with the explicit message of the Enlightenment:

> Oh Liberty, sacred Liberty / Goddess of an enlightened people
> Rule today within these walls. / Through you this temple is purified.
> Liberty! Before you reason chases out deception, / Error flees, fanaticism is beaten
>   down.
> Our gospel is nature / And our cult is virtue.
> To love one's country and one's brothers, / To serve the Sovereign People
> These are the sacred tenets / And pledge of a Republican.[11]

Elsewhere too the French Revolution evoked images of starting over. Witnessing that revolution in 1790, the young William Wordsworth, later a famous British Romantic poet, imagined "human nature seeming born again." "Bliss it was in that dawn to be alive," he wrote. "But to be young was very heaven."

The French Revolution also differed from the American Revolution in the way its influence spread. At least until the United States became a world power at the end of the nineteenth century, what inspired others was primarily the example of its revolution and its constitution. French influence, by contrast, spread through conquest, largely under the leadership of **Napoleon Bonaparte** (r. 1799–1815). A highly successful general who seized power in 1799, Napoleon is often credited with taming the revolution in the face of growing disenchantment with its more radical features and with the social conflicts it generated. He preserved many of its more moderate elements, such as civil equality, a secular law code, religious freedom, and promotion by merit, while reconciling with the Catholic Church and suppressing the revolution's more democratic elements in a military dictatorship. In short, Napoleon kept the revolution's emphasis on social equality for men but dispensed with liberty.

Like many of the revolution's ardent supporters, Napoleon was intent on spreading its benefits far and wide. In a series of brilliant military campaigns, his forces subdued most of Europe, thus creating the continent's largest empire since the days of the Romans (see Map 16.2). Within that empire, Napoleon imposed such revolutionary practices as ending feudalism, proclaiming equality of rights, insisting on religious toleration, codifying the laws, and rationalizing government administration. In many places, these reforms were welcomed, and seeds of further change were planted. But French domination was also resented and resisted, stimulating national consciousness throughout Europe. That too was a seed that bore fruit in the century that followed. More immediately, national resistance, particularly from Russia and Britain, brought down Napoleon and his amazing empire by 1815 and marked an end to the era of the French Revolution, though not to the potency of its ideas.

MAP 16.2 Napoleon's European Empire
The French Revolution spawned a French Empire, under Napoleon's leadership, that encompassed most of Europe and served to spread the principles of the revolution.

The Haitian Revolution, 1791–1804

Nowhere did the example of the French Revolution echo more loudly than in the French Caribbean colony of Saint Domingue, later renamed Haiti (see Map 16.3, page 468). Widely regarded as the richest colony in the world, Saint Domingue boasted 8,000 plantations, which in the late eighteenth century produced some 40 percent of the world's sugar and perhaps half of its coffee. A slave labor force of about 500,000 people made up the vast majority of the colony's population. Whites numbered about 40,000, sharply divided between very well-to-do plantation owners, merchants, and lawyers and those known as *petits blancs* (peh-TEE blahnk), or poor whites. A third social group consisted of some 30,000 *gens de couleur libres* (free people of color), many of them of mixed-race background. Given its enormous inequalities and its rampant exploitation, this Caribbean colony was primed for explosion.

In such a volatile setting, the ideas and example of the French Revolution lit several fuses and set in motion a spiral of violence that engulfed the colony for more than a decade. The principles of the revolution, however, meant different things to different people. To the *grands blancs*—the rich white landowners—it suggested greater autonomy for the colony and fewer economic restrictions on trade, but they resented the demands of the *petits blancs*, who sought equality of citizenship for all whites. Both white groups were adamantly opposed to the insistence of free people of color that the "rights of man" meant equal treatment for all free people regardless of race. To the slaves, the promise of the French Revolution was a personal freedom that challenged the entire slave labor system. In a massive revolt beginning in 1791, triggered by rumors that the French king had already declared an end to slavery, slaves burned 1,000 plantations and killed hundreds of whites as well as mixed-race people.

Soon warring factions of slaves, whites, and free people of color battled one another. Spanish and British forces, seeking to enlarge their own empires at the expense of the French, only added to the turmoil. Amid the confusion, brutality, and massacres of the 1790s, power gravitated toward the slaves, now led by the astute Toussaint Louverture, himself a former slave. He and his successor overcame internal resistance, outmaneuvered the foreign powers, and even defeated an attempt by Napoleon to reestablish French control.

When the dust settled in the early years of the nineteenth century, it was clear that something remarkable and unprecedented had taken place, a revolution unique in the Atlantic world and in world history. Socially, the last had become first. In the only completely successful slave revolt in world history, "the lowest order of the society—slaves—became equal, free, and independent citizens."[12] Politically, they had thrown off French colonial rule, creating the second independent republic in the Americas and the first non-European state to emerge from Western colonialism. They renamed their country "Haiti," a term meaning "mountainous" or "rugged" in the language of the original Taino people. It was a symbolic break with Europe and represented an effort to connect with the long-deceased native inhabitants of the land. Some, in fact, referred to themselves as "Incas." At the formal declaration of Haiti's independence on January 1, 1804, Jean-Jacques Dessalines, the new country's first head of state, declared: "I have given the French cannibals blood for blood; I have avenged America."[13] In defining all Haitian citizens as "black" and legally equal regardless of color or class, Haiti directly confronted elite preferences for lighter skin even as it disallowed citizenship for most whites. Economically, the country's plantation system, oriented wholly toward the export of sugar and coffee, had been largely destroyed. As whites fled or were killed, both private and state lands were redistributed among former slaves and free blacks, and Haiti became a nation of small-scale farmers producing mostly for their own needs, with a much smaller export sector.

The destructiveness of the **Haitian Revolution**, its bitter internal divisions of race and class, and continuing external opposition contributed much to Haiti's abiding poverty as well as to its authoritarian and unstable politics. So too did the enormous "independence debt" that the French forced on the fledgling republic in 1825, a financial burden that endured for well over a century. "Freedom" in Haiti came to mean primarily the end of slavery rather than the establishment of political rights for all. In the early nineteenth century, however, Haiti was a source of enormous hope and of great fear. Within weeks of the Haitian slave uprising in 1791, Jamaican slaves had composed songs in its honor, and it was not long before slave owners in the Caribbean and North America observed a new "insolence" in their slaves. Certainly, its example inspired other slave rebellions, gave a boost to the dawning abolitionist movement, and has been a source of pride for people of African descent ever since.

To whites throughout the hemisphere, the cautionary saying "Remember Haiti" reflected a sense of horror at what had occurred there and a determination not to allow political change to reproduce that fearful outcome again. Particularly in Latin America, the events in Haiti injected a deep caution and social conservatism in the elites who led their countries to independence in the early nineteenth century. Ironically, though, the Haitian Revolution also led to a temporary expansion of slavery elsewhere. Cuban plantations and their slave workers considerably increased their production of sugar as that of Haiti declined. Moreover, Napoleon's defeat in Haiti

The Haitian Revolution This early nineteenth-century engraving, titled *Revenge Taken by the Black Army*, shows black Haitian soldiers hanging a large number of French soldiers, thus illustrating both the violence and the racial dimension of the upheaval in Haiti. (From "An Historic Account of the Black Empire of Haiti," 1805, engraving by Marcus Rainsford [ca. 1750–1805]/Private Collection/ Bridgeman Images)

persuaded him to sell to the United States the French territories known as the Louisiana Purchase, from which a number of "slave states" were carved out. Nor did the example of Haiti lead to successful independence struggles in the rest of the thirty or so Caribbean colonies. Unlike mainland North and South America, Caribbean decolonization had to await the twentieth century. In such contradictory ways did the echoes of the Haitian Revolution reverberate in the Atlantic world.

Latin American Revolutions, 1808–1825

The final act in a half century of Atlantic revolutionary upheaval took place in the Spanish and Portuguese colonies of mainland Latin America (see Map 16.3). These **Latin American revolutions** were shaped by preceding events in North America, France, and Haiti as well as by their own distinctive societies and historical experiences.

MAP 16.3   Latin American Independence
With the exception of Haiti, Latin American revolutions brought independence to new states but offered little social change or political opportunity for the vast majority of people.

As in British North America, native-born elites (known as *creoles*) in the Spanish colonies were offended and insulted by the Spanish monarchy's eighteenth century efforts to exercise greater power over its colonies and to subject them to heavier taxes and tariffs. Creole intellectuals had also become familiar with ideas of popular sovereignty, republican government, and personal liberty derived from the European Enlightenment. But these conditions, similar to those in North America, led initially only to scattered and uncoordinated protests rather than to outrage, declarations of independence, war, and unity, as had occurred in the British colonies. Why did Spanish colonies win their independence almost fifty years later than those of British North America?

Spanish colonies had long been governed in a rather more authoritarian fashion than their British counterparts and were more sharply divided by class. In addition, whites throughout Latin America were vastly outnumbered by Native Americans, people of African ancestry, and those of mixed race. All of this inhibited the growth of a movement for independence, notwithstanding the example of North America and similar provocations.

Despite their growing disenchantment with Spanish rule, creole elites did not so much generate a revolution as have one thrust upon them by events in Europe. In 1808, Napoleon invaded Spain and Portugal, deposing the Spanish king Ferdinand VII and forcing the Portuguese royal family into exile in Brazil. With legitimate royal authority now in disarray, Latin Americans were forced to take action. The outcome, ultimately, was independence for the various states of Latin America, established almost everywhere by 1826. But the way in which independence occurred and the kind of societies it generated differed greatly from the experience of both North America and Haiti.

The process lasted more than twice as long as it did in North America, partly because Latin American societies were so divided by class, race, and region. In North America, violence was directed almost entirely against the British and seldom spilled over into domestic disputes, except for some bloody skirmishes with loyalists. In Mexico, by contrast, the move toward independence began in 1810–1811 in a peasant insurrection, driven by hunger for land and by high food prices and led successively by two priests, Miguel Hidalgo and José Morelos. Alarmed by the social radicalism of the **Hidalgo-Morelos rebellion**, creole landowners, with the support of the Church, raised an army and crushed the insurgency. Later that alliance of clergy and creole elites brought Mexico to a more socially controlled independence in 1821. Such violent conflict among Latin Americans, along lines of race, class, and ideology, accompanied the struggle against Spain in many places.

The entire independence movement in Latin America took place under the shadow of a great fear — the dread of social rebellion from below — that had little counterpart in North America. The extensive violence of the French and Haitian revolutions was a lesson to Latin American elites that political change could easily get out of hand and was fraught with danger to themselves. An abortive rebellion of Native Americans in Peru in the early 1780s, led by **Tupac Amaru**, a man who claimed direct descent from the last Inca emperor, reminded whites that they sat atop a potentially explosive society, most of whose members were exploited and oppressed people of color. So too did the Hidalgo-Morelos rebellion in Mexico.

And yet the creole sponsors of independence movements, both regional military leaders such as Simón Bolívar and José de San Martín and their civilian counterparts, required the support of "the people," or at least some of them, if they were to prevail against Spanish forces. The answer to this dilemma was found in nativism, which cast all of those born in the Americas — creoles, Indians, mixed-race people, free blacks — as

Americanos, while the enemy was defined as those born in Spain or Portugal.[14] This was no easy task, because many creole whites and mestizos saw themselves as Spanish and because great differences of race, culture, and wealth divided the Americanos. Nonetheless, nationalist leaders made efforts to mobilize people of color into the struggle with promises of freedom, the end of legal restrictions, and social advancement. Many of these leaders were genuine liberals who had been influenced by the ideals of the Enlightenment, the French Revolution, and Spanish liberalism. In the long run, however, few of those promises were kept. Certainly, the lower classes, Native Americans, and slaves benefited little from independence. "The imperial state was destroyed in Spanish America," concluded one historian, "but colonial society was preserved."[15]

Nor did women as a group gain much from the independence struggle, though they had participated in it in various ways. Upper-class or wealthy women gave and raised money for the cause and provided safe havens for revolutionary meetings. In Mexico, some women disguised themselves as men to join the struggle, while numerous working-class and peasant women served as cooks and carriers of supplies in a "women's brigade." A considerable number of women were severely punished for their disloyalty to the Crown, with some forty-eight executed in Colombia. Yet, after independence, few social gains rewarded these efforts. General San Martín of Argentina accorded national recognition to a number of women, and modest improvement in educational opportunities for women appeared. But Latin American women continued to be wholly excluded from political life and remained under firm legal control of the men in their families.

A further difference in the Latin American situation lay in the apparent impossibility of uniting the various Spanish colonies, so much larger than the small British territories of North America, despite several failed efforts to do so. Thus no United States of Latin America emerged. Distances among the colonies and geographic obstacles to effective communication were certainly greater than in the Eastern Seaboard colonies of North America, and their longer colonial experience had given rise to distinct and deeply rooted regional identities. Shortly before his death in 1830, the prominent independence leader Simón Bolívar, who so admired George Washington and had so ardently hoped for greater unity, wrote in despair to a friend: "[Latin] America is ungovernable. Those who serve the revolution plough the sea."[16]

The aftermath of independence in Latin America marked a reversal in the earlier relationship of the two American continents. The United States, which began its history as the leftover "dregs" of the New World, grew increasingly wealthy, industrialized, democratic, internationally influential, and generally stable, with the major exception of the Civil War. The Spanish colonies, which took shape in the wealthiest areas and among the most sophisticated cultures of the Americas, were widely regarded as the more promising region compared to England's North American territories, which had a backwater reputation. But in the nineteenth century, as newly independent countries in both regions launched a new phase of their histories, those in Latin America became relatively underdeveloped, impoverished, undemocratic, politically unstable, and dependent on foreign technology and investment. Begun in broadly similar circumstances, the Latin American and North American revolutions occurred in very different societies and gave rise to very different historical trajectories.

Simón Bolívar Among the heroic figures of Spanish American independence movements, none was more significant than Simón Bolívar, shown here in a moment of triumph entering his hometown of Caracas in present-day Venezuela. But Bolívar was immensely disappointed in the outcomes of independence, as his dream of a unified South America perished amid the rivalries of separate countries. (Chalk lithograph by R. Weibezahl, 1829/ Sammlung Archiv für Kunst und Geschichte, Berlin, Germany/ akg-images)

Echoes of Revolution

The repercussions of the Atlantic revolutions reverberated far beyond their places of origin and persisted long after those upheavals had been concluded. Britain's loss of its North American colonies, for example, fueled its growing interest and interventions in Asia, contributing to British colonial rule in India and the Opium Wars in China. Napoleon's brief conquest of Egypt (1798–1801) opened the way for a modernizing regime to emerge in that ancient land and stimulated westernizing reforms in the Ottoman Empire (see "The Ottoman Empire and the West in the Nineteenth Century" in Chapter 19). During the nineteenth century, the idea of a "constitution" found advocates in Poland, Russia, the Spanish-ruled Philippines, China, the Ottoman Empire, and British-governed India.

Within Europe, which was generally dominated by conservative governments following Napoleon's final defeat, smaller revolutionary eruptions occurred in 1830, more widely in 1848, and in Paris in 1870. They reflected ideas of republicanism, greater social equality, and national liberation from foreign rule. Such ideas and social pressures pushed the major states of Western Europe, the United States, and Argentina to enlarge their voting publics, generally granting universal male suffrage by 1914. An abortive attempt to establish a constitutional regime even broke out in autocratic Russia in 1825, led by aristocratic military officers influenced by French revolutionary ideas. While it quickly failed, it marked the beginning of a revolutionary tradition in Russia, which came to fruition only in 1917. More generally, the American and French revolutions led sympathetic elites in Central Europe and elsewhere to feel that they had fallen behind, that their countries were "sleeping." As early as 1791, a Hungarian poet gave voice to such sentiments: "O you still in the slave's collar . . . And you too! Holy consecrated kings . . . turn your eyes to Paris! Let France set out the fate of both king and shackled slave."[17]

Beyond these echoes of the Atlantic revolutions, three major movements arose to challenge continuing patterns of oppression or exclusion. Abolitionists sought the end of slavery; nationalists hoped to foster unity and independence from foreign rule; and feminists challenged male dominance. Each of these movements bore the marks of the Atlantic revolutions, and although they took root first in Europe and the Americas, each came to have a global significance in the centuries that followed.

The Abolition of Slavery

In little more than a century, from roughly 1780 to 1890, a remarkable transformation occurred in human affairs as slavery, widely practiced and little condemned since at least the beginning of civilization, lost its legitimacy and was largely ended. In this amazing process, the ideas and practices of the Atlantic revolutions played an important role.

Enlightenment thinkers in eighteenth-century Europe had become increasingly critical of slavery as a violation of the natural rights of every person, and the public pronouncements of the American and French revolutions about liberty and equality likewise focused attention on this obvious breach of those principles. To this secular antislavery thinking was added an increasingly vociferous religious voice, expressed first by Quakers and then by Protestant evangelicals in Britain and the United States. To them, slavery was "repugnant to our religion" and a "crime in the sight of God."[18] What made these moral arguments more widely acceptable was the growing belief that, contrary to much earlier thinking, slavery was not essential for economic progress. After all, England and New England were among the most prosperous regions of the Western world in the early nineteenth century, and both were based on free labor. Slavery in this view was out of date, unnecessary in the new era of industrial technology and capitalism. Thus moral virtue and economic success were joined. It was an attractive argument. The actions of slaves themselves likewise hastened the end of slavery. The dramatically successful Haitian Revolution was followed by three major rebellions in the British West Indies, all of which were harshly crushed, in the early nineteenth century. The **Great Jamaica Revolt** of 1831–1832, in which perhaps 60,000 slaves attacked several hundred plantations, was particularly important in prompting Britain to abolish slavery throughout its empire in 1833. These revolts demonstrated clearly that slaves were hardly "contented," and the brutality with which they were suppressed appalled British public opinion. Growing numbers of the British public came to believe that slavery was "not only morally wrong and economically inefficient, but also politically unwise."[19]

These various strands of thinking — secular, religious, economic, and political — came together in an **abolitionist movement**, most powerfully in Britain, which brought growing pressure on governments to close down the trade in slaves and then to ban slavery itself. In the late eighteenth century, such a movement gained wide support among middle- and working-class people in Britain. Its techniques included pamphlets with heartrending descriptions of slavery, numerous petitions to Parliament, lawsuits, and boycotts of slave-produced sugar. Frequent public meetings dramatically featured the testimony of Africans who had experienced the horrors of slavery firsthand. In 1807, Britain forbade the sale of slaves within its empire and in 1834 emancipated those who remained enslaved. Over the next half century, other nations followed suit, responding to growing international pressure, particularly from Britain, then the world's leading economic and military power. British naval vessels patrolled the Atlantic, intercepted illegal slave ships, and freed their human cargoes in a small West African settlement called Freetown, in present-day Sierra Leone. Following their independence, most Latin American countries abolished slavery by the 1850s. Brazil, in 1888, was the last to do so, bringing more than four centuries of Atlantic slavery to an end. A roughly similar set of conditions — fear of rebellion, economic inefficiency, and moral concerns — persuaded the Russian tsar (zahr) to free the many serfs of that huge country in 1861, although there it occurred by fiat from above rather than from growing public pressure.

None of this happened easily. Slave economies continued to flourish well into the nineteenth century, and plantation owners vigorously resisted the onslaught of abolitionists. So did slave traders, both European and African, who together shipped millions of additional captives, mostly to Cuba and Brazil, long after the British had declared the trade illegal. Osei Bonsu, the powerful king of the West African state of Asante, was puzzled as to why the British would no longer buy his slaves. "If they think it bad now," he asked a local British representative in 1820, "why did they think it good before?"[20] Nowhere was the persistence of slavery more evident and resistance to abolition more intense than in the southern states of the United States. It was the only slaveholding society in which the end of slavery occurred through a bitter, prolonged, and highly destructive civil war (1861–1865).

The end of Atlantic slavery during the nineteenth century surely marked a major and quite rapid turn in the world's social history and in the moral thinking of humankind. Nonetheless, the outcomes of that process were often surprising and far from the expectations of abolitionists or the newly freed slaves. In most cases, the economic lives of the former slaves did not improve dramatically. Nowhere in the Atlantic world, except Haiti, did a redistribution of land follow the end of slavery. But freedmen everywhere desperately sought economic autonomy on their own land, and in parts of the Caribbean such as Jamaica, where unoccupied land was available, independent peasant agriculture proved possible for some. Elsewhere, as in the southern United States, various forms of legally free but highly dependent labor, such as sharecropping, emerged to replace slavery and to provide low-paid and often-indebted workers for planters. The understandable reluctance of former slaves to continue working in plantation agriculture created labor shortages and set in motion a huge new wave of global migration. Large numbers of indentured servants from India and China were imported into the Caribbean, Peru, South Africa, Hawaii, Malaya, and elsewhere to work in mines, on plantations, and in construction projects. There they often toiled in conditions not far removed from slavery itself.

Newly freed people did not achieve anything close to political equality, except in Haiti. White planters, farmers, and mine owners retained local authority in the Caribbean, where colonial rule persisted until well into the twentieth century. In the southern United States, a brief period of "radical reconstruction," during which newly freed blacks did enjoy full political rights and some power, was followed by harsh segregation laws, denial of voting rights, a wave of lynchings, and a virulent racism that lasted well into the twentieth century. For most former slaves, emancipation usually meant "nothing but freedom."[21] Unlike the situation in the Americas, the end of serfdom in Russia transferred to the peasants a considerable portion of the nobles' land, but the need to pay for this land with "redemption dues" and the rapid growth of Russia's rural population ensured that most peasants remained impoverished and politically volatile.

In both West and East Africa, the closing of the external slave trade decreased the price of slaves and increased their use within African societies to produce the export crops that the world economy now sought. Thus, as Europeans imposed colonial rule on Africa in the late nineteenth century, they loudly proclaimed their commitment to ending slavery in a continent from which they had extracted slaves for more than four centuries. This was surely among the more ironic outcomes of the abolitionist process.

In the Islamic world, where slavery had long been practiced and elaborately regulated, the freeing of slaves, though not required, was strongly recommended as a mark of piety. Some nineteenth-century Muslim authorities opposed slavery altogether on the grounds that it violated the Quran's ideals of freedom and equality. But unlike Europe and North America, the Islamic world generated no popular grassroots antislavery movements. There slavery was outlawed gradually only in the twentieth century under the pressure of international opinion.

Nations and Nationalism

In addition to contributing to the end of slavery, the Atlantic revolutions also gave new prominence to a relatively recent kind of human community — the nation. By the end of the twentieth century, the idea that humankind was divided into separate nations, each with a distinct culture and territory and deserving an independent political life, was so widespread as to seem natural and timeless. And yet for most of human experience, states did not usually coincide with the culture of a particular people, for all the great empires and many smaller states governed culturally diverse societies. Few people considered rule by foreigners itself a terrible offense because the most important identities and loyalties were local, limited to clan, village, or region, with only modest connection to the larger state or empire that governed them. People might on occasion consider themselves part of larger religious communities (such as Christians or Muslims) or ethno-linguistic groupings such as Greek, Arab, or Maya, but such identities rarely provided the basis for enduring states.

All of that began to change during the era of Atlantic revolutions. Independence movements in both North and South America were made in the name of new nations. The French Revolution declared that sovereignty lay with "the people," and its leaders mobilized this people to defend the "French nation" against its external enemies. In 1793, the revolutionary government of France declared a mass conscription (*levée en masse*) with a stirring call to service:

> Henceforth, until the enemies have been driven from the territory of the Republic, all the French are in permanent requisition for army service. The young men shall go to battle; the married men shall forge arms and transport provisions; the women shall make tents and clothes, and shall serve in the hospitals; the children shall turn old linen into lint; the old men shall repair to the public places, to stimulate the courage of the warriors and preach the unity of the Republic and the hatred of kings.[22]

Napoleon's conquests likewise stimulated national resistance in many parts of Europe. European states had long competed and fought with one another, but increasingly in the nineteenth century, those states were inhabited by people who felt themselves to be citizens of a nation, deeply bound to their fellows by ties of blood, culture, or common experience, not simply common subjects of a ruling dynasty. It was a novel form of political loyalty.

The rise of **nationalism** was also facilitated by Europe's modern transformation, as older identities and loyalties eroded. Science weakened the hold of religion on some. Migration to industrial cities or abroad diminished allegiance to local communities. At the same time, printing and the publishing industry standardized a variety of dialects into a smaller number of European languages, a process that allowed a growing reading public to think of themselves as members of a common linguistic group or nation. All of this encouraged political and cultural leaders to articulate an appealing idea of their particular nations and ensured a growing circle of people receptive to such ideas. Thus the idea of the "nation" was constructed or even invented, but it was often imagined and presented as a reawakening of older linguistic or cultural identities, and it certainly drew on the songs, dances, folktales, historical experiences, and collective memories of earlier cultures (see Map 16.4).

Whatever its precise origins, nationalism proved to be an infinitely flexible and enormously powerful idea in nineteenth-century Europe and beyond. It inspired the political unification of both Italy (1870) and Germany (1871), gathering their previously fragmented peoples into new states. It encouraged Greeks and Serbs to assert their independence from the Ottoman Empire; Czechs and Hungarians to demand more autonomy within the Austrian Empire; Poles and Ukrainians to become more aware of their oppression within the Russian Empire; and the Irish to seek "home rule" and separation from Great Britain. By the end of the nineteenth century, a small Zionist movement, seeking a homeland in Palestine, had emerged among Europe's frequently persecuted Jews.

Popular nationalism made the normal rivalry among European states even more acute and fueled a highly competitive drive for colonies in Asia and Africa. The immensity of the suffering and sacrifice that nationalism generated in Europe was vividly disclosed during the horrors of World War I. Furthermore, nationalism fueled rivalries among the various European-derived states in the Americas, reflected, for example, in the Mexican–United States War of 1846–1848 and the devastating conflict between Paraguay and the Triple Alliance of Argentina, Brazil, and Uruguay between 1864 and 1870, in which about half of Paraguay's population perished.

Governments throughout the Western world now claimed to act on behalf of their nations and deliberately sought to instill national loyalties in their citizens through schools, public rituals, the mass media, and military service. Russian authorities, for example, imposed the use of the Russian language, even in parts of the country where it was not widely spoken. They succeeded, however, only in producing a greater awareness of Ukrainian, Polish, and Finnish nationalism.

As it became more prominent in the nineteenth century, nationalism took on a variety of political ideologies. Some supporters of liberal democracy and representative government, as in France or the United States, saw nationalism, with its emphasis on "the people," as an aid to their aspirations toward wider involvement in political life. Often called civic nationalism, such a view identified the nation with a particular territory and maintained that people of various cultural backgrounds could assimilate into the dominant culture, as

MAP 16.4   The Nations and Empires of Europe, ca. 1880

By the end of the nineteenth century, the national principle had substantially reshaped the map of Europe, especially in the unification of Germany and Italy. However, several major empires remained, each with numerous subject peoples who likewise sought national independence.

in the process of "becoming American." Other versions of nationalism, in Germany, for example, sometimes defined the nation in racial terms that excluded those who did not share an imagined common ancestry, such as Jews. In the hands of conservatives, nationalism could be used to combat socialism and feminism, for those movements allegedly divided the nation along class or gender lines. Thus nationalism generated endless controversy because it provided no clear answer to the questions of who belonged to the nation or who should speak for it.

Nor was nationalism limited to the Euro-American world in the nineteenth century. An "Egypt for the Egyptians" movement arose in the 1870s as British and French intervention in Egyptian affairs deepened. When Japan likewise confronted European aggression in the second half of the nineteenth century, its long sense of itself as a distinct culture

Nationalism in Poland In the eighteenth century, Poland had been divided among Prussia, Austria, and Russia and disappeared as a separate and independent state. Polish nationalism found expression in the nineteenth century in a series of revolts against Poland's Russian occupiers. This painting shows Russian officers surrendering their standards to Polish insurgents during the November Uprising of 1830. The revolt was subsequently crushed, and Poland regained its independence as a nation-state only in 1918 at the end of World War I. (ullstein Bild/ Granger, NYC — All rights reserved)

was readily transformed into an assertive modern nationalism. In British-ruled India, small groups of Western-educated men began to think of their enormously diverse country as a single nation. The Indian National Congress, established in 1885, gave expression to this idea. The notion of the Ottoman Empire as a Turkish national state rather than a Muslim or dynastic empire took hold among a few people. By the end of the nineteenth century, some Chinese intellectuals began to think in terms of a Chinese nation beset both by a foreign ruling dynasty and by predatory Europeans. Along the West African coast, the idea of an "African nation" stirred among a handful of freed slaves and missionary-educated men. Although Egyptian and Japanese nationalism gained broad support, elsewhere in Asia and Africa such movements would have to wait until the twentieth century, when they exploded with enormous power on the stage of world history.

Feminist Beginnings

A third echo of the Atlantic revolutions lay in the emergence of a feminist movement. Although scattered voices had earlier challenged patriarchy, never before had an organized and substantial group of women called into question this most fundamental and accepted feature of all preindustrial civilizations — the subordination of women to men. But in the century following the French Revolution, such a challenge took shape, especially in Europe and North America. Then, in the twentieth century, feminist thinking transformed "the way in which women and men work, play, think, dress, worship, vote, reproduce, make love and make war."[23] How did this extraordinary process get launched in the nineteenth century?

Thinkers of the European Enlightenment had challenged many ancient traditions, including on occasion that of women's intrinsic inferiority (see "Science and Enlightenment" in Chapter 15). The French writer Condorcet, for example, called for "the complete destruction of those prejudices that have established an inequality of rights between the sexes." The French Revolution then raised the possibility of re-creating human societies on new foundations. Many women participated in these events, and a few insisted, unsuccessfully, that the revolutionary ideals of liberty and equality must include women. In neighboring England, the French Revolution stimulated the writer Mary Wollstonecraft to pen her famous *Vindication of the Rights of Woman*, one of the earliest expressions of a feminist consciousness. "Who made man the exclusive judge," she asked, "if woman partake with him of the gift of reason?"

Within the growing middle classes of industrializing societies, more women found both educational opportunities and some freedom from household drudgery. Such women increasingly took part in temperance movements, charities, abolitionism, and missionary work, as well as socialist and pacifist organizations. Some of their working-class sisters became active trade unionists. On both sides of the Atlantic, small numbers of these women began to develop a feminist consciousness that viewed women as individuals with rights equal to those of men. The first organized expression of this new feminism took place at the Women's Rights Convention in Seneca Falls, New York, in 1848. At that meeting, **Elizabeth Cady Stanton** drafted a statement that began by paraphrasing the Declaration of Independence: "We hold these truths to be self-evident, that all men and women are created equal."

From the beginning, feminism became a transatlantic movement in which European and American women attended the same conferences, corresponded regularly, and read one another's work. Access to schools, universities, and the professions were among their major concerns as growing numbers of women sought these previously unavailable opportunities. The more radical among them refused to take their husbands' surname or wore trousers under their skirts. Elizabeth Cady Stanton published a Women's Bible, excising the parts she found offensive. As heirs to the French Revolution, feminists ardently believed in progress and insisted that it must now include a radical transformation of the position of women.

By the 1870s, feminist movements in the West were focusing primarily on the issue of suffrage and were gaining a growing constituency. Now many ordinary middle-class housewives and working-class mothers joined their better-educated sisters in the movement. By 1914, some 100,000 women took part in French feminist organizations, while the National American Woman Suffrage Association claimed 2 million members. Most operated through peaceful protest and persuasion, but the British Women's Social and Political Union organized a campaign of violence that included blowing up railroad stations, slashing works of art, and smashing department store windows. One British activist, Emily Davison, threw herself in front of the king's horse during a race in Britain in 1913 and was trampled to death. By the beginning of the twentieth century in the most highly industrialized countries of the West, the women's movement had become a mass movement.

That movement had some effect. By 1900, upper- and middle-class women had gained entrance to universities, though in small numbers, and women's literacy rates were growing steadily. In the United States, a number of states passed legislation allowing women to manage and control their own property and wages, separate from their husbands. Divorce laws were liberalized in some places. Professions such as medicine opened to a few, and teaching beckoned to many more. In Britain, Florence Nightingale professionalized nursing and attracted thousands of women into it, while Jane Addams in the United States virtually invented "social work," which also became a female-dominated profession. Progress was slower in the political domain. In 1893, New Zealand became the first country to give the vote to all adult women; Finland followed in 1906. Elsewhere widespread voting rights for women in national elections were not achieved until after World War I, in 1920 in the United States, and in France not until 1945.

Beyond these concrete accomplishments, the movement prompted an unprecedented discussion about the role of women in modern society. In Henrik Ibsen's play *A Doll's House* (1879), the heroine, Nora, finding herself in a loveless and oppressive marriage, leaves both her husband and her children. European audiences were riveted, and many were outraged. Writers, doctors, and journalists addressed previously taboo sexual topics, including homosexuality and birth control. Socialists too found themselves divided about women's issues. Did the women's movement distract from the class solidarity that Marxism proclaimed, or did it provide added energy to the workers' cause? Feminists themselves disagreed about the proper basis for women's rights. Some took their stand on the modern idea of human equality: "Whatever is right for a man is right for a woman." Others, particularly in France, based their claims more on the distinctive role of women as mothers. "It is above all this holy function of motherhood," wrote one advocate of **maternal feminism**, "which requires that women watch over the futures of their children and gives women the right to intervene not only in all acts of civil life, but also in all acts of political life."[24]

Not surprisingly, feminism provoked bitter opposition. Some academic and medical experts argued that the strains of education and life outside the home would cause serious reproductive damage and as a consequence depopulate the nation. Thus feminists were viewed as selfish, willing to sacrifice the family or even the nation while pursuing their individual goals. Some saw suffragists, like Jews and socialists, as "a foreign body in our national life." Never before in any society had such a passionate and public debate about the position of women erupted. It was a novel feature of Western historical experience in the aftermath of the Atlantic revolutions.

Like nationalism, a concern with women's rights spread beyond Western Europe and North America, though less widely. An overtly feminist newspaper was established in Brazil in 1852, and an independent school for girls was founded in Mexico in 1869. A handful of Japanese women and men, including the empress Haruko, raised issues about marriage, family planning, and especially education as the country began its modernizing process after 1868, but the state soon cracked down firmly, forbidding women from joining political parties or even attending political meetings. In Russia, the most radical feminist activists operated within socialist or anarchist circles, targeting the oppressive tsarist regime. Within the Islamic world and in China, some modernists came to believe that education and a higher status for women strengthened the nation in its struggles for development and independence and therefore deserved support. Huda Sharawi, founder of the first feminist organization in Egypt, returned to Cairo in 1923 from an international conference in Italy and threw her veil into the sea. Many upper-class Egyptian women soon followed her example.

Nowhere did nineteenth-century feminism have thoroughly revolutionary consequences. But as an outgrowth of the French and Industrial Revolutions, it raised issues that echoed repeatedly and more loudly in the century that followed.

Reflections: Revolutions: Pro and Con

Long after the dust had settled from the Atlantic upheavals, their legacies have continued to provoke controversy. Were these revolutions necessary? Did they really promote the freedoms that they advertised? Did their benefits outweigh their costs in blood and treasure?

To the people who made these revolutions, benefited from them, or subsequently supported them, they represented an opening to new worlds of human possibility, while sweeping away old worlds of oppression, exploitation, and privilege. Modern revolutionaries acted on the basis of Enlightenment ideas, believing that the structure of human societies was not forever ordained by God or tradition and that it was both possible and necessary to reconstruct those societies. They saw themselves as correcting ancient and enduring injustices. To those who complained about the violence of revolutions, supporters pointed to the violence that maintained the status quo and the unwillingness of favored classes to accommodate changes that threatened those unjust privileges. It was persistent injustice that made revolution necessary and perhaps inevitable.

To their victims, critics, and opponents, revolutions appeared in a quite different light. Conservatives generally viewed human societies not as machines whose parts could be easily rearranged but as organisms that evolved slowly. Efforts at radical and sudden change only invited disaster, as the unrestrained violence of the French Revolution at its height demonstrated. The brutality and bitterness of the Haitian Revolution arguably contributed to the unhappy future of that country. Furthermore, critics charged that revolutions were largely unnecessary since societies were in fact changing. France was becoming a modern society, and feudalism was largely gone well before the revolution exploded. Slavery was ended peacefully in many places, and democratic reform proceeded gradually throughout the nineteenth century. Was this not a preferable alternative to revolutionary upheaval?

Historians too struggle with the passions of revolution—both pro and con—as they seek to understand the origins and consequences of these momentous events. Were revolutions the product of misery, injustice, and oppression? Or did they reflect the growing weakness of established authorities, the arrival of new ideas, or the presence of small groups of radical activists able to fan the little fires of ordinary discontent into revolutionary conflagrations? The outcomes of revolutions have been as contentious as their beginnings. Did the American Revolution enable the growth of the United States as an economic and political Great Power? Did the Haitian Revolution stimulate the later end of slavery elsewhere in the Atlantic world? Did the French Revolution and the threat of subsequent revolutions encourage the democratic reforms that followed in the nineteenth century? Such questions have been central to an understanding of the Atlantic revolutions as well as to those that followed in Russia, China, and elsewhere in the twentieth century.

Second Thoughts

WHAT'S THE SIGNIFICANCE?

American Revolution (p. 458)

Declaration of the Rights of Man and Citizen (p. 461)

French Revolution (p. 461)

Robespierre (p. 462)

Napoleon Bonaparte (p. 464)

Haitian Revolution (p. 467)

Latin American revolutions (p. 468)

Hidalgo-Morelos rebellion (p. 469)

Tupac Amaru (p. 469)

Great Jamaica Revolt (p. 472)

abolitionist movement (p. 472)

nationalism (p. 475)

Vindication of the Rights of Woman (p. 478)

Elizabeth Cady Stanton (p. 478)

maternal feminism (p. 479)

BIG PICTURE QUESTIONS

1. Do revolutions originate in oppression and injustice, in the weakening of political authorities, in new ideas, or in the activities of small groups of determined activists?

2. "The influence of revolutions endured long after they ended and far beyond where they started." To what extent does this chapter support or undermine this idea?

3. Did the Atlantic revolutions fulfill or betray the goals of those who made them? Consider this question in both short- and long-term perspectives.

4. **Looking Back:** To what extent did the Atlantic revolutions reflect the influence of early modern historical developments (1450–1750)?

CHRONOLOGY

1754–1763	• Seven Years' War among European Great Powers
1775–1787	• American Revolution
1780–1782	• Tupac Amaru rebellion in Peru
1787	• Establishment of Freetown, a colony of freed slaves in West Africa
1789–1815	• French Revolution and reign of Napoleon
1791–1804	• Haitian Revolution
1798–1801	• Napoleon's invasion of Egypt
1808–1825	• Latin American wars of independence
1810–1811	• Hidalgo-Morales rebellion in Mexico
1815–1840	• *Mfecane*; rise of Zulu kingdom in South Africa

1825	• Anti-tsarist uprising in Russia
1833	• Slavery prohibited in British Empire
1848	• Women's Rights Convention, Seneca Falls, NY
1852	• Feminist newspaper established in Brazil
1861	• Emancipation of serfs in Russia
1861–1865	• U.S. Civil War and abolition of slavery
1870	• Unification of Italy
1870s	• "Egypt for the Egyptians" movement
1871	• Unification of Germany
1885	• Indian National Congress established
1888	• End of slavery in Brazil
1893	• Women's suffrage in New Zealand
1920	• Women's suffrage in the United States

17

Revolutions of Industrialization

1750–1900

IN MID-2017, ERIK SOLHEIM, THE NORWEGIAN HEAD OF THE UN
Environment Program, stated that "humanity's advancement in science, technology and industrialization [is] harming the planet, hence the need to reverse course."[1] At the same time, Dr. Lloyd G. Adu Amoah, a prominent professor at the University of Ghana in West Africa, declared: "We need to industrialize, because if we don't, we are not adding value to what the African continent has."[2]

These two statements represent perhaps the most compelling dilemma facing human-kind in the twenty-first century. How can we embrace the wealth and improvement in human life universally associated with industrialization, while preserving and pro-tecting this fragile planet that sustains us all? That profound dilemma has its origins in the enormously transformative process of the Industrial Revolution, which took place initially in Europe during the century and a half between 1750 and 1900. Not since the Agricultural Revolution some 12,000 years ago have our ways of living and our relationship to the natural world been so fundamentally altered.

In any long-term reckoning, the history of industrialization is very much an unfinished story. Are we at the beginning of a movement leading to worldwide industrialization, stuck in the middle of a world permanently divided into rich and poor countries, or approaching the end of an environmentally unsustainable indus-trial era? Whatever the future holds, this chapter focuses on the early stages of an immense transformation in the global condition of humankind.

Industrialization: The Global Context

The epic economic transformation of the Industrial Revolution took shape as a very substantial increase in human numbers unfolded—from about 375 million people in 1400 to about 1 billion in the early nineteenth century. Accompanying this growth in population was an emerging energy crisis, most pronounced in Western Europe, China, and Japan, as wood and charcoal, the major industrial fuels, became more scarce and more costly. In short, "global energy demands began to push against the existing local and regional ecological limits."[3] In broad terms, the Industrial Rev-olution marked a human response to that dilemma. It was a twofold revolution—drawing on new sources of energy and new technologies—that combined to utterly transform economic and social life on the planet.

In terms of energy, the Industrial Revolution came to rely on fossil fuels such as coal, oil, and natural gas, which supplemented and largely replaced the earlier energy sources of wind, water, wood, and the muscle power of people and animals that had long sustained humankind. It was a breakthrough of unprecedented pro-portions that made available for human use, at least temporarily, immensely greater quantities of energy. During the nineteenth century, yet another fuel became widely available as Europeans learned to exploit guano, or seabird excrement, found on the islands off the coast of Peru. Used as a potent fertilizer, guano enabled highly produc-tive input-intensive farming practices. In much of Western Europe, North America, Australia, and New Zealand, it sustained the production of crops that fed both the draft animals and the growing human populations of the industrializing world.[4]

The technological dimension of the Industrial Revolution has been equally significant. Early signs of the technological creativity that spawned the Industrial Revolution appeared in eighteenth-century Britain, where a variety of innovations transformed cotton textile production. It was only in the nineteenth century, though, that Europeans in general and the British in particular more clearly forged ahead of the rest of the world. (See "Controversies: Debating 'Why Europe?'") The great breakthrough was the coal-fired **steam engine**, which provided an inanimate and almost limitless source of power beyond that of wind, water, or muscle and could be used to drive any number of machines as well as locomotives and oceangoing ships. Soon the Industrial Revolution spread beyond the textile industry to iron and steel production, railroads and steamships, food processing, and construction. Later in the nineteenth century, a so called second Industrial Revolution focused on chemicals, electricity, precision machinery, the telegraph and telephone, rubber, printing, and much more. Agriculture too was affected as mechanical reapers, chemical fertilizers, pesticides, and refrigeration transformed this most ancient of industries. Sustaining this explosion of technological innovation was a "culture of innovation," a widespread and almost obsessive belief that things could be endlessly improved.

Together, these new sources of energy and new technologies gave rise to an enormously increased output of goods and services. In Britain, where the Industrial Revolution began, industrial output increased some fiftyfold between 1750 and 1900. It was a wholly unprecedented and previously unimaginable jump in the capacity of human societies to produce wealth, to extend life expectancies, and to increase human numbers. Furthermore, industrialization soon spread beyond Britain to continental Western Europe and then in the second half of the nineteenth century to the United States, Russia, and Japan. In the twentieth century it became a genuinely global process. More than anything else, industrialization marks the past 250 years as a distinct phase of human history.

In the long run, the Industrial Revolution unarguably improved the material conditions of life for much of humankind. But it also unarguably wrought a mounting impact on the environment. The massive extraction of nonrenewable raw materials to feed and to fuel industrial machinery—coal, iron ore, petroleum, and much more—altered the landscape in many places. Sewers and industrial waste emptied into rivers, turning them into poisonous cesspools. In 1858, the Thames River running through London smelled so bad that the British House of Commons had to suspend its session. Smoke from coal-fired industries and domestic use polluted the air in urban areas and sharply increased the incidence of respiratory illness. For many historians, the Industrial Revolution marked a new era in both human history and the history of the planet that scientists increasingly call the Anthropocene, or the "age of man." More and more, human industrial activity left a mark not only on human society but also on the ecological, atmospheric, and geological history of the earth.

Producing Gas from Coal Coal was central to the Industrial Revolution. An early industrial process in Britain involved the burning of coal to produce "coal gas," used for public lighting. This image from 1822 shows that process in action at one such production facility in London. Those who stoked the furnaces often developed various lung diseases and died early. (Print Collector/Getty Images)

The First Industrial Society

Wherever it took hold, the Industrial Revolution generated, within a century or less, an economic miracle, at least in comparison with earlier technologies. The **British textile industry**, which used 52 million pounds of cotton in 1800, consumed 588 million pounds in 1850, as multiple technological innovations and factory-based production vastly increased output. Britain's production of coal likewise soared from 5.23 million tons in 1750 to 68.4 million tons a century later.[5] Railroads crisscrossed Britain and much of Europe like a giant spider web (see Map 17.1). Most of this dramatic increase in production occurred in mining, manufacturing, and services. Thus agriculture, for millennia the overwhelmingly

MAP 17.1   The Early Phase of Europe's Industrial Revolution

From its beginning in Great Britain, industrialization had spread by 1850 across Western Europe to include parts of France, Germany, Belgium, Bohemia, and Italy.

dominant economic sector in every civilization, shrank in relative importance. In Britain, for example, agriculture generated only 8 percent of national income in 1891 and employed fewer than 8 percent of working Britons in 1914. Accompanying this vast economic change was an epic transformation of social life. "In two centuries," wrote one prominent historian, "daily life changed more than it had in the 7,000 years before."[6] Nowhere were the revolutionary dimensions of industrialization more apparent than in Great Britain, the world's first industrial society.

The social transformation of the Industrial Revolution both destroyed and created. Referring to the impact of the Industrial Revolution on British society, historian Eric Hobsbawm wrote: "In its initial stages it destroyed their old ways of living and left them free to discover or make for themselves new ones, if they could and knew how. But it rarely told them how to set about it."[7] For many people, it was an enormously painful, even traumatic process, full of social conflict, insecurity, and false starts even as it offered new opportunities, an eventually higher standard of living, and greater participation in public life. The human gains and losses associated with the Industrial Revolution have been debated ever since. Amid the arguments, however, one thing is clear: not everyone was affected in the same way.

The British Aristocracy

Individual landowning aristocrats, long the dominant class in Britain, suffered little in material terms from the Industrial Revolution. In the mid-nineteenth century, a few thousand families still owned more than half of the cultivated land in Britain, most of it leased to tenant farmers, who in turn employed agricultural wage laborers to work it. Rapidly growing population and urbanization sustained a demand for food products grown on that land. For most of the nineteenth century, landowners continued to dominate the British Parliament.

As a class, however, the British aristocracy declined as a result of the Industrial Revolution, as have large landowners in every industrial society. As urban wealth became more important, landed aristocrats had to make way for the up-and-coming businessmen, manufacturers, and bankers, newly enriched by the Industrial Revolution. By the end of the century, landownership had largely ceased to be the basis of great wealth, and businessmen, rather than aristocrats, led the major political parties. Even so, the titled nobility of dukes, earls, viscounts, and barons retained great social prestige and considerable personal wealth. Many among them found an outlet for their energies and opportunities for status and enrichment in the vast domains of the British Empire, where they went as colonial administrators or settlers. Famously described as a "system of outdoor relief for the aristocracy," the empire provided a cushion for a declining class.

The Middle Classes

Those who benefited most conspicuously from industrialization were members of that amorphous group known as the middle class. At its upper levels, this middle class contained extremely wealthy factory and mine owners, bankers, and merchants. Such rising businessmen readily assimilated into aristocratic life, buying country houses, obtaining seats in Parliament, sending their sons to Oxford or Cambridge University, and gratefully accepting titles of nobility from Queen Victoria.

Far more numerous were the smaller businessmen, doctors, lawyers, engineers, teachers, journalists, scientists, and other professionals required in any industrial society. Such people set the tone for a distinctly **middle-class society** with its own values and outlooks. Politically they were liberals, favoring constitutional government, private property, free trade, and social reform within limits. Their agitation resulted in the Reform Bill of 1832, which broadened the right to vote to many men of the middle class, but not to middle-class women. Ideas of thrift and hard work, a rigid morality, "respectability," and cleanliness characterized middle-class culture. According to Samuel Smiles's famous book *Self-Help*, an enterprising spirit was what distinguished the prosperous middle class from Britain's poor. The misery of the poorer classes was "voluntary and self-imposed — the results of idleness, thriftlessness, intemperance, and misconduct."[8]

Women in such middle-class families were increasingly cast as homemakers, wives, and mothers, charged with creating an emotional haven for their men and a refuge from a heartless and cutthroat capitalist world. They were also expected to be the moral centers of family life, the educators of "respectability," and the managers of household consumption as "shopping" — a new concept in eighteenth-century Britain — became a central activity for the middle classes. An **ideology of domesticity** defined homemaking, child rearing, charitable endeavors, and "refined" activities such as embroidery, music, and drawing as the proper sphere for women, while paid employment and the public sphere of life outside the home beckoned to men.

The Industrial Middle Class This late nineteenth-century painting shows a prosperous French middle-class family, attended by a servant. (*Family Reunion at the Home of Madame Adolphe Brisson, 1893*, by Marcel André Baschet [1862–1941]/Château de Versailles, France/Bridgeman Images)

Male elites in many civilizations had long established their status by detaching women from productive labor. The new wealth of the Industrial Revolution now allowed larger numbers of families to aspire to that kind of status. With her husband as "provider," such a woman was now a "lady." "She must not work for profit," wrote the Englishwoman Margaretta Greg in 1853, "or engage in any occupation that money can command."[9] Employing even one servant became a proud marker of such middle-class status. But the withdrawal of middle-class women from the labor force turned out to be only a temporary phenomenon. By the late nineteenth century, some middle-class women began to enter the teaching, clerical, and nursing professions, and in the second half of the twentieth century, many more flooded into the labor force. By contrast, the withdrawal of children from productive labor into schools has proved a more enduring phenomenon as industrial economies increasingly required a more educated workforce.

As Britain's industrial economy matured, it also gave rise to a sizable **lower middle class**, which included people employed in the growing service sector as clerks, salespeople, bank tellers, hotel staff, secretaries, telephone operators, police officers, and the like. By the end of the nineteenth century, this growing segment of the middle class represented about 20 percent of Britain's population and provided new employment opportunities for women as well as men. In just twenty years (1881–1901), the number of female secretaries in Britain rose from 7,000 to 90,000. Almost all were single and expected to return to the home after marriage. For both men and women, such employment represented a claim on membership in the larger middle class and a means of distinguishing themselves clearly from a working class tainted by manual labor. The mounting ability of these middle classes to consume all manner of material goods—and their appetite for doing so—were among the factors that sustained the continuing growth of the industrializing process.

The Laboring Classes

The overwhelming majority of Britain's nineteenth-century population—some 70 percent or more—were neither aristocrats nor members of the middle classes. They were manual workers in the mines, ports, factories, construction sites, workshops, and farms of an industrializing Britain. Although their conditions varied considerably and changed over time, it was the **laboring classes** who suffered most and benefited least from the epic transformations of the Industrial Revolution. Their efforts to accommodate, resist, protest, and change those conditions contributed much to the texture of the first industrial society.

The lives of the laboring classes were shaped primarily by the rapid urbanization of the industrial era. Liverpool's population alone grew from 77,000 to 400,000 in the first half of the nineteenth century. By 1851, a majority of Britain's population lived in towns and cities, an enormous change from the overwhelmingly rural life of almost all previous civilizations. By the end of the century, London was the world's largest city, with more than 6 million inhabitants.

These cities were vastly overcrowded and smoky, with wholly insufficient sanitation, periodic epidemics, endless row houses and warehouses, few public services or

DEATH'S DISPENSARY.
OPEN TO THE POOR, GRATIS, BY PERMISSION OF THE PARISH.

The Urban Poor of Industrial Britain This 1866 political cartoon shows an impoverished urban family forced to draw its drinking water from a polluted public well, while a figure of Death operates the pump.

open spaces, and inadequate and often-polluted water supplies. This was the environment in which most urban workers lived in the first half of the nineteenth century. By 1850, the average life expectancy in England was only 39.5 years, less than it had been some three centuries earlier. Nor was there much personal contact between the rich and the poor of industrial cities. Benjamin Disraeli's novel *Sybil*, published in 1845, described these two ends of the social spectrum as "two nations between whom there is no intercourse and no sympathy; who are ignorant of each other's habits, thoughts and feelings, as if they were dwellers in different zones or inhabitants of different planets."

The industrial factories to which growing numbers of desperate people looked for employment offered a work environment far different from the artisan's shop or the tenant's farm. Long hours, low wages, and child labor were nothing new for the poor, but the routine and monotony of work, dictated by the factory whistle and the needs of machines, imposed novel and highly unwelcome conditions of labor. Also objectionable were the direct and constant supervision and the rules and fines aimed at enforcing work discipline. In addition, the ups and downs of a capitalist economy made industrial work insecure as well as onerous.

In the early decades of the nineteenth century, Britain's industrialists favored girls and young unmarried women as employees in the textile mills, for they were often willing to accept lower wages, while male owners believed them to be both docile and more suitable for repetitive tasks such as tending machines. A gendered hierarchy of labor emerged in these factories, with men in supervisory and more skilled positions, while women occupied the less skilled and "lighter" jobs that offered little opportunity for advancement. Nor were women welcome in the unions that eventually offered men some ability to shape the conditions under which they labored.

Thus, unlike their middle-class counterparts, many girls and young women of the laboring classes engaged in industrial work or found jobs as domestic servants for upper- and middle-class families to supplement meager family incomes. But after marriage, they too usually left outside paid employment because a man who could not support his wife was widely considered a failure. Within the home, however, many working-class women continued to earn money by taking in boarders, doing laundry, or sewing clothes in addition to the domestic and child-rearing responsibilities long assigned to women.

Social Protest

For workers of the laboring classes, industrial life "was a stony desert, which they had to make habitable by their own efforts."[10] Such efforts took many forms. By 1815, about 1 million workers, mostly artisans, had created a variety of "friendly societies." With dues contributed by members, these working-class self-help groups provided insurance against sickness, a decent funeral, and an opportunity for social life in an otherwise-bleak environment. Other skilled artisans who had been displaced by machine-produced goods and forbidden to organize in legal unions sometimes wrecked the offending machinery and burned the mills that had taken their jobs. The class consciousness of working people was such that one police informer reported that "most every creature of the lower order both in town and country are on their side."[11] Others acted within the political arena by joining movements aimed at obtaining the vote for working-class men, a goal that was gradually achieved in the second half of the nineteenth century. When trade unions were legalized in 1824, growing numbers of factory workers joined these associations in their efforts to achieve better wages and working conditions. Initially their strikes, attempts at nationwide organization, and threat of violence made them fearful indeed to the upper classes. One British newspaper in 1834 described unions as "the most dangerous institutions that were ever permitted to take root, under shelter of law, in any country,"[12] although they later became rather more "respectable" organizations.

Socialist ideas of various kinds gradually spread within the working class, challenging the assumptions of a capitalist society. Robert Owen (1771–1858), a wealthy British cotton textile manufacturer, urged the creation of small industrial communities where workers and their families would be well treated. He established one such community, with a ten-hour workday, spacious housing, decent wages, and education for children, at his mill in New Lanark in Scotland.

Of more lasting significance was the socialism of **Karl Marx** (1818–1883). German by birth, Marx spent much of his life in England, where he witnessed the brutal conditions of Britain's Industrial Revolution and wrote voluminously about history and economics. His probing analysis led him to conclude that industrial capitalism was an inherently unstable system, doomed to collapse in a revolutionary upheaval that would give birth to a classless socialist society, thus ending forever the ancient conflict between rich and poor.

In Marx's writings, the combined impact of Europe's industrial, political, and scientific revolutions found expression. Industrialization created both the social conditions against which Marx protested so bitterly and the enormous wealth he felt would make socialism possible. The French Revolution, still a living memory in Marx's youth, provided evidence that grand upheavals, giving rise to new societies, had in fact taken place and could do so again. Moreover, Marx regarded himself as a scientist, discovering the laws of social development in much the same fashion as Newton discovered the laws of motion. His was therefore a "scientific socialism," embedded in these laws of historical change; revolution was a certainty and the socialist future was inevitable.

It was a grand, compelling, prophetic, utopian vision of human freedom and community—and it inspired socialist movements of workers and intellectuals amid the grim harshness of Europe's industrialization in the second half of the nineteenth century. Socialists established political parties in most European states and linked them together in international organizations as well. These parties recruited members, contested elections as they gained the right to vote, agitated for reforms, and in some cases plotted revolution.

In the later decades of the nineteenth century, such ideas echoed among more radical trade unionists and some middle-class intellectuals in Britain, and even more so in a rapidly industrializing Germany and elsewhere. By then, however, the British working-class movement was not overtly revolutionary. When a working-class political party, the **Labour Party**, was established in the 1890s, it advocated a reformist program and a peaceful democratic transition to socialism, largely rejecting the class struggle and revolutionary emphasis of classical Marxism. Generally known as "social democracy," this approach to socialism was especially prominent in Germany during the late nineteenth century and spread more widely in the twentieth century, when it came into conflict with the more violent and revolutionary movements calling themselves "communist."

Improving material conditions during the second half of the nineteenth century helped move the working-class movement in Britain, Germany, and elsewhere away from a revolutionary posture. Marx had expected industrial capitalist societies to polarize into a small wealthy class and a huge and increasingly impoverished proletariat. However, standing between "the captains of industry" and the workers was a sizable middle and lower middle class, constituting perhaps 30 percent of the population, most of whom were not really wealthy but were immensely proud that they were not manual laborers. Marx had not foreseen the development of this intermediate social group, nor had he imagined that workers could better their standard of living within a capitalist framework. But they did. Wages rose under pressure from unions; cheap imported food improved working-class diets; infant mortality rates fell; and shops and chain stores catering to working-class families multiplied. As English male workers gradually obtained the right to vote, politicians had an incentive to legislate in their favor, by abolishing child labor, regulating factory conditions, and even, in 1911, inaugurating a system of relief for the unemployed. Sanitary reform considerably cleaned up the "filth and stink" of early nineteenth-century cities, and urban parks made a modest appearance. Contrary to Marx's expectations, capitalist societies demonstrated some capacity for reform.

Further eroding working-class radicalism was a growing sense of nationalism, which bound workers in particular countries to their middle-class employers and compatriots, offsetting to some extent the economic and social antagonism between them. When World War I broke out, the "workers of the world," far from uniting against their bourgeois enemies as Marx had urged them, instead set off to slaughter one another in enormous numbers on the battlefields of Europe. National loyalty had trumped class loyalty.

Nonetheless, as the twentieth century dawned, industrial Britain was hardly a stable or contented society. Immense inequalities still separated the classes. Some 40 percent of the working class continued to live in conditions then described as "poverty." A mounting wave of strikes from 1910 to 1913 testified to the intensity of class conflict. The Labour Party was becoming a major force in Parliament. Some socialists and some feminists were becoming radicalized. "Wisps of violence hung in the English air," wrote Eric Hobsbawm, "symptoms of a crisis in economy and society, which the [country's] self-confident opulence . . . could not quite conceal."[13] The world's first industrial society remained dissatisfied and conflicted.

It was also a society in economic decline relative to industrial newcomers such as Germany and the United States. Britain paid a price for its early lead, for its businessmen became committed to machinery that became obsolete as the century progressed. Latecomers invested in more modern equipment and in various ways had surpassed the British by the early twentieth century.

Europeans in Motion

Europe's Industrial Revolution prompted a massive migratory process that uprooted many millions, setting them in motion both internally and around the globe. Within Europe itself, the movement of men, women, and families from the countryside to the cities involved half or more of the region's people by the mid-nineteenth century. More significant for world history was the exodus between 1815 and 1939 of fully 20 percent of Europe's population, some 50 to 55 million people, who left home for the Americas, Australia, New Zealand, South Africa, and elsewhere (see Map 17.2). They were pushed by poverty, a rapidly growing population, and the displacement of peasant farming and artisan manufacturing. And they were pulled abroad by the enormous demand for labor overseas, the ready availability of land in some places, and the relatively cheap transportation of railroads and steamships. But not all found a satisfactory life in their new homes, and perhaps 7 million returned to Europe.[14]

This huge process had a transformative global impact, temporarily increasing Europe's share of the world's population and scattering Europeans around the world. In 1800, less than 1 percent of the total world population consisted of overseas Europeans and their descendants; by 1930, they represented 11 percent.[15] In particular regions, the impact was profound. Australia and New Zealand became settler colonies, outposts of European civilization in the South Pacific that overwhelmed their native populations through conquest, acquisition of their lands, and disease. By the end of the nineteenth century, New Zealand's European population, based on immigration of free people, outnumbered the native Maori by 700,000 to 40,000. Smaller numbers of Europeans found their way to South Africa, Kenya, Rhodesia, Algeria, and elsewhere, where they injected a sharp racial divide into those colonized territories.

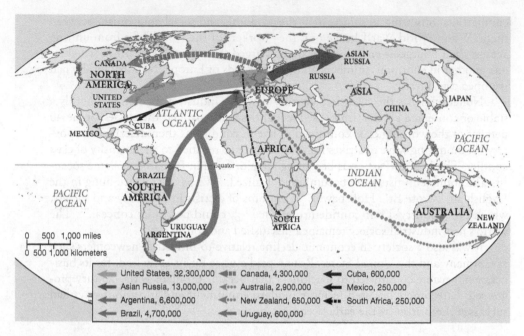

MAP 17.2   European Migration in the Industrial Age
The Industrial Revolution not only transformed European society but also scattered millions of Europeans
to the far corners of the world.

But it was the Americas that felt the brunt of this huge movement of people.
Latin America received about 20 percent of the European migratory stream, mostly
from Italy, Spain, and Portugal, with Argentina and Brazil accounting for some
80 percent of those immigrants. Considered "white," they enhanced the social weight
of the European element in those countries and thus enjoyed economic advantages
over the mixed-race, Indian, and African populations.

In several ways the immigrant experience in the United States was distinctive.
It was far larger and more diverse than elsewhere, with some 32 million newcomers
arriving from all over Europe between 1820 and 1930. Furthermore, the United States
offered affordable land to many and industrial jobs to many more, neither of which
was widely available in Latin America. And the United States was unique in turning
the immigrant experience into a national myth—that of the melting pot. Despite this
ideology of assimilation, the earlier immigrants, mostly Protestants from Britain and
Germany, were anything but welcoming to Catholics and Jews from Southern and
Eastern Europe who arrived later. The newcomers were seen as distinctly inferior, even
"un-American," and blamed for crime, labor unrest, and socialist ideas. Nonetheless,
this surge of immigration contributed much to the westward expansion of the United
States, to the establishment of a European-derived culture in a vast area of North
America, and to the displacement of the native peoples of the region.

In the vast domains of the Russian Empire, a parallel process of European
migration likewise unfolded. After the freeing of the serfs in 1861, some 13 million

Russians and Ukrainians migrated to Siberia, where they overwhelmed the native population of the region, while millions more settled in Central Asia. The availability of land, the prospect of greater freedom from tsarist restrictions and from the exploitation of aristocratic landowners, and the construction of the trans-Siberian railroad—all of this facilitated the continued Europeanization of Siberia. As in the United States, the Russian government encouraged and aided this process, hoping to forestall Chinese pressures in the region and relieve growing population pressures in the more densely settled western lands of the empire.

Variations on a Theme: Industrialization in the United States and Russia

Not for long was the Industrial Revolution confined to Britain. It soon spread to continental Western Europe, and by the end of the nineteenth century it was well under way in the United States, Russia, and Japan. The globalization of industrialization had begun. Everywhere it took hold, industrialization bore a range of broadly similar outcomes. New technologies and sources of energy generated vast increases in production and spawned an unprecedented urbanization as well. Class structures changed as aristocrats, artisans, and peasants declined as classes, while the middle classes and a factory working class grew in numbers and social prominence. Middle-class women generally withdrew from paid labor altogether, and their working-class counterparts sought to do so after marriage. Working women usually received lower wages than their male counterparts, had difficulty joining unions, and were accused of taking jobs from men. Working-class frustration and anger gave rise to trade unions and socialist movements, injecting a new element of social conflict into industrial societies.

Nevertheless, different histories, cultures, and societies ensured that the Industrial Revolution unfolded variously in the diverse countries in which it became established. Differences in the pace and timing of industrialization, the size and shape of major industries, the role of the state, the political expression of social conflict, and many other factors have made this process rich in comparative possibilities. French industrialization, for example, occurred more slowly and perhaps less disruptively than did that of Britain. Germany focused initially on heavy industry—iron, steel, and coal—rather than on the textile industry with which Britain had begun. Moreover, German industrialization was far more highly concentrated in huge companies called cartels, and it generated a rather more militant and Marxist-oriented labor movement than in Britain.

Nowhere were the variations in the industrializing process more apparent than in those two vast countries that lay on the periphery of Europe. To the west across the Atlantic Ocean was the United States, a young, vigorous, democratic, expanding country, populated largely by people of European descent, along with a substantial number of slaves of African origin. To the east was Russia, with its Eastern Orthodox Christianity, an autocratic tsar, a huge population of serfs, and an empire stretching across all of northern Asia. By the early twentieth century, industrialization had turned the United States into a major global power and had spawned in Russia an enormous revolutionary upheaval that made that country the first outpost of global communism.

The United States: Industrialization without Socialism

American industrialization began in the textile factories of New England during the 1820s but grew explosively in the half century following the Civil War (1861–1865) (see Map 17.3). The country's huge size, the ready availability of natural resources, its expanding domestic market, and its relative political stability combined to make the United States the world's leading industrial power by 1914. At that time, it produced 36 percent of the world's manufactured goods, compared to 16 percent for Germany, 14 percent for Great Britain, and 6 percent for France. Furthermore, U.S. industrialization was closely linked to that of Europe. About one-third of the capital investment that financed its remarkable growth came from British, French, and German capitalists. But unlike Latin America, which also received much foreign investment, the United States was able to use those funds to generate an independent Industrial Revolution of its own.

As in other later industrializing countries, the U.S. government played an important role, though less directly than in Germany or Japan. Tax breaks, huge grants of public land to the railroad companies, laws enabling the easy formation of corporations, and the absence of much overt regulation of industry all fostered the rise of very large business enterprises. The U.S. Steel Corporation, for example, by 1901 had an annual budget three times the size of the federal government's budget.

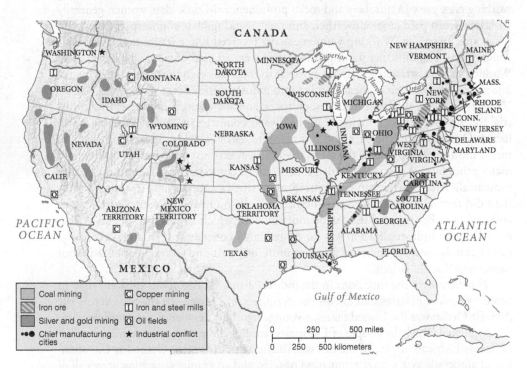

MAP 17.3   The Industrial United States in 1900
By the early twentieth century, manufacturing industries were largely in the Northeast and Midwest, whereas mining operations were more widely scattered across the country.

In this respect, the United States followed the pattern of Germany but differed from that of France and Britain, where family businesses still predominated.

The United States also pioneered techniques of mass production, using interchangeable parts, the assembly line, and "scientific management" to produce for a mass market. The nation's advertising agencies, Sears Roebuck's and Montgomery Ward's mail-order catalogs, and urban department stores generated a middle-class "culture of consumption." When the industrialist Henry Ford in the early twentieth century began producing the Model T at a price that many ordinary people could afford, he famously declared: "I am going to democratize the automobile." More so than in Europe, with its aristocratic traditions, self-made American industrialists of fabulous wealth such as Henry Ford, Andrew Carnegie, and John D. Rockefeller became cultural heroes, widely admired as models of what anyone could achieve with daring and hard work in a land of endless opportunity.

Nevertheless, well before the first Model T rolled off the assembly line, serious social divisions of a kind common to European industrial societies mounted. Preindustrial America had boasted of a relative social equality, quite unlike that of Europe, but by the end of the nineteenth century a widening gap separated the classes. In Carnegie's Homestead steel plant near Pittsburgh, employees worked every day except Christmas and the Fourth of July, often for twelve hours a day. In Manhattan, where millions of European immigrants disembarked, many lived in five- or six-story buildings with four families and two toilets on each floor. In every large city, such conditions prevailed close by the mansions of elite neighborhoods. To some, the contrast was a betrayal of American ideals, while others saw it as a natural outcome of competition and "the survival of the fittest."

As elsewhere, such conditions generated much labor protest, the formation of unions, strikes, and sometimes violence. In 1877, when the eastern railroads announced a 10 percent wage cut for their workers, strikers disrupted rail service across the eastern half of the country, smashed equipment, and rioted. Both state militias and federal troops were called out to put down the movement. Class consciousness and class conflict were intense in the industrial America of the late nineteenth and early twentieth centuries.

Unlike in many European countries, however, no major political party emerged in the United States to represent the interests of the working class. Nor did the ideas of socialism, especially those of Marxism, appeal to American workers nearly as much as they did to European laborers. At its high point, the Socialist Party of America garnered just 6 percent of the vote for its presidential candidate in the 1912 election, whereas socialists at the time held more seats in Germany's Parliament than any other party. Even in the depths of the Great Depression of the 1930s, no major socialist movement emerged to champion American workers. How might we explain the relative weakness of socialism in the United States?

One answer lies in the relative conservatism of major American union organizations, especially the American Federation of Labor. Its focus on skilled workers excluded the more radical unskilled laborers, and its refusal to align with any party limited its influence in the political arena. Furthermore, massive immigration from Europe, beginning in the 1840s, created a very diverse industrial labor force on top of the country's sharp racial divide. This diversity contrasted sharply with the more homogeneous populations of many European countries. Catholics and Protestants;

whites and blacks; English, Irish, Germans, Slavs, Jews, and Italians—such differences undermined the class solidarity of American workers, making it far more difficult to sustain class-oriented political parties and a socialist labor movement. Moreover, the country's remarkable economic growth generated on average a higher standard of living for American workers than their European counterparts experienced. Land was cheaper, and home ownership was more available. Workers with property generally found socialism less attractive than those without. By 1910, a particularly large group of white-collar workers in sales, services, and offices outnumbered factory laborers. Their middle-class aspirations further diluted impulses toward radicalism.

But political challenges to the abuses of capitalist industrialization did arise. In the 1890s, among small farmers in the U.S. South, West, and Midwest, "populists" railed against banks, industrialists, monopolies, the existing money system, and both major political parties, all of which they thought were dominated by the corporate interests of the eastern elites. More successful, especially in the early twentieth century, were the **Progressives**, who pushed for specific reforms, such as wages-and-hours legislation, better sanitation standards, antitrust laws, and greater governmental intervention in the economy. Socialism, however, came to be defined as fundamentally "un-American" in a country that so valued individualism and so feared "big government." It was a distinctive feature of the American response to industrialization.

Russia: Industrialization and Revolution

As a setting for the Industrial Revolution, it would be hard to imagine two more different environments than the United States and Russia. If the United States was the Western world's most exuberant democracy during the nineteenth century, Russia remained the sole outpost of absolute monarchy, in which the state exercised far greater control over individuals and society than anywhere in the Western world.

At the beginning of the twentieth century, Russia still had no national parliament, no legal political parties, and no nationwide elections. The tsar, answerable to God alone, ruled unchecked. Furthermore, Russian society was dominated by a titled nobility of various ranks. Its upper levels included great landowners, who furnished the state with military officers and leading government officials. Until 1861, most Russians were peasant serfs, bound to the estates of their masters, subject to sale, greatly exploited, and largely at the mercy of their owners. A vast cultural gulf separated these two classes. Many nobles were highly westernized, some speaking French better than Russian, whereas their serfs were steeped in a backwoods Orthodox Christianity that incorporated pre-Christian spirits, spells, curses, and magic.

A further difference between Russia and the United States lay in the source of social and economic change. In the United States, such change bubbled up from society as free farmers, workers, and businessmen sought new opportunities and operated in a political system that gave them varying degrees of expression. In autocratic Russia, change was far more often initiated by the state itself, in its continuing efforts to catch up with the more powerful and innovative states of Europe. This kind of "transformation from above" found an early expression in the reign of Peter the Great (r. 1689–1725). (See "Russians and Empire" in Chapter 13.) Such state-directed change continued in the nineteenth century with the freeing of the serfs in 1861, an action stimulated by military defeat at the hands of British and French

Russian Serfs This 1872 photograph shows a wealthy Russian landowner and his wife being pulled in a cart by serfs, who had been legally freed just eleven years earlier but continued to serve their master. They are attending a high-society wedding of another local estate owner. (© SZ Photo/Bridgeman Images)

forces in the Crimean War (1854–1856). To many thoughtful Russians, serfdom seemed incompatible with modern civilization and held back the country's overall development, as did its economic and industrial backwardness. Thus, beginning in the 1860s, Russia began a program of industrial development that was more heavily directed by the state than was the case in Western Europe or the United States.

By the 1890s, Russia's Industrial Revolution was launched and growing rapidly. It focused particularly on railroads and heavy industry and was fueled by a substantial amount of foreign investment. By 1900, Russia ranked fourth in the world in steel production and had major industries in coal, textiles, and oil. Its industrial enterprises, still modest in comparison to those of Europe, were concentrated in a few major cities—Moscow, St. Petersburg, and Kiev, for example—and took place in factories far larger than in most of Western Europe.

All of this contributed to the explosive social outcomes of Russian industrialization. A growing middle class of businessmen and professionals increasingly took shape. As modern and educated people, many in the middle class objected strongly to the deep conservatism of tsarist Russia and sought a greater role in political life, but they were also dependent on the state for contracts and jobs and for suppressing the growing radicalism of the workers, which they greatly feared. Although factory workers constituted only about 5 percent of Russia's total population, they quickly developed a radical class consciousness, based on harsh conditions and the absence of any legal outlet for their grievances. As in Western Europe, millions flocked to the new centers of industrial development. By 1897, over 70 percent of the population in Moscow and St. Petersburg were recent migrants from the rural areas. Their conditions of life resembled those of industrial migrants in New York or Berlin. One observer wrote: "People live in impossible conditions: filth, stench, suffocating heat. They lie down together barely a few feet apart; there is no division between the sexes and adults sleep with children."[16] Until 1897, a thirteen-hour working day was common, while ruthless discipline and overt disrespect from supervisors created resentment. In the absence of legal unions or political parties, these grievances often erupted in the form of large-scale strikes.

In these conditions, a small but growing number of educated Russians found in Marxist socialism a way of understanding the changes they witnessed daily as well as hope for the future in a revolutionary upheaval of workers. In 1898, they created an illegal Russian Social Democratic Labor Party and quickly became involved in workers' education, union organizing, and, eventually, revolutionary action. By the early twentieth century, the strains of rapid change and the state's continued intransigence had reached the bursting point, and in 1905, following its defeat in a naval war with Japan, Russia erupted in spontaneous insurrection (see Map 17.4). Workers in

MAP 17.4
Industrialization and Revolution in Russia, 1905
Only in Russia did industrialization lead to violent revolutionary upheavals, both in 1905 and more successfully in 1917.

Moscow and St. Petersburg went on strike and created their own representative councils, called soviets. Peasant uprisings, student demonstrations, revolts of non-Russian nationalities, and mutinies in the military all contributed to the upheaval. Recently formed political parties, representing intellectuals of various persuasions, came out into the open.

The **Russian Revolution of 1905**, though brutally suppressed, forced the tsar's regime to make more substantial reforms than it had ever contemplated. It granted a constitution, legalized both trade unions and political parties, and permitted the election of a national assembly, called the Duma. Censorship was eased, and plans were under way for universal primary education. Industrial development likewise continued at a rapid rate, so that by 1914 Russia stood fifth in the world in terms of overall output. But in the first half of that year, some 1,250,000 workers, representing about 40 percent of the entire industrial workforce, went out on strike.

Thus the tsar's limited political reforms, which had been granted with great reluctance and were often reversed in practice, failed to tame working-class radicalism or to bring social stability to Russia. In Russian political life, the people generally, and even the middle class, had only a very limited voice. Representatives of even the privileged classes had become so alienated by the government's intransigence that many felt revolution was inevitable. Various revolutionary groups, many of them socialist, published pamphlets and newspapers, organized trade unions, and spread their messages among workers and peasants. Particularly in the cities, these revolutionary parties had an impact. They provided a language through which workers could express their grievances; they created links among workers from different factories; and they furnished leaders who were able to act when the revolutionary moment arrived.

World War I provided that moment. The enormous hardships of that war, coupled with the immense social tensions of industrialization within a still-autocratic political system, sparked the Russian Revolution of 1917 (see Chapter 20). That massive upheaval quickly brought to power the most radical of the socialist groups operating in the country—the Bolsheviks, led by the charismatic Vladimir Ilyich Ulyanov, better known as Lenin. Only in Russia was industrialization associated with violent social revolution. This was the most distinctive feature of Russia's modern historical development. And only in Russia was a socialist political party, inspired by the teachings of Karl Marx, able to seize power, thus launching the modern world's first socialist society, with enormous implications for the twentieth century.

The Industrial Revolution and Latin America in the Nineteenth Century

Beyond the world of Europe and North America, only Japan underwent a major industrial transformation during the nineteenth century, part of that country's overall response to the threat of European aggression. (See "The Japanese Difference: The Rise of a New East Asian Power" in Chapter 19.) Elsewhere—in colonial India, Egypt, the Ottoman Empire, China, and Latin America—very modest experiments in modern industry were undertaken, but nowhere did they drive the kind of major social transformation that had taken place in Britain, Europe,

North America, and Japan. However, even in societies that did not experience their own Industrial Revolution, the profound impact of European and North American industrialization was hard to avoid. Such was the case in Latin America during the nineteenth century. (See Snapshot: The Industrial Revolution and the Global Divide.)

After Independence in Latin America

The struggle for independence in Latin America had lasted far longer and proved far more destructive than in North America. Decimated populations, diminished herds of livestock, flooded or closed silver mines, abandoned farms, shrinking international trade and investment capital, and empty national treasuries—these were the conditions that greeted Latin Americans upon independence. Furthermore, the four major administrative units (viceroyalties) of Spanish America ultimately dissolved into eighteen separate countries, and regional revolts wracked Brazil in the early decades of its independent life. A number of international wars in the post-independence century likewise shook these new nations. Peru and Bolivia briefly united and then broke apart in a bitter conflict (1836–1839); Mexico lost huge territories to the United States (1846–1848); and an alliance of Argentina, Brazil, and Uruguay went to war with Paraguay (1864–1870) in a conflict that devastated Paraguay's small population.

Within these new countries, political life was turbulent and unstable. Conservatives favored centralized authority and sought to maintain the social status quo of the colonial era in alliance with the Catholic Church, which at independence owned perhaps half of all productive land. Their often-bitter opponents were liberals, who attacked the Church in the name of Enlightenment values, sought at least modest

SNAPSHOT   **THE INDUSTRIAL REVOLUTION AND THE GLOBAL DIVIDE**

During the nineteenth century, the Industrial Revolution generated an enormous and unprecedented economic division in the world, as measured by the share of manufacturing output. What patterns can you see in this table?

SHARE OF TOTAL WORLD MANUFACTURING OUTPUT (percentage)

	1750	1800	1860	1880	1900
EUROPE AS A WHOLE	23.2	28.1	53.2	61.3	62.0
United Kingdom	1.9	4.3	19.9	22.9	18.5
France	4.0	4.2	7.9	7.8	6.8
Germany	2.9	3.5	4.9	8.5	13.2
Russia	5.0	5.6	7.0	7.6	8.8
UNITED STATES	0.1	0.8	7.2	14.7	23.6
JAPAN	3.8	3.5	2.6	2.4	2.4
THE REST OF THE WORLD	73.0	67.7	36.6	20.9	11.0
China	32.8	33.3	19.7	12.5	6.2
South Asia (India/Pakistan)	24.5	19.7	8.6	2.8	1.7

Data from Paul Kennedy, *The Rise and Fall of the Great Powers* (New York: Random House, 1987), 149.

social reforms, and preferred federalism. In many countries, conflicts between these factions, often violent, enabled military strongmen known as *caudillos* (kaw-DEE-yos) to achieve power as defenders of order and property, although they too succeeded one another with great frequency. One of them, Antonio López de Santa Anna of Mexico, was president of his country at least nine separate times between 1833 and 1855. Constitutions too replaced one another with bewildering speed. Bolivia had ten constitutions during the nineteenth century, while Ecuador and Peru each had eight.

Social life did not change fundamentally in the aftermath of independence. As in Europe and North America, women remained disenfranchised and wholly outside of formal political life. Slavery was abolished in most of Latin America by midcentury, although it persisted in both Brazil and Cuba until the late 1880s. Most of the legal distinctions among various racial categories also disappeared, and all free people were considered, at least officially, equal citizens. Nevertheless, productive economic resources such as businesses, ranches, and plantations remained overwhelmingly in the hands of creole white men, who were culturally oriented toward Europe. The military provided an avenue of mobility for a few skilled and ambitious mestizo men, some of whom subsequently became caudillos. Other mixed-race men and women found a place in a small middle class as teachers, shopkeepers, or artisans. The vast majority—blacks, Indians, and many mixed-race people of both sexes—remained impoverished, working small subsistence farms or laboring in the mines or on the *haciendas* (ah-see-EHN-duhz) (plantations) of the well-to-do. Only rarely did the poor and dispossessed actively rebel against their social betters. One such case was the Caste War of Yucatán (1847–1901), a prolonged struggle of the Maya people of Mexico aimed at cleansing their land of European and mestizo intruders.

Facing the World Economy

During the second half of the nineteenth century, a measure of political consolidation took hold in Latin America, and countries such as Mexico, Peru, and Argentina entered periods of greater stability. At the same time, Latin America as a whole became more closely integrated into a world economy driven by the industrialization of Western Europe and North America. The new technology of the steamship cut the sailing time between Britain and Argentina almost in half, while the underwater telegraph instantly brought the latest news and fashions of Europe to Latin America.

The most significant economic outcome of this growing integration was a rapid growth of Latin American exports to the industrializing countries, which now needed the food products, raw materials, and markets of these new nations. Latin American landowners, businessmen, and governments proved eager to supply those needs, and in the sixty years or so after 1850, a **Latin American export boom** increased the value of goods sold abroad by a factor of ten.

Mexico continued to produce large amounts of silver, providing more than half the world's new supply until 1860. Now added to the list of raw materials flowing out of Latin America were copper from Chile, a metal that the growing electrical industry required; tin from Bolivia, which met the mounting demand for tin cans; and nitrates from Chile and guano (bird droppings) from Peru, both of which were used for fertilizer. Wild rubber from the Amazon rain forest was in great demand for bicycle and automobile tires, as was sisal from Mexico, used to make binder twine for the proliferating mechanical harvesters of North America. Bananas from Central America, beef from Argentina, cacao from Ecuador, coffee from Brazil and Guatemala, and sugar from Cuba also found eager markets in the rapidly growing and increasingly prosperous world of industrializing countries. In return for these primary products, Latin Americans imported the textiles, machinery, tools, weapons, and luxury goods of Europe and the United States (see Map 17.5).

U.S. Interventions
→ Puerto Rico, 1898–on
→ Panama, 1903
⇒ Cuba, 1898–1902, 1905–09, 1917–21
⇢ Haiti, 1915–34
→ Mexico, 1846–48, 1914, 1916–17
→ Nicaragua, 1909, 1912–25, 1927–32
⇢ Dominican Republic, 1916–24

Exports
🍌 Bananas
◎ Cacao
🐂 Cattle
● Coffee
▬ Copper and tin
🥥 Cotton
■ Guano
◆ Nitrate
⭐ Oil
🌴 Rubber
🐑 Sheep
◇ Silver
✳ Sisal
▣ Sugar
🍃 Tobacco
🌾 Wheat
$161 Foreign investment (in millions of U.S. dollars around 1914)
⬅ European immigration

MEXICO $1329
CUBA $471
DOMINICAN REPUBLIC $16 $44 $19
HAITI
$99 $42
$19 $12
$61
$28
VENEZUELA $161
COLOMBIA $77
ECUADOR $41
PERU $197
BOLIVIA $59
BRAZIL $1913
PARAGUAY $27
ARGENTINA $4001
CHILE $668
URUGUAY $475

MAP 17.5   Latin America and the World, 1825–1935

During the nineteenth and early twentieth centuries, Latin American countries interacted with the industrializing world via investment, trade, immigration, and military intervention from the United States.

Accompanying this burgeoning commerce was large-scale investment of European capital in Latin America, $10 billion alone between 1870 and 1919. Most of this capital came from Great Britain, which invested more in Argentina in the late nineteenth century than in its colony of India, although France, Germany, Italy, and the United States also contributed to this substantial financial transfer. By 1910, U.S. business interests controlled 40 percent of Mexican property and produced half of its oil. Much of this capital was used to build railroads, largely to funnel Latin American exports to the coast, where they were shipped to overseas markets. Mexico had only 390 miles of railroad in 1876; it had 15,000 miles in 1910. By 1915, Argentina, with 22,000 miles of railroad, had more track per person than the United States had.

Becoming like Europe?

To the economic elites of Latin America, intent on making their countries resemble Europe or the United States, all of this was progress. In some respects, they were surely right. Economies were growing, producing more than ever before. The population was also burgeoning; it increased from about 30 million in 1850 to more than 77 million in 1912 as public health measures (such as safe drinking water, inoculations, sewers, and campaigns to eliminate mosquitoes that carried yellow fever) brought down death rates.

Urbanization also proceeded rapidly. By the early twentieth century, wrote one scholar, "Latin American cities lost their colonial cobblestones, white-plastered walls, and red-tiled roofs. They became modern metropolises, comparable to urban giants anywhere. Streetcars swayed, telephones jangled, and silent movies flickered from Montevideo and Santiago to Mexico City and Havana."[17] Buenos Aires, Argentina's metropolitan center, boasted 750,000 people in 1900 and billed itself as the "Paris of South America." There the educated elite, just like the English, drank tea in the afternoon, while discussing European literature, philosophy, and fashion, usually in French.

To become more like Europe, Latin America sought to attract more Europeans. Because civilization, progress, and modernity apparently derived from Europe, many Latin American countries actively sought to increase their "white" populations by deliberately recruiting impoverished Europeans with the promise, mostly unfulfilled, of a new and prosperous life in the New World. Argentina received the largest wave of European immigrants (some 2.5 million between 1870 and 1915), mostly from Spain and Italy. Brazil and Uruguay likewise attracted substantial numbers of European newcomers.

Only a quite modest segment of Latin American society saw any great benefits from the export boom and all that followed from it. Upper-class landowners certainly gained as exports flourished and their property values soared. Middle-class urban dwellers — merchants, office workers, lawyers, and other professionals — also grew in numbers and prosperity as their skills proved valuable in a modernizing society. As a percentage of the total population, however, these were small elites. In Mexico in the mid-1890s, for example, the landowning upper class made up no more than 1 percent and the middle classes perhaps 8 percent of the population. Everyone else was lower class, and most of them were impoverished.[18]

A new but quite small segment of this vast lower class emerged among urban workers who labored in the railroads, ports, mines, and a few factories. They initially organized themselves in a variety of mutual aid societies, but by the end of the nineteenth century they were creating unions and engaging in strikes. To authoritarian governments interested in stability and progress, such activity was highly provocative and threatening, and they acted harshly to crush or repress unions and strikes. In 1906, the Mexican dictator Porfirio Díaz invited the Arizona Rangers to suppress a strike at Cananea, near the U.S. border, an action that resulted in dozens of deaths. The following year in the Chilean city of Iquique, more than 1,000 men, women, and children were slaughtered by police when nitrate miners protested their wages and working conditions.

The vast majority of the lower class lived in rural areas, where they suffered the most and benefited the least from the export boom. Government attacks on communal landholding and peasant indebtedness to wealthy landowners combined to push many farmers off their land or into remote and poor areas where they could barely make a living. Many wound up as dependent laborers or peons on the haciendas of the wealthy, where their wages were often too meager to support a family. Thus women and children, who had earlier remained at home to tend the family plot, were required to join their menfolk as field laborers. Many immigrant Italian farmworkers in Argentina and Brazil were unable to acquire their own farms, as they had expected, and so drifted into the growing cities or returned to Italy.

Although local protests and violence were frequent, only in Mexico did these vast inequalities erupt into a nationwide revolution. There, in the early twentieth century, middle-class reformers joined with workers and peasants to overthrow the long dictatorship of Porfirio Díaz (r. 1876–1911). What followed was a decade of bloody conflict (1910–1920) that cost Mexico some 1 million lives, or roughly 10 percent of the population. Huge peasant armies under charismatic leaders such as Pancho Villa and Emiliano Zapata helped oust Díaz. Intent on seizing land and redistributing it to the peasants, they then went on to attack many of Mexico's large haciendas. But unlike the leaders of the later Russian and Chinese revolutions, whose most radical elements seized state power, Villa and Zapata proved unable to do so on any long-term basis, in part because they were hobbled by factionalism and focused on local or regional issues. Despite this limitation and its own internal conflicts, the **Mexican Revolution** transformed the country. When the dust settled, Mexico had a new constitution (1917) that proclaimed universal male suffrage; provided for the redistribution of land; stripped the Catholic Church of any role in public education and forbade it to own land; announced unheard-of rights for workers, such as a minimum wage and an eight-hour workday; and placed restrictions on foreign ownership of property. Much of Mexico's history in the twentieth century involved working out the implications of these nationalist and reformist changes. The revolution's direct influence, however, was largely limited to Mexico itself and a few places in Central America and the Andes; the upheaval did not have the wider international impact of the Russian and Chinese revolutions.

Perhaps the most significant outcome of the export boom lay in what did *not* happen, for nowhere in Latin America did it jump-start a thorough Industrial Revolution, despite a few factories that processed foods or manufactured textiles, clothing, and building materials. The reasons are many. A social structure that relegated some 90 percent of its population to an impoverished lower class generated only a very small market for manufactured goods. Moreover, economically powerful groups such as landowners and cattlemen benefited greatly from exporting agricultural products and had little incentive to invest in manufacturing. Domestic manufacturing enterprises could only have competed with cheaper and higher-quality foreign goods if they had been protected for a time by high tariffs. But Latin American political leaders had thoroughly embraced the popular European doctrine of prosperity through free trade, and many governments depended on taxing imports to fill their treasuries.

Instead of their own Industrial Revolutions, Latin Americans developed a form of economic growth that was largely financed by capital from abroad and dependent on European and North American prosperity and decisions. Brazil experienced this kind of dependence when its booming rubber industry suddenly collapsed in 1910–1911, after seeds from the wild rubber tree had been illegally exported to Britain and were used to start competing and cheaper rubber plantations in Malaysia.

Later critics saw this **dependent development** as a new form of colonialism, expressed in the power exercised by foreign investors. The influence of the U.S.-owned United Fruit Company in Central America was a case in point. Allied with large landowners and compliant politicians, the company pressured the governments of these "banana republics" to maintain conditions favorable to U.S. business. This indirect or behind-the-scenes imperialism was supplemented by repeated U.S. military intervention in support of American corporate interests in Cuba, Haiti, the Dominican Republic, Nicaragua, and Mexico. The United States also controlled the Panama Canal and acquired Puerto Rico as a territory in the aftermath of the Spanish-American War (see Map 17.5, page 504).

Thus, despite Latin America's domination by people of European descent and its close ties to the industrializing countries of the Atlantic world, that region's historical trajectory in the nineteenth century diverged considerably from that of Europe and North America.

Controversies: Debating "Why Europe?"

The Industrial Revolution marked a dramatic change in the trajectory of human history. But why did that breakthrough occur first in Europe? This question has long been a source of great controversy among scholars.

A "European Miracle"

Does the answer lie in some unique or "miraculous" feature of European history, culture, or society? Perhaps, as one scholar recently suggested, Europeans have been distinguished for several thousand years by a restless, creative, and freedom-loving culture with its roots in the aristocratic warlike societies of early Indo-European invaders, which rendered them uniquely open to change and development.[19] But critics have questioned both the claims to European cultural uniqueness and causal links between industrialization and developments of the distant past.

Or should we focus more narrowly on the period between about 1400 and 1800 for the origins of this "European miracle"?[20] During those centuries distinctive new forms of landowning and farming practices emerged, especially in Britain, which made land and labor available for capitalist agriculture and enabled the accumulation of wealth in the hands of a few. Was this "agricultural revolution" a prelude to the subsequent "industrial revolution"? Or perhaps it was the Scientific Revolution, a distinctly European event that generated a new view of the cosmos, that stimulated industrialization.

It turns out, however, that industrial technologies derived from the workshops of artisans and craftsmen rather than from the laboratories of scientists. And so by the early twenty-first century, many historians were thinking in terms of a broader cultural pattern, an eighteenth-century "Industrial Enlightenment" in which scientific methods and a general belief in an ordered universe mixed with commitment to the ideas of "progress" and human improvement to foster technological innovation.

And what about Europe's many relatively small and highly competitive states? Perhaps their rivalries stimulated innovation and provided an "insurance against economic and technological stagnation," which the larger Chinese, Ottoman, or Mughal empires lacked. In their struggles with other states, European governments desperately needed revenue, and to get it, European authorities developed an unusual alliance with their merchant classes. Small groups of merchant capitalists might be granted special privileges, monopolies, or even tax-collecting responsibilities in exchange for much-needed loans or payments to the state. Governments granted charters and monopolies to private trading companies, and states founded scientific societies and offered prizes to promote innovation. European merchants and other innovators after the fifteenth century became more independent from state control and enjoyed a higher social status than their counterparts in more established civilizations. Such internally competitive semi-capitalist economies, coupled with a highly competitive system of rival states, arguably fostered innovation in the new civilization taking shape in Western Europe. But at the same time, nearly constant war and the destruction that accompanied it also served as a long-term drain on European resources.

Britain especially benefited from several advantages of the "European Miracle," including a spirit of innovation, a lot of easily accessible coal, a growing consumer market, plentiful cheap capital accumulated in agriculture and trade, and its island geography, which frequently shielded it from the worst effects of Europe's wars. It also had a relatively high-wage workforce, which gave British businesses an extraordinary incentive to invent laborsaving technologies.

The "Great Divergence"

But was Europe alone destined to lead the way to modern economic life? To many world historians, such views are both Eurocentric and deterministic; they also fly in the face of much recent research. Historians now know that India, the Islamic world, and especially China had experienced times of great technological and scientific flourishing. For reasons much debated, all of these flowerings of creativity had slowed down considerably or stagnated by the early modern era, when the pace of technological change in Europe began to pick up. But these earlier achievements certainly suggest that Europe was not alone in its capacity for technological innovation.

Nor did Europe enjoy any overall economic advantage as late as 1750. Recent scholars have found rather "a world of surprising resemblances" among major Eurasian societies during the eighteenth century. Economic indicators such as life expectancies, patterns of consumption and nutrition, wage levels, general living standards, widespread free markets, and prosperous merchant communities suggest "a global economic parity" across the major civilizations of Europe and Asia.[21] Thus Europe had no obvious economic lead, even on the eve of the Industrial Revolution. So much for the "European miracle"!

Trade and Empire

But if there was little that was economically distinctive within Europe itself, perhaps it was the spoils of empire and the benefits of global trade after 1500 that allowed Europeans to accumulate the wealth that funded industrial enterprises back home. European empires provided access to an abundance of raw materials—timber, fish, maize, potatoes, slave-produced sugar and cotton—far more than that of other early modern empires. Moreover, these empires generated a global economy that funneled the trade of the world through Europe, offering access to the raw materials and markets of the planet. Demand for Asian goods, including porcelain and especially cotton cloth, also spurred manufacturers in Europe to produce similar items, while production for overseas markets further sparked industry in Europe. The new wealth spawned a growing middle class in Europe whose members bought the products of the Industrial Revolution. As one scholar has put it, "The industrial revolution . . . emerged from the exploitive advantages Europe was already gaining in the world's markets."[22] So rather than something distinctive about European society, perhaps it was Europe's increasing engagement with the wider world that sparked industrialization.

Many or most of these factors likely played some role in Europe's industrialization. But in considering the "Why Europe?" question, historians confront the relative importance of internal and external factors in explaining historical change. Was industrialization primarily spurred by some special combination of elements peculiar to Western Europe, or were broader global relationships of greater significance? Arguments giving great weight to internal features of European life seem to congratulate Europeans on their good fortune or wisdom, while those that contextualize it globally and point to the unique character of European imperial trade and exploitation are rather more critical. Furthermore, the former seem to imply a certain long-term inevitability to European prominence, while the latter see the Industrial Revolution as more of a surprise, the outcome of a unique conjuncture of events . . . in short, luck.

Reflections: History and Horse Races

Historians and students of history seem endlessly fascinated by "firsts"—the first breakthrough to agriculture, the first domestication of horses, the first civilization, the first use of gunpowder, the first printing press, and so on. Each of these firsts presents a problem of explanation: why did it occur in some particular time and place rather than somewhere else or at some other time? Such questions have assumed historical significance because "first achievements" represent something new in the human journey and because many of them conveyed unusual power, wealth, status, or influence on their creators.

Nonetheless, the focus on firsts can be misleading as well. Those who accomplished something first may see themselves as generally superior to those who embraced that innovation later. Historians too can sometimes adopt a winners-and-losers mentality, inviting a view of history as a horse race toward some finish line of accomplishment. Most first achievements in history, however, were not the result of intentional efforts but rather the unexpected outcome of converging circumstances.

The Industrial Revolution is a case in point. Efforts to understand the European beginnings of this immense breakthrough are certainly justified by its pervasive global consequences and its global spread over the past several centuries. In terms of human ability to dominate the natural environment and to extract wealth from it, the Industrial Revolution marks a decisive turning point in the history of our species. But Europeans' attempts to explain their Industrial Revolution have at times stated or implied their own unique genius. In the nineteenth century, many Europeans saw their technological mastery as a sure sign of their cultural and racial superiority as they came to use "machines as the measure of men."[23] In pondering the European origins of the Industrial Revolution, historians too have sometimes sought an answer in some distinct or even superior feature of European civilization.

In emphasizing the unexpectedness of the first Industrial Revolution, and the global context within which it occurred, world historians have attempted to avoid a "history as horse race" outlook. Clearly, the first industrial breakthrough in Britain was not a self-conscious effort to win a race; it was the surprising outcome of countless decisions by many people to further their own interests. Subsequently, however, other societies and their governments quite deliberately tried to catch up, seeking the wealth and power that the Industrial Revolution promised.

The rapid spread of industrialization across the planet, though highly uneven, may diminish the importance of its Europeans beginnings. Just as no one views agriculture as a Middle Eastern phenomenon even though it occurred first in that region, it seems likely that industrialization will be seen increasingly as a global process rather than one uniquely associated with Europe. If industrial society proves to be a sustainable future for humankind—presently a very open question—historians of the future may well be more interested in the pattern of its global spread and in efforts to cope with its social and environmental consequences than in its origins in Western Europe.

Second Thoughts

WHAT'S THE SIGNIFICANCE?

steam engine (p. 484)
British textile industry (p. 486)
middle-class society (p. 488)
ideology of domesticity (p. 488)
lower middle class (p. 489)
laboring classes (p. 489)
Karl Marx (p. 491)
Labour Party (p. 492)

socialism in the United States
   (p. 497)
Progressives (p. 498)
Russian Revolution of 1905 (p. 501)
caudillos (p. 503)
Latin American export boom (p. 503)
Mexican Revolution (p. 506)
dependent development (p. 507)

BIG PICTURE QUESTIONS

1. What did humankind gain from the Industrial Revolution, and what did it lose?
2. In what ways might the Industrial Revolution be understood as a global rather than simply a European phenomenon?
3. The Industrial Revolution transformed social as well as economic life. What evidence might support this statement?
4. How do you think the Industrial Revolution will be viewed 50, 100, or 200 years into the future?
5. **Looking Back:** How did the Industrial Revolution interact with the Scientific Revolution and the French Revolution to generate Europe's modern transformation?

CHRONOLOGY

1780s	• Industrial Revolution begins in England
1811–1850	• Earliest railroads established
1820s	• First textile factories in New England
1824	• Trade unions legalized in Britain
ca. 1825	• Independence from colonial rule achieved in Latin America
1840s	• Beginnings of massive immigration from Europe
1847	• Caste War of Yucatán begins in Mexico
1848	• Marx's *Communist Manifesto* published
1850s	• Beginning of railroad building in Argentina, Cuba, Chile, Brazil
1850–1910	• Export boom
1861	• Freeing of the serfs in Russia
1865–1900	• Socialist parties established
1865–1900	• Rapid industrial growth
1870s–1900	• Labor protests, strikes, violence
1890s	• Russia's industrial takeoff
1898	• Founding of Russian Social Democratic Labor Party
1905	• Insurrection in Russia
1910–1920	• Mexican Revolution
1917	• Russian Revolution

18

Colonial Encounters in Asia, Africa, and Oceania

1750–1950

IN THE EARLY TWENTY-FIRST CENTURY THE PAST DRAMATICALLY resurfaced in both Namibia, a small country in southwest Africa, and in Germany, which had conquered Namibia and ruled it as a colony from 1884 to 1915. In 2013 and again in 2016, angry Namibians had either defaced or forced the removal of several statues that commemorated German soldiers who had been killed while brutally suppressing an uprising in 1904–1907 by the Herero and Nama people. Often called the first genocide of the twentieth century, German efforts to put down that rebellion had killed about 80 percent of the Herero and 50 percent of the Nama. "We as Hereros and we as Namibians don't want German soldiers in front of our State House," declared Uahimisa Kaapehi, one of the leaders of those protests.[1] The push to remove those offending statues came amid sensitive negotiations between Namibia and Germany in which Germany appeared ready to acknowledge its earlier actions as genocide, to issue a formal apology, and to offer financial compensation. In such ways the colonial past has continued to echo more than a century later.

For many millions of Africans, Asians, and Pacific islanders, colonial rule — by the British, French, Germans, Italians, Belgians, Portuguese, Russians, or Americans — was the major new element in their historical experience during the long nineteenth century (1750–1900). Of course, no single colonial experience characterized this vast region. Much depended on the cultures and prior history of various colonized people. Policies of the colonial powers sometimes differed sharply and changed over time. Men and women experienced the colonial era differently, as did traditional elites, Western-educated groups, artisans, peasant farmers, and migrant laborers. Furthermore, the varied actions and reactions of such people, despite their oppression and exploitation, shaped the colonial experience, perhaps as much as the policies, practices, and intentions of their temporary European rulers. All of them — colonizers and colonized alike — were caught up in the flood of change that accompanied this new burst of European imperialism.

Industry and Empire

Behind much of Europe's nineteenth-century expansion lay the massive fact of its Industrial Revolution, a process that gave rise to new economic needs, many of which found solutions abroad. The enormous productivity of industrial technology and Europe's growing affluence now created the need for extensive raw materials and agricultural products: wheat from the American Midwest and southern Russia; meat from Argentina; bananas from Central America; rubber from Brazil; cocoa and palm oil from West Africa, and much more. This demand radically changed patterns of economic and social life in the countries of their origin.

Furthermore, Europe needed to sell its own products abroad, since its factories churned out more goods than its own people could afford to buy. By 1840, for example, Britain was exporting 60 percent of its cotton-cloth production, annually sending 200 million yards to Europe, 300 million yards to Latin America, and 145 million yards to India. Part of European and American fascination with China during the nineteenth and twentieth centuries lay in the enormous market potential represented by its huge population. Much the same could be said for capital, for European investors often found it more profitable to invest their money abroad than at home. Between 1910 and 1913, Britain was sending about half of its savings overseas as foreign investment.

Wealthy Europeans also saw social benefits to foreign markets because they kept Europe's factories humming and its workers employed. The English imperialist Cecil Rhodes confided his fears to a friend in the late nineteenth century:

> Yesterday I attended a meeting of the unemployed in London and having listened to the wild speeches which were nothing more than a scream for bread, I returned home convinced more than ever of the importance of imperialism. . . . In order to save the 40 million inhabitants of the United Kingdom from a murderous civil war, the colonial politicians must open up new areas to absorb the excess population and create new markets for the products of the mines and factories.[2]

Thus imperialism promised to solve the class conflicts of an industrializing society while avoiding revolution or the serious redistribution of wealth.

But what made imperialism so broadly popular in Europe, especially in the last quarter of the nineteenth century, was the growth of mass nationalism. By 1871, the unification of Italy and Germany intensified Europe's already competitive international relations, and much of this rivalry spilled over into the struggle for colonies or economic concessions in Asia, Africa, and Pacific Oceania. Colonies and spheres of influence abroad became symbols of "Great Power" status for a nation, and their acquisition was a matter of urgency, even if they possessed little immediate economic value. After 1875, it seemed to matter, even to ordinary people, whether some remote corner of Africa or some obscure Pacific island was in British, French, or

Colonial Rivalries This image shows Africa as a sleeping giant, while various European countries stake their rival claims to parts of the continent. It was published in 1911 in *Puck*, a British magazine of humor and satire. ("The Sleeping Sickness" by Gordon Ross [1873–1946], from *Puck*, 1911/Library of Congress, Prints and Photographs Division, LC-DIG-ppmsca-27783)

German hands. Imperialism, in short, appealed on economic and social grounds to the wealthy or ambitious, seemed politically and strategically necessary in the game of international power politics, and was emotionally satisfying to almost everyone. It was a potent mix!

If the industrial era made overseas expansion more desirable or even urgent, it also provided new means for achieving those goals. Steam-driven ships moving through the new Suez Canal, completed in 1869, allowed Europeans to reach distant Asian, African, and Pacific ports more quickly and predictably and to penetrate interior rivers as well. The underwater telegraph made possible almost instant communication with far-flung outposts of empire. The discovery of quinine to prevent malaria greatly reduced European death rates in the tropics. Breech-loading rifles and machine guns vastly widened the military gap between Europeans and everyone else.

Industrialization also occasioned a marked change in the way Europeans perceived themselves and others. In earlier centuries, Europeans had defined others largely in religious terms. "They" were heathen; "we" were Christian. With the advent of the industrial age, however, Europeans developed a secular arrogance that fused with or in some cases replaced their notions of religious superiority. They had, after all, unlocked the secrets of nature, created a society of unprecedented wealth, and used both to produce unsurpassed military power. These became the criteria by which Europeans judged both themselves and the rest of the world.

By such standards, it is not surprising that their opinions of other cultures dropped sharply. The Chinese, who had been highly praised in the eighteenth century, were reduced in the nineteenth century to the image of "John Chinaman"—weak, cunning, obstinately conservative, and, in large numbers, a distinct threat, represented by the "yellow peril" in late nineteenth-century European thinking. African societies, which had been regarded even in the slave-trade era as nations and their leaders as kings, were demoted in nineteenth-century European eyes to the status of tribes led by chiefs as a means of emphasizing their "primitive" qualities.

Peoples of Pacific Oceania and elsewhere could be regarded as "big children," who lived "closer to nature" than their civilized counterparts and correspondingly distant from the high culture with which Europeans congratulated themselves. Upon visiting Tahiti in 1768, the French explorer Bougainville concluded: "I thought I was walking in the Garden of Eden."[3] Such views could be mobilized to criticize the artificiality and materialism of modern European life, but they could also serve to justify the conquest of people who were, apparently, doing little to improve what nature had granted them. Writing in 1854, a European settler in Australia declared: "The question comes to this; which has the better right—the savage, born in a country, which he runs over but can scarcely be said to occupy . . . or the civilized man, who comes to introduce into this . . . unproductive country, the industry which supports life?"[4]

Increasingly, Europeans viewed the culture and achievements of Asian and African peoples through the prism of a new kind of racism, which is sometimes called **scientific racism**. Although physical differences had often been a basis of fear or dislike, in the nineteenth century Europeans increasingly used the prestige and apparatus of science to support their racial preferences and prejudices. Phrenologists, craniologists, and sometimes physicians used allegedly scientific methods and numerous instruments to classify the size and shape of human skulls and concluded, not surprisingly, that those of whites were larger and therefore more advanced.

Nineteenth-century biologists, who classified the varieties of plants and animals, applied these notions of rank to varieties of human beings as well. The result was a hierarchy of races, with the whites on top and the less developed "child races" beneath them. Race, in this view, determined human intelligence, moral development, and destiny. "Race is everything," declared the British anatomist Robert Knox in 1850. "Civilization depends on it."[5] Furthermore, as the germ theory of disease took hold in nineteenth-century Europe, it was accompanied by fears that contact with "inferiors" threatened the health and even the biological future of more advanced or "superior" peoples.

These ideas influenced how Europeans viewed their own global expansion. Almost everyone saw it as inevitable, a natural outgrowth of a superior civilization. For many, though, this viewpoint was tempered with a genuine, if condescending, sense of responsibility to the "weaker races" that Europe was fated to dominate. "Superior races have a right, because they have a duty . . . to civilize the inferior races," declared the French politician Jules Ferry in 1883.[6] That **civilizing mission** included bringing Christianity to the heathen, good government to disordered lands, work discipline and production for the market to "lazy natives," a measure of education to the ignorant and illiterate, clothing to the naked, and health care to the sick, all while suppressing "native customs" that ran counter to Western ways of living. In European thinking, this was "progress" and "civilization."

A harsher side to the ideology of imperialism found expression in **social Darwinism**. Its adherents applied Charles Darwin's evolutionary concept of "the survival of the fittest" to human society. This outlook suggested that European dominance inevitably led to the displacement or destruction of backward peoples or "unfit" races. Such views made imperialism, war, and aggression seem both natural and progressive, for weeding out "weaker" peoples of the world would allow the "stronger" to flourish. These were some of the ideas with which industrializing and increasingly powerful Europeans confronted the peoples of Asia and Africa in the nineteenth century.

A Second Wave of European Conquests

If the sixteenth- and seventeenth-century takeover of the Americas represented the first phase of European colonial conquests, the century and a half between 1750 and 1900 was a second and quite distinct round of that larger process. Now it was focused in Asia, Africa, and Oceania rather than in the Western Hemisphere. And it featured a number of new players—Germany, Italy, Belgium, the United States, and Japan—who were not at all involved in the earlier phase, while the Spanish and Portuguese now had only minor roles. In general, Europeans preferred informal control, which operated through economic penetration and occasional military intervention but without a wholesale colonial takeover. Such a course was cheaper and less likely to provoke wars. But where rivalry with other European states made it impossible or where local governments were unable or unwilling to cooperate, Europeans proved more than willing to undertake the expense and risk of conquest and outright colonial rule.

Once established in a region, they frequently took advantage of moments of weakness in local societies to strengthen their control. "Each global drought was the green light for an imperialist landrush," wrote one scholar when examining the climatic instability that caused monsoon rains across Asia and parts of Africa to repeatedly fail in the second half of the nineteenth century.[7] Nowhere was this more evident than in Africa, where, for instance, a drought in the southern part of the continent in 1877 coincided with British success in reining in Zulu independence, and famine in Ethiopia from the late 1880s on coincided with Italian efforts to subdue the Horn of Africa.

The construction of these new European empires in the Afro-Asian world, like empires everywhere, involved military force or the threat of it. Increasingly in the nineteenth century, Europeans possessed overwhelming advantages in firepower, derived from the recently invented repeating rifles and machine guns. Nonetheless, Europeans had to fight, often long and hard, to create their new empires, as countless wars of conquest attest. In the end, though, they prevailed almost everywhere, largely against adversaries who did not have machine guns or in some cases any guns at all.

Thus were African, Asian, and Oceanic peoples of all kinds incorporated within one or another of the European empires. Gathering and hunting bands in Australia, agricultural village societies or chiefdoms on Pacific islands and in parts of Africa, pastoralists of the Sahara and Central Asia, residents of states large and small, and virtually everyone in the large and complex civilizations of India and Southeast Asia—all of them alike lost the political sovereignty and freedom of action they had previously exercised. For some, such as Hindus governed by the Muslim Mughal Empire, it was an exchange of one set of foreign rulers for another. But now all were subjects of a European colonial state.

The passage to colonial status occurred in various ways. For the peoples of India and Indonesia, colonial conquest grew out of interaction with European trading firms, which were authorized to conduct military operations and exercise political and administrative control over large areas. The British East India Company, rather than the British government directly, played the leading role in the colonial takeover of South Asia. The fragmentation of the Mughal Empire and the absence of any overall sense of cultural or political unity both invited and facilitated European penetration. A similar situation of many small and rival states assisted the Dutch acquisition of Indonesia. However, neither the British nor the Dutch had a clear-cut plan for conquest. Rather, in India it evolved slowly as local authorities and European traders made and unmade a variety of alliances with local states over roughly a century (1750–1850). In Indonesia, a few areas held out until the early twentieth century (see Map 18.1).

For most of Africa, mainland Southeast Asia, and the Pacific islands, colonial conquest came later, in the second half of the nineteenth century, and rather more abruptly and deliberately than in India or Indonesia. The **scramble for Africa**," for example, pitted half a dozen European powers against one another as they partitioned the entire continent among themselves in only about twenty-five years (1875–1900). European leaders themselves were surprised by the intensity of their rivalries and the speed with which they acquired huge territories, about which they knew very little.

That process involved endless but peaceful negotiations among the competing Great Powers about "who got what" and extensive and bloody military action, sometimes lasting decades, to make their control effective on the ground. It took the French sixteen years (1882–1898) to finally conquer the recently created

MAP 18.1 Colonial Asia in the Early Twentieth Century
By the early twentieth century, several of the great population centers of Asia had come under the colonial control of Britain, the Netherlands, France, the United States, or Japan.

West African empire led by Samori Toure. Among the most difficult to subdue were those decentralized societies without any formal state structure. In such cases, Europeans confronted no central authority with which they could negotiate or that they might decisively defeat. It was a matter of village-by-village conquest against extended resistance. As late as 1925, one British official commented on the process as it operated in central Nigeria: "I shall of course go on walloping them until they surrender. It's a rather piteous sight watching a village being knocked to pieces and I wish there was some other way, but unfortunately there isn't."[8] Another very difficult situation for the British lay in South Africa, where they were initially defeated by a Zulu army in 1879 at the Battle of Isandlwana. And twenty years later, in what became known as the Boer War (1899–1902), the Boers, white descendants of the earlier Dutch settlers in South Africa, fought bitterly for three years before succumbing to British forces (see Map 18.2). The colonial conquest of Africa was intensely resisted.

Europeans and Americans had been drawn into the world of Pacific Oceania during the eighteenth century through exploration and scientific curiosity, by the missionary impulse for conversion, and by their economic interests in sperm whale oil, coconut oil, guano, mineral nitrates and phosphates, sandalwood, and other

MAP 18.2   Conquest and Resistance in Colonial Africa

By the early twentieth century, the map of Africa reflected the outcome of the scramble for Africa, a conquest that was heavily resisted in many places.

products. Primarily in the second half of the nineteenth century, these entanglements morphed into competitive annexations as Britain, France, the Netherlands, Germany, and the United States, now joined by Australia, claimed control of all the islands of Oceania (see Map 18.1). Chile too, in search of valuable guano and nitrates, entered the fray and gained a number of coastal islands as well as Rapa Nui (Easter Island), the easternmost island of Polynesia.

The colonization of the South Pacific territories of Australia and New Zealand, both of which were taken over by the British during the nineteenth century, was more similar to the earlier colonization of North America than to contemporary patterns of Asian and African conquest. In both places, conquest was accompanied by large-scale European settlement and diseases that reduced native numbers by 75 percent or more by 1900. Like Canada and the United States, these became settler colonies, "neo-European" societies in the Pacific. Aboriginal Australians constituted only about 2.4 percent of their country's population in the early twenty-first century, and the indigenous Maori were a minority of about 15 percent in New Zealand. In other previously isolated regions as well — Polynesia, Amazonia, Siberia — disease took a terrible toll on peoples who lacked immunities to European pathogens. For example, the population of Hawaii declined from around 142,000 in 1823 to only 39,000 in 1896. Unlike these remote areas, most African and Asian regions shared with Europe a broadly similar disease environment and so were less susceptible to the pathogens of the conquerors.

Elsewhere other variations on the theme of imperial conquest unfolded. The westward expansion of the United States, for example, overwhelmed Native American populations and involved the country in an imperialist war with Mexico. Seeking territory for white settlement, the United States practiced a policy of removing, sometimes almost exterminating, Indian peoples. On the "reservations" to which Indians were confined and in boarding schools to which many of their children were removed, reformers sought to "civilize" the remaining Native Americans, eradicating tribal life and culture, under the slogan "Kill the Indian and Save the Man."

Japan's takeover of Taiwan and Korea bore marked similarities to European actions, as that East Asian nation joined the imperialist club. Russian penetration of Central Asia brought additional millions under European control as the Russian Empire continued its earlier territorial expansion. Filipinos acquired new colonial rulers when the United States took over from Spain following the Spanish-American War of 1898. Some 13,000 freed U.S. slaves, seeking greater freedom than was possible at home, migrated to West Africa, where they became, ironically, a colonizing elite in the land they named Liberia.

Ethiopia and Siam (Thailand) were notable for avoiding the colonization to which their neighbors succumbed. Those countries' military and diplomatic skills, their willingness to make modest concessions to the Europeans, and the rivalries of the imperialists all contributed to these exceptions to the rule of colonial takeover in East Africa and Southeast Asia. Ethiopia, in fact, considerably expanded its own empire, even as it defeated Italy at the Battle of Adowa in 1896.

These broad patterns of colonial conquest contained thousands of separate encounters as the target societies of Western empire builders were confronted with decisions about how to respond to encroaching European power in the context of their local circumstances. Many initially sought to enlist Europeans in their own internal struggles for power or in their rivalries with neighboring states or peoples. As pressures mounted and European demands escalated, some tried to play off imperial powers against one another, while others resorted to military action. Many societies were sharply divided between those who wanted to fight and those who believed that resistance was futile. After extended resistance against French aggression, the nineteenth-century Vietnamese emperor Tu Duc argued with those who wanted the struggle to go on:

> Do you really wish to confront such a power with a pack of [our] cowardly soldiers? . . . With what you presently have, do you really expect to dissolve the enemy's rifles into air or chase his battleships into hell?[9]

Still others negotiated, attempting to preserve as much independence and power as possible. The rulers of the East African kingdom of Buganda, for example, saw opportunity in the British presence and negotiated an arrangement that substantially enlarged their state and personally benefited the kingdom's elite class.

Under European Rule

In many places and for many people, incorporation into European colonial empires was a traumatic experience. Especially for small-scale societies, the loss of life, homes, cattle, crops, and land was devastating. In 1902, a British soldier in East Africa described what happened in a single village: "Every soul was either shot or bayoneted. . . . We burned all the huts and razed the banana plantations to the ground."[10]

For the Vietnamese elite, schooled for centuries in Chinese-style Confucian thinking, conquest meant that the natural harmonies of life had been badly disrupted, that "water flowed uphill." Nguyen Khuyen (1835–1909), a senior Vietnamese official, retired to his ancestral village to farm and write poetry after the French conquest, expressing his anguish at the passing of the world he had known. Many others also withdrew into private life, feigning illness when asked to serve in public office under the French.

Cooperation and Rebellion

Although violence was a prominent feature of colonial life both during conquest and after, various groups and many individuals willingly cooperated with colonial authorities to their own advantage. Many men found employment, status, and security in European-led armed forces. The shortage and expense of European administrators and the difficulties of communicating across cultural boundaries made it necessary for colonial rulers to rely heavily on a range of local intermediaries. Thus Indian princes, Muslim emirs, and African rulers, often from elite or governing families, found it possible to retain much of their earlier status and many of their privileges while gaining considerable wealth by exercising authority, legally and otherwise, at the local level. For example, in French West Africa, an area eight times the size of France and with a population of about 15 million in the late 1930s, the colonial state consisted of just 385 French administrators and more than 50,000 African "chiefs." Thus colonial rule rested on and reinforced the most conservative segments of colonized societies.

Both colonial governments and private missionary organizations had an interest in promoting a measure of European education. From this process arose a small Western-educated class, whose members served the colonial state, European businesses, and Christian missions as teachers, clerks, translators, and lower-level administrators.

A few received higher education abroad and returned home as lawyers, doctors, engineers, or journalists. As colonial governments and business enterprises became more sophisticated, Europeans increasingly depended on the Western-educated class at the expense of the more traditional elites.

If colonial rule enlisted the willing cooperation of some, it provoked the bitter opposition of many others. Thus periodic rebellions, both large and small, erupted in colonial regimes everywhere. The most famous among them was the **Indian Rebellion of 1857–1858**, which was triggered by the introduction into the colony's military forces of a new cartridge smeared with animal fat from cows and pigs. Because Hindus venerated cows and Muslims regarded pigs as unclean, both groups viewed the innovation as a plot to render them defiled and to convert them to Christianity. Behind this incident were many groups of people with a whole series of grievances generated by the British colonial presence: local rulers who had lost power; landlords deprived of their estates or their rent; peasants overtaxed and exploited by urban moneylenders and landlords alike; unemployed weavers displaced by machine-manufactured textiles; and religious leaders outraged by missionary preaching. A mutiny among Indian troops in Bengal triggered the rebellion, which soon spread to other regions of the colony and other social groups. Soon much of India was aflame. Some rebel leaders presented their cause as an effort to revive an almost-vanished Mughal Empire and thereby attracted support from those with strong resentments against the British. Although it was crushed in 1858, the rebellion greatly widened the racial divide in colonial India and heightened British intolerance toward Indians, whom they viewed as untrustworthy. Moreover, the rebellion convinced the British government to assume direct control over India, ending the era of British East India Company rule in the subcontinent. Fear of provoking another rebellion also made the British more conservative and cautious about deliberately trying to change Indian society.

Colonial Empires with a Difference

At one level, European colonial empires were but the latest in a very long line of imperial creations, all of which had enlisted cooperation and experienced resistance from their subject peoples, but the nineteenth-century European version of empire was distinctive in several remarkable ways. One was the prominence of race in distinguishing rulers as "superior" to the ruled, as the high tide of scientific racism in Europe coincided with the acquisition of Asian and African colonies. In East Africa, for example, white men expected to be addressed as *bwana* (Swahili for "master"), whereas Europeans regularly called African men "boy." Particularly affected by European racism were those whose Western education and aspirations most clearly threatened the racial divide. For example, a proposal in 1883 to allow Indian judges to hear cases involving whites provoked outrage and massive demonstrations among European inhabitants of India.

In those colonies that had a large European settler population, the expression of racial distinctions was much more pronounced than in places such as Nigeria, which had few permanently settled whites. The most extreme case was South Africa, where a large European population and the widespread use of African labor in mines and industries brought blacks and whites into closer and more prolonged contact than elsewhere. The racial fears that were aroused resulted in extraordinary efforts to establish race as a legal, not just a customary, feature of South African society. This racial system provided for separate "homelands," educational systems, residential areas, public facilities, and much more. In what was eventually known as apartheid, South African whites attempted the impossible task of creating an industrializing economy based on cheap African labor while limiting African social and political integration in every conceivable fashion.

A further distinctive feature of nineteenth-century European empires lay in the extent to which colonial states were able to penetrate the societies they governed. Centralized tax-collecting bureaucracies, new means of communication and transportation, imposed changes in landholding patterns, integration of colonial economies into a global network of exchange, public health and sanitation measures, and the activities of missionaries—all of this touched the daily lives of many people far more deeply than in earlier empires. Not only were Europeans foreign rulers, but they also bore the seeds of a very different way of life, which grew out of their own modern transformation.

Nineteenth-century European colonizers were extraordinary as well in their penchant for counting and classifying their subject people. With the assistance of anthropologists and missionaries, colonial governments collected a vast amount of information, sought to organize it "scientifically," and used it to manage the unfamiliar, complex, varied, and fluctuating societies that they governed. In India, the British found in classical texts and Brahmin ideology an idealized description of the caste system, based on the notion of four ranked and unchanging varnas, that made it possible to bring order out of the immense complexity and variety of caste as it actually

European Master and Indian Servants This image, dating to 1812, shows a young European gentleman attended by multiple servants in colonial India. It illustrates the exalted status available to quite ordinary Europeans in a colonial setting as well as the sharp racial divide separating Europeans and Indians. (Historia/REX/Shutterstock)

operated. Thus the British invented or appropriated a Brahmin version of "traditional India" that they favored and sought to preserve, while scorning as "non-Indian" the new elite who had been educated in European schools and were enthusiastic about Western ways of life. This view of India reflected the great influence of Brahmins on British thinking and clearly served the interests of this Indian upper class.

Likewise, within African colonies Europeans identified, and sometimes invented, distinct tribes, each with its own clearly defined territory, language, customs, and chief. The notion of a "tribal Africa" expressed the Western view that African societies were primitive or backward, representing an earlier stage of human development. It was also a convenient idea, for it reduced the enormous complexity and fluidity of African societies to a more manageable state and thus made colonial administration easier.

Gender too entered into the efforts of Europeans to define both themselves and their newly acquired subject peoples. European colonizers — mostly male — took pride in their "active masculinity" while defining the "conquered races" as soft, passive, and feminine. Indian Bengali men, wrote a British official in 1892, "are disqualified for political enfranchisement by the possession of essentially feminine characteristics."[11] By linking the inferiority of women with that of people of color, imperialists joined gender ideology and race prejudice in support of colonial rule. But the intersection of race, gender, and empire was complex and varied. European men in the colonies often viewed their own women as the bearers and emblems of civilization, "upholding the moral dignity of the white community" amid the darkness of inferior peoples.[12] As such, European women had to be above reproach in sexual matters, protected against the alleged lust of native men by their separation from local African or Asian societies. Furthermore, certain colonized people, such as the Sikhs and Gurkhas in India, the Kamba in Kenya, and the Hausa in Nigeria, were gendered as masculine or "martial races" and targeted for recruitment into British military or police forces.

Finally, the colonial policies of Europeans contradicted their own core values and their practices at home to an unusual degree. While nineteenth-century Britain and France were becoming more democratic, their colonies were essentially dictatorships, offering perhaps order and stability, but certainly not democratic government, because few colonial subjects were participating citizens. Empire, of course, was wholly at odds with European notions of national independence, and ranked racial classifications went against the grain of both Christian and Enlightenment ideas of human equality. Furthermore, many Europeans were distinctly reluctant to encourage within their colonies the kind of modernization — urban growth, industrialization, individual values, religious skepticism — that was sweeping their own societies. They feared that this kind of social change, often vilified as "detribalization," would encourage unrest and challenge colonial rule. As a model for social development, they much preferred "traditional" rural society, with its established authorities and social hierarchies, though shorn of abuses such as slavery and *sati* (widow burning). Such contradictions between what Europeans embraced at home and what they practiced in the colonies became increasingly apparent to many Asians and Africans and played a major role in undermining the foundations of colonial rule in the twentieth century.

Ways of Working: Comparing Colonial Economies

Colonial rule affected the lives of its subject people in many ways, but the most pronounced change was in their ways of working. The colonial state—with its power to tax, to seize land for European enterprises, to compel labor, and to build railroads, ports, and roads—played an important role in these transformations. Even more powerful was the growing integration of colonized societies into a world economy that increasingly demanded their gold, diamonds, copper, tin, rubber, coffee, cotton, sugar, cocoa, and many other products. But the economic transformations born of these twin pressures were far from uniform. Various groups—migrant workers and cash-crop farmers, plantation laborers and domestic servants, urban elites and day laborers, men and women—experienced the colonial era differently as their daily working lives underwent profound changes.

To various degrees, old ways of working were eroded almost everywhere in the colonial world. Subsistence farming, in which peasant families produced largely for their own needs, diminished as growing numbers directed at least some of their energies to working for wages or selling what they produced for a cash income. That money was both necessary to pay taxes and school fees and useful for buying the various products—such as machine-produced textiles, bicycles, and kerosene—that the industrial economies of Europe sent their way. As in Europe, artisans suffered greatly when cheaper machine-manufactured merchandise displaced their own handmade goods. A flood of inexpensive textiles from Britain's new factories ruined the livelihood of tens of thousands of India's handloom weavers. Iron smelting largely disappeared in Africa, and occupations such as blacksmithing and tanning lost ground. Furthermore, Asian and African merchants, who had earlier handled the trade between their countries and the wider world, were squeezed out by well-financed European commercial firms.

Economies of Coercion: Forced Labor and the Power of the State

Many of the new ways of working that emerged during the colonial era derived directly from the demands of the colonial state. The most obvious was required and unpaid labor on public projects, such as building railroads, constructing government buildings, and transporting goods. In French Africa, all "natives" were legally obligated to do "statute labor" for ten to twelve days a year, a practice that lasted through 1946. It was much resented. A resident of British West Africa, interviewed in 1996, bitterly recalled this feature of colonial life: "They [British officials] were rude, and they made us work for them a lot. They came to the village and just rounded us up and made us go off and clear the road or carry loads on our heads."[13]

The most infamous cruelties of forced labor occurred during the early twentieth century in the **Congo Free State**, then governed personally by King Leopold II of Belgium. Private companies in the Congo, operating under the authority of the state, forced villagers to collect rubber, which was much in demand for bicycle and

Colonial Violence in the Congo Horrific photos of mutilated children had an important impact on public opinion about imperial rule in the Congo Free State. They came to symbolize widespread abuses, including murders, rapes, starvation, and the burning of villages, associated with efforts to obtain supplies of wild rubber for use in industrialized societies. (Universal History Archive/ Getty Images)

automobile tires, with a reign of terror and abuse beginning in the 1890s that cost millions of lives. One refugee from these horrors described the process:

> We were always in the forest to find the rubber vines, to go without food, and our women had to give up cultivating the fields and gardens. Then we starved. . . . We begged the white man to leave us alone, saying we could get no more rubber, but the white men and their soldiers said "Go. You are only beasts yourselves. . . ." When we failed and our rubber was short, the soldiers came to our towns and killed us. Many were shot, some had their ears cut off; others were tied up with ropes round their necks and taken away.[14]

Eventually such outrages were widely publicized in Europe, where they created a scandal, forcing the Belgian government to take control of the Congo in 1908 and ending Leopold's private control of the colony and his reign of terror.

A variation on the theme of forced labor took shape in the so-called **cultivation system** of the Netherlands East Indies (Indonesia) during the nineteenth century. Peasants were required to cultivate 20 percent or more of their land in cash crops such as sugar or coffee to meet their tax obligation to the state. Sold to government contractors at fixed and low prices, those crops, when resold on the world market, proved highly profitable for Dutch traders and shippers as well as for the Dutch state and its citizens. According to one scholar, the cultivation system "performed a miracle for the Dutch economy," enabling it to avoid taxing its own people and providing capital for its Industrial Revolution.[15] It also enriched and strengthened the position of those "traditional authorities" who enforced the system, often by using lashings and various tortures, on behalf of the Dutch. For the peasants of Java, however, it meant a double burden of obligations to the colonial state as well as to local lords. Many became indebted to moneylenders when they could not meet those obligations. Those demands, coupled with the loss of land and labor now excluded from food production, contributed to a wave of famines during the mid-nineteenth century in which hundreds of thousands perished.

On occasion, the forced cultivation of cash crops was successfully resisted. In German East Africa, for example, colonial authorities in the late nineteenth century imposed the cultivation of cotton, which seriously interfered with production of local food crops. Here is how one man remembered the experience:

> The cultivation of cotton was done by turns. Every village was allotted days on which to cultivate. . . . After arriving you all suffered very greatly. Your back and your buttocks were whipped and there was no rising up once you stooped to dig. . . . And yet he [the German] wanted us to pay him tax. Were we not human beings?[16]

Such conditions prompted a massive rebellion in 1904–1905, known as Maji Maji, and persuaded the Germans to end the forced growing of cotton. Thus the actions of colonized peoples could alter or frustrate the plans of the colonizers.

Economies of Cash-Crop Agriculture: The Pull of the Market

Many Asian and African peoples had produced quite willingly for an international market long before they were enclosed within colonial societies. They offered for trade items such as peanuts and palm oil in West Africa, cotton in Egypt, spices in Indonesia, and pepper and textiles in India. In some places, colonial rule created conditions that facilitated and increased **cash-crop production** to the advantage of local farmers. British authorities in Burma, for example, acted to encourage rice production among small farmers by ending an earlier prohibition on rice exports, providing irrigation and transportation facilities, and enacting land tenure laws that facilitated private ownership of small farms. Under these conditions, the population of the Irrawaddy Delta boomed, migrants from Upper Burma and India poured into the region, and rice exports soared. Local small farmers benefited considerably because they were now able to own their own land, build substantial houses, and buy imported goods. For several decades in the late nineteenth century, standards of living improved sharply, and huge increases in rice production fed millions of people in other parts of Asia and elsewhere. It was a very different situation from that of peasants forced to grow crops that seriously interfered with their food production.

But that kind of colonial development, practiced also in the Mekong River delta of French-ruled Vietnam, had important environmental consequences. It involved the destruction of mangrove forests and swamplands along with the fish and shellfish that supplemented local diets. New dikes and irrigation channels inhibited the depositing of silt from upstream and thus depleted soils in the deltas of these major river systems. And, unknown to anyone at the time, this kind of agriculture generates large amounts of methane gas, a major contributor to global warming.

Profitable cash-crop farming also developed in the southern Gold Coast (present-day Ghana), a British territory in West Africa. Unlike in Burma, it was African farmers themselves who took the initiative to develop export agriculture. Planting cacao trees in huge quantities, they became the world's leading supplier of cocoa, used to make chocolate, by 1911. Cacao was an attractive crop because, unlike cotton, it was compatible with the continued production of foods and did not require so much labor time. In the early twentieth century, it brought a new prosperity to many local farmers. But that success brought new problems in its wake. A shortage of labor fostered the employment of former slaves as dependent and exploited workers and also generated tensions between the sexes when some men married women for their labor power but refused to support them adequately. Moreover, the labor shortage brought a huge influx of migrants from the drier interior parts of West Africa, generating ethnic and class tensions. Another problem was that many colonies came to specialize in one or two cash crops, creating an unhealthy dependence when world market prices dropped. Thus African and Asian farmers were increasingly subject to the uncertain rhythms of the international marketplace as well as to those of weather and climate.

Economies of Wage Labor: Migration for Work

Yet another new way of working in colonial societies involved wage labor in some European enterprise. Driven by the need for money, by the loss of land adequate to support their families, or sometimes by the orders of colonial authorities, millions of colonial subjects across Asia, Africa, and Oceania sought employment in European-owned plantations, mines, construction projects, and homes. Often this required migration to distant work sites, many of them overseas. In this process, colonized migrants were joined by millions of Chinese, Japanese, and others who lived in more independent states. Together they generated vast streams of migration that paralleled and at least equaled in numbers the huge movement of Europeans during the nineteenth and early twentieth centuries. For Europeans, Asians, and Africans alike, the globalizing world of the colonial era was one of people in motion. (See the Snapshot on long-distance migration on page 529.)

The African segment of this migratory stream moved in several directions. For much of the nineteenth century, the Atlantic slave trade continued, funneling well over 3 million additional people to the Americas, mostly to Brazil. As the slave trade diminished and colonial rule took shape in Africa, internal migration mounted within or among particular colonies. More than in Asia, Africans migrated to farms or plantations controlled by Europeans because they had lost their own land. In the settler colonies of Africa — Algeria, Kenya, Southern Rhodesia (Zimbabwe), and South Africa, for example — permanent European communities, with the help of colonial governments, obtained huge tracts of land, much of which had previously been home to African societies. A 1913 law in South Africa legally defined 88 percent of the land as belonging to whites, who were then about 20 percent of the population. Much of highland Kenya, an enormously rich agricultural region that was home to the Gikuyu and Kamba peoples, was taken over by some 4,000 white farmers. In such places, some Africans stayed on as "squatters," working for the new landowners as the price of remaining on what had been their own land. Others were

| SNAPSHOT | LONG-DISTANCE MIGRATION IN AN AGE OF EMPIRE, 1846–1940 |

The age of empire was also an age of global migration. Beyond the three major patterns of long-distance migration shown here, shorter migrations within particular regions or colonies set millions more into motion.

Origins	Destination	Numbers
Europe	Americas	55–58 million
India, southern China	Southeast Asia, Indian Ocean rim, South Pacific	48–52 million
Northeast Asia, Russia	Manchuria, Siberia, Central Asia, Japan	46–51 million

Data from Adam McKeown, "Global Migration, 1846–1940," *Journal of World History* 15, no. 2 (2004): 156.

displaced to "native reserves," limited areas that could not support their growing populations, and many were thus forced to work for wages on European farms. Most notably in South Africa, such reserved areas, known as Bantustans, became greatly overcrowded: soil fertility declined, hillsides were cleared, forests shrank, and erosion scarred the land. This kind of ecological degradation was among the environmental consequences of African wage labor on European farms and estates.

The gold and diamond mines of South Africa likewise set in motion a huge pattern of labor migration that encompassed all of Africa south of the Belgian Congo. With skilled and highly paid work reserved for white miners, Africans worked largely as unskilled laborers at a fraction of the wages paid to whites. Furthermore, they were recruited on short-term contracts, lived in all-male prison-like barracks that were often surrounded by barbed wire, and were forced to return home periodically to prevent them from establishing a permanent family life near the mines.

Asians too were in motion and in large numbers. Some 29 million Indians and 19 million Chinese migrated variously to Southeast Asia, the South Pacific, East and South Africa, the Caribbean islands, or the lands around the Indian Ocean basin. All across Southeast Asia in the later nineteenth and early twentieth centuries, huge plantations sprouted that were financed from Europe and that grew sugarcane, rubber, tea, tobacco, sisal (used for making rope), and more. Impoverished workers by the hundreds of thousands came from great distances (India, China, Java) to these plantations, where they were subject to strict control, often housed in barracks, and paid poorly, with women receiving 50 to 75 percent of a man's wage. Disease was common, and death rates were at least double that of the colony as a whole. In 1927 in southern Vietnam alone, one in twenty plantation workers died. British colonial authorities in India facilitated the migration of millions of Indians to work sites elsewhere in the British Empire—Trinidad, Jamaica, Fiji, Malaysia, Ceylon, South Africa, Kenya, and Uganda, for example—with some working as indentured laborers, receiving free passage and enough money to survive in return for five to seven years of heavy labor. Others operated as independent merchants. Particularly in the Caribbean region, Indian migration rose as the end of slavery created a need for additional labor. Since the vast majority of these Asian migrants were male, gender

Economic Change in the Colonial World These workers on a Ceylon tea plantation in the early twentieth century are moving sacks of tea into a drying house in preparation for export. The Lipton label on the bags is a reminder of the role of large-scale foreign investment in the economic transformations of the colonial era. (Hulton Deutsch/Getty Images)

ratios were altered in the islands and in their countries of origin, where women faced increased workloads.

Mines were another source of wage labor for many Asians. In the British-ruled Malay States (Malaysia), tin mining accelerated greatly in the late nineteenth century, and by 1895 that colony produced some 55 percent of the world's tin. Operated initially by Chinese and later by European entrepreneurs, Malaysian tin mines drew many millions of impoverished Chinese workers on strictly controlled three-year contracts. Appalling living conditions, disease, and accidents generated extraordinarily high death rates.

Beyond Southeast Asia, Chinese migrants moved north to Manchuria in substantial numbers, encouraged by a Chinese government eager to prevent Russian encroachment in the area. The gold rushes of Australia and California also attracted hundreds of thousands of Chinese, who often found themselves subject to sharp discrimination from local people, including recently arrived European migrants. For example, Dennis Kearney, who led a California anti-immigrant labor organization with the slogan "The Chinese must go," was himself an Irish-born immigrant. Canada, Australia, New Zealand, and the United States all enacted measures to restrict or end Chinese immigration in the late nineteenth century.

A further destination of African and Asian migrants lay in the rapidly swelling cities of the colonial world—Lagos, Nairobi, Cairo, Calcutta, Rangoon, Batavia, Singapore, Saigon. Racially segregated, often unsanitary, and greatly overcrowded, these cities nonetheless were seen as meccas of opportunity for people all across the social spectrum. Traditional elites, absentee landlords, and wealthy Chinese businessmen occupied the top rungs of Southeast Asian cities. Western-educated people everywhere found opportunities as teachers, doctors, and professional specialists, but more often as clerks in European business offices and government bureaucracies. Skilled workers on the railways or in the ports represented a working class elite, while a few labored in the factories that processed agricultural goods or manufactured basic products such as beer, cigarettes, cement, and furniture. Far more numerous were the construction workers, rickshaw drivers, food sellers, domestic servants, prostitutes, and others who made up the urban poor of colonial cities. In 1955, a British report on life in Nairobi, the capital of Kenya, found that low wages, combined with the high cost of housing and food, "makes family life impossible for the majority."[17] After a half century of colonial rule, it was quite an admission.

Women and the Colonial Economy: Examples from Africa

If economic life in European empires varied greatly from place to place, even within the same colony, it also offered a different combination of opportunities and hardships to women than it did to men, as the experience of colonial Africa shows.[18] In precolonial Africa, women were almost everywhere active farmers, with responsibility for planting, weeding, and harvesting in addition to food preparation and child care. Men cleared the land, built houses, herded the cattle, and in some cases assisted with field work. Within this division of labor, women were expected to feed their own families and were usually allocated their own fields for that purpose. Many were also involved in local trading activity. Though clearly subordinate to men, African women nevertheless had a measure of economic autonomy.

As the demands of the colonial economy grew, women's lives increasingly diverged from those of men. In colonies where cash-crop agriculture was dominant, men often withdrew from subsistence production in favor of more lucrative export crops. Among the Ewe people of southern Ghana, men almost completely dominated the highly profitable cacao farming, whereas women assumed nearly total responsibility for domestic food production. In neighboring Ivory Coast, women had traditionally grown cotton for their families' clothing, but when that crop acquired a cash value, men insisted that cotton grown for export be produced on their own personal fields. Thus men acted to control the most profitable aspects of cash-crop agriculture and in doing so greatly increased the subsistence workload of women. One study from Cameroon estimated that women's working hours increased from forty-six per week in precolonial times to more than seventy by 1934.

Further increasing women's workload and differentiating their lives from those of men was labor migration. As growing numbers of men sought employment in the cities, on settler farms, or in the mines, their wives were left to manage the domestic economy almost alone. In many cases, women also had to supply food to men in the cities to compensate for very low urban wages. They often took over such traditionally male tasks as breaking the ground for planting, milking the cows, and supervising the herds, in addition to their normal responsibilities. In South Africa, where the demands of the European economy were particularly heavy, some 40 to 50 percent of able-bodied adult men were absent from the rural areas, and women headed 60 percent of households. In Botswana, which supplied much male labor to South Africa, married couples by the 1930s rarely lived together for more than two months at a time. Increasingly, men and women lived in different worlds, with one focused on the cities and working for wages and the other on village life and subsistence agriculture.

Women coped with these difficult circumstances in a number of ways. Many sought closer relations with their families of birth rather than with their absent husbands' families, as would otherwise have been expected. Among the Luo of Kenya, women introduced laborsaving crops, adopted new farm implements, and earned some money as traders. In the cities, they established a variety of self-help associations, including those for prostitutes and for brewers of beer.

The colonial economy sometimes provided a measure of opportunity for enterprising women, particularly in small-scale trade and marketing. In some parts of West Africa, women came to dominate this sector of the economy by selling foodstuffs, cloth, and inexpensive imported goods, while men or foreign firms controlled the more profitable wholesale and import-export trade. Such opportunities sometimes gave women considerable economic autonomy. By the 1930s, for example, Nupe women in northern Nigeria had gained sufficient wealth as itinerant traders that they were contributing more to the family income than their husbands and frequently lent money to them. Among some Igbo groups in southern Nigeria, men were responsible for growing the prestigious yams, but women's crops — especially cassava — came to have a cash value during the colonial era, and women were entitled to keep the profits from selling them. "What is man? I have my own money" was a popular saying that expressed the growing economic independence of such women.[19]

At the other end of the social scale, women of impoverished rural families, by necessity, often became virtually independent heads of household in the absence of their husbands. Others took advantage of new opportunities in mission schools, towns, and mines to flee the restrictions of rural patriarchy. Such challenges to patriarchal values elicited various responses from men, including increased accusations of witchcraft against women and fears of impotence. Among the Shona in Southern Rhodesia, and no doubt elsewhere, senior African men repeatedly petitioned the colonial authorities for laws and regulations that would criminalize adultery and restrict women's ability to leave their rural villages. The control of women's sexuality and mobility was a common interest of European and African men.

Assessing Colonial Development

Beyond the many and varied changes that transformed the working lives of millions in the colonial world lies the difficult and highly controversial question of the overall economic impact of colonial rule on Asian and African societies. Defenders, both then and now, praise it for jump-starting modern economic growth, but numerous critics cite a record of exploitation and highlight the limitations and unevenness of that growth.

Amid the continuing debates, three things seem reasonably clear. First, colonial rule served, for better or worse, to further the integration of Asian and African economies into a global network of exchange, now centered in Europe. In many places, that process was well under way before conquest imposed foreign rule, and elsewhere it occurred without formal colonial control. Nonetheless, it is apparent that within the colonial world far more land and labor were devoted to production for the global market at the end of the colonial era than at its beginning. Many colonized groups and individuals benefited from their new access to global markets—Burmese rice farmers and West African cocoa farmers, for example. Others were devastated. In India, large-scale wheat exports to Britain continued unchecked—or even increased—despite a major drought and famine that claimed between 6 and 10 million lives in the late 1870s. A colonial government committed to free market principles declined to interfere with those exports or to provide much by way of relief. One senior official declared it "a mistake to spend so much money to save a lot of black fellows."[20]

Second, Europeans could hardly avoid conveying to the colonies some elements of their own modernizing process. It was in their interests to do so, and many felt duty bound to "improve" the societies they briefly governed. Modern administrative and bureaucratic structures facilitated colonial control; communication and transportation infrastructure (railroads, motorways, ports, telegraphs, postal services) moved products to the world market; schools trained the army of intermediaries on which colonial rule depended; and modest health care provisions fulfilled some of the "civilizing mission" to which many Europeans felt committed. These elements of modernization made an appearance, however inadequately, during the colonial era.

Third, nowhere in the colonial world did a major breakthrough to modern industrial society occur. When India became independent after two centuries of colonial rule by the world's first industrial society, it was still one of the poorest of the world's developing countries. The British may not have created Indian poverty, but neither did they overcome it to any substantial degree. Scholars continue to debate the reasons for that failure: was it the result of deliberate British policies, or was it due to the conditions of Indian society? The nationalist movements that surged across Asia and Africa in the twentieth century had their own answer. To their many millions of participants, colonial rule, whatever its earlier promise, had become an economic dead end, whereas independence represented a grand opening to new and more hopeful possibilities. Taking off from a famous teaching of Jesus, Kwame Nkrumah, the first prime minister of an independent Ghana, declared, "Seek ye first the political kingdom, and all these other things [schools, factories, hospitals, for example] will be added unto you."

Believing and Belonging: Identity and Cultural Change

Beyond profound economic transformations, the experience of colonial rule—its racism, its exposure to European culture, its social and economic upheavals—also generated new patterns of identity within Asian, African, and Oceanic societies. Millions of people underwent substantial and quite rapid changes in what they believed and in how they defined the communities to which they belonged. Those new ways of believing and belonging echoed long after European rule had ended.

Education

For an important minority, it was the acquisition of Western education, obtained through missionary or government schools, that generated a new identity. To previously illiterate people, the knowledge of reading and writing of any kind often suggested an almost magical power. Within the colonial setting, it could mean an escape from some of the most onerous obligations of living under European control, such as forced labor. More positively, it meant access to better-paying positions in government bureaucracies, mission organizations, or business firms and to the exciting imported goods that their salaries could buy. Moreover, education often provided social mobility and elite status within colonized peoples' own communities and an opportunity to achieve, or at least approach, equality with whites in racially defined societies. An African man from colonial Kenya described an encounter he had as a boy in 1938 with a relative who was a teacher in a mission school:

> Aged about 25, he seems to me like a young god with his smart clothes and shoes, his watch, and a beautiful bicycle. I worshipped in particular his bicycle that day and decided that I must somehow get myself one. As he talked with us, it seemed to me that the secret of his riches came from his education, his knowledge of reading and writing, and that it was essential for me to obtain this power.[21]

Many such people ardently embraced European culture, dressing in European clothes, speaking French or English, building European-style houses, getting married in long white dresses, and otherwise emulating European ways. Some of the early Western-educated Bengalis from northeastern India boasted about dreaming in English and deliberately ate beef, to the consternation of their elders. In a well-known poem titled "A Prayer for Peace," Léopold Senghor, a highly educated

The Educated Elite Throughout the Afro-Asian world of the nineteenth century, the European presence generated a small group of people who enthusiastically embraced the culture and lifestyle of Europe. Here King Chulalongkorn of Siam poses with the crown prince and other young students, all of them impeccably garbed in European clothing. (Hulton Deutsch/Getty Images)

West African writer and political leader, enumerated the many crimes of colonialism and yet confessed, "I have a great weakness for France." Asian and African colonial societies now had a new cultural divide: between the small numbers who had mastered to varying degrees the ways of their rulers and the vast majority who had not. Literate Christians in the East African kingdom of Buganda referred with contempt to their "pagan" neighbors as "those who do not read."

Many among the Western-educated elite saw themselves as a modernizing vanguard, leading the regeneration of their societies in association with colonial authorities. For them, at least initially, the colonial enterprise was full of promise for a better future. The Vietnamese teacher and nationalist Nguyen Thai Hoc, while awaiting execution in 1930 by the French for his revolutionary activities, wrote about his earlier hopes: "At the beginning, I had thought to cooperate with the French in Indochina in order to serve my compatriots, my country, and my people, particularly in the areas of cultural and economic development."[22] Senghor too wrote wistfully about an earlier time when "we could have lived in harmony [with Europeans]."

In nineteenth-century India, Western-educated men organized a variety of reform societies that drew inspiration from the classic texts of Hinduism while seeking a renewed Indian culture that was free of idolatry, caste restrictions, and other "errors" that had entered Indian life over the centuries. Much of this reform effort centered on improving the status of women. Thus reformers campaigned against *sati*, the ban on remarriage of widows, female infanticide, and child marriages, while advocating women's education and property rights. For a time, some of these Indian reformers saw themselves working in tandem with British colonial authorities. One of them, Keshub Chunder Sen, addressed his fellow Indians in 1877: "You are bound to be loyal to the British government that came to your rescue, as God's ambassador, when your country was sunk in ignorance and superstition. . . . India in her present fallen condition seems destined to sit at the feet of England for many long years, to learn western art and science."[23]

Those who held such hopes for the modernization of their societies within a colonial framework would be bitterly disappointed. Europeans generally declined to treat their Asian and African subjects—even those with a Western education—as equal partners in the enterprise of renewal. The frequent denigration of Asian and African cultures as primitive, backward, uncivilized, or savage certainly rankled, particularly among the well educated. "My people of Africa," wrote the West African intellectual James Aggrey in the 1920s, "we were created in the image of God, but men have made us think that we are chickens, and we still think we are; but we are eagles. Stretch forth your wings and fly."[24] In the long run, the educated classes in colonial societies everywhere found European rule far more of an obstacle to their countries' development than a means of achieving it. Turning decisively against a now-despised foreign imperialism, they led the many struggles for independence that came to fruition in the second half of the twentieth century.

Religion

Religion too provided the basis for new or transformed identities during the colonial era. Most dramatic were those places where widespread conversion to Christianity took place, such as Pacific Oceania and especially non-Muslim Africa. Some 10,000 missionaries had descended on Africa by 1910; by the 1960s, about 50 million Africans, roughly half of the non-Muslim population, claimed a Christian identity. The attractions of the new faith were many. As in the Americas centuries earlier, military defeat shook confidence in the old gods and local practices, fostering openness to new sources of supernatural power that could operate in the wider world now impinging on Oceanic and African societies. Furthermore, Christianity was widely associated with modern education, and, especially in Africa, mission schools were the primary providers of Western education. The young, the poor, and many women — all of them oppressed groups in many African societies — found new opportunities and greater freedom in some association with missions. Moreover, the spread of the Christian message was less the work of European missionaries than of those many thousands of African teachers, catechists, and pastors who brought the new faith to remote villages as well as the local communities that begged for a teacher and supplied the labor and materials to build a small church or school. In Oceania, local authorities, such as those in Fiji, Tonga, and Hawaii, sought to strengthen their position by associating with Christian missionaries, widely regarded as linked to the growing influence of European or American power in the region. In many of these small island societies, mission Christianity with its schools, clinics, political counsel, and new social conventions provided a measure of social cohesion for peoples devastated by disease and other disruptions that accompanied Western incursions.

But missionary teaching and practice also generated conflict and opposition, particularly when they touched on gender roles. A wide range of issues focusing on the lives of women proved challenging for missionaries and spawned opposition from converts or potential converts. Female nudity offended Western notions of modesty. Polygyny contradicted Christian monogamy, though such prescriptions sat uneasily beside the biblical testimony that Old Testament figures such as Abraham, Jacob, David, and Solomon all had multiple wives. And the question of what male converts should do with their additional wives was always difficult. To many missionaries, bride wealth made marriage seem "a mere mercantile transaction." Marriages between Christians and non-Christians remained problematic. Sexual activity outside of monogamous marriage often resulted in disciplinary action or expulsion from the church. Missionaries' efforts to enforce Western gender norms were in part responsible for considerable turnover in the ranks of African church members.

Among the more explosive issues that agitated nascent Christian communities in colonial Kenya was that of **female circumcision**, the excision of a pubescent girl's clitoris and adjacent genital tissue as a part of initiation rites marking her coming-of-age. To the Gikuyu people, among whom it was widely practiced, it was a prerequisite for adult status and marriage. To missionaries, it was physically damaging to girls and brought "unnecessary attention . . . to the non-spiritual aspects of sex."[25] When missionaries in 1929 sought to enforce a ban on the practice among their African converts, outrage ensued. Thousands abandoned mission schools and churches, but they did not abandon Christianity or modern education. Rather, they created a series of independent schools and churches in which they could practice their new faith and pursue their educational goals without missionary intrusion. Some recalled that the New Testament itself had declared that "circumcision is nothing and uncircumcision is nothing." Accordingly, wrote one angry convert to a local missionary, "Has God spoken to you this time and informed you that those who circumcise will not enter in to God's place? It is better for a European like you to leave off speaking about such things because you can make the Gospel to be evil spoken of."[26]

As elsewhere, Christianity in Africa soon adapted to local cultural patterns. This **Africanization of Christianity** took many forms. Within mission-based churches, many converts continued using protective charms and medicines and consulting local medicine men, all of which caused their missionary mentors to speak frequently of "backsliding." Other converts continued to believe in their old gods and spirits but now deemed them evil and sought their destruction. Furthermore, thousands of separatist movements established a wide array of independent churches that were thoroughly Christian but under African rather than missionary control and that in many cases incorporated African cultural practices and modes of worship. It was a twentieth-century "African Reformation."

In India, where Christianity made only very modest inroads, leading intellectuals and reformers began to define their region's endlessly varied beliefs, practices, sects, rituals, and philosophies as a more distinct, unified, and separate religion, now known as **Hinduism**. It was in part an effort to provide for India a religion wholly equivalent to Christianity, "an accessible tradition and a feeling of historical worth when faced with the humiliation of colonial rule."[27] To **Swami Vivekananda** (1863–1902), one of nineteenth-century India's most influential religious figures, as well as others active in reform movements, a revived Hinduism, shorn of its distortions, offered a means of uplifting the country's village communities, which were the heart of Indian civilization. It also served to distinguish a "spiritual East" from a "materialistic West."

This new notion of Hinduism provided a cultural foundation for emerging ideas of India as a nation, but it also contributed to a clearer sense of Muslims as a

The Missionary Factor Among the major change agents of the colonial era were the thousands of Christian missionaries who brought not only a new religion but also elements of European medicine, education, gender roles, and culture. Here is an assembly at a mission school for girls in New Guinea in the early twentieth century. (Library of Congress, Prints and Photographs Division, LC-USZ62-46884)

distinct community in India. Before the British takeover, little sense of commonality united the many diverse communities who practiced Islam—urban and rural dwellers; nomads and farmers; artisans, merchants, and state officials. But the British had created one set of inheritance laws for all Muslims and another set for all Hindus; in their census taking, they counted the numbers of people within these now sharply distinguished groups; and they allotted seats in local councils according to these artificial categories. As some anti-British patriots began to cast India in Hindu terms, the idea of Muslims as a separate community that was perhaps threatened by the much larger number of Hindus began to make sense to some who practiced Islam. In the early twentieth century, a young Hindu Bengali schoolboy noticed that "our Muslim school-fellows were beginning to air the fact of their being Muslims rather more consciously than before and with a touch of assertiveness."[28] Here were the beginnings of what became in the twentieth century a profound religious and political division within the South Asian peninsula.

"Race" and "Tribe"

In Africa as well, intellectuals and ordinary people alike forged new ways of belonging as they confronted the upheavals of colonial life. Central to these new identities were notions of race and ethnicity. By the end of the nineteenth century, a number of African thinkers, familiar with Western culture, began to define the idea of an "**African identity**." Previously, few if any people on the continent had regarded themselves as Africans. Rather, they were members of particular local communities, usually defined by language; some were also Muslims; and still others inhabited some state or empire. Now, however, influenced by the common experience of colonial oppression and by a highly derogatory European racism, well-educated Africans began to think in broader terms, similar to those of Indian reformers who were developing the notion of Hinduism. It was an effort to revive the cultural self-confidence of their people by articulating a larger, common, and respected "African tradition," equivalent to that of Western culture.

This effort took various shapes. One line of argument held that African culture and history in fact possessed the very characteristics that Europeans exalted. Knowing that Europeans valued large empires and complex political systems, African intellectuals pointed with pride to the ancient kingdoms of Axum/Ethiopia, Mali, Songhay, and others. C. A. Diop, a French-educated scholar from Senegal, insisted that Egyptian civilization was in fact the work of black Africans. Reversing European assumptions, Diop argued that Western civilization owed much to Egyptian influence and was therefore derived from Africa. Black people, in short, had a history of achievement fully comparable to that of Europe and therefore deserved just as much respect and admiration.

An alternative approach to defining an African identity lay in praising the differences between African and European cultures. The most influential proponent of such views was **Edward Blyden** (1832–1912), a West African born in the West Indies and educated in the United States who later became a prominent scholar and political official in Liberia. Blyden accepted the assumption that the world's various races were different but argued that each had its own distinctive contribution to make to world civilization. The uniqueness of African culture, Blyden wrote, lay in its communal, cooperative, and egalitarian societies, which contrasted sharply with Europe's highly individualistic, competitive, and class-ridden societies; in its harmonious relationship with nature as opposed to Europe's efforts to dominate and exploit the natural order; and particularly in its profound religious sensibility, which Europeans had lost in centuries of attention to material gain. Like Vivekananda in India, Blyden argued that Africa had a global mission "to be the spiritual conservatory of the world."[29]

In the twentieth century, such ideas resonated with a broader public. Hundreds of thousands of Africans took part in World War I, during which they encountered other Africans as well as Europeans. Some were able to travel widely. Contact with American black leaders, such as Booker T. Washington, W. E. B. DuBois, and Marcus Garvey, as well as various West Indian intellectuals further stimulated among a few a sense of belonging to an even larger pan-African world. Such notions underlay the growing nationalist movements that contested colonial rule as the twentieth century unfolded.

For the vast majority, however, the most important new sense of belonging that evolved from the colonial experience was not the notion of "Africa"; rather, it was the **idea of "tribe"** or, in the language of contemporary scholars, that of ethnic identity. African peoples, of course, had long recognized differences among themselves based on language, kinship, clan, village, or state, but these were seldom clearly defined. Boundaries fluctuated and were hazy; local communities often incorporated a variety of culturally different peoples. The idea of an Africa sharply divided into separate and distinct "tribes" was in fact a European notion that facilitated colonial administration and reflected Europeans' belief in African primitiveness. For example, when the British began to rule the peoples living along the northern side of Lake Tanganyika, in present-day Tanzania, they found a series of communities that were similar to one another in language and customs but that governed themselves separately and certainly had not regarded themselves as a distinct "tribe." It was British attempts to rule them as a single people, first through a "paramount chief" and later through a council of chiefs and elders, that resulted in their being called, collectively, the Nyakyusa. A tribe had been born. By requiring people to identify their tribe on applications for jobs, schools, and identity cards, colonial governments spread the idea of tribe widely within their colonies.

New ethnic identities were not simply imposed by Europeans, for Africans themselves increasingly found ethnic or tribal labels useful. This was especially true in rapidly growing urban areas. Surrounded by a bewildering variety of people and in a setting where competition for jobs, housing, and education was very intense, migrants to the city found it helpful to categorize themselves and others in larger ethnic terms. Thus, in many colonial cities, people who spoke similar languages, shared a common culture, or came from the same general part of the country began to think of themselves as a single people — a new tribe. They organized a rich variety of ethnic or tribal associations to provide mutual assistance while in the cities and to send money back home to build schools or clinics. Migrant workers, far from home and concerned about protecting their rights to land and to their wives and families, found a sense of security in being part of a recognized tribe, with its chiefs, courts, and established authority.

The Igbo people of southeastern Nigeria represent a case in point. Prior to the twentieth century, they were organized in a series of independently governed village groups. Although they spoke related languages, they had no unifying political system and no myth of common ancestry. Occupying a region of unusually dense population, many of these people eagerly seized on Western education and moved in large numbers to the cities and towns of colonial Nigeria. There they gradually discovered what they had in common and how they differed from the other peoples of Nigeria. By the 1940s, they were organizing on a national level and calling on Igbos everywhere to "sink all differences" to achieve "tribal unity, cooperation, and progress of all the Igbos." Fifty years earlier, however, no one had regarded himself or herself as an Igbo. One historian summed up the process of creating African ethnic identities in this way: "Europeans believed Africans belonged to tribes; Africans built tribes to belong to."[30]

Reflections: Who Makes History?

Winners may write history, but they do not make history, at least not alone. Dominant groups everywhere—slave owners, upper classes, men generally, and certainly colonial rulers—have found their actions constrained and their choices limited by the sheer presence of subordinated people and the ability of those people to act. Europeans who sought to make their countries self-sufficient in cotton by requiring colonized Africans to grow it generally found themselves unable to achieve that goal. Missionaries who tried to impose their own understanding of Christianity in the colonies found their converts often unwilling to accept missionary authority or the cultural framework in which the new religion was presented. In the twentieth century, colonial rulers all across Asia and Africa found that their most highly educated subjects became the leaders of those movements seeking to end colonial rule. Clearly, this was not what they had intended.

In recent decades, historians have been at pains to uncover the ways in which subordinated people—slaves, workers, peasants, women, the colonized—have been able to act in their own interests, even within the most oppressive conditions. Historians of women's lives, for example, have sought to show women not only as victims of patriarchy but also as historical actors in their own right. Likewise, colonized people in any number of ways actively shaped the history of the colonial era. On occasion, they resisted and rebelled; in various times and places, they embraced, rejected, and transformed a transplanted Christianity; many eagerly sought Western education but later turned it against the colonizers; women both suffered from and creatively coped with the difficulties of colonial life; and everywhere people created new ways of belonging. None of this diminishes the hardships, the enormous inequalities of power, or the exploitation and oppression of the colonial experience. Rather, it suggests that history is often made through the struggle of unequal groups and that the outcome corresponds to no one's intentions.

Perhaps we might let Karl Marx have the last word on this endlessly fascinating topic: "Men make their own history," he wrote, "but they do not make it as they please nor under conditions of their own choosing." In the colonial experience of the nineteenth and early twentieth centuries, both the colonizers and the colonized "made history," but neither was able to do so as they pleased.

Second Thoughts

WHAT'S THE SIGNIFICANCE?

scientific racism (p. 515)
civilizing mission (p. 516)
social Darwinism (p. 516)
scramble for Africa (p. 517)
Indian Rebellion of 1857–1858
   (p. 522)
Congo Free State (p. 525)
cultivation system (p. 526)

cash-crop production (p. 527)
female circumcision (p. 536)
Africanization of Christianity (p. 537)
Hinduism (p. 537)
Swami Vivekananda (p. 537)
African identity (p. 538)
Edward Blyden (p. 538)
idea of "tribe" (p. 539)

BIG PICTURE QUESTIONS

1. In what ways did colonial rule rest on violence and coercion, and in what
   ways did it elicit voluntary cooperation or generate benefits for some
   people?

2. In what respects were colonized people more than victims of colonial
   conquest and rule? To what extent could they act in their own interests
   within the colonial situation?

3. Was colonial rule a transforming, even a revolutionary, experience, or did
   it freeze or preserve existing social and economic patterns? What evidence
   can you find to support both sides of this argument?

4. **Looking Back:** How would you compare the colonial experience of Asian
   and African peoples during the long nineteenth century to the earlier
   colonial experience in the Americas?

CHRONOLOGY

1750–1900	• Europe's Industrial Revolution
1757–1858	• East India Company governs India
1788	• Initial European settlement of Australia
1820s	• Quinine isolated and mass-produced
1830s	• France invades Algeria
1830s–1870	• Cultivation system in Netherlands East Indies
1846–1848	• Mexican–United States War
1850–1900	• Scientific racism and social Darwinism prominent

1857–1858	• Indian Rebellion against rule of British East India Company
1858–1893	• French conquest of Indochina
1858–1947	• British government rules India
1862	• Development of Gatling gun, a hand-driven machine gun
1869	• Opening of Suez Canal
1875–1900	• Intensification of European rivalries over African territories
1875–1900	• European conquest of Africa
1890s–1908	• King Leopold's reign of terror in the Congo
1896	• Ethiopia defeats Italy at Battle of Adowa
1898	• Spanish-American War
1898	• United States acquires Hawaii and Philippines
1899–1902	• Boer War
1904–1905	• Maji Maji rebellion in German East Africa
1910	• Japanese annexation of Korea

19

Empires in Collision

Europe, the Middle East, and East Asia

1800–1900

"SEVERAL CENTURIES AGO, CHINA WAS STRONG. . . . IN OVER 100 YEARS after the 1840 Opium War, China suffered immensely from aggression, wars and chaos."[1] Speaking in early 2017, Chinese president Xi Jinping thus reminded his listeners of Britain's nineteenth-century violent intrusion into China's history bearing shiploads of highly addictive opium. This conflict marked the beginning of what the Chinese still describe as a "century of humiliation." In official Chinese thinking, it was only the victory of the Chinese Communist Party that enabled China to finally escape from that shameful past. Memories of the Opium War remain a central element of China's "patriotic education" for the young, serving as a warning against uncritical admiration of the West and providing a rejoinder to any Western criticism of China. Almost 180 years after that clash between the Chinese and British empires, the Opium War retains an emotional resonance for many Chinese and offers a politically useful tool for the country's government.

China was among the countries that confronted an aggressive and industrializing West while maintaining its formal independence, unlike the colonized areas discussed in Chapter 18. So too did Japan, the Ottoman Empire, Persia (now Iran), Ethiopia, and Siam (now Thailand). Latin America also falls in this category (see "The Industrial Revolution and Latin America in the Nineteenth Century" in Chapter 17). These states avoided outright incorporation into European colonial empires, retaining some ability to resist European aggression and to reform or transform their own societies. But they shared with their colonized counterparts the need to deal with four dimensions of the European moment in world history. First, they faced the immense military might and political ambitions of the major imperial powers. Second, they became enmeshed in networks of trade, investment, and sometimes migration that arose from an industrializing and capitalist Europe to generate a new world economy. Third, they were touched by various aspects of traditional European culture, as some among them learned the French, English, or German language; converted to Christianity; or studied European literature and philosophy. Fourth, they too engaged with the culture of modernity—its scientific rationalism; its technological achievements; its belief in a better future; and its ideas of nationalism, socialism, feminism, and individualism. In those epic encounters, they sometimes resisted, at other times accommodated, and almost always adapted what came from the West. They were active participants in the global drama of nineteenth-century world history, not simply its passive victims or beneficiaries.

At the same time, these societies were dealing with their own internal issues. Population growth and peasant rebellion wracked China; internal social and economic changes eroded the stability of Japanese public life; the great empires of the Islamic world shrank or disappeared; rivalry among competing elites troubled Latin American societies. China, the Ottoman Empire, and Japan provide a range of experiences, responses, and outcomes and many opportunities for comparison, as they navigated this era of colliding empires.

Reversal of Fortune: China's Century of Crisis

In 1793, just a decade after King George III of Britain lost his North American colonies, he received yet another rebuff, this time from China. In a famous letter to the British monarch, the Chinese emperor Qianlong (chyan-loong) sharply rejected British requests for a less restricted trading relationship with his country. "Our Celestial Empire possesses all things in prolific abundance," he declared. "There was therefore no need to import the manufactures of outside barbarians." Qianlong's snub simply continued the pattern of the previous several centuries, during which Chinese authorities had strictly controlled and limited the activities of European missionaries and merchants. But by 1912, little more than a century later, China's long-established imperial state had collapsed, and the country had been transformed from a central presence in the global economy to a weak and dependent participant in a European-dominated world system in which Great Britain was the major economic and political player. It was a stunning reversal of fortune for a country that in Chinese eyes was the civilized center of the entire world—in their terms, the Celestial Empire or the Middle Kingdom.

The Crisis Within

In some ways, China was the victim of its own earlier success. Its robust economy and American food crops had enabled substantial population growth, from about 100 million people in 1685 to some 430 million in 1853. Unlike in Europe, though, where a similar population spurt took place, no Industrial Revolution accompanied this vast increase in the number of people, nor was agricultural production able to keep up. Neither did China's internal expansion to the west and south generate anything like the wealth and resources that derived from Europe's overseas empires. The result was growing pressure on the land, smaller farms for China's huge peasant population, and, in all too many cases, unemployment, impoverishment, misery, and starvation.

Furthermore, China's governing institutions did not keep pace with the growing population. Thus the state was increasingly unable to effectively perform its many functions, such as tax collection, flood control, social welfare, and public security. Gradually the central state lost power to provincial officials and local gentry. Among such officials, corruption was endemic, and harsh treatment of peasants was common. According to an official report issued in 1852, "Day and night soldiers are sent out to harass taxpayers. Sometimes corporal punishments are imposed upon tax delinquents; some of them are so badly beaten to exact the last penny that blood and flesh fly in all directions."[2] Finally, European military pressure and economic penetration during the first half of the nineteenth century disrupted internal trade routes, created substantial unemployment, and raised peasant taxes.

This combination of circumstances, traditionally associated with a declining dynasty, gave rise to growing numbers of bandit gangs roaming the countryside and, even more dangerous, to outright peasant rebellion. Beginning in the late eighteenth century, such rebellions drew on a variety of peasant grievances and found leadership in charismatic figures proclaiming a millenarian religious message. Increasingly they also expressed opposition to the Qing dynasty because of its foreign Manchu origins. "We wait only for the northern region to be returned to a Han emperor," declared one rebel group in the early nineteenth century.[3]

China's internal crisis culminated in the **Taiping Uprising**, which set much of the country aflame between 1850 and 1864. This was a different kind of peasant upheaval. Its leaders largely rejected Confucianism, Daoism, and Buddhism alike, finding their primary ideology in a unique form of Christianity. Its leading figure, Hong Xiuquan (hong show-chwaan) (1814–1864), proclaimed himself the younger brother of Jesus, sent to cleanse the world of demons and to establish a "heavenly kingdom of great peace." Nor were these leaders content to restore an idealized Chinese society; instead they insisted on genuinely revolutionary change. They called for the abolition of private property, a radical redistribution of land, the end of prostitution and opium smoking, and the organization of society into sexually segregated

Taiping Uprising Western powers generally supported the Qing dynasty during the Taiping Uprising and even provided it with some military support. This image shows a group of the Taiping rebels and a British soldier they have captured. (Private Collection/Peter Newark Military Pictures/Bridgeman Images)

military camps of men and women. Hong fiercely denounced the Qing dynasty as foreigners who had "poisoned China" and "defiled the emperor's throne." His cousin, Hong Rengan, developed plans for transforming China into an industrial nation, complete with railroads, health insurance for all, newspapers, and widespread public education.

Among the most revolutionary dimensions of the Taiping Uprising was its posture toward women and gender roles. This outlook reflected its origins among the minority Hakka people of southern China, where women were notably less restricted than Confucian orthodoxy prescribed. During the uprising, Hakka women, whose feet had never been bound, fought as soldiers in their own regiments, and in liberated regions, Taiping officials ordered that the feet of other women be unbound. The Taiping land reform program promised women and men equal shares of land. Women were now permitted to sit for civil service examinations and were appointed to supervisory positions, though usually ones in which they exercised authority over other women rather than men. Mutual attraction rather than family interests was promoted as a basis for marriage.

None of these reforms were consistently implemented during the short period of Taiping power, and the movement's leadership demonstrated considerable ambivalence about equality for women. Hong himself reflected a much more traditional understanding of elite women's role when he assembled a large personal harem and declared: "The duty of the palace women is to attend to the needs of their husbands;

and it is arranged by Heaven that they are not to learn of the affairs outside."[4] Nonetheless, the Taiping posture toward women represented a sharp challenge to long-established gender roles and contributed to the hostility that the movement generated among many other Chinese, including women.

With a rapidly swelling number of followers, Taiping forces swept out of southern China and established their capital in Nanjing in 1853. For a time, the days of the Qing dynasty appeared to be over. But divisions and indecisiveness within the Taiping leadership, along with their inability to link up with several other rebel groups also operating separately in China, provided an opening for Qing dynasty loyalists to rally and by 1864 to crush this most unusual of peasant rebellions. Western military support for pro-Qing forces likewise contributed to their victory. It was not, however, the imperial military forces of the central government that defeated the rebels. Instead provincial military leaders, fearing the radicalism of the Taiping program, mobilized their own armies, which in the end crushed the rebel forces.

Thus the Qing dynasty was saved, but it was also weakened as the provincial gentry consolidated their power at the expense of the central state. The intense conservatism of both imperial authorities and their gentry supporters postponed any resolution of China's peasant problem, delayed any real change for China's women, and deferred vigorous efforts at modernization until the communists came to power in the mid-twentieth century. More immediately, the devastation and destruction occasioned by this massive civil war seriously disrupted and weakened China's economy. Estimates of the number of lives lost range from 20 to 30 million. In human terms, it was the most costly conflict in the world during the nineteenth century, and it took China more than a decade to recover from its devastation. China's internal crisis in general and the Taiping Uprising in particular also provided a highly unfavorable setting for the country's encounter with a Europe newly invigorated by the Industrial Revolution.

Western Pressures

Nowhere was the shifting balance of global power in the nineteenth century more evident than in China's changing relationship with Europe, a transformation that registered most dramatically in the famous **Opium Wars**. Derived from Arab traders

Addiction to Opium Throughout the nineteenth century, opium imports created a massive addiction problem in China, as this photograph of an opium den from around 1900 suggests. Not until the early twentieth century did the British prove willing to curtail the opium trade from their Indian colony. (Hulton Deutsch/Getty Images)

in the eighth century or earlier, opium had long been used on a small scale as a drinkable medicine; it was regarded as a magical cure for dysentery and described by one poet as "fit for Buddha."[5] It did not become a serious problem until the late eighteenth century, when the British began to use opium, grown and processed in India, to cover their persistent trade imbalance with China. By the 1830s, British, American, and other Western merchants had found an enormous, growing, and very profitable market for this highly addictive drug. From 1,000 chests (each weighing roughly 150 pounds) in 1773, China's opium imports exploded to more than 23,000 chests in 1832. (See Snapshot, below.)

By then, Chinese authorities recognized a mounting problem on many levels. Because opium importation was illegal, it had to be smuggled into China, thus flouting Chinese law. Bribed to turn a blind eye to the illegal trade, many officials were corrupted. Furthermore, a massive outflow of silver to pay for the opium reversed China's centuries-long ability to attract much of the world's silver supply, and this imbalance caused serious economic problems. Finally, China found itself with many millions of addicts—men and women, court officials, students preparing for exams, soldiers going into combat, and common laborers seeking to overcome the pain and drudgery of their work. Following an extended debate at court in 1836 on whether to legalize the drug or crack down on its use, the emperor decided on suppression. An upright official, **Commissioner Lin Zexu** (lin zuh-SHOO), led the campaign against opium use as a kind of "drug czar." The British, offended by the seizure of their property in opium and emboldened by their new military power, sent a large naval expedition to China, determined to end the restrictive conditions under which they had long traded with that country. In the process, they would teach the Chinese a lesson about the virtues of free trade and the "proper" way to conduct relations

---

SNAPSHOT	**CHINESE/BRITISH TRADE AT CANTON, 1835–1836**

What do these figures suggest about the role of opium in British trade with China? Calculate opium exports as a percentage of British exports to China, Britain's trade deficit without opium, and its trade surplus with opium. What did this pattern mean for China?

	Item	Value (in Spanish dollars)
British Exports to Canton	Opium	17,904,248
	Cotton	8,357,394
	All other items (sandalwood, lead, iron, tin, cotton yarn and piece goods, tin plates, watches, clocks)	6,164,981
	Total	32,426,623
British Imports from Canton	Tea (black and green)	13,412,243
	Raw silk	3,764,115
	Vermilion	705,000
	All other goods (sugar products, camphor, silver, gold, copper, musk)	5,971,541
	Total	23,852,899

Data from Hsin-Pao Chang, ed., *Commissioner Lin and the Opium War* (New York: W. W. Norton, 1970), 226–27.

among countries. Thus began the first Opium War (1840–1842), in which Britain's industrialized military might proved decisive. The Treaty of Nanjing, which ended the war in 1842, largely on British terms, imposed numerous restrictions on Chinese sovereignty and opened five ports to European traders. Its provisions reflected the changed balance of global power that had emerged with Britain's Industrial Revolution. To the Chinese, that agreement represented the first of the "**unequal treaties**" that seriously eroded China's independence by the end of the century.

But it was not the last of those treaties. Britain's victory in a second Opium War (1856–1858) was accompanied by the brutal vandalizing of the emperor's exquisite Summer Palace outside Beijing and resulted in further humiliations. Still more ports were opened to foreign traders. Now those foreigners were allowed to travel freely and buy land in China, to preach Christianity under the protection of Chinese authorities, and to patrol some of China's rivers. Furthermore, the Chinese were forbidden to use the character for "barbarians" to refer to the British in official documents. Following later military defeats at the hands of the French (1885) and Japanese (1895), China lost control of Vietnam, Korea, and Taiwan. By the end of the century, the Western nations plus Japan and Russia had all carved out spheres of influence within China, granting themselves special privileges to establish military bases, extract raw materials, and build railroads. Many Chinese believed that their country was being "carved up like a melon" (see Map 19.1).

Coupled with its internal crisis, China's encounter with European imperialism had reduced the proud Middle Kingdom to dependency on the Western powers as it became part of a European-based "**informal empire**," an area dominated by Western powers but retaining its own government and a measure of independence. China was no longer the center of civilization to which barbarians paid homage and tribute, but just one weak and dependent nation among many others. The Qing dynasty remained in power, but in a weakened condition, which served European interests well and Chinese interests poorly. Restrictions imposed by the unequal treaties clearly inhibited China's industrialization, as foreign goods and foreign investment flooded the country largely unrestricted. Chinese businessmen mostly served foreign firms, rather than developing as an independent capitalist class capable of leading China's own Industrial Revolution.

The Failure of Conservative Modernization

Chinese authorities were not passive in the face of their country's mounting internal and external crises. Known as "**self-strengthening**," their policies during the 1860s and 1870s sought to reinvigorate a traditional China while borrowing cautiously from the West. An overhauled examination system, designed to recruit qualified candidates for official positions, sought the "good men" who could cope with the massive reconstruction that China faced in the wake of the Taiping rebellion. Support for landlords and the repair of dikes and irrigation helped restore rural social and economic order. A few industrial factories producing textiles and steel were established, coal mines were expanded, and a telegraph system was initiated. One Chinese general in 1863 confessed his humiliation that "Chinese weapons are far inferior to those of foreign countries."[6] A number of modern arsenals, shipyards, and foreign-language schools sought to remedy this deficiency.

MAP 19.1   China and the World in the Nineteenth Century
As China was reeling from massive internal upheavals during the nineteenth century, it also faced external assaults from Russia, Japan, and various European powers. By the end of the century, large parts of China were divided into spheres of influence, each affiliated with one of the major industrial powers of the day.

Self-strengthening as an overall program for China's modernization was inhibited by the fears of conservative leaders that urban, industrial, or commercial development would erode the power and privileges of the landlord class. Furthermore, the new industries remained largely dependent on foreigners for machinery, materials, and expertise. And they served to strengthen local authorities, who largely controlled those industries, rather than the central Chinese state.

The general failure of "self-strengthening" became apparent at the end of the century, when China suffered a humiliating military defeat by Japan (1894–1895). This failure was only confirmed when an antiforeign movement known as the **Boxer Uprising** (1898–1901) erupted in northern China. Led by militia organizations calling themselves the Society of Righteous and Harmonious Fists, the "Boxers" killed numerous Europeans and Chinese Christians and laid siege to the foreign embassies in Beijing. When Western powers and Japan occupied Beijing to crush the rebellion and imposed a huge payment on China as a punishment, it was clear that China remained a dependent country, substantially under foreign control.

No wonder, then, that growing numbers of educated Chinese, including many in official elite positions, became highly disillusioned with the Qing dynasty, which was both foreign and ineffective in protecting China. By the late 1890s, such people were organizing a variety of clubs, study groups, and newspapers to examine China's desperate situation and to explore alternative paths. The names of these organizations reflect their outlook—the National Rejuvenation Study Society, Society to Protect the Nation, and Understand the National Shame Society. They admired not only Western science and technology but also Western political practices that limited the authority of the ruler and permitted wider circles of people to take part in public life. They believed that only a truly unified nation in which rulers and ruled were closely related could save China from dismemberment at the hands of foreign imperialists. Despite the small number of women who took part in these discussions, traditional gender roles became yet another focus of opposition. No one expressed that issue more forcefully than Qiu Jin (1875–1907), the rebellious daughter of a gentry family who started a women's journal, arguing that liberated women were essential for a strong Chinese nation, and became involved in revolutionary politics. Thus was born the immensely powerful force of Chinese nationalism, directed alike against Western imperialists, the foreign Qing dynasty, and aspects of China's traditional culture.

The Qing dynasty response to these new pressures proved inadequate. A flurry of progressive imperial edicts in 1898, known as the Hundred Days of Reform, was soon squelched by conservative forces. More extensive reform in the early twentieth century, including the end of the old examination system and the promise of a national parliament, was a classic case of too little too late. In 1912 the last Chinese emperor abdicated as the ancient imperial order that had governed China for two millennia collapsed, with only a modest nudge from organized revolutionaries. This **Chinese revolution of 1911–1912** marked the end of a long era in China's long history and the beginning of an immense struggle over the country's future.

The Ottoman Empire and the West in the Nineteenth Century

Like China, the Islamic world represented a highly successful civilization that felt little need to learn from the "infidels" or "barbarians" of the West until it collided with an expanding and aggressive Europe in the nineteenth century. Unlike China, though, Islamic civilization had been a near neighbor to Europe for 1,000 years. Its most prominent state, the Ottoman Empire, had long governed substantial parts of southeastern Europe and had posed a clear military and religious threat to Europe in the sixteenth and seventeenth centuries. But if its encounter with the West was less abrupt than that of China, it was no less consequential. Neither the Ottoman Empire nor China fell under direct colonial rule, but both were much diminished as the changing balance of global power took hold; both launched efforts at "defensive modernization" aimed at strengthening their states and preserving their independence; and in both societies, some people held tightly to old identities and values, even as others embraced new loyalties associated with nationalism and modernity.

"The Sick Man of Europe"

In 1750, the Ottoman Empire was still the central political fixture of a widespread Islamic world. From its Turkish heartland in Anatolia, it ruled over much of the Arab world, from which Islam had come. It protected pilgrims on their way to Mecca, governed Egypt and coastal North Africa, and incorporated millions of Christians in the Balkans. Its ruler, the sultan, claimed the role of caliph, successor to the Prophet Muhammad, and was widely viewed as the leader, defender, and primary representative of the Islamic world. But by the middle, and certainly by the end, of the nineteenth century, the Ottoman Empire was no longer able to deal with Europe from a position of equality, let alone superiority. Among the Great Powers of the West, it was now known as **"the sick man of Europe."** Within the Muslim world, the Ottoman Empire, once viewed as "the strong sword of Islam," was unable to prevent region after region—India, Indonesia, West Africa, Central Asia—from falling under the control of Christian powers.

The Ottoman Empire's own domains shrank considerably at the hands of Russian, British, Austrian, and French aggression (see Map 19.2). In 1798, Napoleon's invasion of Egypt, which had long been a province of the Ottoman Empire, was a particularly stunning blow. A contemporary observer, Abd al-Rahman al-Jabarti, described the French entry into Cairo:

MAP 19.2   The Contraction of the Ottoman Empire

Foreign aggression and nationalist movements substantially diminished the Ottoman Empire during the nineteenth century, but they also stimulated a variety of efforts to revive and reform Ottoman society.

The French entered the city like a torrent rushing through the alleys and streets without anything to stop them, like demons of the Devil's army. . . . And the French trod in the Mosque of al-Azhar with their shoes, carrying swords and rifles. . . . They plundered whatever they found in the mosque. . . . They treated the books and Quranic volumes as trash. . . . Furthermore, they soiled the mosque, blowing their spit in it, pissing and defecating in it. They guzzled wine and smashed bottles in the central court.[7]

When the French left, a virtually independent Egypt pursued a modernizing and empire-building program of its own during the early and mid-nineteenth century and on one occasion came close to toppling the Ottoman Empire itself.

Beyond territorial losses to stronger European powers, other parts of the empire, such as Greece, Serbia, Bulgaria, and Romania, achieved independence based on their own surging nationalism and support from the British or the Russians. The continued independence of the core region of the Ottoman Empire owed much to the inability of Europe's Great Powers to agree on how to divide it up among themselves.

Behind the contraction of the Ottoman Empire lay other problems. As in China, the central Ottoman state had weakened, particularly in its ability to raise necessary revenue, as provincial authorities and local warlords gained greater power. Moreover, the Janissaries, once the effective and innovative elite infantry units of Ottoman military forces, lost their military edge, becoming a highly conservative force within the empire. The technological and military gap with the West was clearly growing.

Economically, the earlier centrality of the Ottoman and Arab lands in Afro-Eurasian commerce diminished as Europeans achieved direct oceanic access to the treasures of Asia. Competition from cheap European manufactured goods hit Ottoman artisans hard and led to urban riots protesting foreign imports. Furthermore, a series of agreements, known as capitulations, between European countries and the Ottoman Empire granted Westerners various exemptions from Ottoman law and taxation. Like the unequal treaties with China, these agreements facilitated European penetration of the Ottoman economy and became widely resented. Such measures eroded Ottoman sovereignty and reflected the changing position of that empire relative to Europe. So too did the growing indebtedness of the Ottoman Empire, which came to rely on foreign loans to finance its efforts at economic development. By 1881, its inability to pay the interest on those debts led to foreign control of much of its revenue-generating system, while a similar situation in Egypt led to its outright occupation by the British. Like China, the Ottoman Empire had fallen into a position of considerable dependency on Europe.

Reform and Its Opponents

The leadership of the Ottoman Empire recognized many of its problems and during the nineteenth century mounted increasingly ambitious programs of "defensive modernization" that were earlier, more sustained, and far more vigorous than the timid and halfhearted measures of self-strengthening in China. One reason perhaps lay in the absence of any internal upheaval, such as the Taiping Uprising in China, which threatened the very existence of the ruling dynasty. Nationalist revolts on the empire's periphery, rather than Chinese-style peasant rebellion at the center, represented the primary internal crisis of nineteenth-century Ottoman history. Nor did the Middle East in general experience the explosive population growth that contributed so much

Ottoman Modernization Railroads were a major element in Ottoman modernization efforts. This photograph shows a celebration in Medina, Arabia, of the opening in 1908 of the Hejaz rail line from Damascus. Part of the larger Ottoman railroad network, the Hejaz line linked Constantinople more firmly to the empire's Arab domains. It also facilitated the movement of Muslim pilgrims undertaking the *hajj* in Mecca and, potentially, the movement of Ottoman troops as well. Financed substantially by German banks, the Hejaz rail line connected to the more famous Berlin to Baghdad railway, constructed at the same time and also with German funding. (Granger, NYC—All rights reserved)

to China's nineteenth-century crisis. Furthermore, the long-established Ottoman leadership was Turkic and Muslim, culturally similar to its core population, whereas China's Qing dynasty rulers were widely regarded as foreigners from Manchuria.

Ottoman reforms began in the late eighteenth century when Sultan Selim III (r. 1789–1807) sought to reorganize and update the army, drawing on European advisers and techniques. Even these modest innovations stirred the hostility of powerful factions among both the *ulama* (religious scholars) and the elite military corps of Janissaries, who saw them in conflict with both Islam and their own institutional interests. Opposition to his measures was so strong that Selim was overthrown in 1807 and then murdered. Subsequent sultans, however, crushed the Janissaries and brought the ulama more thoroughly under state control than elsewhere in the Islamic world.

Then, in the several decades after 1839, more far-reaching reformist measures, known as **Tanzimat** (tahn-zee-MAHT) (reorganization), took shape as the Ottoman leadership sought to provide the economic, social, and legal underpinnings for a strong and newly recentralized state. Factories producing cloth, paper, and armaments; modern mining operations; reclamation and resettlement of agricultural land;

telegraphs, steamships, railroads, and a modern postal service; Western-style law codes and courts; new elementary and secondary schools—all of these new departures began a long process of modernization and westernization in the Ottoman Empire.

Even more revolutionary, at least in principle, were changes in the legal status of the empire's diverse communities, which now gave non-Muslims equal rights under the law. An imperial proclamation of 1856 declared:

> Every distinction or designation tending to make any class whatever of the subjects of my Empire inferior to another class, on account of their religion, language or race shall be forever effaced. . . . No subject of my Empire shall be hindered in the exercise of the religion that he professes. . . . All the subjects of my Empire, without distinction of nationality, shall be admissible to public employment.

This declaration represented a dramatic change that challenged the fundamentally Islamic character of the state. Mixed tribunals with representatives from various religious groups were established to hear cases involving non-Muslims. More Christians were appointed to high office. A mounting tide of secular legislation and secular schools, drawing heavily on European models, now competed with traditional Islamic institutions.

Although Tanzimat-era reforms did not directly address gender issues, they did stimulate modest educational openings for women, mostly in Istanbul, with a training program for midwives in 1842, a girls' secondary school in 1858, and a teacher training college for women in 1870. Furthermore, the reform-minded class that emerged from the Tanzimat era generally favored greater opportunities for women as a means of strengthening the state, and a number of upper- and middle-class women were involved in these discussions. During the 1870s and 1880s, the prominent female poet Sair Nigar Hanim held weekly "salons" in which reformist intellectuals of both sexes participated.

The reform process raised profound and highly contested questions. What was the Ottoman Empire, and who were its people? Were they Ottoman subjects of a dynastic state, Turkish citizens of a national state, or Muslim believers in a religiously defined state? For decades, the answers oscillated, as few people wanted to choose decisively among these alternative identities.

To those who supported the reforms, the Ottoman Empire was an inclusive state, all of whose people were loyal to the dynasty that ruled it. This was the outlook of a new class spawned by the reform process itself—lower-level officials, military officers, writers, poets, and journalists, many of whom had a modern Western-style education. Dubbed the **Young Ottomans**, they were active during the middle decades of the nineteenth century, as they sought major changes in the Ottoman political system itself. They favored a more European-style parliamentary and constitutional regime that could curtail the absolute power of the sultan. Only such a political system, they felt, could mobilize the energies of the country to overcome backwardness and preserve the state against European aggression. Known as Islamic modernism, such ideas found expression in many parts of the Muslim world in the second half of the century. Muslim societies, the Young Ottomans argued, needed to embrace Western technical and scientific knowledge, while rejecting its materialism. Islam in their view could accommodate a full modernity without sacrificing its essential religious character. After all, the Islamic world had earlier hosted impressive scientific achievements and had incorporated elements of Greek philosophical thinking.

In 1876, the Young Ottomans experienced a short-lived victory when **Sultan Abd al-Hamid II** (r. 1876–1909) accepted a constitution and an elected parliament, but not for long. Under the pressure of war with Russia, the sultan soon suspended the reforms and reverted to an older style of despotic rule for the next thirty years, even renewing the claim that he was the caliph, the successor to the Prophet and the protector of Muslims everywhere.

Opposition to this revived despotism soon surfaced among both military and civilian elites known as the **Young Turks**. Largely abandoning any reference to Islam, they advocated a militantly secular public life, were committed to thorough modernization along European lines, and increasingly thought about the Ottoman Empire as a Turkish national state. "There is only one civilization, and that is European civilization," declared Abdullah Cevdet, a prominent figure in the Young Turk movement. "Therefore we must borrow western civilization with both its rose and its thorn."[8]

A military coup in 1908 finally allowed the Young Turks to exercise real power. They pushed for a radical secularization of schools, courts, and law codes; permitted elections and competing parties; established a single Law of Family Rights for all regardless of religion; and encouraged Turkish as the official language of the empire. They also opened modern schools for women, including access to Istanbul University; allowed women to wear Western clothing; restricted polygamy; and permitted women to obtain divorces in some situations. Women established a number of publications and organizations, some of them linked to British suffrage groups. In the western cities of the empire, some women abandoned their veils.

But the nationalist Turkish conception of Ottoman identity antagonized non-Turkic peoples and helped stimulate Arab and other nationalisms in response. For some, a secular nationality was becoming the most important public loyalty, with Islam relegated to private life. Nationalist sentiments contributed to the complete disintegration of the Ottoman Empire following World War I, but the secularizing and westernizing principles of the Young Turks informed the policies of the Turkish republic that replaced it.

Outcomes: Comparing China and the Ottoman Empire

By the beginning of the twentieth century, both China and the Ottoman Empire, recently centers of proud and vibrant civilizations, had experienced the consequences of a rapidly shifting balance of global power. Now they were "semi-colonies" within the "informal empires" of Europe, although they retained sufficient independence for their governments to launch catch-up efforts of defensive modernization, the Ottomans earlier and the Chinese later. But neither was able to create the industrial economies or strong states required to fend off European intrusion and restore their former status in the world. Despite their diminished power, however, both China and the Ottoman Empire gave rise to new nationalist conceptions of society that were initially small and limited in appeal but of great significance for the future.

In the early twentieth century, that future witnessed the end of both the Chinese and Ottoman empires. In China, the collapse of the imperial system in 1912 was followed by a vast revolutionary upheaval that by 1949 led to a communist regime within largely the same territorial space as the old empire. By contrast, the collapse of the Ottoman Empire following World War I led to the creation of the new but much smaller nation-state of Turkey in the Anatolian heartland of the old empire, which lost its vast Arab and European provinces.

China's twentieth-century revolutionaries rejected traditional Confucian culture far more thoroughly than the secularizing leaders of modern Turkey rejected Islam. Almost everywhere in the Islamic world, including Turkey, traditional religion retained its hold on the private loyalties of most people and later in the twentieth century became a basis for social renewal in many places. Islamic civilization, unlike its Chinese counterpart, had many independent centers and was never so closely associated with a single state. Furthermore, it was embedded in a deeply religious tradition that was personally meaningful to millions of adherents, in contrast to the more elitist and secular outlook of Confucianism. Many Chinese, however, retained traditional Confucian values such as filial piety, and Confucianism has made something of a comeback in China over the past several decades. Nonetheless, Islam retained a hold on its civilization in the twentieth century rather more firmly than Confucianism did in China.

The Japanese Difference: The Rise of a New East Asian Power

Like China and the Ottoman Empire, the island country of Japan confronted the aggressive power of the West during the nineteenth century. This threat took shape as U.S. commodore Matthew Perry's "black ships" steamed into Tokyo Bay in 1853 and forcefully demanded that this reclusive nation open up to more "normal" relations with the world. However, the outcome of that encounter differed sharply from the others. In the second half of the nineteenth century, Japan undertook a radical transformation of its society — a "revolution from above," according to some historians — that turned it into a powerful, modern, united, industrialized nation. It was an achievement that neither China nor the Ottoman Empire was able to duplicate. Far from succumbing to Western domination, Japan joined the club of imperialist countries by creating its own East Asian empire at the expense of China and Korea. In building a society that was both modern and distinctly Japanese, Japan demonstrated that modernity was not a uniquely European phenomenon. This "Japanese miracle," as some have called it, was both promising and ominous for the rest of Asia.

The Tokugawa Background

For 250 years prior to Perry's arrival, Japan had been governed by a shogun (a military ruler) from the Tokugawa family who acted in the name of a revered but powerless emperor who lived in Kyoto, 300 miles away from the seat of power in Edo (Tokyo). The chief task of this Tokugawa shogunate was to prevent the return of civil war among some 260 rival feudal lords, known as daimyo, each of whom had a cadre of armed retainers, the famed samurai warriors of Japanese tradition.

Based on their own military power and political skills, successive shoguns gave Japan more than two centuries of internal peace (1600–1850). To control the restive daimyo, they required these local authorities to create second homes in Edo, the country's capital, where they had to live during alternate years. When they left for their rural residences, families stayed behind, almost as hostages. Nonetheless, the daimyo, especially the more powerful ones, retained substantial autonomy in their own domains and behaved in some ways like independent states, with separate military forces, law codes, tax systems, and currencies. With no national army, no uniform currency, and little central authority at the local level, **Tokugawa Japan** was "pacified . . . but not really unified."[9] To further stabilize the country, the Tokugawa regime issued highly detailed rules governing the occupation, residence, dress, hairstyles, and behavior of the four hierarchically ranked status groups into which Japanese society was divided—samurai at the top, then peasants, artisans, and, at the bottom, merchants.

During these 250 years of peace, much was changing within Japan in ways that belied the control and orderliness of Tokugawa regulations. For one thing, the samurai, in the absence of wars to fight, evolved into a salaried bureaucratic or administrative class amounting to 5 to 6 percent of the total population, but they remained fiercely devoted to their daimyo lords and to their warrior code of loyalty, honor, and self-sacrifice.

More generally, centuries of peace contributed to a remarkable burst of economic growth, commercialization, and urban development. Entrepreneurial peasants, using fertilizers and other agricultural innovations, grew more rice than ever before and engaged in a variety of rural manufacturing enterprises as well. By 1750, Japan had become perhaps the world's most urbanized country, with about 10 percent of its population living in sizable towns or cities. Edo, with perhaps a million residents, was among the world's largest cities. Well-functioning networks of exchange linked urban and rural areas, marking Japan as an emerging market economy. The influence of Confucianism encouraged education and generated a remarkably literate population, with about 40 percent of men and 15 percent of women able to read and write. Although no one was aware of it at the time, these changes during the Tokugawa era provided a solid foundation for Japan's remarkable industrial growth in the late nineteenth century.

Such changes also undermined the shogunate's efforts to freeze Japanese society in the interests of stability. Some samurai found the lowly but profitable path of commerce too much to resist. "No more shall we have to live by the sword," declared one of them in 1616 while renouncing his samurai status. "I have seen that great profit can be made honorably. I shall brew *sake* and soy sauce, and we shall prosper."[10] Many merchants, though hailing from the lowest-ranking status group, prospered in the new commercial environment and supported a vibrant urban culture, while not a few daimyo found it necessary, if humiliating, to seek loans from these social inferiors. Thus merchants had money, but little status, whereas samurai enjoyed high status but were often indebted to inferior merchants. Both resented their positions.

Despite prohibitions to the contrary, many peasants moved to the cities, becoming artisans or merchants and imitating the ways of their social betters. A decree of 1788 noted that peasants "have become accustomed to luxury and forgetful of their status." They wore inappropriate clothing, used umbrellas rather than straw hats in the rain, and even left the villages for the city. "Henceforth," declared the shogun, "all luxuries should be avoided by the peasants. They are to live simply and devote themselves to farming."[11] This decree, like many others before it, was widely ignored.

More than social change undermined the Tokugawa regime. Corruption was widespread, to the disgust of many. The shogunate's failure to deal successfully with a severe famine in the 1830s eroded confidence in its effectiveness. At the same time, a mounting wave of local peasant uprisings and urban riots expressed the many grievances of the poor. The most striking of these outbursts left the city of Osaka in flames in 1837. Its leader, Oshio Heihachiro, no doubt spoke for many ordinary people when he wrote:

> We must first punish the officials who torment the people so cruelly; then we must execute the haughty and rich Osaka merchants. Then we must distribute the gold, silver, and copper stored in their cellars, and bands of rice hidden in their store-houses.[12]

From the 1830s on, one historian concluded, "there was a growing feeling that the *shogunate* was losing control."[13]

American Intrusion and the Meiji Restoration

It was foreign intervention that brought matters to a head. Since the expulsion of European missionaries and the harsh suppression of Christianity in the early seventeenth century, Japan had deliberately limited its contact with the West to a single port, where only the Dutch were allowed to trade. (See "Asians and Asian Commerce" in Chapter 14.) By the early nineteenth century, however, various European countries and the United States were knocking at the door. All were turned away, and even shipwrecked sailors or whalers were expelled, jailed, or executed. As it happened, it was the United States that forced the issue, sending Commodore Perry in 1853 to demand humane treatment for castaways, the right of American vessels to refuel and buy provisions, and the opening of ports for trade. Authorized to use force if necessary, Perry presented his reluctant hosts with, among other gifts, a white flag for surrender should hostilities follow.

In the end, the Japanese avoided war. Aware of what had happened to China as a result of resisting European demands, Japan agreed to a series of unequal treaties with various Western powers. That humiliating capitulation to the demands of the "foreign devils" further eroded support for the shogunate, triggered a brief civil war, and by 1868 led to a political takeover by a group of young samurai from southern Japan. This decisive turning point in Japan's history was known as the **Meiji Restoration**, for the country's new rulers claimed that they were restoring to power the young emperor, then a fifteen-year-old boy whose throne name was Meiji (MAY-jee), or Enlightened Rule. Despite his youth, he was regarded as the most recent link in a chain of descent that traced the origins of the imperial family back to the sun goddess Amaterasu. Having eliminated the shogunate, the patriotic young men who led the takeover soon made their goals clear—to save Japan from foreign domination not by futile resistance, but by a thorough transformation of Japanese society drawing on all that the modern West had to offer. "Knowledge shall be sought throughout the world," they declared, "so as to strengthen the foundations of imperial rule."

Japan now had a government committed to a decisive break with the past, and it had acquired that government without massive violence or destruction. By contrast, the defeat of the Taiping Uprising had deprived China of any such opportunity for a fresh start, while saddling it with enormous devastation and massive loss of life. Furthermore, Japan was of less interest to Western powers than either China, with its huge potential market and reputation for riches, or the Ottoman Empire, with its strategic location at the crossroads of Asia, Africa, and Europe. The American Civil War and its aftermath likewise deflected U.S. ambitions in the Pacific for a time, further reducing the Western pressure on Japan.

Modernization Japanese-Style

These circumstances gave Japan some breathing space, and its new rulers moved quickly to take advantage of that unique window of opportunity. Thus they launched a cascading wave of dramatic changes that rolled over the country in the last three decades of the nineteenth century. Like the more modest reforms of China and the Ottoman Empire, Japanese modernizing efforts were defensive, based on fears that Japanese independence was in grave danger. Those reforms, however, were revolutionary in their cumulative effect, transforming Japan far more thoroughly than even the most radical of the Ottoman efforts, let alone the limited "self-strengthening" policies of the Chinese.

The first task was genuine national unity, which required an attack on the power and privileges of both the daimyo and the samurai. In a major break with the past, the new regime soon ended the semi-independent domains of the daimyo, replacing them with governors appointed by and responsible to the national government. The central state, not the local authorities, now collected the nation's taxes and raised a national army based on conscription from all social classes.

Thus the samurai relinquished their ancient role as the country's warrior class and with it their cherished right to carry swords. The old Confucian-based social order with its special privileges for various classes was largely dismantled, and almost all Japanese became legally equal as commoners and as subjects of the emperor. Limitations on travel and trade likewise fell as a nationwide economy came to parallel the centralized state. Although there was some opposition to these measures, including a brief rebellion of resentful samurai in 1877, it was on the whole a remarkably peaceful process in which a segment of the old ruling class abolished its own privileges. Many, but not all, of these displaced elites found a soft landing in the army, bureaucracy, or business enterprises of the new regime, thus easing a painful transition.

Accompanying these social and political changes was a widespread and eager fascination with almost everything Western. Knowledge about the West — its science and technology; its various political and constitutional arrangements; its legal and educational systems; its dances, clothing, and hairstyles — was enthusiastically sought out by official missions to Europe and the United States, by hundreds of students sent to study abroad, and by many ordinary Japanese at home. Western writers were translated into Japanese. "Civilization and Enlightenment" was the slogan of the time, and both were to be found in the West. The most prominent popularizer of Western knowledge, Fukuzawa Yukichi, summed up the chief lesson of his studies in the mid-1870s — Japan was backward and needed to learn from the West: "If we compare the knowledge of the Japanese and Westerners, in letters, in technique, in commerce, or in industry, from the largest to the smallest matter, there is not one thing in which we excel. . . . In Japan's present condition there is nothing in which we may take pride vis-à-vis the West."[14]

After this initial wave of uncritical enthusiasm for everything Western receded, Japan proceeded to borrow more selectively and to combine foreign and Japanese elements in distinctive ways. For example, the Constitution of 1889, drawing heavily on German experience, introduced an elected parliament, political parties, and democratic ideals, but that constitution was presented as a gift from a sacred emperor descended from the sun goddess. The parliament could advise, but ultimate power, and particularly control of the military, lay theoretically with the emperor and in practice with an oligarchy of prominent reformers acting in his name. Likewise, a modern educational system, which achieved universal primary schooling by the early twentieth century, was laced with Confucian-based moral instruction and exhortations of loyalty to the emperor. Christianity made little headway in Meiji Japan, but Shinto, an ancient religious tradition featuring ancestors and nature spirits, was elevated to the status of an official state cult. Japan's earlier experience in borrowing massively but selectively from Chinese culture perhaps served it better in these new circumstances than either the Chinese disdain for foreign cultures or the reluctance of many Muslims to see much of value in the infidel West.

Like their counterparts in China and the Ottoman Empire, some reformers in Japan—male and female alike—argued that the oppression of women was an obstacle to the country's modernization and that family reform was essential to gaining the respect of the West. Fukuzawa Yukichi, who was widely read, urged an end to concubinage and prostitution, advocated more education for girls, and called for gender equality in matters of marriage, divorce, and property rights. But most male reformers understood women largely in the context of family life, seeing them as "good wife, wise mother." By the 1880s, however, a small feminist movement arose, demanding—and modeling—a more public role for women. Some even sought the right to vote at a time when only a small fraction of men could do so. A leading feminist, Kishida Toshiko, not yet twenty years old, astonished the country in 1882 when she undertook a two-month speaking tour during which she addressed huge audiences. Only "equality and equal rights," she argued, would allow Japan "to build a new society." Japan must rid itself of the ancient habit of "respecting men and despising women."

While the new Japanese government included girls in its plans for universal education, it was with a gender-specific curriculum and in schools segregated by sex. Any thought of women playing a role in public life was harshly suppressed. A Peace Preservation Law of 1887, in effect until 1922, forbade women from joining political parties and even from attending meetings where political matters were discussed. The Civil Code of 1898 accorded absolute authority to the male head of the family, while grouping all wives with "cripples and disabled persons" as those who "cannot undertake any legal action." To the authorities of Meiji Japan, a serious transformation of gender roles was more of a threat than an opportunity.

At the core of Japan's effort at defensive modernization lay its state-guided industrialization program. More than in Europe or the United States, the government itself established a number of enterprises, later selling many of them to private investors. It also acted to create a modern infrastructure by building rail-roads, creating a postal service, and establishing a national currency and banking system. From the 1880s on, the Japanese government developed a distinctive form of "labor-intensive industrialization" that relied more heavily on the country's abundant workforce and less on the replacement of labor by machinery and capital than in Western Europe or North America.[15] By the early twentieth century, Japan's industrialization, organized around a number of large firms called *zaibatsu*, was well under way. The country became a major exporter of textiles, in part as a way to pay for needed imports of raw materials, such as cotton, owing to its limited natural resources. Soon the country was able to produce its own munitions and industrial goods as well. Its major cities enjoyed mass-circulation newspapers, movie theaters, and electric lights. All of this was accomplished through its own resources and without the massive foreign debt that so afflicted Egypt and the Ottoman Empire. No other country outside of Europe and North America had been able to launch its own Industrial Revolution in the nineteenth century. It was a distinctive feature of Japan's modern transformation.

Less distinctive, however, were the social results of that process. Taxed heavily to pay for Japan's ambitious modernization program, many peasant families slid into poverty. Their sometimes-violent protests peaked in 1883–1884 as the Japanese countryside witnessed infanticide, the sale of daughters, and starvation.

While state authorities rigidly excluded women from political life and denied them adult legal status, they badly needed female labor in the country's textile industry, which was central to Japan's economic growth. Accordingly, the majority of Japan's textile workers were young women from poor families in the countryside. Recruiters toured rural villages, contracting with parents for their daughters' labor in return for a payment that the girls had to repay from their wages. That pay was low and their working conditions were terrible. Most lived in factory-provided dormitories and worked twelve or more hours per day. While some committed suicide or ran away and many left after earning enough to pay off their contracts, others organized strikes and joined the anarchist or socialist movements that were emerging among a few intellectuals. One such woman, Kanno Sugako, was hanged in 1911 for participating in a plot to assassinate the emperor. Efforts to create unions and organize strikes, both illegal in Japan at the time, were met with harsh repression even as corporate and state authorities sought to depict the company as a family unit to which workers should give their loyalty, all under the beneficent gaze of the divine emperor.

Japan and the World

Japan's modern transformation soon registered internationally. By the early twentieth century, its economic growth, openness to trade, and embrace of "civilization and enlightenment" from the West persuaded the Western powers to revise the unequal treaties in Japan's favor. This had long been a primary goal of the Meiji regime, and the Anglo-Japanese Treaty of 1902 now acknowledged Japan as an equal player among the Great Powers of the world.

Not only did Japan escape from its semi-colonial entanglements with the West, but it also launched its own empire-building enterprise, even as European powers and the United States were carving up much of Asia, Africa, and Pacific Oceania into

Japanese Women Workers Young women were prominent in Japan's emerging textile industry. The women in this photograph from a silk factory around 1900 are spinning silk threads from raw cocoons. (Pictures from History/Bridgeman Images)

colonies or spheres of influence. It was what industrializing Great Powers did in the late nineteenth century, and Japan followed suit, in part to compensate for the relative poverty of its natural resource base. A successful war against China (1894–1895) established Japan as a formidable military competitor in East Asia, replacing China as the dominant power in the region. Ten years later in the **Russo-Japanese War** (1904–1905), which was fought over rival imperial ambitions in Korea and Manchuria, Japan became the first Asian state to defeat a major European power. Through those victories, Japan also gained colonial control of Taiwan and Korea and a territorial foothold in Manchuria. And in the aftermath of World War I, Japan acquired a growing influence in China's Shandong Peninsula and control over a number of Micronesian islands under the auspices of the League of Nations.

Japan's entry onto the broader global stage was felt in many places (see Map 19.3). It added yet one more imperialist power to those already burdening a beleaguered China. Defeat at the hands of Japanese upstarts shocked Russia and triggered the 1905 revolution in that country. To Europeans and Americans, Japan was now an economic, political, and military competitor in Asia.

In the world of subject peoples, the rise of Japan and its defeat of Russia generated widespread admiration among those who saw Japan as a model for their own modern development and perhaps as an ally in the struggle against imperialism. Some Poles, Finns, and Jews viewed the Russian defeat in 1905 as an opening for their own liberation from the Russian Empire and were grateful to Japan for the opportunity. Despite Japan's aggression against their country, many Chinese reformers and nationalists found in the Japanese experience valuable lessons for themselves. Thousands flocked to Japan to study its achievements. Newspapers throughout the Islamic world celebrated Japan's victory over Russia as an "awakening of the East" that might herald Muslims' own liberation. Some Turkish women gave their children Japanese names. Indonesian Muslims from Aceh wrote to the Meiji emperor asking

MAP 19.3   The Rise of Japan
As Japan modernized after the Meiji Restoration, it launched an empire-building program that provided a foundation for further expansion in the 1930s and during World War II.

for help in their struggle against the Dutch, and Muslim poets wrote odes in his honor. The Egyptian nationalist Mustafa Kamil spoke for many when he declared: "We are amazed by Japan because it is the first Eastern government to utilize Western civilization to resist the shield of European imperialism in Asia."[16]

Those who directly experienced Japanese imperialism in Taiwan or Korea no doubt had a less positive view, for its colonial policies matched or exceeded the brutality of European practices. In the twentieth century, China and much of Southeast Asia suffered bitterly under Japanese imperial aggression. Nonetheless, both the idea of Japan as a liberator of Asia from the European yoke and the reality of Japan as an oppressive imperial power in its own right derived from the country's remarkable modern transformation and its distinctive response to the provocation of Western intrusion.

Reflections: Success and Failure in History

Beyond describing what happened in the past and explaining why, historians often find themselves evaluating the events they study. When they make judgments about the past, notions of success and failure frequently come into play. Should Europe's Industrial Revolution and its rise to global power be regarded as a success? If so, does that imply that other civilizations were failures? Should we consider Japan more successful than China or the Ottoman Empire during the nineteenth century? Three considerations suggest that we should be very careful in applying these ideas to the complexities of the historical record.

First, and most obviously, is the question of criteria. If the measure of success is national wealth and power, then the Industrial Revolution surely counts as a great accomplishment, at least for some. But if preservation of the environment, spiritual growth, and the face-to-face relationships of village life are more highly valued, then industrialization, as Gandhi argued, might be more reasonably considered a disaster. Certainly the expectation of endless economic growth, which derived from the Industrial Revolution, has been a primary factor in generating the climate changes that threaten modern society in the twenty-first century.

Second, there is the issue of "success for whom?" British artisans who lost their livelihood to industrial machines as well as Japanese women textile workers who suffered through the early stages of industrialization might be forgiven for not appreciating the "success" of their countries' transformation, even if their middle-class counterparts and subsequent generations benefited. In such cases, issues of both social and generational justice complicate any easy assessment of the past.

Third, and finally, success is frequently associated with good judgment and wise choices, yet actors in the historical drama are never completely free in making their decisions, and none, of course, have the benefit of hindsight, which historians enjoy. Did the leaders of China and the Ottoman Empire fail to push industrial development more strongly, or were they not in a position to do so? Were Japanese leaders wiser and more astute than their counterparts elsewhere, or did their knowledge of China's earlier experience and their unique national history simply provide them with circumstances more conducive to modern development? Such questions regarding the possibilities and limitations of human action have no clear-cut answers, but they might caution us about any easy assessment of success and failure.

Second Thoughts

WHAT'S THE SIGNIFICANCE?

Taiping Uprising (p. 545)
Opium Wars (p. 547)
Commissioner Lin Zexu (p. 548)
unequal treaties (p. 549)
informal empire (p. 549)

self-strengthening (p. 549)
Boxer Uprising (p. 550)
Chinese revolution of 1911–1912
　(p. 551)
"the sick man of Europe" (p. 552)

Tanzimat (p. 554)   Tokugawa Japan (p. 558)
Young Ottomans (p. 555)   Meiji Restoration (p. 559)
Sultan Abd al-Hamid II (p. 556)   Russo-Japanese War (p. 563)
Young Turks (p. 556)

BIG PICTURE QUESTIONS

1. "The response of each society to European imperialism grew out of its larger historical development and its internal problems." What evidence might support this statement?

2. "Deliberate government policies were more important than historical circumstances in shaping the history of China, the Ottoman Empire, and Japan during the nineteenth century." How might you argue for and against this statement?

3. What kinds of debates, controversies, and conflicts were generated by European intrusion within each of the societies examined in this chapter?

4. **Looking Back:** How did the experiences of China, the Ottoman Empire, Japan, and Latin America, all of which retained their independence despite much European pressure, differ from those of Africa, India, Southeast Asia, and Pacific Oceania, which fell under formal colonial rule?

CHRONOLOGY

1789–1807	• Reforms of Sultan Selim III
1793	• China rejects British request for open trade
1830s	• Famine, peasant uprisings, urban protests in Japan
1839–1876	• Tanzimat reforms in Ottoman Empire
1840–1842	• First Opium War
1850–1864	• Taiping Uprising
1853	• Commodore Perry's arrival in Japan
1856–1858	• Second Opium War
1868	• Meiji Restoration
1870	• Teacher training college for women opened in Istanbul
1876–1909	• Reign of Sultan Abd al-Hamid II
1880s	• Small feminist movement emerges in Japan

1898–1901	• Boxer Uprising in China
1889	• Japanese constitution proclaimed
1894–1895	• Japan defeats China
1904–1905	• Japan defeats Russia
1908	• Military coup by Young Turks
1911–1912	• Chinese revolution; end of Qing dynasty

The Big Picture

The Long Twentieth Century: A New Period in World History?

The years since 1900, or perhaps a little earlier, appear to many historians as a new and distinct phase of the human journey, in large part because the pace of change has so sharply accelerated during this relatively brief time. The world wars during the first half of the twentieth century were far more destructive than earlier conflicts, and the development of nuclear weapons has provided humankind a completely unprecedented capacity for destruction. Both fascism and communism challenged established Western values as they presented new political ideologies to the world. The architecture of global politics changed several times — from a world dominated by European imperial powers, to one structured around the rivalry of two superpowers among some 200 independent states, and by the end of the twentieth century to a global system with one military superpower and a widening array of other centers of economic, military, and political influence.

Beneath the surface of these dramatic events, more significant and enduring processes likewise accelerated at an unprecedented rate. Industrialization quickly became a genuinely global phenomenon, accompanied by a massive increase in energy consumption and overall wealth, a soaring population, and rapid urbanization. Furthermore, long-distance migration mixed the world's peoples in novel ways, generating new social patterns and cultural identities. Feminists mounted an unprecedented attack on patriarchal attitudes and practices, while religious fundamentalists renewed their faith, often in opposition to established political and religious authorities.

But the most fundamental of these processes involved an extraordinary and mounting human impact on the environment. The well-known world historian David Christian has written that "the big story of the twentieth century is how one species began to dominate the energy and resources of the biosphere as a whole."[1]

By the late twentieth century, that dominance had taken humankind well into what many scientists have been calling the Anthropocene era, the age of man, in which human activity is leaving an enduring and global mark on the geological, atmospheric, and biological history of the planet itself. All of this has been part of an astonishing and sometimes disorienting rate of change in human life.

A further distinctive feature of the human story during the past 100 years or so lies in an increasingly thick network of connectedness or entanglement that we commonly refer to as "globalization." It found expression in the worldwide empires of major European powers, in a great increase of international trade and investment, in the flow of ideas and cultural patterns around the world, in the large-scale movements of people, and in the global spread of diseases. War, economic crises, communism, fundamentalism, feminism, and the warming of the planet all operated on a global scale. The speed with which this globalizing world took shape and the density of the connections it forged—these too arguably mark the past century or more as a new era in world history.

But if speed and change mark the past century or so, there were also elements of continuity with the more distant past. Interaction among distinct societies, civilizations, and regions has a very long history. "Contact with strangers possessing new and unfamiliar skills," wrote world historian William McNeill, has long been "the principal factor promoting historically significant social change."[2] In that sense, modern globalization has an ancient pedigree. Furthermore, the collapse of empires during the past century resonates with the dissolution of many earlier empires. Technological innovation too has been a feature of human societies since the beginning, and human activity has left its mark on the planet since our gathering and hunting ancestors decimated a number of large animal species. Billions of people continue to operate in the tradition of long-established religions. Not everything has been new since 1900.

And even if world historians emphasize global networks and connections, what was local, regional, and particular continued to matter. Communism may have been a global phenomenon, but its Russian, Chinese, and Cuban variants were hardly identical. Feminism in the Global North certainly differed from that of the Global South. Economic globalization elicited both a warm embrace among corporate and technological elites and bitter rejection from those whose livelihoods and values were threatened by global linkages. Family, village, city, and nation remain deeply meaningful communities even in an interconnected world. Not everything has been global in this most recent era of world history.

In recounting this history, the four chapters of Part 6 do emphasize what was new, what was rapidly changing, and what was global, but with an eye on what persisted from the past and what was unique to particular places. Chapters 20 and 21 highlight the major events or "milestones" of this era. Thus Chapter 20 focuses on the first half of the twentieth century: the world wars, the Great Depression, the rise of fascist and authoritarian movements and states, and the beginnings of communism in Russia and China, all of this cast in a global context. Chapter 21 then carries this narrative of events from roughly 1950 to 2018. It examines the postwar recovery of Europe, the Soviet Union, and Japan; the emergence of a distinctive Chinese communism; the cold war; the end of European empires in Asia and Africa; the emergence of dozens of new states on the global stage; the demise of communism; and international tensions in the quarter century since the end of the cold war.

With these "milestones" of the past century in mind, Chapters 22 and 23 turn to the larger and perhaps even more consequential processes occurring beneath the surface of major public events. Chapter 22 treats the enormous acceleration of technological innovation as a decisive driver of a deeply interconnected world economy and of pervasive social change. Chapter 23 then turns the spotlight on the explosive growth of human numbers, on the movement of many people to the cities and to new lives abroad, and on the cultural transformations that accompanied modern life during the past century. The chapter—and the book—conclude by examining the enormous and continuing impact of human activity on the entire biosphere, which represents by far the most significant long-term process of this new era and the most critical challenge of the next century.

The accelerating changes of this globalizing century have elicited a wide range of responses. Some individuals and communities welcomed changes that brought them unheard-of levels of material comfort and opportunities for an enriched personal life. Others resisted, denied, or sought to endure and adapt to changes that produced loss, disappointment, impoverishment, and sometimes horror beyond imagination. Reflecting on the flux and flow of this tumultuous era allows all of us—historians and students of history alike—to assess these recent transformations of the human condition, to locate ourselves in this torrent of change, and to ponder what lies ahead.

20

Milestones of the Past Century

War and Revolution

1900–1950

"THE FIRST WORLD WAR WAS DESCRIBED AT THE TIME AS THE WAR TO end all wars. It did nothing of the sort." So said UN secretary general Ban Ki-moon at an event in 2014 marking one hundred years since the outbreak of that global conflict. And in 2017, the one-hundredth anniversary of the Russian Revolution, Russian president Vladimir Putin offered a largely negative commentary on that event. "Could we not have evolved by way of gradual and consistent forward movement," he asked, "rather than at a cost of destroying our statehood and the ruthless fracturing of millions of human lives."[1]

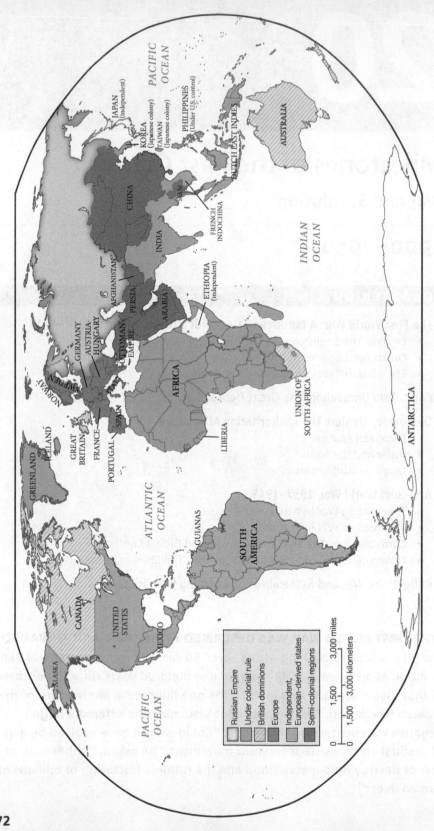

JAPAN (independent)

KOREA (Japanese colony)

TAIWAN (Japanese colony)

PHILIPPINES (Under U.S. control)

DUTCH EAST INDIES

AUSTRALIA

PACIFIC OCEAN

CHINA

SIAM

INDIA

FRENCH INDOCHINA

AFGHANISTAN

PERSIA

ARABIA

ETHIOPIA (independent)

INDIAN OCEAN

GERMANY

AUSTRIA-HUNGARY

SWEDEN

OTTOMAN EMPIRE

NORWAY

ITALY

SPAIN

PORTUGAL

FRANCE

GREAT BRITAIN

ICELAND

GREENLAND

AFRICA

LIBERIA

UNION OF SOUTH AFRICA

ANTARCTICA

ATLANTIC OCEAN

GUIANAS

SOUTH AMERICA

MEXICO

UNITED STATES

CANADA

ALASKA

PACIFIC OCEAN

Russian Empire

Under colonial rule

British dominions

Europe

Independent, European-derived states

Semi-colonial regions

0   1,500   3,000 miles

0   1,500   3,000 kilometers

However they are evaluated, these two immense upheavals—World War I and the Russian Revolution—initiated a chain of events that shaped much of world history during the past century. They were followed by the economic meltdown of the Great Depression, by the rise of Nazi Germany and the horror of the Holocaust, and by an even bloodier and more destructive World War II, a struggle that encompassed much of the world. Among the major outcomes of that war was the Chinese revolution, which brought a modern communist party to power in that ancient land. Within the colonial world of Africa, Asia, and the Middle East, these events set in motion processes of change that would shortly put an end to Europe's global empires. It was, to put it mildly, an eventful half century, and many of its developments had their origins in the First World War and the Russian Revolution.

The First World War: A European Crisis with a Global Impact, 1914–1918

Since 1500, Europe had assumed an increasingly prominent position on the global stage, reflected in its military capacity, its colonial empires, and its Scientific and Industrial Revolutions (see Map 20.1). That unique situation provided the foundation for Europeans' pride, self-confidence, and sense of superiority. In 1900, few could have imagined that this "proud tower" of European dominance would lie shattered less than a half century later. The starting point in that unraveling was the First World War.

Origins: The Beginnings of the Great War

Europe's modern transformation and its global ascendancy were certainly not accompanied by a growing unity or stability among its own peoples—in fact, quite the opposite. The historical rivalries of its competing nation-states further sharpened as both Italy and Germany joined their fragmented territories into two major new powers around 1870. A powerful and rapidly industrializing Germany, seeking its "place in the sun," was a particularly disruptive new element in European political life, especially for the more established powers, such as Britain, France, and Russia. Since the defeat of Napoleon in 1815, a fragile and fluctuating balance of power had generally maintained the peace among Europe's major countries. By the early twentieth century, that balance of power was expressed in two rival alliances, the Triple Alliance of Germany, Italy, and the Austro-Hungarian Empire and the Triple Entente of Russia, France, and Britain. Those commitments, undertaken in the interests of national security, transformed a relatively minor incident in the Balkans (southeastern Europe) into a conflagration that consumed almost all of Europe.

That incident occurred on June 28, 1914, when a Serbian nationalist assassinated the heir to the Austro-Hungarian throne, Archduke Franz Ferdinand. To the rulers of

< **MAP 20.1   The World in 1914**
A map of the world in 1914 shows an unprecedented situation in which one people—Europeans or those of European descent—exercised enormous control and influence over virtually the entire planet.

Austria-Hungary, the surging nationalism of Serbian Slavs was a mortal threat to the cohesion of their fragile multinational empire, which included other Slavic peoples as well. Thus they determined to crush it. But behind Austria-Hungary lay its far more powerful ally, Germany; and behind tiny Serbia lay Russia, with its self-proclaimed mission of protecting other Slavic peoples. Allied to Russia were the French and the British. Thus a system of alliances intended to keep the peace created obligations that drew these Great Powers of Europe into a general war by early August 1914 (see Map 20.2).

The outbreak of **World War I** was something of an accident, in that none of the major states planned or predicted the archduke's assassination or deliberately sought

MAP 20.2 Europe on the Eve of World War I

Despite many elements of common culture, Europe in 1914 was a powder keg, with its major states armed to the teeth and divided into two rival alliances. In the early stages of the war, Italy changed sides to join the French, British, and Russians.

a prolonged conflict, but the system of rigid alliances made Europe vulnerable to that kind of accident. Moreover, behind those alliances lay other factors that contributed to the eruption of war and shaped its character. One of them was a mounting popular nationalism (see "Nations and Nationalism" in Chapter 16). The rulers of the major countries of Europe saw the world as an arena of conflict and competition among rival nation-states. Schools, mass media, and military service had convinced millions of ordinary Europeans that their national identities were profoundly and personally meaningful. The public pressure of these competing nationalisms allowed statesmen little room for compromise and ensured widespread popular support, at least initially, for the decision to go to war. Many men rushed to recruiting offices, fearing that the war might end before they could enlist, and celebratory parades sent them off to the front. For conservative governments, the prospect of war was a welcome occasion for national unity in the face of the mounting class- and gender-based conflicts in European societies.

Also contributing to the war was an industrialized militarism. Europe's armed rivalries had long ensured that military men enjoyed great social prestige, and most heads of state wore uniforms in public. All of the Great Powers had substantial standing armies and, except for Britain, relied on conscription (compulsory military service) to staff them. Furthermore, each of the major states had developed elaborate "war plans" that spelled out in great detail the movement of men and materials that should occur immediately upon the outbreak of war. Such plans created a hair-trigger mentality since each country had an incentive to strike first so that its particular strategy could be implemented on schedule and without interruption or surprise. The rapid industrialization of warfare generated an array of novel weapons, including submarines, tanks, airplanes, poison gas, machine guns, and barbed wire. This new military technology contributed to the staggering casualties of the war, including some 10 million deaths, the vast majority male; perhaps twice that number were wounded, crippled, or disfigured. For countless women, as a result, there would be no husbands or children.

Europe's imperial reach around the world likewise shaped the scope and conduct of the war. It funneled colonial troops and laborers by the hundreds of thousands into the war effort, with men from Africa, India, China, Southeast Asia, Australia, New Zealand, and Canada taking part in the conflict. British and French forces seized German colonies in Africa and the South Pacific. Japan, allied with Britain, took various German possessions in China and the Pacific and demanded territorial and economic concessions from China itself. The Ottoman Empire, which entered the conflict on the side of Germany, became the site of intense military actions and witnessed an Arab revolt against Ottoman Turkish control. Finally, the United States, after initially seeking to avoid involvement in European quarrels, joined the war in 1917 when German submarines threatened American shipping. Thus the war, though centered in Europe, had global dimensions and certainly merited its title as a "world war."

Outcomes: Legacies of the Great War

The Great War shattered almost every expectation. Most Europeans believed in the late summer of 1914 that "the boys will be home by Christmas," but instead the war ground relentlessly on for more than four years before ending in a German defeat in November 1918. Moreover, it had become a "**total war**," requiring the mobilization of each country's entire population. Thus the authority of governments expanded greatly. As the German state, for example, assumed further control over the economy, its policies became known as "war socialism," thus continuing a long-term strengthening of state power across much of Europe. Vast propaganda campaigns sought to arouse citizens by depicting a cruel and inhuman enemy who killed innocent children and violated women. Labor unions agreed to suspend strikes and accept sacrifices for the common good, while women, replacing the men who had left the factories for the battlefront, temporarily abandoned the struggle for the vote.

No less surprising were the longer-term outcomes of the war. In the European cockpit of that conflict, unprecedented casualties, particularly among elite and well-educated groups, and physical destruction, especially in France, led to a widespread disillusionment among intellectuals with their own civilization. For many, the war seemed to mock the Enlightenment values of progress, tolerance, and rationality, and some began to doubt that the West was superior or that its vaunted science and technology were unquestionably good things. In the most famous novel to emerge from the war, the German veteran Erich Remarque's *All Quiet on the Western Front*, one soldier expressed what many no doubt felt: "It must all be lies and of no account when the culture of a thousand years could not prevent this stream of blood being poured out."

The aftermath of war also brought substantial social and cultural changes to ordinary Europeans and Americans. Women were urged to leave the factory work they had taken up during the war and return to their homes, where they would not compete against returning veterans for "men's jobs." Nonetheless, the war had loosened the hold of tradition in various ways. Enormous casualties promoted social mobility, allowing the less exalted to move into positions previously dominated by the upper classes. As the war ended, suffrage movements revived and women received the right to vote in a number of countries—Britain, the United States, Germany, the Soviet Union, Hungary, and Poland—in part perhaps because of the sacrifices they had made during the conflict. Young middle-class women, sometimes known as "flappers," began to flout convention by appearing at nightclubs, smoking, dancing, drinking hard liquor, cutting their hair short, wearing revealing clothing, and generally expressing a more open sexuality. Technological innovations, mass production, and pent-up demand after the austerities of wartime fostered a new consumerism, particularly in the United States, encouraging those who could to acquire cars, washing machines, vacuum cleaners, electric irons, gas ovens, and other newly available products. Radio and the movies now became vehicles of popular culture, transmitting American jazz to Europe and turning Hollywood stars into international celebrities.

The war also transformed international political life. From the collapse of the German, Russian, and Austro-Hungarian empires emerged a new map of Central Europe with an independent Poland, Czechoslovakia, Yugoslavia, and other nations (see Map 20.3). Such new states were based on the principle of "national self-determination," a concept championed by U.S. president Woodrow Wilson, but each of them also contained dissatisfied ethnic minorities who claimed the same principle. By the **Treaty of Versailles**, which formally concluded the war in 1919, Germany

MAP 20.3   Europe and the Middle East after World War I

The Great War brought into existence a number of new states that were carved out of the old German, Austro-Hungarian, Russian, and Ottoman empires. Turkey and the new states in Europe were independent, but those in the Middle East—Syria, Palestine, Iraq, and Transjordan—were administered by Britain or France as mandates of the League of Nations.

lost its colonial empire and 15 percent of its European territory, was required to pay heavy reparations to the winners, had its military forces severely restricted, and was required to accept sole responsibility for the outbreak of the war. All of this created immense resentment in Germany. One of the country's many demobilized and disillusioned soldiers declared in 1922: "It cannot be that two million Germans should have fallen in vain. . . . No, we do not pardon, we demand—vengeance."[2] His name was Adolf Hitler, and within two decades he had begun to exact that vengeance.

The Great War generated profound changes in the world beyond Europe as well. During the conflict, Ottoman authorities, suspecting that some of their Armenian subjects were collaborating with the Russian enemy, massacred or deported an estimated 1 million Armenians. Although the term "genocide" had not yet been invented, some historians have applied it to those atrocities, arguing that they established a precedent on which the Nazis later built. The war also brought a final end to a declining Ottoman Empire, creating the modern map of the Middle East, with the new states of Turkey, Syria, Iraq, Transjordan, and Palestine. Thus Arabs emerged from Turkish rule, but many of them were governed for a time by the British or French, as "mandates" of the League of Nations (see Map 20.3). Conflicting British promises to both Arabs and Jews regarding Palestine set the stage for an enduring struggle over that ancient and holy land. And in the world of European colonies, the war echoed loudly. Millions of Asian and African men had watched Europeans butcher one another without mercy, had gained new military skills and political awareness, and returned home with less respect for their rulers and with expectations for better treatment as a reward for their service. To gain Indian support for the war, the British had publicly promised to put that colony on the road to self-government, an announcement that set the stage for the independence struggle that followed. In East Asia, Japan emerged strengthened from the war, with European support for its claim to take over German territory and privileges in China. That news enraged Chinese nationalists, particularly among the young, and pushed many of them into a more revolutionary posture, as it seemed to signify the continuation of an arrogant imperialist attitude among Europeans toward the Chinese people.

Furthermore, the First World War brought the United States to center stage as a global power. Its manpower had contributed much to the defeat of Germany, and its financial resources turned the United States from a debtor nation into Europe's creditor. When the American president Woodrow Wilson arrived in Paris for the peace conference in 1919, he was greeted with an almost religious enthusiasm. His famous Fourteen Points seemed to herald a new kind of international life, one based on moral principles rather than secret deals and imperialist machinations. Particularly appealing to many was his idea for the League of Nations, a new international peacekeeping organization committed to the principle of "collective security" and intended to avoid any repetition of the horrors that had just ended. Wilson's idealistic vision largely failed, however. Germany was treated more harshly than he had wished. National self-determination in the multiethnic states of Europe and elsewhere was very difficult, and Wilson's rhetoric inspired hopes in the colonies that could not be immediately fulfilled. In his own country, the U.S. Senate refused to join the League, which was established in 1920, fearing that Americans would be forced to bow to "the will of other nations." That refusal seriously weakened the League of Nations as a vehicle for Wilson's new international order.

The Russian Revolution and Soviet Communism

Among the most significant outcomes of World War I was the beginning of world communism, which played such an enormous role in the history of the twentieth century. Modern communism found its political and philosophical roots in nineteenth-century European socialism, inspired by the teachings of Karl Marx. Most European socialists had come to believe that they could achieve their goals peacefully and through the democratic process, but not so in Russia, where democracy barely existed. Many Russian socialists therefore advocated uncompromising revolution as the only possible route to a socialist future. That revolution occurred during World War I in 1917. (For the background to the Russian Revolution, see "Russia: Industrialization and Revolution" in Chapter 17.)

The catalyst for the **Russian Revolution** was World War I, which was going very badly for the Russians. Under this pressure the accumulated tensions of Russian society exploded. Workers—men and women alike, along with the wives of soldiers—took to the streets to express their outrage at the incompetence and privileges of the elites. Activists organized demonstrations, published newspapers, and plotted revolution. By early 1917, Tsar Nicholas II had lost almost all support and was forced to abdicate the throne, thus ending the Romanov dynasty, which had ruled Russia for more than three centuries. What followed was a Provisional Government, led by major political figures from various parties. But the Russian Revolution had only begun.

The tsar's abdication opened the door for a massive social upheaval. Ordinary soldiers, seeking an end to a terrible war and despising their upper-class officers, deserted in substantial numbers. In major industrial centers such as St. Petersburg and Moscow, new trade unions arose to defend workers' interests, and some workers seized control of their factories. Grassroots organizations of workers and soldiers, known as soviets, emerged to speak for ordinary people. Peasants, many of whom had been serfs only a generation or two earlier, seized landlords' estates, burned their manor houses, and redistributed the land among themselves. Non-Russian nationalists in Ukraine, Poland, Muslim Central Asia, and the Baltic region demanded greater autonomy or even independence (see Map 21.1, page 605).

This was social revolution, and it provided an environment in which a small socialist party called the Bolsheviks was able to seize power by the end of 1917 under the leadership of its determined and charismatic leader, Vladimir Ilyich Ulyanov, more commonly known as **Lenin**. In the desperate circumstances of 1917, his party's message—an end to the war, land for the peasants, workers' control of factories, self-determination for non-Russian nationalities—resonated with an increasingly rebellious public mood, particularly in the major cities.

A three-year civil war followed in which the Bolsheviks, now officially calling their party "communist," battled an assortment of enemies—tsarist officials, landlords, disaffected socialists, and regional nationalist forces, as well as troops from the United States, Britain, France, and Japan, all of which were eager to crush the fledgling communist regime. Remarkably, the Bolsheviks held on and by 1921 had staggered to victory over their divided and uncoordinated opponents. They renamed their country the Union of Soviet Socialist Republics (USSR or Soviet Union) and set about its transformation. For the next twenty-five years, the Soviet Union remained a communist island in a capitalist sea.

Once they had consolidated power and resolved their leadership struggles, Russian communists soon began the task of constructing a socialist society under the control of Joseph **Stalin** (1878–1953), who emerged as the principal Soviet leader by the late 1920s. To Stalin and communists generally, building socialism meant first of all the modernization and industrialization of a backward Russian society. They sought, however, a distinctly socialist modernity with an emphasis on social equality and the promotion of cultural values of selflessness and collectivism.

Those imperatives generated a political system thoroughly dominated by the Communist Party. Top-ranking party members enjoyed various privileges but were expected to be exemplars of socialism in the making by being disciplined, selfless, and utterly loyal to their country's Marxist ideology. The party itself penetrated society in ways that Western scholars called "totalitarian," for other parties were forbidden, the state controlled almost the entire economy, and political authorities ensured that the arts, education, and the media conformed to approved ways of thinking. Mass organizations for women, workers, students, and various professional groups operated under party control, with none of the independence that characterized civil society in the West.

In the rural areas, building socialism meant the end of private ownership of land and **collectivization of agriculture**. Between 1928 and 1933, peasants were forced, often against great resistance, into large-scale collective farms, which were supposedly more productive and better able to utilize modern agricultural machinery than the small family farms that had emerged from the revolution. Stalin singled out the richer peasants, known as *kulaks* (koo-LAHKS), for exclusion from the new collective farms. Some were killed, and many others were deported to remote areas of the country. With little support or experience in the countryside, the urban activists who enforced collectivization were viewed as intrusive outsiders in Russian peasant villages. A terrible famine ensued, with some 5 million deaths from starvation or malnutrition.

In the cities, the task was rapid industrialization. The Soviet approach to industrial development, so different from that of the capitalist West, involved state ownership of property, centralized planning embodied in successive five-year plans, priority to heavy industry, massive mobilization of the nation's human and material resources,

Mobilizing Women for Communism As the Soviet Union mobilized for rapid economic development in the 1930s, women entered the workforce in great numbers. Here two young women are mastering the skills of driving a tractor on one of the large collective farms that replaced the country's private agriculture. (Sovfoto/Getty Images)

and intrusive Communist Party control of the entire process. For a time, it worked. During the 1930s, while the capitalist world floundered amid the massive unemployment of the Great Depression, the Soviet Union largely eliminated unemployment and constructed the foundations of an industrial society that proved itself in the victory over Nazi Germany in World War II. In addition, the USSR achieved massive improvements in literacy rates and educational opportunities, allowing far greater social mobility for millions of people than ever before. As in the West, industrialization fostered rapid urbanization, exploitation of the countryside to provide resources for modern industry in the cities, and the growth of a privileged bureaucratic and technological elite intent on pursuing their own careers and passing on their new status to their children.

Despite its totalitarian tendencies, the communist society of the Soviet Union was laced with conflict. Under Stalin's leadership, those conflicts erupted in a search for enemies that terribly disfigured Soviet life. An elastic concept of "enemy" came to include not only surviving remnants from the prerevolutionary elites but also, and more surprisingly, high-ranking members and longtime supporters of the Communist Party, who allegedly had been corrupted by bourgeois ideas, as evidenced by their opposition to some of Stalin's harsh policies. Refracted through the lens of Marxist thinking, these people became "class enemies" who had betrayed the revolution and were engaged in a vast conspiracy, often linked to foreign imperialists, to subvert the socialist enterprise and restore capitalism.

That process culminated in the Terror, or the Great Purges, of the late 1930s, which enveloped tens of thousands of prominent communists, including virtually all of Lenin's top associates, and millions of more ordinary people. Based on suspicious associations in the past, denunciations by colleagues, connections to foreign countries, or simply bad luck, such people were arrested, usually in the dead of night, and then tried and sentenced either to death or to long years in harsh and remote labor camps known as the gulag. A series of show trials publicized the menace that these "enemies of the people" allegedly posed to the country and its revolution. Close to 1 million people were executed between 1936 and 1941. An additional 4 or 5 million were sent to the gulag, where they were forced to work in horrendous conditions and died in appalling numbers. Such was the outcome of the world's first experiment with communism.

Capitalism Unraveling: The Great Depression

While the Soviet Union was constructing the world's first communist society, the capitalist world languished in the **Great Depression**, which began with an abrupt stock market crash in October 1929 and then lasted for a decade. If World War I represented the political collapse of Europe, this economic catastrophe suggested that Western capitalism was likewise failing, as Marx had predicted. All across the Euro-American heartland of the industrialized capitalist world, this vaunted economic system seemed to unravel. For the rich, it meant contracting stock prices that wiped out paper fortunes almost overnight. Banks closed, and many people lost their life savings. Investment dried up, world trade dropped by 62 percent within a few years, and businesses contracted or closed. Unemployment soared everywhere, and in both Germany and the United States it reached 30 percent or more by 1932 (see Snapshot: Comparing the Impact of the Depression, below). Vacant factories, soup kitchens, bread lines, shantytowns, and beggars came to symbolize the human reality of this economic disaster.

This economic breakdown began in the United States, which had experienced a booming economy during the 1920s. By the end of that decade, its farms and factories were producing more goods than could be sold, either at home or abroad. Meanwhile, a speculative stock market frenzy had driven up stock prices to an unsustainable level. When that bubble burst in late 1929, its ripple effects quickly encompassed the industrialized economies of Europe, which were intimately connected to the United States through ties of trade, debt, and investment.

Much as Europe's worldwide empires had globalized the Great War, so too its economic linkages globalized the Great Depression. Countries or colonies tied to exporting one or two products were especially hard-hit. Colonial Southeast Asia, the world's major rubber-producing region, saw the demand for its primary export drop dramatically as automobile sales in Europe and the United States were cut in half. In Britain's West African colony of the Gold Coast (present-day Ghana), farmers who had staked their economic lives on producing cocoa for the world market were badly hurt by the collapse of commodity prices. Latin American countries saw the value of their exports cut by half, generating widespread unemployment and social tensions. In response to these problems, governments sought to steer their economies away from exports toward producing for the internal market, a policy known as import substitution. In Mexico, the Depression opened the way to reviving the principles of the Mexican Revolution under the leadership of Lázaro Cárdenas (1934–1940), who

SNAPSHOT   **COMPARING THE IMPACT OF THE DEPRESSION**

As industrial production dropped during the Depression, unemployment soared. Yet the larger Western capitalist countries differed considerably in the duration and extent of this unemployment. Note especially the differences between Germany and the United States. How might you account for this difference?

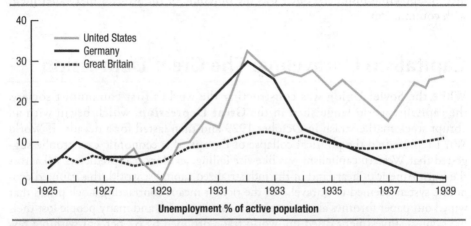

Adapted from Lynn Hunt et al., *The Making of the West: Peoples and Cultures* (Boston: Bedford/St. Martin's, 2001), 1024.

pushed land reform, favored Mexican workers against foreign interests, and nationalized an oil industry dominated by American capital.

The Great Depression also sharply challenged the governments of industrialized capitalist countries. The apparent failure of a market economy to self-correct led many people to look twice at the Soviet Union. There, the dispossession of the propertied classes and a state-controlled economy had generated an impressive economic growth with almost no unemployment in the 1930s, even as the capitalist world was reeling. No Western country opted for the dictatorial and draconian socialism of the Soviet Union, but in Britain, France, and Scandinavia, the Depression energized a "democratic socialism" that sought greater regulation of the economy and a more equal distribution of wealth through peaceful means and electoral politics. The Great Depression, like the world wars, strengthened the power of the state.

The United States illustrated this trend as President Franklin Roosevelt's New Deal (1933–1942) took shape, permanently altering the relationship among government, the private economy, and individual citizens. The New Deal involved immediate programs of public spending (for dams, highways, bridges, and parks); longer-term reforms, such as the Social Security system, the minimum wage, and various relief and welfare programs; support for labor unions; and subsidies for farmers. A mounting number of government agencies marked a new degree of federal regulation and supervision of the economy.

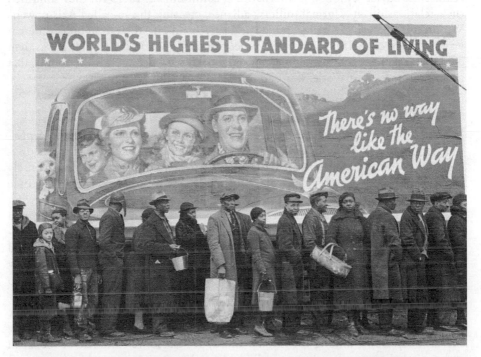

Contrasts of the Great Depression This 1937 *Life* magazine image by famed photographer Margaret Bourke-White shows black victims of a flood in Louisville, Kentucky, standing in a breadline during the Depression while behind them rises a billboard depicting a happy and prosperous white family. (Margaret Bourke-White/The LIFE Picture Collection/Getty Images)

Ultimately, none of the New Deal's programs worked very well to end the Great Depression. Not until the massive government spending required by World War II kicked in did economic disaster abate in the United States. The most successful efforts to cope with the Depression came from unlikely places—Nazi Germany and an increasingly militaristic Japan.

Democracy Denied: The Authoritarian Alternative

Despite the victory of the democratic powers in World War I—Britain, France, and the United States—their democratic political ideals and their cultural values celebrating individual freedom came under sharp attack in the aftermath of that bloody conflict. One challenge derived from communism, which was initiated in the Russian Revolution of 1917. In the 1920s and 1930s, however, the more immediate challenge to the victors in the Great War came from highly authoritarian, intensely nationalistic, territorially aggressive, and ferociously anticommunist regimes, particularly those that took shape in Italy, Germany, and Japan. The common political goals of these three countries drew them together by 1936–1937 in an alliance directed against the Soviet Union and international communism. In 1940, they solidified their relationship in a formal military alliance, creating the so-called Axis powers. Within this alliance, Germany and Japan clearly stand out, though in quite different ways, in terms of their impact on the larger patterns of world history, for it was their efforts to "establish and maintain a new order of things," as the Axis Pact put it, that generated the Second World War both in East Asia and in Europe.

European Fascism

Between 1919 and 1945, a new political ideology, known as **fascism**, found expression across parts of Europe. While communists celebrated class conflict as the driving force of history, for fascists it was the conflict of nations. Fascism was intensely nationalistic, seeking to revitalize and purify the nation and to mobilize its people for some grand task. Its spokesmen praised violence against enemies as a renewing force in society, celebrated action rather than reflection, and placed their faith in a charismatic leader. Fascists also bitterly condemned individualism, liberalism, feminism, parliamentary democracy, and communism, all of which, they argued, divided and weakened the nation. In their determination to overthrow existing regimes, they were revolutionary; in their embrace of traditional values and their opposition to much of modern life, however, they were conservative or reactionary.

Such ideas appealed to aggrieved people all across the social spectrum. In the devastation that followed the First World War, the numbers of such people grew substantially. Some among the middle and upper classes felt the rise of socialism and communism as a dire threat; small-scale merchants, artisans, and farmers feared the loss of their independence to either big business or socialist revolution; demobilized soldiers had few prospects and nursed many resentments; and intellectuals were appalled by the materialism and artificiality of modern life. Such people had lost faith in the capacity of liberal democracy and capitalism to create a good society and to protect their interests. Some among them proved a receptive audience for the message of fascism. Fascist or other highly authoritarian movements appeared in many European countries, such as Spain, Romania, and Hungary, and some in Latin America, but it was in Italy and Germany that such movements achieved prolonged power in major states, with devastating consequences for Europe and the world.

The fascist alternative took shape first in Italy. That nation had become a unified state only in 1870 and had not yet developed a thoroughly industrialized economy or a solidly democratic culture. The First World War gave rise to resentful veterans, many of them unemployed, and to patriots who believed that Italy had not gained the territory it deserved from the Treaty of Versailles. During the serious economic downturn after World War I, trade unions, peasant movements, and various communist and socialist parties threatened the established social order with a wave of strikes and land seizures.

Into this setting stepped a charismatic orator and a former journalist with a socialist background, Benito **Mussolini** (1883–1945). With the help of a private army of disillusioned veterans and jobless men known as the Black Shirts, Mussolini swept to power in 1922 amid considerable violence, promising an alternative to communism, order in the streets, an end to bickering party-based politics, and the maintenance of the traditional social order. That Mussolini's government allegedly made the trains run on time became evidence that these promises might be fulfilled.

In Mussolini's thinking, fascism was resolutely anticommunist, "the complete opposite . . . of Marxist socialism," and equally antidemocratic. "Fascism combats the whole complex system of democratic ideology, and repudiates it," he wrote. At the core of Mussolini's fascism was his conception of the state. "Fascism conceives of the State as an absolute, in comparison with which all individuals and groups are relative, only to be conceived of in their relation to the State." The state was a conscious entity with "a will and a personality" that represented the "spirit of the nation." Its expansion in war and empire building was "an essential manifestation of vitality."

Mussolini's government suspended democracy and imprisoned, deported, or sometimes executed opponents. Italy's fascist regime also disbanded independent labor unions and peasant groups as well as all opposing political parties. In economic life, a "corporate state" took shape, at least in theory, in which workers, employers, and various professional groups were organized into "corporations" that were supposed to settle their disagreements and determine economic policy under the supervision of the state.

Culturally, fascists invoked various aspects of traditional Italian life. Though personally an atheist, Mussolini embraced the Catholic culture of Italy in a series of agreements with the Church, known as the Lateran Accords of 1929, that made the Vatican a sovereign state and Catholicism Italy's national religion. In fascist propaganda, women were portrayed in highly traditional domestic terms, particularly as mothers creating new citizens for the fascist state, with no hint of equality or liberation. Nationalists were delighted when Italy invaded Ethiopia in 1935, avenging the embarrassing defeat that Italians suffered at the hands of Ethiopians in 1896. In the eyes of Mussolini and fascist believers, all of this was the beginning of a "new Roman Empire" that would revitalize Italian society and give it a global mission.

Hitler and the Nazis

Far more important in the long run was the German expression of European fascism, which took shape as the **Nazi Party** under the leadership of Adolf **Hitler** (1889–1945). In many respects, it was similar to its Italian counterpart. Both espoused an extreme nationalism, openly advocated the use of violence as a political tool, generated a single-party dictatorship, were led by charismatic figures, despised parliamentary democracy, hated communism, and viewed war as a positive and ennobling experience.[3] The circumstances that gave rise to the Nazi movement were likewise broadly similar to those of Italian fascism, although the Nazis did not achieve national power until 1933. Germany too was a new European nation, lacking a long-term democratic tradition. As in Italy, resentment about the Treaty of Versailles was widespread, especially among unemployed veterans. Fear of socialism or communism was prevalent among middle- and upper-class groups. But it was the Great Depression that provided the essential context for the victory of German fascism. The German economy largely ground to a halt in the early 1930s amid massive unemployment among workers and the middle class alike. Everyone demanded decisive action from the state.

This was the context in which Adolf Hitler's National Socialist, or Nazi, Party gained growing public support. Its message expressed an intense German nationalism cast in terms of racial superiority, bitter hatred for Jews as an alien presence, passionate opposition to communism, a determination to rescue Germany from the

The Faces of European Fascism Benito Mussolini (left) and Adolf Hitler came to symbolize fascism in Europe in the several decades between the two world wars. In this photograph from September 1937, they are reviewing German troops in Munich during Mussolini's visit to Germany, a trip that deepened the growing relationship between their two countries. (Luce/Getty Images)

humiliating requirements of the Treaty of Versailles, and a willingness to decisively tackle the country's economic problems. All of this resonated widely, enabling the Nazis to win 37 percent of the vote in the election of 1932. The following year, Hitler was legally installed as the chancellor of the German government. Thus a weak democratic regime that never gained broad support gave way to the Third Reich.

Once in power, Hitler moved quickly to consolidate Nazi control of Germany. All other political parties were outlawed; independent labor unions were ended; thousands of opponents were arrested; and the press and radio came under state control. Far more thoroughly than Mussolini in Italy, Hitler and the Nazis established their control over German society.

By the late 1930s, Hitler apparently had the support of a considerable majority of the population, in large measure because his policies successfully brought Germany out of the Depression. The government invested heavily in projects such as superhighways, bridges, canals, and public buildings and, after 1935, in rebuilding and rearming the country's diminished military forces. These policies drove down the number of unemployed Germans from 6.2 million in 1932 to fewer than 500,000 in 1937. Two years later Germany had a labor shortage. Erna Kranz, a teenager in the 1930s, later remembered the early years of Nazi rule as "a glimmer of hope . . . not just for the unemployed but for everybody because we all knew that we were downtrodden. . . . It was a good time . . . there was order and discipline."[4] Millions agreed with her.

Other factors as well contributed to Nazi popularity. Like Italian fascists, Hitler appealed to rural and traditional values that many Germans feared losing as their country modernized. In Hitler's thinking and in Nazi propaganda, Jews became the symbol of the urban, capitalist, and foreign influences that were undermining traditional German culture. Thus the Nazis reflected and reinforced a broader and long-established current of anti-Semitism that had deep roots in much of Europe. In his book *Mein Kampf* (My Struggle), Hitler outlined his case against the Jews and his call for the racial purification of Germany in vitriolic terms.

Far more than in Italy or elsewhere, this insistence on a racial revolution was a central feature of the Nazi program. Upon coming to power, Hitler implemented policies that increasingly restricted Jewish life. Soon Jews were excluded from universities, professional organizations, and civil employment. In 1935, the Nuremberg Laws ended German citizenship for Jews and forbade marriage or sexual relations between Jews and Germans. On the night of November 9, 1938, known as Kristallnacht ("Night of Crystal" or "Night of Broken Glass"), persecution gave way to terror, when Nazis smashed and looted Jewish shops. Such actions made clear the Nazis' determination to rid Germany of its Jewish population, thus putting into effect the most radical element of Hitler's program. Still, it was not yet apparent that this "racial revolution" would mean the mass killing of Europe's Jews. That horrendous development emerged only in the context of World War II.

Beyond race, gender too figured prominently in Nazi thought and policies. While Soviet communists sought to enroll women in the country's industrialization effort, Nazis wanted to limit women largely to the home, removing them from the paid workforce. To Hitler, the state was the natural domain of men, while the home was the realm of women. "Woman in the workplace is an oppressed and tormented being," declared a Nazi publication. Concerned about declining birthrates, Italy and Germany alike promoted a cult of motherhood, glorifying and rewarding women who produced children for the state. Accordingly, fascist regimes in both countries generally opposed abortion, contraception, family planning, and sex education, all of which were associated with feminist thinking. Yet such an outlook did not necessarily coincide with conservative or puritanical sexual attitudes. In Germany, a state-sponsored system of brothels was initiated in the mid-1930s, for it was assumed that virile men would be promiscuous and that soldiers required a sexual outlet if they were to contribute to the nation's military strength.

Also sustaining Nazi rule were massive torchlight ceremonies celebrating the superiority of the German race and its folk culture. In these settings, Hitler was the mystical leader, the Führer, a mesmerizing orator who would lead Germany to national greatness and individual Germans to personal fulfillment.

If World War I and the Great Depression brought about the political and economic collapse of Europe, the Nazi phenomenon represented a rejection of some of the values—rationalism, tolerance, democracy, human equality—that for many people had defined the core of Western civilization since the Enlightenment. On the other hand, Nazis claimed the legacy of modern science, particularly in their concern to classify and rank various human groups. Thus they drew heavily on the "scientific racism" of the late nineteenth century and its expression in phrenology, which linked the size and shape of the skull to human behavior and personality (see "Industry and Empire" in Chapter 18). Moreover, in their effort to purify German society, the Nazis reflected the Enlightenment confidence in the perfectibility of humankind and in the social engineering necessary to achieve it.

By 1940, the European political landscape had altered dramatically from what it had been just a few decades earlier. At the beginning of the twentieth century, major European countries had embraced largely capitalist economies and to varying degrees increasingly democratic political systems with multiple parties and elected parliaments. But by the time World War II broke out, Europe's largest country, the Soviet Union, had altogether rejected capitalism in favor of a state-controlled economy and a political system dominated by a single communist political party. The fascist states of Germany and Italy likewise dismantled multiparty democracies, replacing them with highly authoritarian dictatorships. While they retained major private ownership of property, the state played a large role in economic affairs. Communist and fascist states alike rejected the individualistic liberalism of the remaining democracies, celebrating the collective identities of "class" in the case of the Soviet Union and of nation or race in Italy and Germany.

Japanese Authoritarianism

In various ways, the modern history of Japan paralleled that of Italy and Germany. All three were newcomers to Great Power status, with Japan joining the club of industrializing and empire-building states only in the late nineteenth century as its sole Asian member (see "The Japanese Difference" in Chapter 19). Like Italy and Germany, Japan had a rather limited experience with democratic politics, for its elected parliament was constrained by a very small electorate (only 1.5 million men in 1917) and by the exalted position of a semi-divine emperor and his small coterie of elite advisers. During the 1930s, Japan too moved toward authoritarian government and a denial of democracy at home, even as it launched an aggressive program of territorial expansion in East Asia. But in sharp contrast to Italy and Germany, Japan's participation in World War I was minimal, and its economy grew considerably as other industrialized countries were consumed by the European conflict. At the peace conference ending that war, Japan was seated as an equal participant, allied with the winning side of democratic countries such as Britain, France, and the United States.

During the 1920s, Japan seemed to be moving toward more democratic politics and Western cultural values. Universal male suffrage was achieved in 1925, and a two-party system began to emerge. Supporters of these developments, mostly urban and well-to-do, generally embraced the dignity of the individual, free expression of ideas, and greater gender equality. Education expanded; an urban consumer society developed; middle-class women entered new professions; and young women known as *moga* (modern girls) sported short hair and short skirts, while dancing with *mobo* (modern boys) at jazz clubs and cabarets. To such people, the Japanese were becoming global citizens and their country was becoming "a province of the world" as they participated increasingly in a cosmopolitan and international culture.

In this environment, the accumulated tensions of Japan's modernizing and industrializing processes found expression. "Rice riots" in 1918 brought more than a million people into the streets of urban Japan to protest the rising price of that essential staple. Union membership tripled in the 1920s as some factory workers began to think in terms of entitlements and workers' rights rather than the benevolence of their employers. In rural areas, tenant unions multiplied, and disputes with landowners increased amid demands for a reduction in rents. A mounting women's movement advocated a variety of feminist issues, including suffrage and the end of legalized prostitution. "All the sleeping women are now awake and moving," declared Yosano Akiko, a well-known poet, feminist, and social critic in 1911. A number of "proletarian (working class) parties" — the Labor-Farmer Party, the Socialist People's Party, and a small Japan Communist Party — promised in various ways to promote radical social change.

For many people in established elite circles — bureaucrats, landowners, industrialists, military officials — all of this was both appalling and alarming, suggesting echoes of the Russian Revolution of 1917. As in Germany, however, it was the impact of the Great Depression that paved the way for harsher and more authoritarian action. That worldwide economic catastrophe hit Japan hard. Shrinking world demand for silk impoverished millions of rural dwellers who raised silkworms. Japan's exports fell by half between 1929 and 1931, leaving a million or more urban workers unemployed. Many young workers returned to their rural villages only to find food scarce, families forced to sell their daughters to urban brothels, and neighbors unable to offer the customary money for the funerals of their friends. In these desperate circumstances, many began to doubt the ability of parliamentary democracy and capitalism to address Japan's "national emergency." Such conditions energized a growing movement in Japanese political life known as Radical Nationalism or the **Revolutionary Right**. Expressed in dozens of small groups, it was especially appealing to younger army officers. The movement's many separate organizations shared an extreme nationalism, hostility to parliamentary democracy, a commitment to elite leadership focused around an exalted emperor, and dedication to foreign expansion.

The manifesto of one of those organizations, the Cherry Blossom Society, expressed these sentiments clearly in 1930:

> As we observe recent social trends, top leaders engage in immoral conduct, political parties are corrupt, capitalists and aristocrats have no understanding of the masses, farming villages are devastated, unemployment and depression are serious. . . . The rulers neglect the long term interests of the nation, strive to win only the pleasure of foreign powers and possess no enthusiasm for external expansion. . . . The people are with us in craving the appearance of a vigorous and clean government that is truly based upon the masses, and is genuinely centered around the Emperor.[5]

In sharp contrast to developments in Italy and Germany, however, no right-wing or fascist party gained wide popular support in Japan, and no such party was able to seize power. Nor did Japan produce any charismatic leader on the order of Mussolini or Hitler. People arrested for political offenses were neither criminalized nor exterminated, as in Germany, but instead were subjected to a process of "resocialization" that brought the vast majority of them to renounce their "errors" and return to the "Japanese way." Japan's established institutions of government were sufficiently strong, and traditional notions of the nation as a family headed by the emperor were sufficiently intact, to prevent the development of a widespread fascist movement able to take control of the country.

In the 1930s, though, Japanese public life clearly changed in ways that reflected the growth of right-wing nationalist thinking. The military in particular came to exercise a more dominant role in Japanese political life, reflecting the long-standing Japanese respect for the samurai warrior class. Censorship limited the possibilities of free expression, and a single news agency was granted the right to distribute all national and most international news to the country's newspapers and radio stations. Established authorities also adopted many of the ideological themes of the

The Growth of Japanese Militarism This poster celebrating the Japanese navy was created by the National Defense Women's Association in 1938. It reflects the increasing role of the military in Japanese national life and seeks to encourage female support for it. (Pictures from History/Bridgeman Images)

Revolutionary Right. In 1937, the Ministry of Education issued a new textbook, *Cardinal Principles of the National Entity of Japan*, for use in all Japanese schools. That document proclaimed the Japanese to be "intrinsically quite different from the so-called citizens of Occidental [Western] countries." Those nations were "conglomerations of separate individuals" with "no deep foundation between ruler and citizen to unite them." In Japan, by contrast, an emperor of divine origin related to his subjects as a father to his children. It was a natural, not a contractual, relationship, expressed most fully in the "sacrifice of the life of a subject for the Emperor."

The state's success in quickly bringing the country out of the Depression likewise fostered popular support. As in Nazi Germany, state-financed credit, large-scale spending on armaments, and public works projects enabled Japan to emerge from the Depression more rapidly and more fully than major Western countries. "By the end of 1937," noted one Japanese laborer, "everybody in the country was working."[6] By the mid-1930s, the government increasingly assumed a supervisory or managerial role in economic affairs. Private property, however, was retained, and the huge industrial enterprises called *zaibatsu* continued to dominate the economic landscape.

Although Japan during the 1930s shared some common features with fascist Italy and Nazi Germany, it remained, at least internally, a less repressive and more pluralistic society than either of those European states. Japanese intellectuals and writers had to contend with government censorship, but they retained some influence in the country. Generals and admirals exercised great political authority as the role of an elected parliament declined, but they did not govern alone. Political prisoners were few and were not subjected to execution or deportation as in European fascist states. Japanese conceptions of their racial purity and uniqueness were directed largely against foreigners rather than an internal minority. Nevertheless, like Germany and Italy, Japan developed extensive imperial ambitions. Those projects of conquest and empire building collided with the interests of established imperial powers such as the United States and Britain, launching a second, and even more terrible, global war.

A Second World War, 1937–1945

World War II, even more than the Great War, was a genuinely global conflict with independent origins in both Asia and Europe. Dissatisfied states in both continents sought to fundamentally alter the international arrangements that had emerged from World War I. Many Japanese, like their counterparts in Italy and Germany, felt stymied by Britain and the United States as they sought empires that they regarded as essential for their national greatness and economic well-being.

The Road to War in Asia

World War II began in Asia before it occurred in Europe. In the late 1920s and the 1930s, Japanese imperial ambitions mounted as the military became more powerful in Japan's political life and as an earlier cultural cosmopolitanism gave way to more nationalist sentiments. An initial problem was the rise of Chinese nationalism, which seemed to threaten Japan's sphere of influence in Manchuria, acquired by Japan after the Russo-Japanese War of 1904–1905. Acting independently of civilian authorities in Tokyo, units of the Japanese military seized control of Manchuria in 1931 and established a puppet state called Manchukuo. This action was condemned by China, the United States, and the League of Nations alike, but there was no effective military response to the Japanese aggression. The condemnation, however, prompted Japan to withdraw from the League of Nations and in 1936 to align more closely with Germany and Italy. By that time, relations with an increasingly nationalist China had deteriorated further, leading to a full-scale attack on heartland China in 1937 and escalating a bitter conflict that would last another eight years. **World War II in Asia** had begun (see Map 20.4).

MAP 20.4 World War II in Asia and the Pacific
Japanese aggression temporarily dislodged the British, French, Dutch, and Americans from their colonial possessions in Asia, while inflicting vast devastation on China. Much of the American counterattack involved "island hopping" across the Pacific until the dropping of the atomic bombs on Hiroshima and Nagasaki finally prompted the Japanese surrender in August 1945.

As Japan's war against China unfolded, the view of the world held by Japanese authorities and many ordinary people hardened. Increasingly, they felt isolated, surrounded, and threatened. Anti-Japanese immigration policies in the United States convinced some Japanese that racism prevented the West from acknowledging Japan as an equal power. Furthermore, Japan was quite dependent on foreign and especially American sources of strategic goods—oil, for example—even as the United States was becoming increasingly hostile to Japanese ambitions in Asia. Moreover, Western imperialist powers—the British, French, and Dutch—controlled resource-rich colonies in Southeast Asia. Finally, the Soviet Union, proclaiming an alien communist ideology, loomed large in northern Asia. To growing numbers of Japanese, their national survival was at stake.

Thus in 1940–1941, Japan extended its military operations to the French, British, Dutch, and American colonies of Southeast Asia—Malaya, Burma, Indonesia, Indochina, and the Philippines—in an effort to acquire those resources that would free it from dependence on the West. In carving out this Pacific empire, the Japanese presented themselves as liberators and modernizers, creating an "Asia for Asians" and freeing their continent from European and American dominance. Experience soon showed that Japan's concern was far more for Asia's resources than for its liberation and that Japanese rule exceeded in brutality even that of the Europeans.

A decisive step in the development of World War II in Asia lay in the Japanese attack on the United States at Pearl Harbor in Hawaii in December 1941. Japanese authorities undertook that attack with reluctance and only after negotiations to end American hostility to Japan's empire-building enterprise proved fruitless and an American oil embargo was imposed on Japan in July 1941. In the face of this hostility, Japan's leaders felt that the alternatives for their country boiled down to either an acceptance of American terms, which they feared would reduce Japan to a second- or third-rank power, or a war with an uncertain outcome. Given those choices, the decision for war was made more with foreboding than with enthusiasm. A leading Japanese admiral made the case for war in this way in late 1941: "The government has decided that if there were no war the fate of the nation is sealed. Even if there is a war, the country may be ruined. Nevertheless a nation that does not fight in this plight has lost its spirit and is doomed."[7]

As a consequence of the attack on Pearl Harbor, the United States entered the war in the Pacific, beginning a long and bloody struggle that ended only with the use of atomic bombs against Hiroshima and Nagasaki in 1945. Since Japan was allied with Germany and Italy, the Pearl Harbor action also joined the Asian theater of the war with the ongoing conflict in Europe into a single global struggle that pitted Germany, Italy, and Japan (the Axis powers) against the United States, Britain, and the Soviet Union (the Allies).

The Road to War in Europe

If Japan was the dissatisfied power in Asia, Nazi Germany occupied that role in Europe. As a consequence of their defeat in World War I and the harsh terms of the Treaty of Versailles, many Germans harbored deep resentments about their country's position in the international arena. Taking advantage of those resentments, the Nazis pledged to rectify the treaty's perceived injustices. Thus, to most historians, the origins of **World War II in Europe** lie squarely in German aggression, although with many twists and turns and encouraged by the initial unwillingness of Britain, France, or the Soviet Union to confront that aggression forcefully. If World War I was accidental and unintended, World War II was deliberate and planned—perhaps even desired—by the German leadership and by Hitler in particular.

Slowly at first and then more aggressively, Hitler rearmed the country for war as he also pursued territorial expansion, annexing Austria and the German-speaking parts of Czechoslovakia. At a famous conference in Munich in that year, the British and the French gave these actions their reluctant blessing, hoping that this "appeasement" of Hitler could satisfy his demands and avoid all-out war. But it did not. On September 1, 1939, Germany unleashed a devastating attack on Poland, triggering the Second World War in Europe, as Britain and France declared war on Germany. Quickly defeating France, the Germans launched a destructive air war against Britain and in 1941 turned their war machine loose on the Soviet Union. By then, most of Europe was under Nazi control (see Map 20.5).

The Second World War was quite different from the first. It was not welcomed with the kind of mass enthusiasm across Europe that had accompanied the opening of World War I in 1914. The bitter experience of the Great War suggested to most people that only suffering lay ahead. The conduct of the two wars likewise differed. The first war had quickly bogged down in trench warfare that emphasized defense, whereas in the second war the German tactic of *blitzkrieg* (lightning war) coordinated the rapid movement of infantry, tanks, and airpower over very large areas.

Such military tactics were initially successful and allowed German forces, aided by their Italian allies, to sweep over Europe, the western Soviet Union, and North Africa. The tide began to turn in 1942 when the Soviet Union absorbed the German onslaught and then began to counterattack, slowly and painfully moving westward toward the German heartland. The United States, with its enormous material and human resources, joined the struggle against Germany in 1942 and led the invasion of northern France in 1944, opening a long-awaited second front in the struggle against Hitler's Germany. Years of bitter fighting ensued before these two huge military movements ensured German defeat in May 1945.

Consequences: The Outcomes of a Second Global Conflict

The Second World War was the most destructive conflict in world history, with total deaths estimated at around 60 million, some six times that of World War I. More than half of those casualties were civilians. Partly responsible for this horrendous toll were the new technologies of warfare—heavy bombers, jet fighters, missiles, and atomic weapons. Equally significant, though, was the almost complete blurring of the traditional line between civilian and military targets, as entire cities and whole populations came to be defined as the enemy. Nowhere was that blurring more complete than in the Soviet Union, which accounted for more than 40 percent of the total deaths in the war—probably around 25 million, with an equal number made homeless and thousands of towns, villages, and industrial enterprises destroyed. In China as well, perhaps 15 million deaths and uncounted refugees grew out of prolonged Chinese resistance and the shattering Japanese response, including the killing of every person and every animal in many villages. Within a few months, during the

MAP 20.5 World War II in Europe and Africa

For a brief moment during World War II, Nazi Germany came close to bringing all of Europe and North Africa under its rule. Then in late 1942, the Allies began a series of counterattacks that led to German surrender in May 1945.

infamous Rape of Nanjing in 1937–1938, some 200,000 to 300,000 Chinese civilians were killed and often mutilated, and countless women were sexually assaulted. Indiscriminate German bombing of British cities and the Allied firebombing of Japanese and German cities likewise reflected the new morality of total war, as did the dropping of atomic bombs on Hiroshima and Nagasaki, which in a single instant vaporized tens of thousands of people. This was total war with a scale, intensity, and indiscriminate brutality that exceeded even the horrors of World War I.

A further dimension of total war lay in governments' efforts to mobilize their economies, their people, and their propaganda machines even more extensively than before. Colonial resources were harnessed once again. The British in particular made extensive use of colonial troops and laborers from India and Africa. Japan compelled several hundred thousand women from Korea, China, and elsewhere to serve the sexual needs of Japanese troops as so-called comfort women, who often accommodated twenty to thirty men a day.

As in World War I, though on a much larger scale, the needs of the war drew huge numbers of women into both industry and the military. In the United States, "Rosie the Riveter" represented those women who now took on heavy industrial jobs, which previously had been reserved for men. In the Soviet Union, women constituted more than half of the industrial workforce by 1945 and almost completely dominated agricultural production. Soviet women also participated actively in combat, with some 100,000 of them winning military honors. A much smaller percentage of German and Japanese women were mobilized for factory work, but a Greater Japan Women's Society enrolled some 19 million members, who did volunteer work and promised to lay aside their gold jewelry and abandon extravagant weddings. As always, war heightened the prestige of masculinity, and given the immense sacrifices that men had made, few women were inclined to directly challenge the practices of patriarchy immediately following the war.

Among the most haunting outcomes of the war was the **Holocaust**. The outbreak of war closed off certain possibilities, such as forced emigration, for implementing the Nazi dream of ridding Germany of its Jewish population. It also brought millions of additional Jews in Poland and the Soviet Union under German control and triggered among Hitler's enthusiastic subordinates various schemes for a "final solution" to the Jewish question. From this emerged the death camps that included Auschwitz, Treblinka, and Sobibór. Altogether, some 6 million Jews perished in a technologically sophisticated form of mass murder that set a new standard for human depravity. Millions more whom the Nazis deemed inferior, undesirable, or dangerous—Russians, Poles, and other Slavs; Gypsies, or the Roma; mentally or physically handicapped people; homosexuals; communists; and Jehovah's Witnesses—likewise perished in Germany's efforts at racial purification.

Although the Holocaust was concentrated in Germany, its significance in twentieth-century world history has been huge. It has haunted postwar Germany in particular and the Western world in general. How could such a thing have occurred in a Europe bearing the legacy of both Christianity and the Enlightenment? More specifically, it sent many of Europe's remaining Jews fleeing to Israel and gave urgency to the establishment of a modern Jewish nation in the ancient Jewish homeland. That action outraged many Arabs, some of whom were displaced by the arrival of the Jews, and has fostered an enduring conflict in the Middle East. Furthermore, the Holocaust defined a new category of crimes against humanity—genocide, the attempted elimination of entire peoples.

On an even larger scale than World War I, this second global conflict rearranged the architecture of world politics. As the war ended, Europe was impoverished, its industrial infrastructure shattered, many of its great cities in ruins, and millions of its people homeless or displaced. Within a few years, this much-weakened Europe was effectively divided, with its western half operating willingly under an American security umbrella and the eastern half subject to Soviet control, but less willingly. It was clear that Europe's dominance in world affairs was finished. Not only had the war weakened both the will and the ability of European powers to hold on to their colonies, but it had also emboldened nationalist and anticolonial movements everywhere (see "Toward Independence in Asia and Africa" in Chapter 21). Japanese victories in Southeast Asia had certainly damaged European prestige. Furthermore, tens of thousands of Africans had fought for the British or the French, had seen white people die, had enjoyed the company of white women, and had returned home with very different ideas about white superiority and the permanence of colonial rule. Colonial subjects everywhere were very much aware that U.S. president Franklin Roosevelt and British prime minister Winston Churchill had solemnly declared in 1941 that "we respect the right of all peoples to choose the form of government under which they will live." Increasingly, Asian and African leaders demanded that such principles should apply to them as well.

The horrors of two world wars within a single generation prompted a renewed interest in international efforts to maintain the peace in a world of competing and sovereign states. The chief outcome was the United Nations (UN), established in 1945 as a successor to the moribund League of Nations. As a political body dependent on agreement among its most powerful members, the UN proved more effective as a forum for international opinion than as a means of resolving the major conflicts of the postwar world, particularly the Soviet/American hostility during the cold war decades. Further evidence for a growing internationalism lay in the creation in late 1945 of the World Bank and International Monetary Fund, whose purpose was to regulate the global economy, prevent another depression, and stimulate economic growth, especially in the poorer nations. What these initiatives shared was the dominant presence of the United States, as the half century following the end of World War II witnessed its emergence as a global superpower. This was among the major outcomes of the Second World War and a chief reason for the remarkable recovery of a badly damaged and discredited Western civilization.

Communist Consolidation and Expansion: The Chinese Revolution

Yet another outcome of World War II lay in the consolidation and extension of the communist world. The Soviet victory over the Nazis, though bought at an unimaginable cost in blood and treasure, gave immense credibility to that communist regime and to its leader, Joseph Stalin. Whatever atrocities he had committed, many in the Soviet Union credited Stalin with leading the country's heroic struggle against Nazi aggression. Furthermore, Stalin also presided over a major expansion of communist control in Eastern Europe, much of which was occupied by Soviet forces as the war ended. He insisted that Soviet security required "friendly" governments in the region to permanently end the threat of invasion from the West. Stalin also feared that large-scale American aid for Europe's economic recovery, which began in 1948, sought to incorporate Eastern Europe into a Western and capitalist economic network. Thus he acted to install fully communist governments, loyal to himself, in Poland, East Germany, Czechoslovakia, Hungary, Romania, and Bulgaria. Backed by the pressure and presence of the Soviet army, **communism in Eastern Europe** was largely imposed from the outside rather than growing out of a domestic revolution, as had happened in Russia itself. The situation in Yugoslavia differed sharply from the rest of Eastern Europe. There a genuinely popular communist movement had played a leading role in the struggle against Nazi occupation and came to power on its own with little Soviet help. Its leader, Josef Broz, known as Tito, openly defied Soviet efforts to control Yugoslav communism, claiming that "our goal is that everyone should be master in his own house."

In Asia too communism took root after World War II. Following Japan's defeat, its Korean colony was partitioned, with the northern half coming under Soviet and therefore communist control. In Vietnam, a much more locally based communist movement, active since the mid-1920s under the leadership of **Ho Chi Minh** (1890–1969), embodied both a socialist vision and Vietnamese nationalism as it battled Japanese, French, and later American invaders and established communist control first in the northern half of the country and after 1975 throughout the whole country. The victory of the Vietnamese communists spilled over into neighboring Laos and Cambodia, where communist parties took power in the mid-1970s.

Far and away the most striking expansion of communism occurred in China, where that country's Communist Party triumphantly seized power in 1949. As in Russia, that victory came on the heels of war and domestic upheaval. But the **Chinese Revolution of 1949**, which was a struggle of decades rather than a single year, was far different from its earlier Russian counterpart. The Chinese imperial system had collapsed in 1911, under the pressure of foreign imperialism, its own inadequacies, and mounting internal opposition (see "The Failure of Conservative Modernization" in Chapter 19). Unlike in Russia, where intellectuals had been discussing socialism for half a century or more before the revolution, the ideas of Karl Marx were barely known in China in the early twentieth century. Not until 1921 was a small Chinese Communist Party (CCP) founded, aimed initially at organizing the country's minuscule urban working class.

Over the next twenty-eight years, that small party, with an initial membership of only sixty people, grew enormously, transformed its strategy, found a charismatic leader in **Mao Zedong** (1893–1976), engaged in an epic struggle with its opponents, fought the Japanese heroically, and in 1949 emerged victorious as the rulers of the world's most populous country. That victory was all the more surprising because the CCP faced a far more formidable foe than the weak Provisional Government over which the Bolsheviks had triumphed in Russia. That opponent was the **Guomindang** (GWOH-mihn-dahng) (Nationalist Party), which governed China after 1928. Led by a military officer, Chiang Kai-shek, that party promoted a measure of modern development (railroads, light industry, banking, airline services) in the decade that followed. However, the impact of these achievements was limited largely to the cities, leaving the rural areas, where most people lived, still impoverished. The Guomindang's base of support was also narrow, deriving from urban elites, rural landlords, and Western powers.

Whereas the Bolsheviks had found their primary audience among workers in Russia's major cities, Chinese communists, in a striking adaptation of European Marxism, increasingly looked to the country's peasant villages for support. But Chinese peasants did not rise up spontaneously against their landlords, as Russian peasants had. Instead, years of guerrilla warfare, experiments with land reform in areas

Mao Zedong and the Long March An early member of China's then-minuscule Communist Party, Mao rose to a position of dominant leadership during the Long March of 1934–1935, when beleaguered communists from southeastern China trekked to a new base area in the north. This photograph shows Mao on his horse during that epic journey. (© Collection J.A. Fox/ Magnum Photos)

under communist control, and the creation of a communist military force to protect liberated areas slowly gained for the CCP a growing measure of respect and support among China's peasants, particularly during the 1930s. In the process, Mao Zedong, the son of a prosperous Chinese peasant family and a professional revolutionary since the early 1920s, emerged as the party's leader. A central event in Mao's rise to prominence was the Long March of 1934–1935, when beleaguered communist forces in southern China made a harrowing but successful retreat to a new base area in the northwest of the country, an epic journey of some 5,600 miles that soon acquired mythical dimensions in communist lore.

To recruit women for the revolution, communists drew on a theoretical commitment to their liberation and in the areas under their control established a Marriage Law that outlawed arranged or "purchased" marriages, made divorce easier, and gave women the right to vote and own property. Women's associations enrolled hundreds of thousands of women and promoted literacy, fostered discussions of women's issues, and encouraged handicraft production such as making clothing, blankets, and shoes, so essential for the revolutionary forces. But resistance to such radical measures from more traditional rural villagers, especially the male peasants and soldiers on whom the communists depended, persuaded the party leaders to modify these measures. Women were not permitted to seek divorce from men on active military duty. Women's land deeds were often given to male family heads and were regarded as family property. Female party members found themselves limited to work with women or children.

It was Japan's brutal invasion of China that gave the CCP a decisive opening, for that attack destroyed Guomindang control over much of the country and forced it to retreat to the interior, where it became even more dependent on conservative landlords. The CCP, by contrast, grew from just 40,000 members in 1937 to more than 1.2 million in 1945, while the communist-led People's Liberation Army mushroomed to 900,000 men, supported by an additional 2 million militia troops.

Much of this growing support derived from the vigor with which the CCP waged war against the Japanese invaders. Using guerrilla warfare techniques learned in the struggle against the Guomindang, communist forces established themselves behind enemy lines and, despite periodic setbacks, offered a measure of security to many Chinese faced with Japanese atrocities. The Guomindang, by contrast, sometimes seemed to be more interested in eliminating the communists than in actively fighting the Japanese. Furthermore, in the areas it controlled, the CCP reduced rents, taxes, and interest payments for peasants; taught literacy to adults; and mobilized women for the struggle. As the war drew to a close, more radical action followed. Teams of activists encouraged poor peasants to "speak bitterness" in public meetings, to "struggle" with landlords, and to "settle accounts" with them.

Thus the CCP frontally addressed both of China's major problems—foreign imperialism and peasant exploitation. It expressed Chinese nationalism as well as a demand for radical social change. It gained a reputation for honesty that contrasted sharply with the massive corruption of Guomindang officials. It put down deep roots among the peasantry in a way that the Bolsheviks never did. And whereas the Bolsheviks gained support by urging Russian withdrawal from the highly unpopular First World War, the CCP won support by aggressively pursuing the struggle against Japanese invaders during World War II. In 1949, four years after the war's end, the Chinese communists swept to victory over the Guomindang, many of whose followers fled to Taiwan. Mao Zedong announced triumphantly that "the Chinese people have stood up."

Reflections: War and Remembrance: Learning from History

When asked about the value of studying history, most students respond with some version of the Spanish-born philosopher George Santayana's famous dictum: "Those who cannot remember the past are condemned to repeat it." At one level, this notion of learning from the "lessons of history" has much to recommend it, for there is, after all, little else except the past on which we can base our actions in the present. And yet historians in general are notably cautious about drawing particular lessons from the past and applying them to present circumstances.

For one thing, the historical record is sufficiently rich and complex to allow many people to draw quite different lessons from it. The world wars of the twentieth century represent a case in point, as writer Adam Gopnik has pointed out:

> The First World War teaches that territorial compromise is better than full-scale war, that an "honor-bound" allegiance of the great powers to small nations is a recipe for mass killing, and that it is crazy to let the blind mechanism of armies and alliances trump common sense. The Second teaches that searching for an accommodation with tyranny by selling out small nations only encourages the tyrant, that refusing to fight now leads to a worse fight later on. . . . The First teaches us never to rush into a fight, the Second never to back down from a bully.[8]

Did the lessons of the First World War lead Americans to ignore the rise of fascism until the country was directly threatened by Japanese attack? Did the lessons of World War II contribute to unnecessary wars in Vietnam and Iraq? There are no easy answers to such questions, for the lessons of history are many, varied, and changing.

Behind any such lesson is the common assumption that history repeats itself. This too is a notion to which historians bring considerable skepticism. They are generally more impressed with the complexity and particularity of major events such as wars rather than with any clear-cut "laws" or patterns of historical development. Thus historians are often reluctant to speculate about the future based on drawing lessons from the past.

That reluctance is also grounded in historians' awareness of the unexpected outcomes of the wars of the past century. Few people in 1914 anticipated the duration and carnage of World War I. The Holocaust was literally unimaginable when Hitler took power in 1933 or even at the outbreak of the Second World War in 1939. Who would have expected an American defeat at the hands of the Vietnamese? And suicide bombings by Islamic radicals have been a novel and unpredictable development in the history of warfare. History repeats itself most certainly only in its unexpectedness.

Second Thoughts

WHAT'S THE SIGNIFICANCE?

World War I (p. 574)
total war (p. 576)
Treaty of Versailles (p. 576)
Russian Revolution (p. 579)
Lenin (p. 579)
Stalin (p. 579)
collectivization of agriculture
   (p. 580)
Great Depression (p. 581)
fascism (p. 584)
Mussolini (p. 585)
Nazi Party (p. 586)

Hitler (p. 586)
Revolutionary Right (Japan) (p. 589)
World War II in Asia (p. 592)
World War II in Europe (p. 594)
Holocaust (p. 596)
communism in Eastern Europe
   (p. 597)
Ho Chi Minh (p. 598)
Chinese Revolution of 1949 (p. 598)
Mao Zedong (p. 598)
Guomindang (p. 598)

BIG PICTURE QUESTIONS

1. What explains the disasters that befell Europe in the first half of the twentieth century?

2. To what extent did the two world wars settle the issues that caused them? What legacies for the future did they leave?

3. In what ways did Europe's internal conflicts between 1914 and 1945 have global implications?

4. In what ways did communism have an impact on world history in the first half of the twentieth century?

5. **Looking Back:** In what ways were the major phenomena of the first half of the twentieth century—world wars, communist revolutions, the Great Depression, fascism, the Holocaust, the emergence of the United States as a global power—rooted in earlier times?

CHRONOLOGY

1910–1920	• Mexican Revolution
1911	• Collapse of Qing dynasty China
1914–1918	• World War I
1917	• U.S. joins World War I
1917	• Russian Revolution
1918–1920	• Collapse of Ottoman Empire
1919	• Treaty of Versailles
1920	• League of Nations established
1921	• Chinese Communist Party established
1922–1943	• Mussolini in power in Italy
1929–1939	• The Great Depression
1929–1953	• Stalin in power in Soviet Union
1933–1943	• New Deal in the U.S.
1933–1945	• Hitler in power in Germany
1936–1940	• Italy, Germany, Japan form Axis alliance
1937–1945	• World War II
1939–1945	• The Holocaust
1945	• UN, World Bank, International Monetary Fund established
1945–1950	• Imposition of communism in Eastern Europe
1945–1950	• Israel, Indonesia, and India establish independence
1945–1950	• Beginnings of cold war
1949	• Chinese Communist Party comes to power

21

Milestones of the Past Century

A Changing Global Landscape

1950–present

"TODAY MARKS EXACTLY TWENTY YEARS SINCE THE DAWN OF freedom and democracy in our country," declared South African president Jacob Zuma on April 27, 2014. "We gained equal citizenship in the land of our birth."[1] It was the twentieth anniversary of the end of apartheid and white domination as well as the election of the highly regarded Nelson Mandela as the country's first African leader. But not everyone was ready to celebrate. The activist Archbishop Desmond Tutu said: "I am glad that

603

[Mandela] is dead. . . . I didn't think there would be disillusionment so soon."[2] He was referring to widespread corruption in official circles and frustration with the slow pace of movement toward overcoming the poverty and inequalities of the apartheid era.

The end of European empires and the arrival of many newly independent nations on the global stage marked a dramatic change in the political landscape of the world in the second half of the twentieth century. So too did the continuing struggles of their people to create stable, unified, and prosperous societies. But this epic transformation intersected with other profound changes during the more than seventy years that followed World War II. A devastated Europe rebuilt its modern economy and moved toward greater union. Communism expanded its reach into Eastern Europe, China, Southeast Asia, and Cuba. A cold war between the United States and the Soviet Union, both of them armed with nuclear weapons of unprecedented destructive power, structured much of international life until the communist experiment largely collapsed at the end of the twentieth century. By the early twenty-first century, China had become a powerful and prominent player in the global arena, while the Middle East emerged as a center of conflict and instability.

These are among the major milestones of world history during the past seven decades. Each of them had roots in the past, and each had a profound impact on many millions of people. Together they transformed the texture of human life all across the planet.

Recovering from the War

The tragedies that afflicted Europe in the first half of the twentieth century—fratricidal war, economic collapse, the Holocaust—were wholly self-inflicted, and yet that civilization had not permanently collapsed. In the twentieth century's second half, Europeans rebuilt their industrial economies and revived their democratic political systems. Three factors help to explain this astonishing recovery. One is the apparent resiliency of an industrial society, once it has been established. The knowledge, skills, and habits of mind that enabled industrial societies to operate effectively remained intact, even if the physical infrastructure had been substantially destroyed. Thus even the most terribly damaged countries—Germany, the Soviet Union, and Japan—had largely recovered by 1960, amid a worldwide economic boom during the 1950s.

A second factor lay in the ability of the major Western European countries to integrate their recovering economies, putting aside some of their prickly nationalism in return for enduring peace and common prosperity. That process took shape during the 1950s, giving rise to the **European Economic Community** (EEC), established in 1957, whose members reduced their tariffs and developed common trade policies. Over the next half century, the EEC expanded its membership to include almost all of Europe, including many former communist states. In 1994, the EEC was renamed the European Union, and in 2002 twelve of its members, later increased to seventeen, adopted a common currency, the euro (see Map 21.1). All of this sustained Europe's remarkable economic recovery and expressed a larger European identity.

Original members of EU

New members, 1973–1986

New members, 1990–2017

Candidates for membership, 2018

ATLANTIC
OCEAN

North
Sea

FINLAND

NORWAY

SWEDEN

ESTONIA

RUSSIAN
FEDERATION

IRELAND

UNITED
KINGDOM

DENMARK

LATVIA

LITHUANIA

RUSS. FED.

BELARUS

2016: British vote to
exit from EU

NETHERLANDS

POLAND

BELGIUM   GERMANY

LUXEMBOURG

CZECH
REP.

UKRAINE

SLOVAKIA

FRANCE

SWITZ.

AUSTRIA

MOLDOVA

HUNGARY

SLOVENIA

CROATIA

ROMANIA

PORTUGAL

BOSNIA-
HERZEGOVINA

SERBIA

Black Sea

SPAIN

ITALY

KOSOVO

MONTENEGRO

MACEDONIA

BULGARIA

ALBANIA

Mediterranean Sea

GREECE

TURKEY

MALTA

CYPRUS

MAP 21.1   The Growth of European Integration

During the second half of the twentieth century, Europeans gradually put aside their bitter rivalries and entered into various forms of economic cooperation with one another, although these efforts fell short of complete political union. This map illustrates the growth of what is now called the European Union (EU).

A third element of European recovery lay in the United States, which emerged after 1945 as the dominant center of Western civilization and a global superpower. An early indication of the United States' intention to exercise global leadership took shape in its effort to rebuild and reshape shattered European economies. Known as the **Marshall Plan**, that effort funneled into Europe some $12 billion (roughly $121 billion in 2017 dollars), together with numerous advisers and technicians. It was motivated by some combination of genuine humanitarian concern, a desire to prevent a new depression by creating overseas customers for American industrial goods, and an interest in undermining the growing appeal of European communist parties.

This economic recovery plan, along with access to American markets, was success-ful beyond all expectations. Between 1948 and the early 1970s, Western European economies grew rapidly, generating a widespread prosperity and improving liv-ing standards. Beyond economic assistance, the American commitment to Europe soon came to include political and military security against the distant possibility of renewed German aggression and the more immediate communist threat from the Soviet Union. Thus was born the military and political alliance known as the North Atlantic Treaty Organization (NATO) in 1949. It committed the United States and its nuclear arsenal to the defense of Europe against the Soviet Union, and it firmly anchored West Germany within the Western alliance. It also allowed West-ern Europe to avoid heavy military expenditures.

A parallel process in Japan, which was under American occupation between 1945 and 1952, likewise revived that country's devastated but already industrial-ized economy. In the two decades following the occupation, Japan's economy grew remarkably, and the nation became an economic giant on the world stage. The dem-ocratic constitution imposed on Japan by American occupation authorities required that "land, sea, and air forces, as well as other war potential, will never be main-tained." This meant that Japan, even more so than Europe, depended on the United States for its military security.

Recovery in the Soviet Union, so terribly damaged by the war, occurred under very different conditions from that of Japan and Western Europe. The last years of Stalin's rule (1945–1953) were extraordinarily harsh, with no tolerance for dissent of any kind. One result was a huge and growing convict labor force of 3 to 4 million people who provided a major source of cheap labor for the recovery effort. Further-more, that program was a wholly state-planned effort that favored heavy industry, agricultural production, and military expenditure at the expense of basic consumer goods, such as shoes and clothing. But Stalin's regime did gain some popular support by substantially lowering the price of bread and other essentials. Finally, the Soviet Union benefited greatly from its seizure of industrial complexes, agricultural goods, raw materials, gold, and European art from Germany, Poland, and elsewhere. Viewed as looting or plunder in the West, this appropriation in Soviet eyes was seen as the "spoils of war" and justified by the massive damage, both human and material, that the Nazi invasion had caused in the USSR. By the mid-1950s, economic recovery was well under way.

Communism Chinese-Style

While Europe, Japan, and the Soviet Union were emerging from the chaos of World War II, China was likewise recovering from decades of civil war and from its devastat-ing struggle against Japanese imperialism. And it was doing so under the direction of the Chinese Communist Party and its leader Mao Zedong. In a longer-term perspec-tive, China's revolution represented the real beginning of that country's emergence from a century of imperialist humiliation and semi-colonial rule, the development of a distinctive Chinese approach to modern development, and its return to a position of prominence on the global stage.

As a communist country, China began its task of "building socialism" in a very different international environment than its Soviet counterpart had experienced. In 1917 Russian Bolsheviks faced a hostile capitalist world alone, while Chinese communists, coming to power over thirty years later, had an established Soviet Union as a friendly northern neighbor and ally. Furthermore, Chinese revolutionaries had actually governed parts of their huge country for decades, gaining experience that the new Soviet rulers had altogether lacked, since they had come to power so quickly. And the Chinese communists were firmly rooted in the rural areas and among the country's vast peasant population, while their Russian counterparts had found their support mainly in the cities.

If these comparisons generally favored China in its efforts to "build socialism," in economic terms that country faced even more daunting prospects than did the Soviet Union. Its population was far greater, its industrial base far smaller, and the availability of new agricultural land far more limited than in the Soviet Union. China's literacy and modern education, as well as its transportation network, were likewise much less developed. Even more than the Soviets, Chinese communists had to build a modern society from the ground up.

Building a Modern Society

Initially China sought to follow the Soviet model of socialist modernization, though with important variations. In sharp contrast to the Soviet experience, the collectivization of agriculture in China during the 1950s was a generally peaceful process, owing much to the close relationship between the Chinese Communist Party and the peasantry that had been established during three decades of struggle. China, however, pushed collectivization even further than the Soviet Union did, particularly in huge "people's communes" during the **Great Leap Forward** in the late 1950s. It was an effort to mobilize China's enormous population for rapid development and at the same time to move toward a more fully communist society with an even greater degree of social equality and collective living.

China's industrialization program was also modeled on the earlier Soviet experience, with an emphasis on large-scale heavy industries, urban-based factories, centralized planning by state and party authorities, and the mobilization of women for the task of development. As in the Soviet Union, impressive economic growth followed, as did substantial migration to the cities and the emergence of a bureaucratic elite of planners, managers, scientists, and engineers (see Snapshot). And both countries favored urban over rural areas and privileged an educated, technically trained elite over workers and peasants. Stalin and his successors largely accepted these inequalities, while Mao certainly did not. Rather, he launched recurrent efforts to combat these perhaps inevitable tendencies of any industrializing process and to revive and preserve the revolutionary spirit that had animated the Communist Party during its long struggle for power.

By the mid-1950s, Mao and some of his followers had become persuaded that the Soviet model of industrialization was leading China away from socialism and toward new forms of inequality, toward individualistic and careerist values, and toward an urban bias that favored the cities at the expense of the countryside. The

The Great Leap Forward This Chinese poster from 1960 celebrates both the agricultural and industrial efforts of the Great Leap Forward. The caption reads: "Start the movement to increase production and practice thrift, with foodstuffs and steel at the center, with great force!" The great famine that accompanied this "great leap" belied the optimistic outlook of the poster. (Stefan R. Landsberger Collections/International Institute of Social History, Amsterdam/www.chineseposters.net)

Great Leap Forward of 1958–1960 marked Mao's first response to these distortions of Chinese socialism. It promoted small-scale industrialization in the rural areas rather than focusing wholly on large enterprises in the cities; it tried to foster widespread and practical technological education for all rather than relying on a small elite of highly trained technical experts; and it envisaged an immediate transition to full communism in the "people's communes" rather than waiting for industrial development to provide the material basis for that transition. The Great Leap, however, generated a national catastrophe and an unprecedented human tragedy that temporarily discredited Mao's radicalism. Administrative chaos, disruption of marketing networks, and bad weather combined to produce a massive famine, the worst in human history according to some scholars, that killed some 30 million people or more between 1959 and 1962, dwarfing the earlier Soviet famine.

Nonetheless, in the mid-1960s, Mao launched yet another campaign — the Great Proletarian **Cultural Revolution** — to combat the capitalist tendencies that he believed had penetrated even the highest ranks of the Communist Party itself. The Cultural Revolution also involved new efforts to bring health care and education to the countryside and to reinvigorate earlier attempts at rural industrialization under

| SNAPSHOT | CHINA UNDER MAO, 1949–1976 |

The following table reveals some of the achievements, limitations, and tragedies of China's communist experience during the era of Mao Zedong.

Steel production	from 1.3 million to 23 million tons
Coal production	from 66 million to 448 million tons
Electric power generation	from 7 million to 133 billion kilowatt-hours
Fertilizer production	from 0.2 million to 28 million tons
Cement production	from 3 million to 49 million tons
Industrial workers	from 3 million to 50 million
Scientists and technicians	from 50,000 to 5 million
"Barefoot doctors" posted to countryside	1 million
Annual growth rate of industrial output	11 percent
Annual growth rate of agricultural output	2.3 percent
Total population	from 542 million to 1 billion
Average population growth rate per year	2 percent
Per capita consumption of rural dwellers	from 62 to 124 yuan annually
Per capita consumption of urban dwellers	from 148 to 324 yuan annually
Overall life expectancy	from 35 to 65 years
Counterrevolutionaries killed (1949–1952)	between 1 million and 3 million
People labeled "rightists" in 1957	550,000
Deaths from famine during Great Leap Forward	30 million to 45 million
Deaths during Cultural Revolution	500,000
Officials sent down to rural labor camps during Cultural Revolution	3 million or more
Urban youth sent down to countryside	17 million (1967–1976)

Such figures are often highly controversial. See Maurice Meisner, *Mao's China and After* (New York: Free Press, 1999), 413–25; and Roderick MacFarquhar, ed., *The Politics of China* (Cambridge: Cambridge University Press, 1997), 243–45.

local rather than central control. In these ways, Mao struggled, though without great success, to overcome the inequalities associated with China's modern development and to create a model of socialist modernity quite distinct from that of the Soviet Union.

Eliminating Enemies

China under Mao, like the Soviet Union under Stalin, found itself caught up in a gigantic search for enemies beginning in the 1950s. In the Soviet Union, that process occurred under the clear control of state authorities. In China, however, it became much more public, escaping the control of the leadership, particularly during the most intense phase of the Cultural Revolution (1966–1969). Convinced that many within the Communist Party had been seduced by capitalist values of self-seeking and materialism, Mao called for rebellion against the Communist Party itself. Millions of young people responded, and, organized as Red Guards, they set out to rid China of those who were "taking the capitalist road." Following gigantic and ecstatic rallies in Beijing, they fanned out across the country and attacked local party and government officials, teachers, intellectuals, factory managers, and others they defined as enemies. Many were "sent down" to the countryside for hard physical labor and to "learn from the peasants." Others were humiliated, beaten, and sometimes killed. Rival revolutionary groups soon began fighting with one another, violence erupted throughout the country, and civil war threatened China. Mao was forced to call in the military to restore order and Communist Party control. Both the Soviet Terror and the Chinese Cultural Revolution badly discredited the very idea of socialism and contributed to the ultimate collapse of the communist experiment at the end of the century.

East versus West: A Global Divide and a Cold War

Not only did communist regimes bring revolutionary changes to the societies they governed, but their very existence launched a global conflict that restructured international life and touched the lives of almost everyone, particularly in the twentieth century's second half. That rift had begun soon after the Russian Revolution when the new communist government became the source of fear and loathing to many in the Western capitalist world. The common threat of Nazi Germany temporarily made unlikely allies of the Soviet Union, Britain, and the United States, but a few years after World War II ended, that division erupted again in what became known as the **cold war**. Underlying that conflict were the geopolitical and ideological realities of the postwar world. The Soviet Union and the United States were now the world's major political and military powers, replacing the shattered and diminished states of Western Europe, but they represented sharply opposed views of history, society, politics, and international relations. In retrospect, conflict seemed almost inevitable, as both sides felt they were riding the tides of historical progress.

Military Conflict and the Cold War

The initial arena of the cold war was Eastern Europe, where Soviet insistence on security and control clashed with American and British desires for open and democratic societies with ties to the capitalist world economy. What resulted were rival military alliances. The **North Atlantic Treaty Organization (NATO)**, created in 1949, brought the United States and various West European countries together to defend themselves against the threat of Soviet aggression. Then in 1955 the **Warsaw Pact** joined the Soviet Union and East European communist countries in an alliance intended to provide a counterweight to NATO and to prevent Western influence in the communist bloc. These alliances created a largely voluntary American sphere of influence in Western Europe and an imposed Soviet sphere in Eastern Europe. The heavily fortified border between Eastern and Western Europe came to be known as the Iron Curtain. Thus Europe was bitterly divided. But although tensions flared across this dividing line, particularly in Berlin, no shooting war occurred between the two sides (see Map 21.2).

By contrast, the extension of communism into Asia — China, Korea, and Vietnam — globalized the cold war and occasioned its most destructive and prolonged "hot wars." A North Korean invasion of South Korea in 1950 led to both Chinese and American involvement in a bitter three-year conflict (1950–1953), which ended in an essential standoff that left the Korean peninsula still divided in the early twenty-first century. Likewise in Vietnam, military efforts by South Vietnamese communists and the already communist North Vietnamese government to unify their country prompted massive American intervention in the 1960s. To American authorities, a communist victory would open the door to further communist expansion in Asia and beyond. Armed and supported by the Soviets and Chinese and willing to endure enormous losses, the Vietnamese communists bested the Americans, who were hobbled by growing protest at home. The Vietnamese united their country under communist control by 1975.

A third major military conflict of the cold war era occurred in Afghanistan, where a Marxist party had taken power in 1978. Soviet leaders were delighted at this extension of communism on their southern border, but radical land reforms and efforts to liberate Afghan women soon alienated much of this conservative Muslim country and led to a mounting opposition movement. Fearing the overthrow of a new communist state and its replacement by Islamic radicals, Soviet forces intervened militarily and were soon bogged down in a war they could not win. For a full decade (1979–1989), that war was a "bleeding wound," sustained in part by U.S. aid to Afghan guerrillas. Under widespread international pressure, Soviet forces finally withdrew in 1989, and the Afghan communist regime soon collapsed. In Vietnam and Afghanistan, both superpowers painfully experienced the limits of their power.

The most haunting battle of the cold war era was one that never happened. The setting was Cuba, where a communist regime under the leadership of Fidel Castro had emerged by the early 1960s. Intense American hostility to this nearby outpost of communism prompted the Soviet leader Nikita Khrushchev (KROOSH-chef), who had risen to power after Stalin's death in 1953, to secretly deploy nuclear-tipped Soviet missiles to Cuba, believing that this would deter further U.S. action against Castro. When the missiles were discovered in October 1962, the world held its breath for thirteen days as American forces blockaded the island and prepared for an invasion. A nuclear exchange between the superpowers seemed imminent, but that catastrophe was averted by a compromise between Khrushchev and U.S. president John F. Kennedy. Under its terms, the Soviets removed their missiles from Cuba in return for an American promise not to invade the island. That promise was kept and a communist regime persisted in Cuba, though much changed, well into the twenty-first century.

Nuclear Standoff and Third-World Rivalry

The **Cuban missile crisis** gave concrete expression to the most novel and dangerous dimension of the cold war — the arms race in nuclear weapons. An initial American monopoly on those weapons prompted the Soviet Union to redouble its efforts to acquire them, and in 1949 it succeeded. Over the next forty years, the world moved

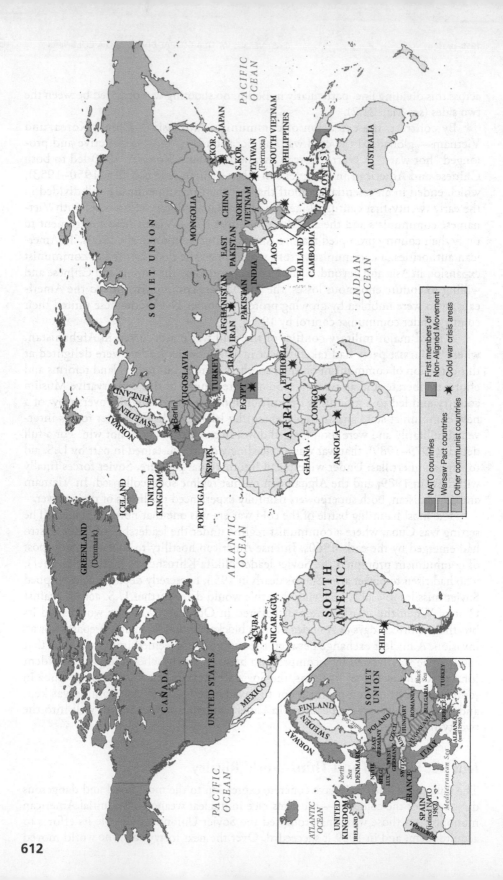

from a mere handful of nuclear weapons to a global arsenal of close to 60,000 warheads. Delivery systems included submarines, bomber aircraft, and missiles that could rapidly propel numerous warheads across whole continents and oceans with accuracies measured in hundreds of feet. During those decades, the entire world lived in the shadow of weapons whose destructive power is scarcely within the bounds of human imagination.

Awareness of this power is surely the primary reason that no shooting war of any kind occurred between the two superpowers, for leaders on both sides knew beyond any doubt that a nuclear war would produce only losers and utter catastrophe. Already in 1949, Stalin had observed that "atomic weapons can hardly be used without spelling the end of the world."[3] Particularly after the frightening Cuban missile crisis of 1962, both sides carefully avoided further nuclear provocation, even while continuing the buildup of their respective arsenals. Moreover, because they feared that a conventional war would escalate to the nuclear level, they implicitly agreed to sidestep any direct military confrontation at all.

Still, opportunities for conflict abounded as the U.S.-Soviet rivalry spanned the globe. Using military and economic aid, educational opportunities, political pressure, and covert action, both sides courted countries emerging from colonial rule. The Soviet Union aided anticolonial and revolutionary movements in many places, including South Africa, Mozambique, Vietnam, and Cuba. Cold war fears of communist penetration prompted U.S. intervention, sometimes openly and often secretly, in Iran, the Philippines, Guatemala, El Salvador, Chile, the Congo, and elsewhere. In the process the United States frequently supported anticommunist but corrupt and authoritarian regimes. However, neither superpower was able to completely dominate its supposed allies, many of whom resisted the role of pawns in superpower rivalries. Some countries, such as India, took a posture of nonalignment in the cold war, while others tried to play off the superpowers against each other. Indonesia received large amounts of Soviet and Eastern European aid, but that did not prevent it from destroying the Indonesian Communist Party in 1965, killing half a million suspected communists in the process. When the Americans refused to assist Egypt in building the Aswan Dam in the mid-1950s, that country developed a close relationship with the Soviet Union. Later, in 1972, Egypt expelled 21,000 Soviet advisers, following disagreements over the extent of Soviet military aid, and again aligned more clearly with the United States.

The Cold War and the Superpowers

World War II and the cold war provided the context for the emergence of the United States as a global superpower. Much of that effort was driven by the perceived demands of the cold war, during which the United States spearheaded the Western

< **MAP 21.2   The Global Cold War**
The cold war witnessed a sharp division between the communist world and the Western democratic world. It also divided the continent of Europe; the countries of China, Korea, Vietnam, and Germany; and the city of Berlin. In many places, it also sparked crises that brought the nuclear-armed superpowers of the United States and the USSR to the brink of war, although in every case they managed to avoid direct military conflict between themselves. Many countries in Africa and Asia claimed membership in a Non-Aligned Movement that sought to avoid entanglements in cold war conflicts.

effort to contain a worldwide communist movement that seemed to be advancing. By 1970, one writer observed, "the United States had more than 1,000,000 soldiers in 30 countries, was a member of four regional defense alliances and an active participant in a fifth, had mutual defense treaties with 42 nations, was a member of 53 international organizations, and was furnishing military or economic aid to nearly 100 nations across the face of the globe."[4] Sustaining this immense international effort was a flourishing U.S. economy and an increasingly middle-class society. The United States was the only major industrial country to escape the physical devastation of war on its own soil. As World War II ended with Europe, the Soviet Union, and Japan in ruins, the United States was clearly the world's most productive economy.

On the communist side, the cold war was accompanied by considerable turmoil within and among the various communist states. In the Soviet Union, the superpower of the communist world, the mid-1950s witnessed devastating revelations of Stalin's many crimes, shocking the communist faithful everywhere. And in Hungary (1956–1957), Czechoslovakia (1968), and Poland (early 1980s), various reform movements registered sharp protest against highly repressive and Soviet-dominated communist governments.

Many in the West had initially viewed world communism as a monolithic force whose disciplined members meekly followed Soviet dictates in cold war solidarity against the West. And Marxists everywhere contended that revolutionary socialism would erode national loyalties as the "workers of the world" united in common opposition to global capitalism. Nonetheless, the communist world experienced far more bitter and divisive conflict than did the Western alliance, which was composed of supposedly warlike, greedy, and highly competitive nations.

In Eastern Europe, Yugoslav leaders early on had rejected Soviet domination of their internal affairs and charted their own independent road to socialism. Fearing that reform might lead to contagious defections from the communist bloc, Soviet forces actually invaded their supposed allies in Hungary and Czechoslovakia to crush such movements, and they threatened to do so in Poland. Such actions gave credibility to Western perceptions of the cold war as a struggle between tyranny and freedom and badly tarnished the image of Soviet communism as a reasonable alternative to capitalism.

Even more startling, the two communist giants, the Soviet Union and China, found themselves sharply opposed, owing to territorial disputes, ideological differences, and rivalry for communist leadership. In 1960, the Soviet Union backed away from an earlier promise to provide China with the prototype of an atomic bomb and abruptly withdrew all Soviet advisers and technicians who had been assisting Chinese development. By the late 1960s, China on its own had developed a modest nuclear capability, and the two countries were at the brink of war, with the Soviet Union hinting at a possible nuclear strike on Chinese military targets. Beyond this central conflict, communist China in fact went to war against communist Vietnam in 1979, even as Vietnam invaded communist Cambodia. Nationalism, in short, proved more powerful than communist solidarity, even in the face of cold war hostilities with the capitalist West.

Despite its many internal conflicts, world communism remained a powerful global presence during the 1970s, achieving its greatest territorial reach. China was emerging from the chaos of the Cultural Revolution, while the Soviet Union had matched U.S. military might. Despite American hostility, Cuba remained a communist outpost in the Western Hemisphere, with impressive achievements in education and health care for its people and a commitment to supporting revolutionary movements in Africa and Latin America. Communism triumphed in Vietnam, dealing a major setback to the United States. A number of African countries also affirmed their commitment to Marxism. Few people anywhere expected that within two decades most of the twentieth century's experiment with communism would be gone.

Toward Freedom: Struggles for Independence

From an American or Soviet perspective, cold war struggles dominated international life from the 1940s through the early 1990s. But viewed from the world of Asia and Africa, a rather different global struggle was unfolding. Its central focus was colonial rule, subordination, poverty, and racism. Variously called the struggle for independence or **decolonization**, that process marked a dramatic change in the world's political architecture, as nation-states triumphed over the empires that had structured much of the world's political life in the nineteenth and early twentieth centuries. It mobilized millions of people, thrusting them into political activity and sometimes into violence and warfare. Decolonization signaled the declining legitimacy of both empire and race as a credible basis for political or social life. It promised not only national freedom but also personal dignity, opportunity, and prosperity.

In 1900, European colonial empires in Africa, Asia, the Caribbean region, and Pacific Oceania appeared as enduring features of the world's political landscape. Well before the end of the twentieth century, they were gone. The first major breakthroughs occurred in Asia and the Middle East in the late 1940s, when the Philippines, India, Pakistan, Burma, Indonesia, Syria, Iraq, Jordan, and Israel achieved independence. The decades from the mid-1950s through the mid-1970s were an age of African independence as colony after colony, more than fifty in total, emerged into what was then seen as the bright light of freedom. During the 1970s, many of the island societies of Pacific Oceania—Samoa, Fiji, Tonga, the Solomon Islands, Kiribati—joined the ranks of independent states, almost entirely peacefully and without much struggle as the various colonial powers willingly abandoned their right to rule. Hawaiians, however, sought incorporation as a state within the United States, rather than independence. Finally, a number of Caribbean societies—the Bahamas, Barbados, Belize, Jamaica, Trinidad, and Tobago—achieved independence during the 1960s and 1970s, informed by a growing awareness of a distinctive Caribbean culture. Cuba, although formally independent since 1902, dramatically declared its rejection of American control in its revolutionary upheaval in 1959. By 1983 the Caribbean region hosted sixteen separate independent states.

The End of Empire in World History

At one level, this vast process was but the latest case of imperial dissolution, a fate that had overtaken earlier empires, including those of the Assyrians, Romans, Arabs, and Mongols. But never before had the end of empire been so associated with the mobilization of the masses around a nationalist ideology. More comparable perhaps was that earlier decolonization in which the European colonies in the Americas

NORTH KOREA 1948 *From Japan*

SOUTH KOREA 1948

JAPAN

PACIFIC OCEAN

PHILIPPINES 1946

PAPUA NEW GUINEA 1975 *From Australia*

EAST TIMOR *From Portugal, 1975; from Indonesia, 2002*

Unified 1975

SOUTH VIETNAM 1954 *From Great Britain*

BRUNEI 1984

INDONESIA 1949

CHINA

NORTH VIETNAM 1954

LAOS 1949

CAMBODIA 1954

MALAYSIA 1963

SINGAPORE 1965

MYANMAR (BURMA) 1948

PAKISTAN 1947 (BANGLADESH 1971)

SRI LANKA (CEYLON) 1948

INDIA 1947

INDIAN OCEAN

MAURITIUS 1968 *From Great Britain*

SOVIET UNION

AFGHANISTAN

PAKISTAN 1947

IRAN

KUWAIT 1961

IRAQ 1932

JORDAN 1946

BAHRAIN 1971

QATAR 1971

UNITED ARAB EMIRATES 1971

YEMEN 1967

P.D.R. YEMEN

SOMALIA 1960

SEYCHELLES 1976

COMOROS 1975

MADAGASCAR 1960

TURKEY

SYRIA 1944

LEBANON 1944

ISRAEL 1948

MALTA 1964

CYPRUS 1960 *From G.B.*

EGYPT 1922

ERITREA 1950 *Federated with Ethiopia*

DJIBOUTI 1977

ETHIOPIA 1941

SUDAN 1956

UGANDA 1962

KENYA 1963

TANZANIA 1964

MALAWI 1964

ZAMBIA 1964

SWAZILAND 1968

LESOTHO 1966

ITALY

LIBYA 1951

CHAD 1960

CENTRAL AFR. REP. 1960

DEMOCRATIC REP. OF CONGO 1960

RWANDA 1962

BURUNDI 1962

ZIMBABWE 1980

MOZAMBIQUE 1974

BOTSWANA 1966

SOUTH AFRICA (Republic 1961; black majority rule, 1994)

ANGOLA 1975

TUNISIA 1957

ALGERIA 1962

MALI 1960

NIGER 1960

NIGERIA 1960

CAMEROON 1960

GABON 1960

REP. OF CONGO 1960

EQUATORIAL GUINEA 1968 *From Spain*

BURKINA FASO 1960

BENIN 1960

TOGO 1960

NAMIBIA 1985 *From South Africa*

SPAIN

PORTUGAL

MOROCCO 1956

WESTERN SAHARA (Morocco) 1975 *From Spain*

MAURITANIA 1960

SENEGAL 1960

GAMBIA 1965

GUINEA-BISSAU 1961 *From Portugal*

GUINEA 1958

SIERRA LEONE 1961

LIBERIA 1820s

IVORY COAST 1960

GHANA 1957

SÃO TOMÉ AND PRINCIPE 1975 *From Portugal*

ATLANTIC OCEAN

1960 Year of independence

Belgium
France
Great Britain
Italy
Netherlands
Portugal
United States
Other

0   500   1,000 miles
0 500 1,000 kilometers

616

had thrown off British, French, Spanish, or Portuguese rule during the late eighteenth and early nineteenth centuries (see "Comparing Atlantic Revolutions" in Chapter 16). Like their earlier counterparts, the new nations of the mid-to-late twentieth century claimed an international status equivalent to that of their former rulers. In the Americas, however, many of the colonized people were themselves of European origin, sharing much of their culture with their colonial rulers. In that respect, the freedom struggles of the twentieth century were very different, for they not only asserted political independence but also affirmed the vitality of their cultures, which had been submerged and denigrated during the colonial era.

The twentieth century witnessed the demise of many empires. The Austrian and Ottoman empires collapsed following World War I, giving rise to a number of new states in Europe and the Middle East. The Russian Empire also unraveled, although it was soon reassembled under the auspices of the Soviet Union. World War II ended the German and Japanese empires. African and Asian movements for independence shared with these other end-of-empire stories the ideal of national self-determination. This novel idea — that humankind was naturally divided into distinct peoples or nations, each of which deserved an independent state of its own — was loudly proclaimed by the winning side of both world wars. It gained a global acceptance, particularly in the colonial world, during the twentieth century and rendered empire illegitimate in the eyes of growing numbers of people.

Empires without territory, such as the powerful influence that the United States exercised in Latin America, likewise came under attack from highly nationalist governments. An intrusive U.S. presence was certainly one factor stimulating the Mexican Revolution, which began in 1910. One of the outcomes of that upheaval was the nationalization in 1937 of Mexico's oil industry, much of which was owned by American and British investors. Similar actions accompanied Cuba's revolution of 1959–1960 and also occurred in other places throughout Latin America and elsewhere. National self-determination and freedom from Soviet control likewise lay behind the Eastern European revolutions of 1989. The disintegration of the Soviet Union itself in 1991 brought to an inglorious end one of the last major territorial empires of the twentieth century and the birth of fifteen new national states. China's Central Asian empire, however, remained intact despite considerable resistance in Tibet and elsewhere. Although the winning of political independence for Europe's African and Asian colonies was perhaps the most spectacular challenge to empire in the twentieth century, that process was part of a larger pattern in modern world history (see Map 21.3).

Toward Independence in Asia and Africa

As the twentieth century closed, the end of European empires seemed in retrospect almost inevitable, for colonial rule had lost any credibility as a form of political order. What could be more natural than for people to seek to rule themselves? Yet at the

< **MAP 21.3 The End of Empire in Africa and Asia**
In the second half of the twentieth century, under pressure from nationalist movements, Europe's Asian and African empires dissolved into dozens of new independent states, dramatically altering the structure of international life.

beginning of the century, few observers were predicting the collapse of these empires, and the idea that "the only legitimate government is national self-government" was not nearly so widespread as it subsequently became. How might historians explain the rapid collapse of European colonial empires and the emergence of a transformed international landscape with dozens of new nation-states?

One approach focuses attention on fundamental contradictions in the entire colonial enterprise. The rhetoric of Christianity, Enlightenment thought, and material progress sat awkwardly with the realities of colonial racism, exploitation, and poverty. The increasingly democratic values of European states ran counter to the essential dictatorship of colonial rule. The ideal of national self-determination was profoundly at odds with the possession of colonies that were denied any opportunity to express their own national character. The enormously powerful force of nationalism, having earlier driven the process of European empire building, now played a major role in its disintegration. From this perspective, colonial rule dug its own grave because its practice ran counter to established European values of democracy and national self-determination.

But why did this "fatal flaw" of European colonial rule lead to independence in the post–World War II decades rather than earlier or later? Here, historians have found useful the notion of "conjuncture": the coming together of several separate developments at a particular time. At the international level, the world wars had weakened Europe while discrediting any sense of European moral superiority. Both the United States and the Soviet Union, the new global superpowers, generally opposed the older European colonial empires, even as they created empire-like international relationships of their own. Meanwhile, the United Nations provided a prestigious platform from which to conduct anticolonial agitation. Within the colonies, the dependence of European rulers on the cooperation of local elites, and increasingly on Western-educated men, rendered those empires vulnerable to the withdrawal of that support. All of this contributed to the global illegitimacy of empire, a novel and stunning transformation of social values that was enormously encouraging to anticolonial movements everywhere.

At the same time, social and economic processes within the colonies themselves generated the human raw material for anticolonial movements. By the early twentieth century in Asia and the mid-twentieth century in Africa, a second or third generation of Western-educated elites, largely male, had arisen throughout the colonial world. These young men were thoroughly familiar with European culture; they were deeply aware of the gap between its values and its practices; they no longer viewed colonial rule as a vehicle for their peoples' progress as their fathers had; and they increasingly insisted on immediate independence. Moreover, growing numbers of ordinary people—women and men alike—were receptive to this message. Veterans of the world wars; young people with some education but few jobs commensurate with their expectations; a small class of urban workers who were increasingly aware of their exploitation; small-scale female traders resentful of European privileges; rural dwellers who had lost land or suffered from forced labor; impoverished and insecure newcomers to the cities—all of these groups had reason to believe that independence held great promise. And as populations grew across the colonial world, the pressure of numbers enhanced these grievances.

Such pressures increasingly placed colonial rulers on the defensive. As the twentieth century wore on, these colonial rulers began to plan—tentatively at first—for

Military Struggles for Independence While many colonies won their independence through peaceful political pressure, others found it necessary to adopt a military strategy. This photograph shows an assembly of Algerian fighters from the National Liberation Front (NLF) in 1960. Established in 1954, the NLF was the major nationalist organization in Algeria that led the country to independence from France in 1962 following a bitter and violent eight-year struggle. (Kharbine-Tapabor/REX/Shutterstock)

a new political relationship with their Asian and African subjects. The colonies had been integrated into a global economic network, and local elites were largely committed to maintaining those links. In these circumstances, Europeans could imagine retaining profitable economic interests in Asia, Africa, and Oceania without the expense and trouble of formal colonial governments. Deliberate planning for decolonization included gradual political reforms; investments in railroads, ports, and telegraph lines; the holding of elections; and the writing of constitutions. To some observers, it seemed as if independence was granted by colonial rulers rather than gained or seized by anticolonial initiatives.

But these reforms, and independence itself, occurred only under considerable pressure from mounting nationalist movements. Creating such movements was no easy task. Leaders, drawn everywhere from the ranks of the educated few and almost always male, organized political parties, recruited members, plotted strategy, developed an ideology, and negotiated with one another and with the colonial state. The most prominent among them became the "fathers" of their new countries as independence dawned—Gandhi and Nehru in India, Sukarno in Indonesia, Ho Chi Minh in Vietnam, Nkrumah in Ghana, and Mandela in South Africa. In places where colonial rule was particularly intransigent—settler-dominated colonies such as Algeria, Kenya, and Rhodesia and Portuguese territories, for example—leaders also directed military operations and administered liberated areas. While such movements drew on memories of earlier, more localized forms of resistance, nationalist leaders did not seek to restore a vanished past. Rather, they looked forward to joining the world of independent nation-states, to membership in the United Nations, and to the wealth and power that modern technology promised.

A further common task of the nationalist leadership involved recruiting a mass following, and to varying degrees, they did. Millions of ordinary men and women joined Gandhi's nonviolent campaigns in India; tens of thousands of freedom fighters waged guerrilla warfare in Algeria, Kenya, Mozambique, and Zimbabwe; in West Africa workers went on strike and market women joined political parties, as did students, farmers, and the unemployed.

But struggles for independence were rarely if ever cohesive movements of uniformly oppressed people. More often, they were fragile alliances representing different classes, ethnic groups, religions, or regions. Beneath the common goal of independence, they struggled with one another over questions of leadership, power, strategy, ideology, and the distribution of material benefits, even as they fought and negotiated with their colonial rulers. Sometimes the relationship between nationalist leaders and their followers was fraught with tension. One such Indonesian leader, educated in Holland, spoke of his difficulty in relating to the common people: "Why am I vexed by the things that fill their lives, and to which they are so attached? Why are the things that contain beauty for them . . . only senseless and displeasing for me? We intellectuals here are much closer to Europe or America than we are to the primitive Islamic culture of Java and Sumatra."[5] In colonial Nigeria, the independence movement took shape as three major political parties, each of them identified primarily with a particular ethnic group, Igbo, Yoruba, or Hausa. Thus the very notion of "national self-government" posed obvious but often contentious questions: What group of people constituted the "nation" that deserved to rule itself? And who should speak for it?

India's independence movement, which found expression in the **Indian National Congress** or Congress Party, provides a compelling example of these divisions and controversies. Its primary leader, **Mohandas Gandhi**, rejected modern industrialization as a goal for his country, while his own chief lieutenant, Jawaharlal Nehru, thoroughly embraced science, technology, and industry as essential to India's future. Nor did everyone accept Gandhi's nonviolent philosophy or his inclusive definition of India as embracing all religions, regions, and castes. Some believed that Gandhi's efforts to improve the position of women or untouchables were a distraction from the chief task of gaining independence. Whether to participate in British-sponsored legislative bodies prior to complete independence also became a divisive issue. Furthermore, a number of smaller parties advocated on behalf of particular regions or castes.

By far the most serious threat to a unified movement derived from the growing divide between the country's Hindu and Muslim populations. As a distinct minority within India, some Muslims feared that their voice could be swamped by numerically dominant Hindus, despite Gandhi's inclusive sensibility. Some Hindu politicians confirmed those fears when they cast the nationalist struggle in Hindu religious terms, hailing their country, for example, as a goddess, Bande Mataram (Mother India). This approach, as well as Hindu efforts to protect cows from slaughter, antagonized Muslims. Their growing skepticism about the possibility of a single Indian

Mahatma Gandhi on the Salt March The most widely recognized and admired figure in the global struggle against colonial rule was Mohandas Gandhi, often known as Mahatma, or "Great Soul." He is shown here with his granddaughter Ava (left) and his personal physician Dr. Sushila Nayar (right). (Bettmann/Getty Images)

state found expression in the **Muslim League**, whose leader, Muhammad Ali Jinnah (JIN-uh), argued that those parts of India that had a Muslim majority should have a separate political status. They called it Pakistan, the land of the pure. In this view, India was not a single nation, as Gandhi had long argued. Jinnah put his case succinctly: "The Muslims and Hindus belong to two different religious philosophies, social customs, and literatures. They neither intermarry nor interdine [eat] together and, indeed, they belong to two different civilizations."[6] With great reluctance and amid mounting violence, Gandhi and the Congress Party finally agreed to partition as the British declared their intention to leave India after World War II.

Thus colonial India became independent in 1947 as two countries—a Muslim Pakistan, itself divided into two wings 1,000 miles apart, and a mostly Hindu India governed by a secular state. Dividing colonial India in this fashion was horrendously painful. A million people or more died in the communal violence that accompanied partition, and some 12 million refugees moved from one country to the other to join their religious compatriots. Gandhi himself, desperately trying to stem the mounting tide of violence, refused to attend the independence celebrations. Only a year after independence, he was assassinated by a Hindu extremist. The great triumph of independence, secured from the powerful British Empire, was overshadowed by the great tragedy of violent partition.

Beyond their internal divisions, nationalist movements seeking independence differed sharply from one another. In some places, that struggle, once begun, produced independence within a few years, four in the case of the Belgian Congo. Elsewhere it was measured in decades. Nationalism had surfaced in Vietnam in the early

1900s, but the country achieved full political independence only in the mid-1970s, having fought French colonial rulers, Japanese invaders during World War II, and U.S. military forces in the 1960s and 1970s, as well as Chinese forces during a brief war in 1979. And the struggle in South Africa was distinctive in many ways. It was not waged against a distant colonial power, but against a white settler minority representing about 20 percent of the population that had already been granted independence from Great Britain in 1910. It took place in a mature industrialized and urbanized nation and in the face of the world's most rigid and racially repressive regime, known as apartheid. These factors help to explain why South Africa gained its "independence" from colonial oppression only in 1994.

Tactics too varied considerably. In many places, such as West Africa, nationalists relied on peaceful political pressure—demonstrations, strikes, mass mobilization, and negotiations—to achieve independence. Elsewhere armed struggle was required. Eight years of bitter guerrilla warfare preceded Algerian independence from France in 1962.

While all nationalist movements sought political independence for modern states, their ideologies and outlooks also differed. Many in India and the Islamic world viewed their new nations through the prism of religion, while elsewhere more secular outlooks prevailed. In Indonesia an early nationalist organization, the Islamic Union, appealed on the basis of religion, while later groups espoused Marxism. Indonesia's primary nationalist leader, Sukarno, sought to embrace and reconcile these various outlooks. "What is Sukarno?" he asked. "A nationalist? An Islamist? A Marxist? . . . Sukarno is a mixture of all these isms."[7] Nationalist movements led by communist parties, such as those in Vietnam and China, sought major social transformations as well as freedom from foreign rule, while those in most of Africa focused on ending racial discrimination and achieving political independence with little concern about emerging patterns of domestic class inequality.

However it was achieved, the collapse of colonial rule and the emergence of these new nations onto the world stage as independent and assertive actors have been distinguishing features of world history in this most recent century.

After Freedom

Having achieved the long-sought status of independent nation-states, how would those states be governed? And how would they undertake the tasks of nation building and modern development? Those were the questions that confronted both the former colonies and those already independent, such as China, Thailand, Ethiopia, Iran, Turkey, and Central and South America. Together they formed the bloc of nations known variously as the third world, the developing countries, or the Global South.

All across the developing world, efforts to create a new political order had to contend with a set of common conditions. Populations were exploding, and expectations for independence ran very high, often exceeding the available resources. Many developing countries were culturally very diverse, with little loyalty to a central state. Nonetheless, public employment mushroomed as the state assumed greater responsibility for economic development. In conditions of widespread poverty and weak private economies, groups and individuals sought to capture the state, or parts of it, both for the salaries and status it offered and for the opportunities for private enrichment that public office provided.

This was the formidable setting in which developing countries had to hammer out new political systems. The range of that effort was immense: Communist Party control in China, Vietnam, and Cuba; multiparty democracy in India and South Africa; one-party democracy in Mexico, Tanzania, and Senegal; military regimes for a time in much of Latin America, Africa, and the Middle East; personal dictatorships in Iraq, Uganda, and the Philippines. In many places, one kind of political system followed another in kaleidoscopic succession.

As colonial rule drew to a close, European authorities in many places attempted to transplant democratic institutions to colonies they had long governed with such a heavy and authoritarian hand. They established legislatures, permitted elections, allowed political parties to operate, and in general anticipated the development of constitutional, parliamentary, multiparty democracies similar to their own.

It was in India that such a political system established its deepest roots. There Western-style democracy, including regular elections, multiple parties, civil liberties, and peaceful changes in government, has been practiced almost continuously since independence. Elsewhere in the colonial world, democracy proved a far more fragile transplant. Among the new states of Africa, for example, few retained their democratic institutions beyond the initial post-independence decade. Many of the apparently popular political parties that had led the struggle for independence lost mass support and were swept away by military coups. When the army took power in Ghana in 1966, no one lifted a finger to defend the party that had led the country to independence only nine years earlier. Other states evolved into one-party systems, and still others degenerated into corrupt personal tyrannies or "Big Man" dictatorships. Freedom from colonial rule certainly did not automatically generate the internal political freedoms associated with democracy.

Across much of Africa, economic disappointments, class resentments, and ethnic conflicts provided the context for numerous military takeovers. By the early 1980s, the military had intervened in at least thirty of Africa's forty-six independent states and actively governed more than half of them. Army officers swept aside the old political parties and constitutions and vowed to begin anew, while promising to return power to civilians and restore democracy at some point in the future.

A similar wave of military interventions swept over Latin America during the 1960s and 1970s, leaving Brazil, Argentina, Peru, Chile, Uruguay, Bolivia, the Dominican Republic, and other countries governed at times by their military officers. However, the circumstances in Latin America were quite different from those in Africa. While military rule was something new and unexpected in Africa, Latin American armed forces had long intervened in political life. The region had also largely escaped the bitter ethnic conflicts that afflicted so many African states, though its class antagonisms were more clearly defined and expressed. Furthermore, Latin American societies in general were far more modernized and urbanized than those of Africa. And while newly independent African states remained linked to their former European rulers, long-independent Latin American states lived in the shadow of a dominant United States. "Poor Mexico," bemoaned Porfirio Díaz, that country's dictator before the Mexican Revolution, "so far from God and so close to the United States."

The late twentieth century witnessed a remarkable political reversal, a **globalization of democracy**, that brought popular movements, multiparty elections, and new constitutions to many countries all around the world. This included the end of military and autocratic rule in Spain, Portugal, and Greece as well as the stunning rise of democratic movements, parties, and institutions amid the collapse of communism in the Soviet Union and Eastern Europe. But the most extensive expression of this global reemergence of democracy lay in the developing countries. By 2000, almost all Latin American countries had abandoned their military-controlled regimes and returned to some form of democratic governance. So too did most African states previously ruled by soldiers, dictators, or single parties. In Asia, authoritarian regimes, some long established, gave way to more pluralistic and participatory political systems in South Korea, Taiwan, Thailand, the Philippines, Iraq, and Indonesia. And in 2011, mass movements in various Arab countries—Tunisia, Egypt, Libya, Syria, Bahrain, Yemen—challenged or ended the hold of entrenched, corrupt, and autocratic rulers, while proclaiming their commitment to democracy, human dignity, and honest government. What might explain this global pattern and its expression in the Global South in particular?

One factor surely was the untethering of the ideas of democracy and human rights from their Western origins. By the final quarter of the twentieth century, democracy increasingly was viewed as a universal political principle to which all could aspire rather than an alien and imposed system deriving from the West. Democracy, like communism, feminism, modern science, and Christianity, was a Western import that took root in a globalizing world and partly lost its association with the West. It was therefore increasingly available as a vehicle for social protest in the rest of the world.

Perhaps the most important internal factor favoring a revival of democracy lay in the apparent failure of authoritarian governments to remedy disastrous economic situations, to raise standards of living, to provide jobs for the young, and to curb pervasive corruption. The oppressive and sometimes brutal behavior of repressive governments humiliated and outraged many. Furthermore, the growth of civil society with its numerous voluntary groups provided a social foundation, independent of the state, for demanding change. Disaffected students, professionals, urban workers, religious organizations, women's groups, and more joined in a variety of grassroots movements, some of them mobilized through social media, to insist on democratic change as a means to a better life. Such movements found encouragement in the demands for democracy that accompanied the South African struggle against apartheid and the collapse of Soviet and Eastern European communism. And the end of the cold war reduced the willingness of the major industrial powers to underwrite their authoritarian client states.

But the consolidation of democratic practice was an uncertain and highly variable process. Some elected leaders, such as Hugo Chávez in Venezuela, Vladimir Putin in Russia, and Recip Erdogan in Turkey, turned authoritarian once in office. Even where parliaments existed, they were often quite circumscribed in their powers. Outright electoral fraud tainted democratic institutions in many places, while established elites and oligarchies found it possible to exercise considerable influence even in formal democracies, and not only in the Global South. Chinese authorities brutally crushed a democratic movement in 1989. The Algerian military sponsored elections in 1992 and then abruptly canceled them when an Islamic party seemed poised to win. And the political future of the Arab Spring remained highly uncertain, as a military strongman became a civilian politician and returned to power in Egypt in 2014 and Syria degenerated into brutal civil war. Nonetheless, this worldwide revival of democracy represented the globalization of what had been a Western idea and the continuation of the political experiments that had begun with independence.

The End of the Communist Era

As the emergence of dozens of "new nations" from colonial rule reshaped the international political landscape during the second half of the twentieth century, so too did the demise of world communism during the last quarter of that century. It effectively ended the cold war, diminished the threat of a nuclear holocaust, and marked the birth of another twenty or so new nation-states.

Surprisingly enough, the communist era came to an end far more peacefully than it had begun. That ending might be viewed as a drama in three acts. Act One began in China during the late 1970s, following the death of its towering revolutionary leader **Mao Zedong** in 1976. Over the next several decades, the CCP gradually abandoned almost everything that had been associated with Maoist communism, even as the party retained its political control of the country. Act Two took place in Eastern Europe in the "miracle year" of 1989, when popular movements toppled despised communist governments one after another all across the region. The climactic act in this "end of communism" drama occurred in 1991 in the Soviet Union, where the entire "play" had opened seventy-four years earlier. There the reformist leader Mikhail Gorbachev (GORE-beh-CHOF) had come to power in 1985 intending to revive and save Soviet socialism from its accumulated dysfunctions. Those efforts, however, only exacerbated the country's many difficulties and led to the political disintegration of the Soviet Union on Christmas Day 1991. The curtain had fallen on the communist era.

Behind these separate stories lay two general failures of the communist experiment, measured both by communists' own standards and by those of the larger world. The first was economic. Despite their early successes, communist economies by the late 1970s showed no signs of catching up to the more advanced capitalist countries. The highly regimented Soviet economy in particular was largely stagnant; its citizens were forced to stand in long lines for consumer goods and complained endlessly about their poor quality and declining availability. This was enormously embarrassing, for it had been the proud boast of communist leaders everywhere that they had found a better route to modern prosperity than their capitalist rivals. Furthermore, these unflattering comparisons were increasingly well known, thanks to the global information revolution. They had political and national security implications as well, for economic growth, even more than military capacity, was increasingly the measure of state power and widely expected among the general population as consumerism took hold around the world. The second failure was moral. The horrors of Stalin's Terror and the gulag, of Mao's Cultural Revolution, of something approaching genocide in communist Cambodia—all of this wore away at communist claims to moral superiority over capitalism. Moreover, this erosion occurred as global political culture more widely embraced democracy and human rights as the universal legacy of humankind, rather than the exclusive possession of the capitalist West. In both economic and moral terms, the communist path to the modern world was increasingly seen as a road to nowhere.

Communist leaders were not ignorant of these problems, and particularly in China and the Soviet Union, they moved aggressively to address them. But their approach to doing so varied greatly, as did the outcomes of those efforts. Thus, much as the Russian and Chinese revolutions differed and their approaches to building socialism diverged, so too did these communist giants chart distinct paths during the final years of the communist experiment.

Beyond Mao in China

In China the reform process took shape under the leadership of **Deng Xiaoping** (dung shee-yao-ping), who emerged as China's "paramount leader" in 1976, following the death of Mao Zedong. Particularly dramatic were Deng's dismantling of the country's system of collectivized farming and a return to something close to small-scale private agriculture. Impoverished Chinese peasants eagerly embraced these new opportunities and pushed them even further than the government had intended. Industrial reform proceeded more gradually. Managers of state enterprises were given greater authority and encouraged to act like private owners, making many of their own decisions and seeking profits. China opened itself to the world economy and welcomed foreign investment in "special enterprise zones" along the coast, where foreign capitalists received tax breaks and other inducements. Local governments and private entrepreneurs joined forces in thousands of flourishing "township and village enterprises" that produced food, clothing, building materials, and much more.

The outcome of these reforms was stunning economic growth and a new prosperity for millions. Better diets, lower mortality rates, declining poverty, massive urban construction, and surging exports—all of this accompanied China's state-directed rejoining of the world economy and contributed to a much-improved material life for millions of its citizens. China was the rising economic giant of the twenty-first century. That economic success provided the foundation for China's emergence as one of the Great Powers of the new century, able to challenge American dominance in eastern Asia and the Pacific.

On the other hand, the country's burgeoning economy also generated massive corruption among Chinese officials, sharp inequalities between the coast and the interior, a huge problem of urban overcrowding, terrible pollution in major cities, and periodic inflation as the state loosened its controls over the economy. Urban vices such as street crime, prostitution, gambling, drug addiction, and a criminal underworld, which had been largely eliminated after 1949, surfaced again in China's booming cities. Nonetheless, something remarkable had occurred in China: a largely capitalist economy had been restored, and by none other than the Communist Party itself. Mao's worst fears had been realized, as China "took the capitalist road."

Although the party was willing to abandon many communist economic policies, it was adamantly unwilling to relinquish its political monopoly or to promote democracy at the national level. "Talk about democracy in the abstract," Deng Xiaoping declared, "will inevitably lead to the unchecked spread of ultra-democracy and anarchism, to the complete disruption of political stability, and to the total failure of our modernization program. . . . China will once again be plunged into chaos, division, retrogression, and darkness."[8] Such attitudes associated democracy with the chaos and uncontrolled mass action of the Cultural Revolution. Thus, when a democracy movement spearheaded by university and secondary school students surfaced in the late 1980s, Deng ordered the brutal crushing of its brazen demonstration in Beijing's Tiananmen Square before the television cameras of the world.

The Collapse of the Soviet Union

A parallel reform process unfolded quite differently in the USSR under the leadership of **Mikhail Gorbachev**, beginning in the mid-1980s. Like Deng Xiaoping in China, Gorbachev was committed to aggressively tackling the country's many problems—economic stagnation, a flourishing black market, public apathy, and cynicism about the party. His economic program, launched in 1987 and known as *perestroika* (per-uh-STROI-kuh) (restructuring), paralleled aspects of the Chinese approach by freeing state enterprises from the heavy hand of government regulation, permitting small-scale private businesses called cooperatives, offering opportunities for private farming, and cautiously welcoming foreign investment in joint enterprises.

But in cultural and political affairs, Gorbachev moved far beyond Chinese reforms. His policy of *glasnost* (GLAHS-nohst) (openness) now permitted an unprecedented range of cultural and intellectual freedoms. In the late 1980s, glasnost hit the Soviet Union like a bomb. Newspapers and TV exposed social pathologies—crime, prostitution, child abuse, suicide, elite corruption, and homelessness—that previously had been presented solely as the product of capitalism. "Like an excited boy reads a note from his girl," wrote one poet, "that's how we read the papers today."[9] Plays, poems, films, and novels that had long been buried "in the drawer" were now released to a public that virtually devoured them. Films broke the ban on nudity and explicit sex. Soviet history was also reexamined as revelations of Stalin's crimes poured out of the media. The Bible and the Quran became more widely available, atheistic propaganda largely ceased, and thousands of churches and mosques were returned to believers and opened for worship. And beyond glasnost lay democratization and a new parliament with real powers, chosen in competitive elections. When those elections occurred in 1989, dozens of leading communists were rejected at the polls. In foreign affairs, Gorbachev moved to end the cold war by making unilateral cuts in Soviet military forces, engaging in arms control negotiations with the United States, and refusing to intervene as communist governments in Eastern Europe were overthrown.

But almost nothing worked out as Gorbachev had anticipated. Far from strengthening socialism and reviving a stagnant Soviet Union, the reforms led to its further weakening and collapse. In a dramatic contrast with China's booming economy, the Soviet Union spun into a sharp decline as its planned economy was dismantled before a functioning market-based system could emerge. Inflation mounted; consumer goods were in short supply, and ration coupons reappeared; many feared the loss of their jobs. Unlike Chinese peasants, few Soviet farmers were willing to risk the jump into private farming, and few foreign investors found the Soviet Union a tempting place to do business.

Furthermore, the new freedoms provoked demands that went far beyond what Gorbachev had intended. A democracy movement of unofficial groups and parties now sprang to life, many of them seeking a full multiparty democracy and a market-based economy. They were joined by independent labor unions, which actually went on strike, something unheard of in the "workers' state." Most corrosively, a multitude of nationalist movements used the new freedoms to insist on greater autonomy, or even independence, from the Soviet Union. In the face of these mounting demands, Gorbachev resolutely refused to use force to crush the protesters, another sharp contrast with the Chinese experience.

Events in Eastern Europe intersected with those in the Soviet Union. Gorbachev's reforms had lit a fuse in these Soviet satellites, where communism had been imposed and maintained from outside. If the USSR could practice glasnost and hold competitive elections, why not Eastern Europe as well? This was the background for the "miracle year" of 1989. Massive demonstrations, last-minute efforts at reforms, the breaching of the Berlin Wall, the surfacing of new political groups—all of this and more overwhelmed the highly unpopular communist regimes of Poland, Hungary, East Germany, Bulgaria, Czechoslovakia, and Romania, which were quickly swept away. This success then emboldened nationalists and democrats in the Soviet Union. If communism had been overthrown in Eastern Europe, perhaps it could be overthrown in the USSR as well. Soviet conservatives and patriots, however, were outraged. To them, Gorbachev had stood idly by while the political gains of World War II, for which the Soviet Union had paid in rivers of blood, vanished before their eyes. It was nothing less than treason.

A brief and unsuccessful attempt to restore the old order through a military coup in August 1991 triggered the end of the Soviet Union and its communist regime. From the wreckage there emerged fifteen new and independent states, following the internal political divisions of the USSR. Arguably the Soviet Union had collapsed less because of its multiple problems and more from the unexpected consequences of Gorbachev's efforts to address them. The Soviet collapse represented a unique phenomenon in the world of the late twentieth century. Simultaneously, the world's largest state and its last territorial empire vanished; the world's first Communist Party disintegrated; a powerful command economy broke down; an official socialist ideology was repudiated; and a forty-five-year global struggle between the East and the West ended, at least temporarily. In Europe, Germany was reunited, and a number of former communist states joined NATO and the European Union, ending the division of the continent. At least for the moment, capitalism and democracy seemed to triumph over socialism and authoritarian governments. In many places, the end of communism allowed simmering ethnic tensions to explode into open conflict. Beyond the disintegration of the Soviet Union, both Yugoslavia and Czechoslovakia fragmented. Chechens in Russia, Abkhazians in Georgia, Russians in the Baltic states and Ukraine, Tibetans and Uighurs in China—all of these minorities found themselves in opposition to the states in which they lived.

After Communism

As the twenty-first century dawned, the communist world had shrunk considerably from its high point just three decades earlier. In the Soviet Union and Eastern

Breaching the Berlin Wall In November 1989, anticommunist protesters broke through the Berlin Wall dividing the eastern and western sections of the city, even as East Berlin citizens joyfully entered their city's western zone. That event has become an iconic symbol of the collapse of communism in Eastern Europe and heralded the reunification of Germany and the end of the cold war, which had divided Europe since the late 1940s. (Tom Stoddart/Reportage via Getty Images)

Europe, communism had disappeared entirely as the governing authority and dominant ideology. In the immediate aftermath of the Soviet collapse, Russia experienced a sharply contracting economy, widespread poverty and inequality, and declining life expectancy. Not until 2006 did its economy recover to the level of 1991. China had largely abandoned its communist economic policies as a market economy took shape, spurring remarkable economic growth. Like China, Vietnam and Laos remained officially communist, even while they pursued Chinese-style reforms, though more cautiously. Even Cuba, which was beset by economic crisis in the 1990s after massive Soviet subsidies ended, allowed small businesses, private food markets, and tourism to grow, while harshly suppressing opposition political groups. Cubans were increasingly engaged in private enterprise, able to buy and sell cars and houses, and enthusiastically embracing mobile phones and computers. In 2015 diplomatic relations with the United States were restored after more than a half century of hostility between the two countries. An impoverished and highly nationalistic North Korea, armed with nuclear weapons, remained the most unreformed and repressive of the remaining communist countries. But either as a primary source of international conflict or as a compelling path to modernity and social justice, communism was effectively dead. The brief communist era in world history had ended.

The end of the cold war and the thorough discrediting of communism, however, did not usher in any extended period of international tranquility as many had hoped, for the rivalries of the Great Powers had certainly not ended. As the bipolar world of the cold war faded away, the United States emerged as the world's sole superpower, but Russia and China alike continued to challenge American dominance in world affairs. Russian president Vladimir Putin deeply resented the loss of his country's international stature after the breakup of the Soviet Union and what he regarded as U.S. efforts to intrude upon Russia's legitimate interests. Issues such as the eastward expansion of NATO, Russia's intervention in the Ukraine and its outright annexation of the Crimea, rival involvements in Syria's civil war, and Russian meddling in American elections had brought the relationship of Russia and the United States by 2016 to something resembling cold war era hostility, though without the sharp ideological antagonism of that earlier conflict. And the rising economic and military power of China generated many tensions in its relationship with the United States and Japan as China sought to assert its interests and influence in East Asia, the South China Sea, and the global economic arena.

Beyond the antagonisms among the major world powers, the Middle East emerged as a vortex of instability and conflict that echoed widely across the world. The struggles between the new Jewish state of Israel, granted independence in 1948, and the adjacent Palestinian Muslim territories generated periodic wars and upheavals that have persisted into the post–cold war era. Both near neighbors, such as Syria, Jordan, Turkey, and Egypt, as well as distant powers, such as the United States and Russia, have been drawn into the **Israeli-Palestinian Conflict** on both sides. The **Iranian revolution** of 1979 established a radically Islamist government in that ancient land, helped to trigger a long and bloody war with neighboring Iraq during the 1980s, posed a serious threat to Israel, and launched a continuing rivalry with Saudi Arabia for dominant influence in the region. Iran's alleged efforts to acquire nuclear weapons capability generated widespread efforts to forestall that possibility, which came to fruition in a contentiously negotiated international agreement in 2015.

But the most globally unsettling and novel aspect of post–cold war international life has been the proliferation of "terrorist" attacks undertaken by radical Islamist groups such as the Taliban, al-Qaeda, Boko Haram, and the Islamic State or by individuals inspired by their message. (See "Religion and Global Modernity" in Chapter 23.) The random character of these attacks, their unpredictability, and their targeting of civilians have generated immense fear and insecurity in many places. In terms of their international consequences, the most significant of these attacks was that launched against several U.S. targets, including the World Trade Center, in September of 2001, for that event prompted large-scale U.S. military intervention and prolonged wars in both Afghanistan and Iraq. In both places old regimes were replaced by new ones amid enormous and continuing conflict and carnage. But the United States has certainly not been the sole target of terrorist violence. Many European and Russian cities have experienced such attacks in the twenty-first century, and terrorism has claimed far more victims in the Islamic world itself, as Islamic radicals have sought to oust what they view as corrupt and un-Islamic governments. Thus terrorism and the so-called war on terrorism have become a global issue in the post–cold war era.

A final source of international tension deriving from the Middle East has been the flood of refugees from war-torn and economically desperate societies in the region and adjacent African states, many of them headed for Europe. The **Syrian civil war**, beginning in 2011, had by itself generated over 12 million refugees by mid-2016, with about 1 million seeking asylum in Europe, almost 5 million relocated to Turkey and other neighboring countries, and another 6.5 million displaced within Syria. That conflict became thoroughly internationalized as Russia, the United States, and various Muslim governments and radical groups took sides. It also sharpened the regional rivalry between Iran and Saudi Arabia, which contained both an ethnic Persian/Arab dimension and a religious Shia/Sunni element.

Beyond the Middle East, conflicts between India and Pakistan, between North Korea and its various neighbors, and between China and Taiwan continued to roil the waters of international life. That all of these countries except Taiwan possessed nuclear weapons compounded the potential dangers of these conflicts. Furthermore, the East-West struggles of the cold war era gave way to tension between the wealthy countries of the Global North and the developing countries of the Global South, led by such emerging powers as India, Indonesia, Brazil, Mexico, and South Africa. And any number of civil wars or ethnically based separatist movements took shape in Yugoslavia, Rwanda, Russia, Ukraine, Myanmar (Burma), Iraq, Somalia, Afghanistan, and Libya, among other places.

The pattern of global military spending in the postcommunist era reflected all of these continuing or emerging tensions in international life. After a brief drop during the 1990s, global military spending rose during the early twenty-first century to exceed cold war levels by 2010. The United States led this global pattern, with sharp spending increases after the attacks of 2001, as the "war on terror" took hold. Although the United States accounted for roughly 35 to 40 percent of this spending in the twenty-first century, China has steadily increased its military budget during this time and is now second only to the United States in expenditures for war. Clearly, no prolonged period of international stability and no lasting "peace dividend" accompanied the passing of the cold war into history.

Reflections: To Judge or Not to Judge

Should historians or students of history make moral judgments about the people and events they study? On the one hand, some would argue, scholars do well to act as detached and objective observers of the human experience. The task is to describe what happened and to explain why things turned out as they did. Whether we approve or condemn the outcomes of the historical process is, in this view, beside the point. On the other hand, all of us, scholars and students alike, stand somewhere. We are members of particular cultures; we have values and outlooks on the world that inevitably affect the way we think about the past. Perhaps it is better to recognize and acknowledge these realities than to pretend to some unattainable objectivity that places us above it all. Furthermore, making judgments is a way of caring about the past, of affirming our continuing relationship with those who have gone before us.

The question of making judgments informs historical analysis of everything from the Agricultural Revolution of 12,000 years ago to the events and processes of the past century. Consider as an example the communist phenomenon. In a United States lacking a major socialist tradition, sometimes saying anything positive about communism or even noting its appeal to millions of people has brought charges of whitewashing its crimes. Within the communist world, even modest criticism was usually regarded as counterrevolutionary and was largely forbidden and harshly punished. Certainly few observers were neutral in their assessment of the communist experiment.

Were the Russian and Chinese revolutions a blow for human freedom and a cry for justice on the part of oppressed people, or did they simply replace one tyranny with another? Was Stalinism a successful effort to industrialize a backward country or a ferocious assault on its moral and social fabric? Did Chinese reforms of the late twentieth century represent a return to sensible policies of modernization, a continued denial of basic democratic rights, or an opening to capitalist inequalities, corruption, and acquisitiveness? Passionate debate continues on all of these questions.

Communism, like many human projects, has been an ambiguous enterprise. On the one hand, communism brought hope to millions by addressing the manifest injustices of the past; by providing new opportunities for women, workers, and peasants; by promoting rapid industrial development; and by ending Western domination. On the other hand, communism was responsible for mountains of crimes — millions killed and wrongly imprisoned; massive famines partly caused by radical policies; human rights violated on an enormous scale; lives uprooted and distorted by efforts to achieve the impossible.

Studying communism challenges our inclination to want definitive answers and clear moral judgments. Can we hold contradictory elements in some kind of tension? Can we affirm our own values while acknowledging the ambiguities of life, both past and present? Doing so is arguably among the essential tasks of growing up and achieving a measure of intellectual maturity. In that undertaking, history can be helpful.

Second Thoughts

WHAT'S THE SIGNIFICANCE?

European Economic Community (p. 604)
Marshall Plan (p. 605)
Great Leap Forward (p. 607)
Cultural Revolution (p. 608)
cold war (p. 610)
North Atlantic Treaty Organization(NATO) (p. 610)
Warsaw Pact (p. 610)
Cuban missile crisis (p. 611)
decolonization (p. 615)

Indian National Congress (p. 620)
Mohandas Gandhi (p. 620)
Muslim League (p. 621)
globalization of democracy (p. 623)
Mao Zedong (p. 625)
Deng Xiaoping (p. 626)
Mikhail Gorbachev (p. 627)
Israeli-Palestinian Conflict (p. 630)
Iranian revolution (p. 630)
Syrian civil war (p. 630)

BIG PICTURE QUESTIONS

1. What was the global significance of the cold war?

2. How would you compare the historical experiences of India and China since World War II?

3. In what ways did the struggle for independence shape the agenda of developing countries in the second half of the twentieth century?

4. "The end of communism was as revolutionary as its beginning." Do you agree with this statement?

5. Looking Back: To what extent did the struggle for independence and the postcolonial experience of African and Asian peoples in the twentieth century parallel or diverge from that of the earlier "new nations" in the Americas in the eighteenth and nineteenth centuries?

CHRONOLOGY

1947	• Independence of India
1948–1952	• Marshall Plan for European recovery
1949–1955	• Formation of NATO and Warsaw Pact as rival military alliances
1949–1976	• Mao Zedong rules China
1950–1953	• Korean War
1955–1975	• Vietnam War
1957	• European Economic Community established
1957	• Independence of Ghana
1959	• Cuban Revolution
1959–1990	• Military governments in Africa and Latin America
1962	• Cuban missile crisis
1978–1989	• Deng Xiaoping reforms in China
1979	• Iranian revolution
1979–1989	• Soviet war in Afghanistan
1987	• Gorbachev reforms begin in Soviet Union
1989	• Collapse of Eastern European communism
1990	• German reunification

1991	• End of cold war
1991	• Collapse of Soviet Union
1994	• EU established
1994	• End of apartheid in South Africa
2011	• Beginning of Syrian civil war
2016	• British vote to exit from EU

22

Global Processes
Technology, Economy, and Society

1900–present

THE LIVES OF THREE YOUNG INDONESIANS IN THE EARLY TWENTY-FIRST century reflect the changing conditions of a globalized world. The first, Memey, was a young uneducated widow from Java who was caught up in sex work in neighboring Malaysia in a desperate effort to support her young child.[1] The second, Samysuddin, was a fisherman who found his livelihood threatened as coral reefs degraded in the face of global warming and fish became scarce.[2] The third was M. Arie Kurniawan, a twenty-one-year-old engineer who won first place and a $7,000 prize in an international technology competition sponsored by General Electric.[3]

For all three of these young Indonesians, life in the early twenty-first century was shaped not so much by war, revolution, or liberation struggles, but by powerful though less visible processes such as migration and sex trafficking for Memey, climate change and impoverishment for Samysuddin, and technological innovation and economic globalization for Kurniawan. And so it has been for billions of others during the past century. Therefore, the two final chapters of Part 6 turn the historical spotlight away from the dominant events of the past century, recounted in Chapters 20 and 21, to focus more explicitly on such immensely transformative processes, all of which have played out on a deeply interconnected global stage.

Technology: The Acceleration of Innovation

Behind both the major events and the global processes of the past century lies the decisive power of technological innovation. Technological breakthroughs—such as electrical grids, antibiotics, nuclear weapons, airplanes, automobiles, cell phones, and the Internet—occurred largely within Western Europe, the United States, and Japan, where the Industrial Revolution had first taken shape during the nineteenth century. The accumulated wealth and experience derived from this early industrialization enabled these countries to maintain their momentum as the primary source of global innovation well into the twentieth century.

Particularly after World War II, a potent combination of universities, governments, and large corporations relentlessly drove the process of technological development. University-based scientific research provided the foundational knowledge from which all manner of technical applications emerged. Governments enmeshed in wars and concerned about national security developed weaponry, medicine, communications, aircraft, rocketry, and computing that often had civilian applications. And large corporations, eager for profits and motivated to create or meet consumer demand, invested heavily in new products.

Thanks to the deepening linkages of globalization, many of these innovations spread rapidly to the rest of the world. By the end of the twentieth century, major industrial enterprises had been established in Mexico and Brazil, China and Vietnam, and India and Indonesia. About 45 percent of Nigerians were Internet users and 82 percent had access to mobile phone service in 2015. Some of these countries—China and India, for example—were making their own contribution to global technological development, even as vast disparities in access to technology remained firmly entrenched.

Generating Energy: Fossil Fuel Breakthroughs

Access to the stored energy of fossil fuels—coal, oil, and natural gas—has provided the foundation of the modern world economy, beginning with the Industrial Revolution in the nineteenth century. But it was the twentieth century that became the

*An exajoule is a large-scale unit of energy.

FIGURE 22.1   Sources of World Energy Consumption, 1820–2010
It was access to fossil fuels that allowed world energy production to skyrocket during
the twentieth century. (Gail Tverberg, OurFiniteWorld.com, from https://ourfiniteworld.com/2012/03/12/
world-energy-consumption-since-1820-in-charts)

age of fossil fuels as their consumption skyrocketed. (See Figure 22.1.) Coal production increased by some 700 percent during that century, and in its second half
oil overtook coal as the dominant source of energy. Natural gas became a growing
element in the energy equation in the latter decades of the century. And beyond fossil
fuels, the energy contained within the nucleus of atoms, as well as that derived from
wind, flowing water, and sunlight, added modestly to global energy consumption.
Nonetheless, by 2000 fossil fuels still provided about 80 percent of the energy that
powered the world economy.

Technological innovations allowed humankind to turn the potential energy of
fossil fuels into useful energy. One such innovation involved the generation of electricity, the basic principles of which were discovered in the early nineteenth century in Great Britain. The subsequent development of coal-, oil-, or gas-fired power
stations, alternating current, transformers, and batteries permitted electricity to be
generated on a commercial scale, moved across great distances, and stored.

This more widespread availability of electricity was the product of electric grids,
which generated power and transmitted it widely to homes and businesses. The
development of such grids began in the late nineteenth century in the already industrialized countries, but it spread rapidly in capitalist, communist, colonial, and developing countries alike. By 2014, some 85 percent of the world's population had access
to electricity, though not always reliably. Europe, Russia, North America, and Japan
achieved 100 percent electrification first, but China, North Africa, Latin America,
and parts of India achieved or approached that figure in the early twenty-first century.[4] By any historical standard, global electrification represents a very rapid transition to new ways of living.

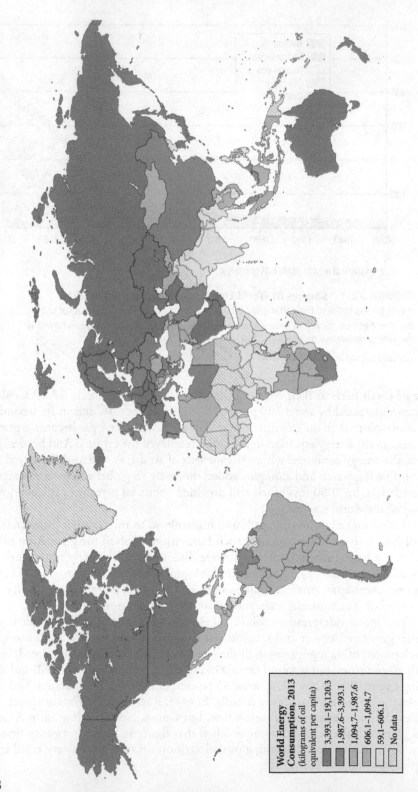

World Energy Consumption, 2013
(kilograms of oil equivalent per capita)

- 3,393.1–19,120.3
- 1,987.6–3,393.1
- 1,094.7–1,987.6
- 606.1–1,094.7
- 59.1–606.1
- No data

Electrification lit up the world, especially at night, and much more cheaply than oil or gas lighting, allowing students to study, people to play, and employees to work around the clock. Electric motors powered all manner of industrial machinery far more productively than steam engines, and they made possible a vast array of consumer goods. Electrification became a crucial component of all economic development planning.

Another breakthrough in the generation of useful energy via fossil fuels was the gasoline- or oil-driven internal combustion engine, pioneered in the late nineteenth century in Western Europe and applied widely throughout the world in the twentieth century. That innovation created a huge new industry that became central to modern economic life; it led to a sharp decline in the use of horses; it enabled the far more rapid and efficient movement of goods and people, transforming the patterns of daily life for much of humankind; and it has been a potent source of the greenhouse gases that have driven climate change. Together, electricity and the internal combustion engine have enormously increased the energy available to humankind, even as access to that energy has favored the most highly industrialized economies. (See Map 22.1.)

Harnessing Energy: Transportation Breakthroughs

Nowhere did this new availability of energy register more dramatically than in the technology of transportation, which built upon the revolutionary development of railroads and steamships in the nineteenth century. To those innovations, the twentieth century added cars, buses, and trucks, containerized shipping and supertankers, airplanes and air freight. This technological infrastructure has made possible the surging movement of goods and people in the globalized world of recent times. By the early twenty-first century, the planet was densely crisscrossed on land by roads, railways, and pipelines, on the seas by shipping routes, and in the air by flight patterns.

Among these transportation technologies, none achieved a greater social and cultural impact than the automobile. In 1900, there were only about 10,000 cars in the global inventory, all of them expensive luxury items for the rich and most of them driven by steam or electric power. But the growing availability of cheap gasoline established the internal combustion engine as the means of propulsion for cars for the next century. It was Henry Ford's Model T, initially built in 1908, that launched the democratization of the automobile and made the United States the first country to market cars for the masses, followed by European countries and Japan after World War II. By 2010, the world had over 1 billion cars, with developing countries contributing substantially to that number. China and India alone produced 28 percent of the world's cars in that year. The age of the automobile had become a global phenomenon.

Cars have shaped modern society and culture in many ways. Ownership of a car conveyed a sense of freedom, individuality, personal empowerment, and status. The early driver was a mounted knight, observed British intellectual Kenneth Boulding, while pedestrians and those using public transportation were merely peasants.[5] Like electrification, the car linked remote rural areas more firmly into national life.

< **MAP 22.1   World Energy Consumption per Capita, 2013**
While global energy production soared during the past century, access to that energy remained highly uneven in the early twenty-first century when measured on a per person basis. (Data from World Bank)

A farmwife in Georgia wrote to Henry Ford in 1918 about the Model T: "Your car lifted us out of the mud. It brought joy into our lives."[6] In urban areas, car ownership facilitated the growth of burgeoning suburbs. In doing so, it also created pervasive traffic jams and contributed much to air pollution, greenhouse gas emissions, and traffic fatalities. Like most technologies, the car conveyed both great benefits and heavy costs, but the world's love affair with the automobile has shown few signs of waning.

Harnessing Energy: Communication and Information Breakthroughs

The past century has also witnessed a flurry of innovations in communication and information that have transformed life for almost everyone. The modern **communication revolution**, like that of transportation, began in the nineteenth century with the telegraph and telephone, both of them using electricity to transmit information along a wire. In the twentieth century, innovation piled on innovation: vacuum tubes, transistors, integrated circuits, microprocessors, and fiber-optic cables. These novel technologies enabled radios, motion pictures, televisions, and most recently computers, cell phones, and the Internet. While these technologies and products were initially created in the West or Japan, they have taken root globally in less than a century, albeit unevenly. Radios have spread most widely, with over 75 percent of households in developing countries having access to a radio in 2012. TV coverage is more variable but surprisingly widespread. In much of Latin America, North Africa, the Middle East, and East Asia, 90 percent or more of households had a TV in the early twenty-first century. Internet access has soared globally

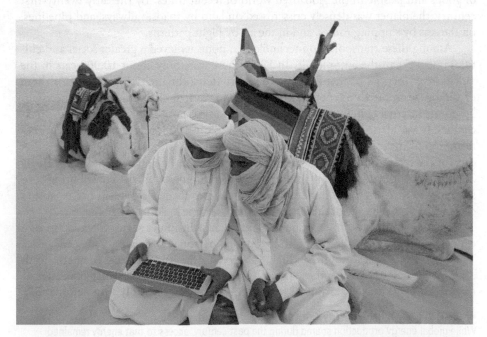

Computers and Camels The global penetration of computer technology is illustrated in this 2012 image of two Tunisian Bedouins consulting their laptop in the Sahara Desert. (Philippe Liccac/Godong/UIG/akg-images)

since the introduction of web browsers in 1991, connecting slightly over half of the world's population by 2017. The availability of cell phones has also spread very rapidly since the first mobile call in 1973 and the first smart phone in 1992. In much of Africa, for example, close to 80 percent of adults had access to a cell phone in 2015, allowing much of the continent to avoid installing more expensive land lines.

These communication technologies have reshaped human life across the planet and have spawned numerous debates about their consequences. Radio enabled even remote villagers to become aware of national and international events, even as it empowered authoritarian and democratic governments alike. Hitler's minister of propaganda, Joseph Goebbels, claimed in 1933 that "it would not have been possible for us [Nazis] to take power or to use it in the ways we have without the radio."[7] And Franklin Roosevelt used his radio "fireside chats" to reassure the American public during the Depression and World War II. But radio also challenged governments that sought to restrict their people's access to information. The availability of short-wave radio broadcasts from Europe and the United States eroded the capacity of the Soviet regime to monopolize the mass media and contributed to the collapse of Communist Party rule in the Soviet Union. Television and the movies have generated a particularly sharp debate. Supporters have praised their ability to inform, educate, and entertain, but critics fear that American or Western domination of the media might erode local or national cultures, regret the generally low cultural level of TV programming, lament the effects of TV violence on children, and argue about the portrayal of women, minorities, Muslims, and others.

The impact of personal computers and their numerous uses (the Internet, e-mail, social media, cell phones) has been pervasive and contested ever since they began to be widely available, at least in the West, during the 1980s. They made possible virtually unlimited access to information, enabling people the world over to participate creatively in this technological revolution. Education in many parts of the world has been transformed as online courses, "smart" classrooms, and digital books have proliferated, while computer science has become a major new field of study. Computer applications have become central to almost every aspect of business and economic life, spawning entirely new industries and forms of commerce. In many African countries, mobile banking has allowed millions to access financial services, with some 61 percent of Kenyans using their cell phones for this purpose. Online commerce has grown rapidly in the twenty-first century. China has become the world's largest e-commerce country, with its Internet giant, the Alibaba Group, replacing Walmart as the world's leading retailer in 2014.

Computer applications have also transformed personal life as online dating has spread to urban areas all around the world. Internet pornography has also become pervasive, though it is legally banned in China, India, the Islamic world, and elsewhere. Facebook, launched in 2004, had connected some 2.234 billion active users, almost 30 percent of the world's population, to an array of "friends" by 2017. Recreation also has been transformed as computer-based gaming has spread globally, with China emerging as the largest video game market in the world.

Beyond their many advantages, these information technologies have generated anxieties and criticism. Individuals fear being bullied by peers, monitored and controlled by governments, and manipulated by corporations able to track their buying preferences. Debate has arisen as to whether the Internet facilitates or undermines personal relationships. Hacking of government records and corporate secrets has raised concerns about cyber-warfare, while the entire complex system remains vulnerable to outages, sabotage, and natural disaster.

Harnessing Energy: Military Breakthroughs

A final example of accelerated innovation lies in technologies of destruction. The late nineteenth-century development of high-power explosives such as dynamite as well as machine guns found application in World War I, along with other new technologies such as submarines, tanks, poison gas, radio, and military aircraft. World War II refined and enhanced these technologies, while adding radar, computers, jet engines, battle tanks, fighter aircraft, aircraft carriers, and atomic bombs to the mix. The cold war generated ever-more-sophisticated nuclear weapons, from enormous hydrogen bombs to smaller tactical nuclear weapons. New means of delivering them also emerged using ballistic missiles launched from airplanes, land-based silos, or submarines with almost pinpoint accuracies. At the height of the cold war and ever since, we have been able to imagine, realistically, a nuclear war that would result in instant death for tens of millions of people, the collapse of modern civilization, and perhaps the extinction of the human species. Military technologies, of course, have also had numerous civilian spin-offs, including radar, nuclear power plants, the Internet, space exploration, and communication satellites.

The Global Economy: The Acceleration of Entanglement

Accelerating technological innovation decisively shaped the world economy of the past century, enabling what we now refer to as **economic globalization**. Precisely when this most recent phase of global connectivity began is a matter of some dispute among historians. (See "Controversies: Debating Globalization.") But almost all scholars agree that the seven decades following World War II have marked an extraordinary surge in economic globalization. A central element of that process has been the spread of industrialization among the peoples of the Global South.

The Globalization of Industrialization: Development in the Global South

As decolonization, independence, and revolution rolled over much of Africa, Asia, and Latin America, economic development and industrialization became everywhere a central priority. It was an essential promise of all revolutions and independence struggles, and it was increasingly the standard by which people measured and granted legitimacy to their governments.

Achieving economic development, however, was no easy or automatic task for societies sharply divided by class, religion, ethnic group, and gender and facing explosive population growth. In many places, colonial rule had provided only the most slender foundations for modern development, as new nations often came to independence with low rates of literacy, few people with managerial experience, a weak private economy, and little industrial infrastructure. Furthermore, the entire effort occurred in a world split by rival superpowers and economically dominated by the powerful capitalist economies of the West.

Beyond these difficulties lay the vexing question of what strategies to pursue. Should state authorities take the lead, or was it wiser to rely on private enterprise and the market? Should industrial production be aimed at the domestic market in an "import substitution" approach, or was it more effective to specialize in particular products, such as cars, clothing, or electronics, for an export market?

For developing countries, it was an experimental process, and the outcomes varied considerably. (See Snapshot, page 647.) In general, East Asian countries that produced products primarily for export have had the strongest record of economic growth. South Korea, Taiwan, Singapore, and Hong Kong were dubbed **Asian Tigers** or newly industrialized countries. Following the death of Mao Zedong in 1976, China soon became a spectacular economic success story, boasting the most rapid economic growth in the world by the end of the twentieth century while replacing Japan as the world's second-largest economy and edging up on the United States. In the 1990s, Asia's other giant, India, opened itself more fully to the world market and launched rapid economic growth with a powerful high-tech sector and major steel, chemical, automotive, and pharmaceutical industries. Oil-producing countries reaped a bonanza when they were able to demand much higher prices for that essential commodity in the 1970s and after. By 2016, Mexico, Turkey, Malaysia, Thailand, Vietnam, India, and Indonesia numbered in the top twenty of the most competitive manufacturing countries, with China ranking number one. Limited principally to Europe, North America, and Japan in the nineteenth century, industrialization and modern economic growth had become a global phenomenon by the early twenty-first century.

But not everywhere. In most of Africa, much of the Arab world, and parts of Asia — regions representing about one-third of the world's population — there was little sign of rapid economic development and frequent examples of declining standards of living since the end of the 1960s. Between 1980 and 2000, the average income in forty-three of Africa's poorest countries dropped by 25 percent, pushing living standards for many below what they had been at independence. But in the early twenty-first century, a number of African countries began to experience encouraging economic growth, an expanding middle class with some money to spend, and more international investment. Some observers began to speak about "Africa Rising."

Scholars and politicians alike argue about the reasons for such sharp differences in economic performance. Variables such as geography and natural resources, differing colonial experiences, variations in regional cultures, the degree of political stability and social equality, state economic policies, population growth rates, and varying forms of involvement with the world economy — all of these have been invoked to explain the widely diverging trajectories among developing countries.

Re-globalization: Deepening Economic Connections

Accompanying the worldwide spread of modern development and industrial growth was a tightening network of global economic relationships that cut across the world's separate countries and regions, binding them together more closely, but also more contentiously, during the second half of the twentieth century. This was the economic face of globalization. (See "Controversies: Debating Globalization.") In some respects, it was a "re-globalization," for the aftermath of World War I and the Great Depression had wreaked havoc on an increasingly globalized world economy. International trade, investment, and labor migration dropped sharply as major states turned inward, favoring high tariffs and economic autonomy, in the face of a global economic collapse. In this context, what occurred after World War II signaled a renewal and a great acceleration of earlier trends that had linked the economies of the world more tightly together.

The capitalist victors in World War II, led by the United States, were determined to avoid any return to the kind of economic contraction and nationalist excesses that had followed World War I. At a conference in Bretton Woods, New Hampshire, in 1944, they forged a set of agreements and institutions (the World Bank and the International Monetary Fund [IMF]) that laid the foundation for postwar globalization. This "**Bretton Woods system**" negotiated the rules for commercial and financial dealings among the major capitalist countries, while promoting relatively free trade, stable currency values linked to the U.S. dollar, and high levels of capital investment.

By the 1970s, leading figures in capitalist countries such as the United States and Great Britain, as well as in major international lending agencies such as the World Bank, increasingly viewed the entire world as a single market. This approach to the world economy, widely known as neoliberalism, favored the reduction of tariffs, the free global movement of capital, a mobile and temporary workforce, the privatization of many state-run enterprises, the curtailing of government efforts to regulate the economy, and both tax and spending cuts. In this view, the market, operating both globally and within nations, was the most effective means of generating the holy grail of economic growth. As communism collapsed by the end of the twentieth century, "capitalism was global and the globe was capitalist."[8]

Such policies, together with major changes in transportation and communication technology, accompanied a dramatic quickening of global economic transactions

Containerized Shipping The growth of global trade has been facilitated by containerized shipping, a highly mechanized process of moving goods that requires far fewer workers and has substantially reduced transportation costs. This photograph illustrates that process as it occurred in the Chinese port of Qingdao in mid-2017. (STR/Getty Images)

after World War II, expressed in the accelerating circulation of both goods and capital. World trade, for example, skyrocketed from a value of some $57 billion in 1947 to about $18.3 trillion in 2012. In wealthy countries and for elites everywhere, increasing global trade meant access to the goods of the world. In varying degrees, it also meant employment. In the United States in 2008, exports supported some 10 million jobs and represented about 13 percent of its gross domestic product (GDP). Many developing countries, however, were far more dependent on exports, usually raw materials and agricultural products. Ghana, for example, relied on exports for 44 percent of its GDP in 2014, mostly gold, cocoa beans, and timber products. Cocoa alone supported some 700,000 farming families. Mounting trade entangled the peoples of the world to an unprecedented degree.

Economic entanglement was financial as well as commercial. "Foreign direct investment," whereby a firm in, say, the United States opens a factory in China or Mexico, exploded after 1960 as companies in rich countries sought to take advantage of cheap labor, tax breaks, and looser environmental regulations in developing countries. Money also surged around the planet as investors and financiers annually spent trillions of dollars purchasing foreign currencies or stocks likely to increase in value and often sold them quickly thereafter, with unsettling consequences. The personal funds of individuals likewise achieved a new mobility as international credit cards took hold almost everywhere.

Central to the acceleration of economic globalization have been huge global businesses known as **transnational corporations** (TNCs), which produce goods or deliver services simultaneously in many countries. Toyota, the world's largest automaker in 2016, sold cars around the world and had manufacturing facilities in some twenty-eight countries on five continents. Burgeoning in number since the 1960s, TNCs such as Royal Dutch Shell, Sony, and General Motors often were of such an enormous size and had such economic clout that their assets and power dwarfed that of many countries. By 2000, 51 of the world's 100 largest economic units were in fact TNCs, not countries. In the permissive economic climate of recent decades, such firms have been able to move their facilities quickly from place to place in search of the lowest labor costs or the least restrictive environmental regulations. During one five-year period, for example, Nike closed twenty factories and opened thirty-five others, often thousands of miles apart.

Growth, Instability, and Inequality

The impact of these tightening economic linkages has prompted enormous debate and controversy. (See "Controversies: Debating Globalization.") Amid the swirl of contending opinion, one thing seemed reasonably clear: economic globalization accompanied, and arguably helped generate, the most remarkable spurt of economic growth in world history. On a global level, total world output grew from a value of $7 trillion in 1950 to $73 trillion in 2009 and on a per capita basis from $2,652 to $10,728.[9] While world population quadrupled, or increased by a factor of 4, during the twentieth century, the output of the world economy grew by a factor of 14 and industrial output by a factor of 40. This represents an immense, rapid, and unprecedented creation of wealth with a demonstrable impact on human welfare. Everywhere people lived longer. Global average life expectancy has more than doubled since 1900, approaching an average of about seventy years in 2012. Everywhere, far fewer children died before the age of five: in 1960 the global average was 18.2 percent; in 2015, 4.3 percent. And everywhere more people were literate. Some

80 percent of adults could read and write at some level by 2000, while only 21 percent could do so in 1900. The UN Human Development Report in 1997 concluded that "in the past 50 years, poverty has fallen more than in the previous 500."

Far more problematic have been the instability of this emerging world economy and the distribution of the immense wealth it has generated. Amid overall economic growth, periodic crises and setbacks have shaped recent world history. Soaring oil prices in 1973–1974 resulted in several years of economic stagnation for many industrialized countries, great hardship for many developing countries, and an economic windfall for oil-producing countries. Inability to repay mounting debts triggered a major financial crisis in Latin America during the 1980s and resulted in a "lost decade" in terms of economic development. Another financial crisis in Asia during the late 1990s resulted in the collapse of many businesses, widespread unemployment, and political upheaval in Indonesia and Thailand. And in 2008 an inflated housing market—or "bubble"—in the United States collapsed, triggering millions of home foreclosures, growing unemployment, the tightening of credit, and declining consumer spending. Soon this crisis rippled around the world. Iceland's rapidly growing economy collapsed almost overnight as three major banks failed, the country's stock market dropped by 80 percent, and its currency lost more than 70 percent of its value—all in a single week. In Sierra Leone, some 90 percent of the country's diamond-mine workers lost their jobs. Impoverished Central American and Caribbean families, dependent on money sent home by family members working abroad, suffered further as those remittances dropped sharply. Contracting economies contributed to debt crises in Greece, Italy, and Spain and threatened to unravel European economic integration. Whatever the overall benefits of globalization, economic stability and steady progress were not among them.

Nor did globalization resolve the problem of inequality. (See Snapshot, page 647.) Despite substantial gains in life expectancy, infant mortality, literacy, and the reduction of poverty, economic inequality on a global level has been stubbornly persistent and by some measures growing. In 1870 the average per capita income in the world's ten richest countries was six times that of the ten poorest countries. By 2002 that ratio was 42 to 1.[10] That gap has been evident, often tragically, in great disparities in incomes, medical care, availability of clean drinking water, educational and employment opportunities, access to the Internet, and dozens of other ways. It has shaped the life chances of practically everyone. Even among developing countries, great inequalities were apparent. The oil-rich economies of the Middle East had little in common with the banana-producing countries of Central America. The rapidly industrializing states of China, India, and South Korea had quite different economic agendas than impoverished African countries.

Economic globalization has contributed to inequalities not only among countries and regions, but also within individual nations, rich and poor alike. In the United States, for example, income inequality has sharply increased since the late 1970s. The American economy shed millions of manufacturing jobs, with some companies moving their operations to Asia or Latin America, where labor costs were lower. More important, however, was automation. The U.S. steel industry, for example, lost 75 percent of its workforce between 1962 and 2005, while producing roughly the same amount of steel. This left many American workers in the lurch, forcing them to work in the low-wage service sector, even as other Americans were growing prosperous in emerging high-tech industries. Globalization divided Mexico as well. The northern part of the country, with close business and manufacturing ties to the United States, grew much

SNAPSHOT	GLOBAL DEVELOPMENT AND INEQUALITY, 2011

This table shows thirteen commonly used indicators of "development" and their variations in 2011 across four major groups of countries defined by average level of per capita income. In which areas has the Global South most nearly caught up with the Global North?

Gross National Income per Capita with Sample Countries	Low Income: $995 or Less (Congo, Kenya, Ethiopia, Afghanistan, Myanmar)	Lower Middle Income: $996–$3,945 (India, China, Egypt, Algeria, Indonesia, Nigeria)	Upper Middle Income: $3,946–$12,195 (Mexico, Brazil, Turkey, Russia, Iran)	Upper Income: $12,196 or More (USA, Western Europe, Japan, South Korea, Australia)
Life expectancy: M/F in years	58/60	66/70	68/75	77/83
Deaths under age 5 per 1,000 live births	120	60	24	7
Deaths from infectious disease: %	36	14	11	7
Access to toilets: %	35	50	84	99
Years of education	7.9	10.3	13.8	14.5
Literacy rate: %	66	80	93	99
Population growth: % annual	2.27	1.27	.96	.39
Urban population: %	27	41	74	78
Cell phones per 100 people	22	47	92	106
Internet users per 100 people	2.3	13.7	29.9	68.3
Personal computers per 100 people	1.2	4.3	11.9	60.4
Cars per 1,000 people	5.8	20.3	125.2	435.1
Carbon dioxide emissions: metric tons per capita	1	3	5	13

Data from "Map Supplement," *National Geographic* (Washington, DC: National Geographic Society, March 2011).

more prosperous than the south, which was a largely rural agricultural area and had a far more slowly growing economy. China's rapid economic growth likewise fostered mounting inequality between its rural households and those in its burgeoning cities, where income by 2000 was three times that of the countryside. Economic globalization may have brought people together as never before, but it has also divided them sharply.

Pushback: Resistance to Economic Globalization

The movement toward a thoroughly entangled world economy was accompanied by much conflict, criticism, resistance, and protest from those who felt unfairly treated, left behind, or overwhelmed by a tsunami of change in a globalizing process they could not control. One expression of this resistance derived from the Global South. As the East/West division of capitalism and communism faded, differences between the rich nations of the Global North and the developing countries of the Global South assumed greater prominence in world affairs. Highly contentious issues have included the rules for world trade, availability of and terms for foreign aid, representation in international economic organizations, the mounting problem of indebtedness, and environmental and labor standards. In the 1970s, for example, a large group of developing countries joined together to demand a "new international economic order" that was more favorable to the poor countries, though the effort met with little success. Developing countries have often contested protectionist restrictions on their agricultural exports imposed by the rich countries seeking to safeguard their own politically powerful farmers.

In the 1990s a growing popular movement, featuring a highly critical posture toward globalization, emerged as an international coalition of political activists, concerned scholars and students, trade unions, women's and religious organizations, environmental groups, and others, hailing from rich and poor countries alike. Though reflecting a variety of viewpoints, that opposition largely agreed that market-driven corporate globalization had lowered labor standards, fostered ecological degradation, prevented poor countries from protecting themselves against financial speculators, ignored local cultures, disregarded human rights, and enhanced global inequality, while favoring the interests of large corporations and rich countries.

This movement appeared dramatically on the world's radar screen in 1999 in Seattle at a meeting of the **World Trade Organization (WTO)**. An international body representing 149 nations and charged with negotiating the rules for global commerce and promoting free trade, the WTO had become a major target of globalization critics. "The central idea of the WTO," argued one such critic, "is that *free trade*—actually the values and interests of global corporations—should supersede all other values."[11] Tens of thousands of protesters from all over the world descended on Seattle in what became a violent, chaotic, and much-publicized protest. Such protests stimulated the creation in 2001 of the World Social Forum, an annual gathering of alternative globalization activists to coordinate strategy, exchange ideas, and share experiences, under the slogan "Another world is possible."

Local activists in various places likewise resisted the impact of globalization. In 1994 in southern Mexico, peasant resentment boiled over against the Mexican government and its privatizing of communally held land, which was related to the country's recent entry into the **North American Free Trade Agreement (NAFTA)**. The leader of this peasant upheaval referred to globalization as a "process to eliminate that multitude of people who are not useful to the powerful." Likewise in southern India, activist farmers during the late 1990s organized protests against the opening of Kentucky Fried Chicken outlets as well as against the giant American chemical corporation Monsanto, uprooting and burning fields where Monsanto grew genetically modified cotton.

Opposition to globalization also emerged from more conservative circles, especially after the sharp economic downturn beginning in 2008. Britain's vote in 2016 to

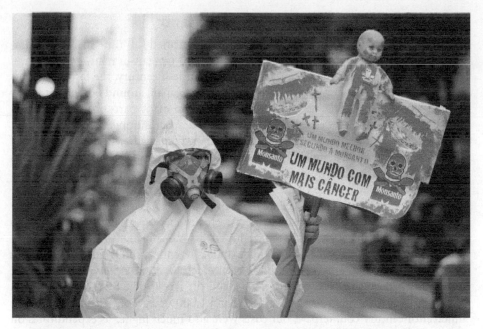

Anti-Globalization Protest A demonstrator in São Paulo, Brazil, in 2013, part of a worldwide protest against the biotech giant Monsanto, holds a sign reading: "A better world according to Monsanto is a world with more cancer." (Nelson Antoine/AP Images)

leave the European Union clearly represented a backlash against globalization, even as movements hostile to a more united Europe gained support in many countries. So too did the U.S. election of 2016, in which all of the candidates expressed reservations about international trade agreements as threatening American jobs. The most vociferous voice was that of the winner, Donald Trump, who in early 2017 withdrew the United States from the Trans-Pacific Partnership trade agreement and demanded a renegotiation of NAFTA with Mexico and Canada. Elsewhere as well — in Turkey, Russia, China, and India, for example — political leaders increasingly appealed to national pride and cultural purity. Observers wondered if this represented a rejection of earlier assumptions that international cooperation in reducing trade barriers fostered peace and prosperity for all concerned.

Producing and Consuming: The Shapes of Modern Societies

Technological innovation and economic globalization during the past century have dramatically reshaped human societies around the world. Further contributing to this reshaping of social structures have been the actions of state authorities through their laws, regulations, and policies. Broad global patterns such as the declining role of peasant farmers and the growing role of middle-class professionals found expression in many variations across the multiple divides of the modern world.

Life on the Land: The Decline of the Peasantry

A little over 20 percent of the world's population farmed full time in 2000, a dramatic drop from 66 percent in 1950 and around 80 percent in many preindustrial agricultural societies. In the second half of the twentieth century, the farming population declined by 80 percent in Western Europe and Japan, around 60 percent in the United States and Canada, and 50 percent or more in many parts of Latin America, North Africa, and Southwest Asia. In communist Eastern Europe, the Soviet Union, and China, similar declines occurred a little later and especially when collectivization was abandoned after the late 1980s. One historian has described this development as "the death of the peasantry," which has allowed "an absurdly tiny percentage" of the population "to flood . . . the world with untold quantities of food."[12]

What caused this dramatic decline? A major factor was mechanization, as machinery such as tractors and combines made farmers more productive, earlier in North America and Australia and later elsewhere in the world. Furthermore, many farmers in the Global North and some regions of the Global South (India, Argentina, and Brazil) also embraced Green Revolution innovations, including chemical fertilizers and new types of seed, that were initially developed between the 1930s and the late 1960s. By the 1970s a corn farmer in the United States was between 100 and 1,000 times more productive than his nineteenth-century counterpart, but costs were also much higher as expenditures on machinery, fertilizer, and diesel fuel soared. Both family farmers and managers for agribusiness companies had to master often complex new farming practices. Describing the impact of technology on his work, Ken Grimsdell, whose company raised crops in the Midlands of England, noted in 2015: "A tractor can be controlled by satellite, drones can fly over a crop, record pictures and send them back to the office. The technology has made for better farming."[13] It also made for fewer farmers.

Many of the most mechanized and efficient farms in the world remained dependent on seasonal labor at crucial moments in the agricultural year. The work of migrant laborers, often organized into teams that moved from place to place, was intense, repetitive, and sometimes dangerous, especially as the use of toxic pesticides increased with the Green Revolution. Migrant workers typically were outsiders in the communities where they worked and in the United States were often undocumented or possessed temporary work visas. Nevertheless, this difficult life attracted millions of Latin American and Caribbean migrants to the fields of the United States and similar numbers of Eastern Europeans to the farms of Western Europe following the enlargement of the European Union in the early twenty-first century.

Ever cheaper transportation costs created an increasingly global market for food, forcing farmers, often on different continents, to compete with each other. Trade deals exposed small-scale farmers in the Global South to the mechanized and heavily subsidized farming industries of the Global North. In 1994, NAFTA allowed corn from the United States to flood the Mexican market, forcing 2 million small farmers in Mexico to abandon its cultivation. In 2006, Tirso Alvares Correa worried that no one would be left to work land that his family had tilled for generations. "Free trade has been a disaster for us. . . . Corn from abroad is taking a toll. . . . We can't sell our corn anymore."[14] Some displaced farmers found work on large estates geared toward raising crops like avocados for export. Many others immigrated to the United States, with some finding work on American farms.

While farmers as a percentage of the population declined dramatically in the second half of the twentieth century, some 27 percent of the world's population, about

1.8 billion people, still earned their living from the land in 2006, more than the total world population in 1850. Most remained small-scale or subsistence cultivators, and in some regions farming populations grew rapidly, paralleling the growth of population generally. In Africa the number of full time farmers nearly doubled between 1960 and 2000. Land reform movements also served to keep people on the land. In Mexico, for example, "land to the tiller of the soil" was a powerful rallying cry of the Mexican Revolution of 1910 in a country where some 97 percent of the land was owned by 1 percent of the population. Enshrined in a new constitution, land reform laws redistributed about half the total land to those who farmed between 1920 and 1940. Meanwhile, in the communist world, collectivization movements in the Soviet Union from the 1920s and in Eastern Europe and China in the immediate aftermath of World War II also had the effect of employing large numbers in agriculture even as collectives brought an end to private ownership of land. Nonetheless, after millennia during which 80 percent or more of people toiled on the land, the past century has witnessed those who farm shrink to a distinct minority of humankind.

The Changing Lives of Industrial Workers

The opening decades of the twentieth century brought considerable changes to the lives of millions who labored in factories. American industry pioneered the moving production line and "scientific management" that broke down more complex activities into simple steps. While increasing productivity substantially, these changes fundamentally altered the pace and nature of factory work. More jobs became repetitive and boring. The moving assembly line removed nearly all control over the pace of work from those who performed it. Some employers, like the car manufacturer Henry Ford, offered better pay and somewhat shorter hours to his workers to entice them into his factories, while union movements and social reformers pressed for worker's rights, sometimes through strikes. Elements of these American innovations spread to factories in Europe, the Soviet Union, and to a lesser extent Japan by the 1930s.

In many heavily unionized industries, the two-day weekend became standard by the 1920s and along with higher wages created a growing culture of leisure and consumption, often called **consumerism**. In summarizing this development, one scholar has stated that "industrial cities became places of leisure as well as labor."[15] Shopping at department stores and attending movies or sporting events emerged as popular pastimes among working-class families, who also increasingly purchased prepared foods rather than cooking. Fish and chips (French fries) became a particular favorite of the British working class, with over 30,000 shops across the country offering this new convenience food by the 1920s.

Plant closures during the Great Depression significantly disrupted the lives of factory workers, as did World War II through the rationing and physical destruction of wartime. But the shortage of wartime labor drew women into factories across the industrialized world in unprecedented numbers and also allowed them to fill positions traditionally reserved for men. After the war many women were forced to abandon the factories altogether or at least abandon "male" jobs. In the 1950s and 1960s, stable and well-paid workforces often represented by strong unions typified the industrial sectors of Japan, the United States, and Western Europe. After decades of depression and wartime scarcity, industrial workers everywhere reacted to the good times by embracing consumerism. By 1970 nearly all urban households in Japan owned the "big three"—a television, washing machine, and refrigerator. Between 1945 and 1960 companies in the United States quadrupled their collective advertising expenditure, reflecting the buying power of the American worker. Europeans consumed more but also emphasized leisure, as one month of paid annual vacation became standard in many industries. In the communist world, large factory workforces enjoyed similar job security, even if their economies proved unable to produce the variety of consumer goods available to workers elsewhere.

Further changes awaited factory workers in the later twentieth century. Liberalization of global trade, automation and robots, relocation of factories to places with cheaper labor costs, and the rapid growth of manufacturing in the Global South—all of this led to the decline or "rusting out" of many well-established industrial centers in parts of Western Europe and the United States and the displacement of many less-skilled workers. As the former Soviet Union and China opened up to global trade in the 1990s, many state-owned manufacturing enterprises collapsed or fell into decline, displacing many workers, even as a new factory working class formed in China's coastal regions, where foreign investors had created new industrial operations. Closure of factories around the world tore at the social fabric of communities and led many to seek better employment opportunities elsewhere. Speaking in 2015 about his two teenage daughters, Mark Semande, a former worker at the closed Maytag appliance plant in Galesburg, Illinois, mused: "Maybe they could find jobs and live in the community but not if they want to do as well as [my wife and I]."[16] Nonetheless, in some heavily industrialized regions, new, more efficient automated manufacturing allowed factories to survive and compete in the global market, but with far fewer and more highly skilled workers.

Even as manufacturing declined in many of its traditional heartlands in the later twentieth century, it took root and thrived in new regions. Between 1980 and 2007 the global manufacturing workforce grew from 1.9 to 3.1 billion people, offering many new employment opportunities, especially in the developing world. Countries competed to attract manufacturers, luring them with weak labor laws, low wages, tax incentives, and special **export-processing zones (EPZs)** where international companies could operate with expedited building permits, exemptions from certain taxes and customs duties, and other benefits.

Many of the conditions for workers remained much as they had been during the first Industrial Revolution. Women made up an important part of the global industrial workforce and typically earned less than men. At the turn of the twenty-first century, around 74 percent of the workers in the Philippine's EPZs were women who earned on average 54 percent of what their male counterparts did. Also mirroring the first Industrial Revolution, workers frequently labored in dangerous conditions that resulted in tragedies like the collapse of the Rana Plaza garment factory in Bangladesh in April 2013, which killed 1,135 workers and injured a further 2,500. In some regions like South Africa during the apartheid era or China during the 1980s and 1990s, migrants from the countryside who worked in industrial zones commonly lacked official residency and work privileges, limiting their ability to oppose the demands of their employers and access services like education or health care. But as manufacturing became established in new regions, workers often voiced dissatisfaction and sought better pay and working conditions. In Brazil, South Africa, and South Korea, labor movements emerged within a generation of the auto industry establishing major production facilities.

The Service Sector and the Informal Economy

Beyond farm and factory, employment opportunities grew significantly in service indus-tries, sales, and the knowledge economy, which included government, medicine, edu-cation, finance, communication, information technology, and media. Growth in these areas was driven in part by an emerging consumerism and increasing population and was encouraged by new communication and computation technologies, including the type-writer, telephone, and later the computer and the Internet. Some of these **service sector** enterprises employed highly educated, well-paid workers such as doctors, computer cod-ers, and bankers, but many more were lower-skilled, lower-paid occupations such as cleaners, shopkeepers, taxi drivers, secretaries, and typists. Everywhere race and gender pay differentials existed, with jobs gendered female—manicurist, nurse, teacher—pay-ing less than those gendered male—plumber, bank manager, engineer.

The last decades of the twentieth century witnessed a trend toward less stable employment in service industries and the knowledge economies of more developed regions as employers outsourced jobs to freelancers, independent contractors, contract workers, and temporary staffing agencies. Advances in telecommunications and the Internet allowed companies to relocate jobs in the service industry (call centers, data entry) and knowledge economy (computer coding, editing) to lower-wage countries. At the opening of the twenty-first century, zero-hour contracts, which required employees to be on call without any guarantee of work, grew more common in the retail sector, and new ride-sharing apps competed with taxi firms. In what has been described as the new "gig economy," jobs came with greater flexibility for workers but also less security, fewer fringe benefits, looser relationships with employers, and often longer workdays.

The **informal economy** (or "shadow" economy), which operated "off the books" and largely outside government regulation and taxation, grew rapidly as fewer employ-ees worked in stable, permanent jobs. This growth occurred most notably in the Global South, where new immigrants to rapidly expanding cities often found employment as day laborers or small-scale traders and lived in crowded shantytowns, but it was also evident in the Global North. Greece's black market reached 20 to 25 percent of its total economy in 2017, and in the United States, an estimated $2 trillion of unreported income in 2012 suggested a substantial shadow economy. The expansion of such infor-mal economies over the past several decades has led some scholars to conclude that the stable and well-defined workplaces in the mid-twentieth-century industrialized North were an aberration rather than a new norm in the world of work.

Global Middle Classes and Life at the Top

A prosperous middle class in the Global North was a defining feature of the twen-tieth century. By the 1950s factory workers, tradesmen, and increasing numbers of service, sales, clerical, and knowledge economy workers came to view themselves as "middle class," for they were earning stable wages that allowed them to live comfort-ably, own their homes, and secure access to health care, education, entertainment, and travel. In much of the Global South, "middle class" was defined differently—as those households earning significantly above the poverty line but less than the highest earners in their communities. In most developing countries, a large middle class of this kind only emerged at the opening of the twenty-first century. But by 2009, an estimated 1.8 billion people globally were "middle class."[17] The shifting of manufacturing and some service and knowledge economy employment to the Global South was an important driver in this remarkable growth.

However, at the opening of the twenty-first century, many in the global middle class felt that their position in society was insecure or under threat. In Europe, the United States, Japan, and other places in the industrial north, the middle class as a proportion of society has been stagnant or shrinking since the 1970s, and the living standards of many declined even as economic growth continued in these regions. As one Chicago steelworker whose plant shut down in the 1980s put it: "I'm working harder, making less money, got less of a future."[18] Less secure employment, the loss of manufacturing jobs, immigration, and the decline of labor unions have all taken their toll on the middle class, sparking populist political backlashes such as Britain's announced exit from the European Union in 2016 and the election of President Donald Trump in the United States. In the Global South as well, many in the middle class find their positions precarious. More than 60 percent of the middle class in Bolivia, Brazil, Chile, and Mexico work precariously within the informal economy, often running their own very small businesses.

The last several decades also produced economic winners. Never before had the richest 1 percent controlled so much wealth as they did at the opening of the twenty-first century. In 2016 an OXFAM study concluded that the eight richest people in the world possessed roughly the same amount of wealth as the poorest

Middle-Class Life in Nigeria One sign of an emerging middle class in the Global South was the proliferation of malls and huge retail outlets such as this Shoprite store, located in the new Delta Mall in Warri, Nigeria. Shoprite is Africa's largest food retailer, selling food, liquor, household goods, and small appliances. A recent customer commented: "A middle-class person can come into this mall and feel a sense of belonging."[19] (Glenna Gordon/© The New York Times/Redux)

3.5 billion. The gap between the pay of top executives and employees at major firms has widened dramatically. One commentator in 2011 described it as "The Winner-Take-Most Economy" where a small number of "superstar" performers enjoyed most of the newly generated wealth.[20]

The richest 1 percent looked very different in 2000 than a century earlier. More were self-made, with fewer having inherited their wealth. In the West and some other places, the globalization and deregulation of the financial industry from the 1980s on allowed some in the banking, private equity, and hedge fund industries to make fortunes even as a series of financial bubbles and collapses made finance more risky. At the same time, the remarkable growth of high tech and especially Internet businesses made billionaires out of a lucky few. Some 1 percenters from the Global South made their fortunes following decolonization by taking over the structures of the state, often through direct corruption, as in Nigeria, where billions in oil revenues were siphoned off into the personal accounts of officials. Similarly, following the collapse of the Soviet Union, well-connected individuals who frequently had held elite positions in the former regime purchased state assets on the cheap, becoming billionaires in the process.

The newly enriched rubbed shoulders with one another and with more traditional elites while living global lifestyles almost unimaginable to the rest. Owning multiple houses in desirable locations—London, Dubai, Hong Kong, New York—and moving between them on private jets or on luxury yachts established their place in the new elite, as did participation in exclusive gatherings like the annual DAVOS summit in Switzerland. More so than in the past, the superrich possessed a shared international outlook, educational background, and experiences that made them a self-conscious global class. "A person in Africa who runs a big African bank and went to Harvard Business School has more in common with me than he does with his neighbors, and I have more in common with him than I do with my neighbors," observed the private equity banker Glen Hutchins.[21] At the opening of the twenty-first century, humankind had never been so collectively wealthy. That wealth lifted billions out of poverty and created a growing global middle class, but it also accumulated in the hands of a privileged few, creating an unprecedentedly wealthy global plutocracy.

Getting Personal: Transformations of Private Life

The public face of social life, expressed in work, class, income, and wealth, has a more private counterpart, experienced in marriage, family, sexuality, and gender roles. These elements of personal life also changed dramatically amid the technological and economic transformations of the past century. Increasingly, individuals had to makes choices about intimate matters that were previously regarded as determined by custom or law—who to marry, how many children to bear, when to begin sexual activity, and what it meant to be male or female. Amid much diversity and variation, many people the world over have experienced and celebrated those changes as liberation from ancient constraints and social oppression, while many others have felt them as an assault on the natural order of things and a threat to ways of living sanctioned by religion and traditional moral codes. These diverse reactions have driven matters long considered private or unspeakable into the public sphere of controversy, debate, and political action.

Modernity and Personal Life

Among the agents of change in personal life, none have been more fundamental than the multiple processes widely associated with modernity—science and technology, industrialization and urbanization, and globalization and migration. Consider, for example, their impact on family life, experienced earlier and most fully in the industrialized societies of Europe, North America, and Japan, but also more recently in the Global South.

As industrial and urban life took hold across the world during the past two centuries, large business enterprises and the state took over functions that families had previously performed. Production moved from family farms and workshops to factories, offices, and large-scale agricultural enterprises, and opportunities for work outside the home beckoned to growing numbers of women as well as men. Education became the task of state-run schools rather than families, and the primary role of children became that of student rather than worker. Families increasingly functioned primarily to provide emotional and financial security in a turbulent and rapidly changing world. In this setting, modern families became smaller as children were increasingly seen as economic burdens and as both men and women married later. Furthermore, family life grew less stable as divorce became far more frequent and the stigma attached to it diminished. Modern life also witnessed an increasing variety of family patterns across the world: patriarchal families of several generations living together; small nuclear families of mother, father, and children; single-parent families, usually headed by women; unmarried couples living together, sometimes with children and often without; blended families as a result of second marriages; polygamous families; and gay and lesbian families.

These broad patterns of change in family life at the global level hid a great deal of diversity. While family size has dropped sharply in much of Asia and Latin America during the past century, it has remained quite high in sub-Saharan Africa, where women in the early twenty-first century produced on average 5 children during their reproductive years, compared to a global average of 2.5. Divorce rates too varied widely in the early twenty-first century, with 50 percent or more of marriages ending in divorce in the United States, France, Spain, Cuba, Hungary, and the Czech Republic, compared to much lower rates in Chile (3 percent), Brazil (21 percent), Egypt (17 percent), Iran (22 percent), and South Africa (17 percent). Since the mid-1990s, China has experienced a dramatic increase in divorce, prompting the Chinese government to intervene to address the issue. Most of the world's marriages during the past century have involved one man and one woman, though polygamy remains legal in much of Africa and the Islamic Middle East, while same-sex marriages have gained a measure of acceptance at least in some cultures in recent decades. While the past century has generally favored free choice or "love" marriages, many families in India and elsewhere still arrange marriages for their children.

Modern life has also deeply impacted sexuality. Technologies of contraception—condoms, IUDs, diaphragms, and above all "the pill"—have allowed many people to separate sexual life from reproduction. Especially since the 1960s, this has contributed to the emergence of a highly sexualized public culture in many parts of the world, expressed in advertising and in an enormous pornography industry with a global reach. One investigator reported on a remote village in the West African country of Ghana: "The village has no electricity, but that doesn't stop a generator from being wheeled in, turning a mud hut into an impromptu porn cinema."[22] Sex tourism has also become big business, with major destinations in Thailand, Indonesia, the Philippines, Columbia, Brazil, and the Netherlands. Movies, TV, newspapers, and magazines openly display or discuss all manner of sexual topics that would have been largely forbidden in public discourse only a century ago: premarital sex, homosexuality, gay marriage, LGBT rights, sexually transmitted diseases, birth control, abortion, teen pregnancy, and much more. Sex education in schools has spread globally to varying degrees, while provoking sharp controversy in many places.

Sex, in short, has come out of the closet during the past century. Unsurprisingly, this has been associated with a considerable increase in premarital sex in many parts of the world, with the vast majority of Americans and Europeans participating in such activity by the late 1960s. A rapidly industrializing China has witnessed the frequency of premarital sex skyrocket since 1989, approaching levels in the United States.

But all of this has occurred in the face of much controversy and opposition. The hierarchies of the Catholic Church and many fundamentalist or evangelical Christian leaders have remained steadfastly opposed to the "sexual revolution" of the past century, even as many of their parishioners participate in it. Despite the sexual revolution, over 90 percent of Muslims in Indonesia, Jordan, Pakistan, Turkey, and Egypt found premarital sex unacceptable in the early twenty-first century, while fewer than 10 percent of the people in France, Germany, and Spain felt the same way.[23] Greater openness and assertiveness among gays and lesbians have triggered legal action against them, especially in Africa, where many countries have passed harsh antigay legislation, citing the AIDS crisis, a defense of traditional marriage, and the supposedly "un-African" character of homosexuality.

The State and Personal Life

States too have shaped personal life in the past century, as they grew more powerful and intrusive and as matters of marriage, family, gender, and sexuality became ever more entangled with politics. Nazi Germany, for example, prohibited birth control and rewarded large families during the 1930s in an effort to produce as many "good Germans" as possible. At the same time, they sterilized or executed those deemed "undesirable" and forbade marriage or sexual relations between Jews and Germans to prevent "contamination" of the Aryan race. For similar racial reasons, South Africa under the apartheid regime legally prohibited both sexual relationships and marriage between whites and nonwhites. In the aftermath of World War II, the Soviet Union sharply limited access to all contraception in an effort to rebuild a population devastated by war.

But as concerns about population growth mounted in the 1970s and beyond, some states moved to limit the numbers of their people. Acting under a state of emergency, the government of India sterilized some 11 million men and women between 1975 and 1977, using a combination of incentives and compulsion to gain consent. China pursued population control on an even larger scale through its **one-child family policy**, which lasted from 1980 until 2014. Under the pressure of financial incentives and penalties and intense pressure from local authorities, over 300 million women "agreed" to have IUD devices implanted, over 100 million were sterilized, and many were forced to undergo abortions.

一对夫妇只生一个孩子

China's One-Child Family China's vigorous efforts to limit its population growth represented a radical intrusion of state power into the private lives of its people. It was accompanied by a massive propaganda effort, illustrated by this urban billboard. (Barry Lewis/Alamy)

Communist regimes intervened in personal life in other ways as well. Among the earliest and most revolutionary actions of the new communist government in the Soviet Union were efforts at liberating and mobilizing women. Almost immediately upon coming to power, communist authorities in the Soviet Union declared full legal and political equality for women; marriage became a civil procedure among freely consenting adults; divorce was legalized and made easier, as was abortion; illegitimacy was abolished; women no longer had to take their husbands' surnames; pregnancy leave for employed women was mandated; and women were actively mobilized as workers in the country's drive to industrialization. During the 1920s, a special party organization called the **Women's Department** (Zhenotdel) organized numerous conferences for women, trained women to run day-care centers and medical clinics, published newspapers and magazines aimed at a female audience, provided literacy and prenatal classes, and encouraged Muslim women to take off their veils.

Elsewhere as well, states acted in favor of women's rights and gender equality, most notably in Turkey, a thoroughly Muslim country, during the 1920s and 1930s. Turkey had emerged as an independent state, led by Kemal Atatürk, from the ashes of the Ottoman Empire following World War I. In Atatürk's view, the emancipation of women was a cornerstone of the new Turkey and a mark of the country's modernization. In a much-quoted speech, he declared:

If henceforward the women do not share in the social life of the nation . . . we shall remain irremediably backward, incapable of treating on equal terms with the civilizations of the West.[24]

Thus polygamy was abolished; women were granted equal rights in divorce, inheritance, and child custody; and in 1934 Turkish women gained the right to vote and hold public office, a full decade before French women gained that right. Public beaches were opened to women, and Atatürk encouraged them to discard the veil or head covering, long associated with Muslim piety, in favor of Western styles of dress. As in the early Soviet Union, this was a state-directed feminism, responsive to Atatürk's modern views, rather than reflecting popular demands from women themselves.

But what the state granted to women, the state could also take away, as it did in Iran in the years following that country's Islamic revolution in 1979. The country's new Islamic government, headed by the Ayatollah Khomeini, moved to sharply tighten religiously inspired restrictions on women, while branding feminism and women's rights as a Western evil. By 1983, all women were required to wear the modest head-to-toe covering known as hijab, a regulation enforced by roving groups of militants, or "revolutionary guards." Sexual segregation was imposed in schools, parks, beaches, and public transportation. The legal age of marriage for girls, set at eighteen under the prerevolutionary regime, was reduced to nine with parental consent. Married women could no longer file for divorce or attend school. Yet, despite such restrictions, many women supported the revolution and over the next several decades found far greater opportunities for employment and higher education than before. By the early twenty-first century, almost 60 percent of university students were women, women's right to vote remained intact, and some loosening of earlier restrictions on women had become apparent.

Feminism and Personal Life

A third source of change in personal life during the past century derived from social movements committed to liberation from ancient patterns of inequality and oppression. No expression of this global culture of liberation held a more profound potential for social change than feminism, for it represented a rethinking of the most fundamental and personal of all human relationships—that between women and men. Although feminism had begun in the West in the nineteenth century, it became global in the twentieth, as organized efforts to address the concerns of women took shape across the world.

Western feminism had lost momentum as an organized movement by the end of the 1920s, when many countries in Western Europe and North America had achieved women's suffrage. But it revived in the 1960s with a quite different agenda as women's participation in the paid workforce mounted rapidly. In France, for example, *The Second Sex*, by the writer and philosopher Simone de Beauvoir, appeared in 1949 arguing that women had historically been defined as "other," or deviant from the "normal" male sex. The book soon became a central statement of a reviving women's movement. Across the Atlantic, millions of American women responded to Betty Friedan's book, *The Feminine Mystique* (1963), which disclosed the identity crisis of educated women, unfulfilled by marriage and motherhood. Some adherents of this **second-wave feminism** took up the equal rights agenda of their nineteenth-century predecessors, but with an emphasis now on employment and education rather than voting rights. A more radical expression of American feminism, widely known as "women's liberation," took broader aim at patriarchy as a system of domination, similar to those of race and class. One manifesto from 1969 declared:

> We are exploited as sex objects, breeders, domestic servants, and cheap labor. We are considered inferior beings, whose only purpose is to enhance men's lives. . . . Because we live so intimately with our oppressors, we have been kept from seeing our personal suffering as a political condition.[25]

Thus liberation for women meant becoming aware of their own oppression, a process that took place in thousands of consciousness-raising groups across the United States. Favoring direct action, some of these women disrupted the Miss America contest of 1968 while disposing of girdles, bras, high-heeled shoes, tweezers, and other "instruments of oppression" in a Freedom Trashcan. They also brought into open discussion issues involving sexuality, insisting that free love, lesbianism, and celibacy should be accorded the same respect as heterosexual marriage.

Yet another strand of Western feminism emerged from women of color. For many of them, the concerns of white, usually middle-class, feminists were hardly relevant to their oppression. Black women had always worked outside the home and so felt little need to be liberated from the chains of homemaking. Whereas white women might find the family oppressive, African American women viewed it as a secure base from which to resist racism and poverty. Solidarity with black men, rather than separation from them, was essential in confronting a racist America.

As women mobilized across Asia, Africa, and Latin America, they too faced very different situations than did white women in the United States and Europe. The predominant issues for **feminism in the Global South**—colonialism, racism, poverty, development, political oppression, and sometimes revolution—were not always directly related to gender. To many African feminists in the 1970s and later, the concerns of their American or European sisters were too individualistic, too focused on sexuality, and insufficiently concerned with issues of motherhood, marriage, and poverty to be of much use. Furthermore, they resented Western feminists' insistent interest in cultural matters such as female genital mutilation and polygamy, which sometimes echoed the concerns of colonial-era missionaries and administrators. Western feminism could easily be seen as a new form of cultural imperialism.

During the colonial era, much of women's political activity was aligned with the struggle for independence. Later, women's movements in the Global South took shape around a wide range of issues. In the East African country of Kenya, a major form of mobilization was the "women's group" movement. Some 27,000 small associations of women, an outgrowth of traditional self-help groups, provided support for one another during times of need, such as weddings, births, and funerals, and took on community projects, such as building water cisterns, schools, and dispensaries. Some groups became revolving loan societies or bought land or businesses. One woman testified to the sense of empowerment she derived from membership in her group:

> I am a free woman. I bought this piece of land through my group. I can lie on it, work on it, keep goats or cows. What more do I want? My husband cannot sell it. It is mine.[26]

Elsewhere, other issues and approaches predominated. In the North African Islamic kingdom of Morocco, a more centrally directed and nationally focused feminist movement targeted the country's Family Law Code, which still defined women as minors. In 2004, a long campaign by Morocco's feminist movement, often with the help of supportive men and a liberal king, resulted in a new Family Law Code that recognized women as equals to their husbands and allowed them to initiate divorce and to claim child custody, all of which had previously been denied.

In Chile, a women's movement emerged as part of a national struggle against the military dictatorship of General Augusto Pinochet, who ruled the country from 1973 to 1990. Because they were largely regarded as "invisible" in the public sphere, women were able to organize extensively, despite the repression of the Pinochet regime. From this explosion of organizing activity emerged a women's movement that crossed class lines and party affiliations. Poor urban women by the tens of thousands organized soup kitchens, craft workshops, and shopping collectives, all aimed at the economic survival of their families. Smaller numbers of middle-class women brought more distinctly feminist perspectives to the movement and argued pointedly for "democracy in the country and in the home." This diverse women's movement was an important part of the larger national protest that returned Chile to democratic government in 1990.

Perhaps the most impressive achievement of feminism in the twentieth century was its ability to project the "woman question" as a global issue and to gain international recognition for the view that "women's rights are human rights." Like slavery and empire before it, patriarchy lost at least some of its legitimacy during this most recent century. Feminism registered as a global issue when the United Nations (UN), under pressure from women activists, declared 1975 as International Women's Year and the next ten years as the Decade for Women. By 2006, 183 nations, though not the United States, had ratified a UN Convention on the Elimination of All Forms of Discrimination against Women, which committed them to promote women's legal equality, to end discrimination, to actively encourage women's development, and to protect women's human rights. Clearly, this international attention to women's issues set a global standard to which feminists operating in their own countries could aspire.

But feminism generated a global backlash among those who felt that its agenda undermined family life, the proper relationship of men and women, and civilization generally. To Phyllis Schlafly, a prominent American opponent of equal rights for women, feminism was a "disease" that brought in its wake "fear, sickness, pain, anger, hatred, danger, violence, and all manner of ugliness."[27] In the Islamic world, Western-style feminism, with its claims of gender equality and open sexuality, was highly offensive to many and fueled movements of religious revivalism that invited or compelled women to wear the veil and sometimes to lead highly restricted lives. The Vatican, some Catholic and Muslim countries, and at times the U.S. government took strong exception to aspects of global feminism, particularly its emphasis on reproductive rights, including access to abortion and birth control. Many African governments and many African men defined feminism of any kind as "un-African" and associated with a hated colonialism. Feminist support for gay and lesbian rights only solidified opposition to women's rights activists within socially conservative circles internationally. Thus feminism was global as the twenty-first century dawned, but it was very diverse and much contested.

Controversies: Debating Globalization

By the early 1990s, "globalization" had become a buzzword among scholars, journalists, and ordinary people alike because it succinctly captured something of the deeply connected and entangled world of the late twentieth century. The economists, sociologists, and political scientists who first embraced the term presented "globalization" as novel and unprecedented: the world was becoming "a single place," and human history was entering a wholly new era of global connectedness and global consciousness.

World historians, however, were not so sure about the novelty of "globalization." They had, after all, long traced patterns of interaction, communication, and exchange among distant regions and civilizations: the Silk Road commercial networks across Eurasia; the movement of technologies and disease; the transcontinental spread of Buddhism, Christianity, and Islam; the making of an Atlantic world linking Europe, Africa, and the Americas; and the globe-spanning empires of Europe. Did all of this count as "globalization," pushing its origins deep into the past?

Yet another controversy involved the "drivers" of globalization. For some, they were impersonal forces — "the inexorable integration of markets, nation-states, and technologies" — according to leading journalist Thomas Friedman. In such a view, no one was in control, and the process, once begun, was inevitable and unstoppable. Others believed that powerful economic elites and political leaders, acting from a free market ideology, deliberately shaped policies (such as low tariffs) and institutions (the World Trade Organization, for example) that opened the door to corporate globalization.

The economic outcomes of recent globalization have also generated much debate. Did globalization increase or reduce inequality? Answers depend very much on what is being measured. If the measure is income, most economists think that inequality on a global level has substantially increased. One study concluded that the per capita income gap between the United States and various regions of the Global South roughly tripled since 1960.[28] The rich were getter richer much faster than the poor were gaining income.

But if the measure of economic outcomes involves "quality of life indicators," the picture changes considerably. Average global life expectancy, for example, more than doubled since 1900, reaching 71.4 years in 2014. Thus many countries in the Global South now approach the 79-year life span of U.S. citizens: China, 76 years; Iran, 75; Brazil, 74; India, 68. Even poorer countries have dramatically increased their life expectancies, with sub-Saharan African rates improving from 40 years in 1960 to 59 years in 2014.[29] Clearly, despite growing inequality in income, inequality in longevity has lessened. So which is the more important measure of inequality: income measured in dollars or life expectancy measured in years?

Yet another controversy involves the impact of globalization on nation-states. Many elements of the globalized world have arguably diminished the ability of nation-states to act freely in their own interests — agreements favoring free trade and the power of huge transnational corporations, for example. The more enthusiastic advocates of globalization have imagined a future in which the nation-state has vanished, or at least greatly weakened, in the face of global flows of people, capital, goods, services, and ideas.

Others, however, view such opinions as exaggerated. It was, after all, the decisions of some states that created a free trade international system after World War II, even as other states, especially in the communist bloc, refused to take part in it. And what states create they can also change. China joined the World Trade Organization in 2001 after decades of declining to take part in the global marketplace; the United Kingdom decided in 2016 to leave the European Union; the Trump administration in the United States announced American withdrawal from the Trans-Pacific Partnership agreement in early 2017. Even developing countries have some leverage. Both Mexico and Cuba have nationalized American industries in their countries in the twentieth century. And the oil-producing states of the Middle East upended the global markets in the late 1970s when they dramatically raised the price of oil. All of this testifies to the continuing power of state action to shape the world economy.

Cultural globalization too prompted debate and controversy. Has the world become more culturally homogeneous in the global age? Many feared that the answer was "yes" as "cultural imperialism" in the shape of westernization or Americanization swept the planet, displacing many established cultural patterns and ways of living. The prevalence of English and modern science; the popularity of McDonald's, blue jeans, Barbie dolls, and American films; shopping malls and Western-style consumerism across the world; cell phones and the Internet—all of this and much more suggested the emergence of a "global culture."

But perhaps globalization produces or reinforces cultural difference as well as commonality. The rise of Islamic fundamentalism represented strong resistance to the intrusion of Western secular culture. French efforts to prevent the importation of too many American films or TV programs and to prohibit the wearing of headscarves by Muslim women likewise reflected a desire to preserve major elements of French national culture in an age of globalization. A proliferation of ethnic nationalist movements articulated demands to ensure the integrity of particular and local cultures. Furthermore, a phenomenon known as "glocalization" refers to the process by which foreign products or practices are adapted to local cultural patterns. Yoga in the West often became a form of exercise or relaxation, losing much of its original spiritual significance, while McDonald's restaurants in India and China now include various rice-based menu offerings.

Globalization is commonly regarded as a still-unfolding process leading to an uncertain destination, often called "globality" or "entanglement on a global scale." Two prominent historians have recently contested this understanding, arguing that "globality" has long been a "done deal," a condition already achieved. The question then is not whether to participate in this globalized world, but rather "how to change in order to keep pace with, hold out against, or adapt to a world of continuous and inescapable interactivity."[30]

And yet, is it possible to imagine global connections unraveling? Is globalization really a "done deal"? Various events of the early twenty-first century have caused many to wonder: something close to a global economic collapse in 2008; the exit of Great Britain from the European Union; the election of Donald Trump promising that "Americanism not globalism will be our credo"; the reaction against immigration in the United States and Western Europe; and the rise of assertive nationalist movements in much of Europe, Turkey, Iran, China, India, and elsewhere. Does this mean that globalization is in retreat? The debate continues, as it does for almost everything related to globalization.

Reflections: History in the Middle of the Stream

Historians are usually more at ease telling stories that have clear endings, such as those that describe ancient Egyptian civilization, the Atlantic slave trade, or the French Revolution. There is a finality to these stories and a distance from them that makes it easier for historians to assume the posture of detached observers, even if their understandings of those events change over time. Finality, distance, and detachment are harder to come by when historians are describing the events and processes of the past century, for many of these stories are clearly unfinished. Technological innovation, population growth, globalization, and climate change—all of these are ongoing processes, their outcomes unknown and unknowable. In dealing with such matters, historians write from the middle of the stream, often uncomfortably, rather than from the banks, where they might feel more at ease.

In part, that discomfort arises from questions about the future that such issues inevitably raise. Should historians speculate about "what's next?" when the processes they describe in the past bump up against the present and future? Many people expect that some understanding of the past gives historians a unique insight into what is coming next. But historians themselves are often rather cautious about predictions because they are so aware of the unexpectedness and surprising quality of historical change. Fifty years ago, who could have anticipated the Internet or China's massive industrial growth?

And yet questions about the future are legitimate and important. Present-day issues and their possible futures encourage historians to look at the past in different ways. It is surely no accident that women's history and environmental history have flourished in recent decades, as feminism and environmentalism have achieved global prominence. And for individuals seeking guidance about the future, history is just about the only guide we have. As the nineteenth-century Danish philosopher Søren Kierkegaard remarked: "Life can only be understood backward, but it is lived forward." So, like everyone before us, we stumble on, both individually and collectively, largely in the dark, using analogies from the past, tentatively, as we make our way ahead.

These vast uncertainties about the future provide a useful reminder that although we know the outcomes of earlier human stories—the Asian and African struggles for independence, for example—those who lived that history did not. Such awareness can perhaps engender in us a measure of humility and greater sympathy with those whose lives we study. However we may differ from our ancestors across time and place, we share with them an immense ignorance about what the future holds.

Second Thoughts

WHAT'S THE SIGNIFICANCE?

age of fossil fuels (p. 637)
communication revolution (p. 640)
economic globalization (p. 642)
Asian Tigers (p. 643)

Bretton Woods system (p. 644)
transnational corporations (p. 645)
World Trade Organization (WTO)
   (p. 648)

North American Free Trade
   Agreement (NAFTA) (p. 648)
consumerism (p. 651)
export-processing zones (EPZs) (p. 652)
service sector (p. 653)
informal economy (p. 653)

one-child family policy (China)
   (p. 657)
Women's Department (p. 658)
second-wave feminism (p. 659)
feminism in the Global South
   (p. 660)

BIG PICTURE QUESTIONS

1. How did the energy and technology revolutions impact economic development during the past century?
2. What have been the costs and benefits of globalization for the world economy and the lives of workers since 1900?
3. What social, political, and cultural norms were challenged by women in the twentieth century?
4. How have the global developments examined in this chapter shaped your own life and community?
5. Looking Back: To what extent did the processes discussed in this chapter (energy and technological change, globalization, and feminism) have roots in the more distant past? In what respects did they represent something new?

CHRONOLOGY

1882–1920	• Electric grids developed in industrial countries
1908	• Mass production of automobiles begins
1920–1940	• Land reform in Mexico
1923–1938	• Women's emancipation in Turkey
1929–1940	• The Great Depression
1930s–1970	• Green Revolution technologies developed and applied
1940s	• Earliest digital computers
1945–1970	• Postwar economic boom
1960	• Birth control pill approved in U.S.
1960s	• Second-wave feminism begins

1970s	• Developing countries demand "new international economic order"
1975	• United Nations: International Women's Year
1978–2013	• Rapid economic growth in China
1979	• Islamic revolution in Iran
1980–2014	• China's one-child family policy
1991	• Earliest web browser released
1999	• Seattle protests against the WTO
2004	• Morocco's Family Law Code advances women's rights
2006	• UN Convention on the Elimination of All Forms of Discrimination against Women ratified by 183 nations
2016	• Britain's exit from EU announced
2017	• U.S. withdraws from Trans-Pacific Partnership

23

Global Processes

Demography, Culture, and the Environment

1900–present

IN THE EARLY TWENTY-FIRST CENTURY, A FORTY-FIVE-YEAR-OLD
vegetable grower named Omar Imma Assayar moved with his wife and ten children from their rural village in the West African country of Chad to the capital city of N'Djamena. While living in the village, he had to get up early and carry his produce to the market in the city by bicycle. "My life is easier now," he explained. "I live right next to the market. I have more time to be with my family, and I can get a better price for my vegetables as well. . . . My one big wish is for my children to go to school."[1]

667

Omar and his family have both witnessed and participated in some of the major drivers of world history during the past century. His ten children have contributed to the enormous increase in human numbers. In moving to the capital of Chad, Omar joined millions of others in Africa, Asia, and Latin America who are seeking a better life in the city. In his desire to educate his children, he has also taken part in the vast expansion of literacy that has swept the planet during the past century. Not far from his new home is Lake Chad, which has shrunk drastically in response to climate change and overuse, linking his country to global patterns of environmental degradation. The life of this single individual then is connected to the global processes that conclude this account of the human journey during the twentieth century and beyond—massive population growth, widespread movement of people, changing patterns of cultural identity, and unprecedented human impact on the environment that sustains us all.

More People: Quadrupling Human Numbers

From about 1.65 billion people in 1900, world population soared to approximately 7.5 billion in 2017. In little more than a century, the human species had more than quadrupled its numbers. It had taken humankind several hundred thousand years to reach 1 billion people in the early nineteenth century. That number then reached 2 billion in roughly 1930, 3 billion in 1960, 4 billion in 1975, 5 billion in 1987, 6 billion in 1999, and 7.6 billion in 2018. The speed and extent of this twentieth-century **population explosion** have no parallel in the human past or in the history of primate life on the planet.[2] Equally striking is the distribution of this massive growth, as some 90 percent of it occurred in the developing countries of Asia, Africa, the Middle East, and Latin America. (See Snapshot: World Population Growth, 1950–2100, page 669.) A striking shift in the demographic weight of the world's various peoples was clearly under way, with more to come in the twenty-first century.

The explanation for this massive demographic change lies in lower death rates. In 1945 roughly 20 people died each year for every 1,000 people in the world's population. By 2014 that figure was 8.[3] Infant mortality has dropped even more quickly, especially since the 1960s. New medical technologies such as antibiotics, disinfectants, vaccines, and x-rays played a major role in this unprecedented change. Many governments, including colonial regimes, as well as international agencies such as the United Nations, established public health programs to push improved sanitation and clean drinking water, while widening access to medical services. Various mosquito control measures sharply reduced death from malaria and yellow fever, while extensive vaccination campaigns eradicated smallpox by 1977.

As populations grew, innovations in agriculture enabled food production globally to keep up with, and even exceed, growing human numbers. A new **"Green Revolution"** greatly increased agricultural output through the use of tractors and mechanical harvesters; the massive application of chemical fertilizers, pesticides, and herbicides; and the development of high-yielding varieties of wheat and rice. All of this sustained the enormous population growth in developing countries.

By the end of the twentieth century, the rate of global population growth had begun to slow, as birth rates dropped all around the world. This transition to fewer births had occurred first in the more industrialized countries, where birth control

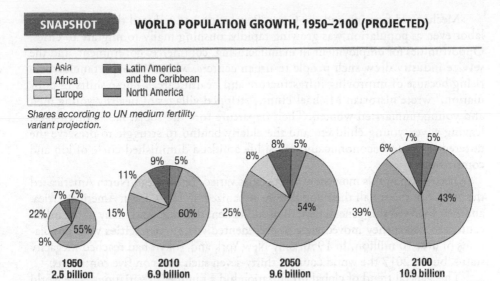

SNAPSHOT   **WORLD POPULATION GROWTH, 1950–2100 (PROJECTED)**

Legend:
- Asia
- Africa
- Europe
- Latin America and the Caribbean
- North America

Shares according to UN medium fertility variant projection.

1950 — 2.5 billion: 22%, 7%, 7%, 55%, 9%

2010 — 6.9 billion: 11%, 9%, 5%, 60%, 15%

2050 — 9.6 billion: 8%, 8%, 5%, 54%, 25%

2100 — 10.9 billion: 6%, 7%, 5%, 43%, 39%

The European Environment Agency

measures were widely available, women were educated and pursuing careers, and large families were economically burdensome. By 1983, in a dozen or more countries in Europe, population growth had stopped altogether and then began to decline in a number of places. More recently, this pattern began to take hold in developing countries as well, associated with urbanization, with growing educational opportunities for girls, and with vigorous family-planning programs in many places. China's famous one-child family policy, introduced in 1980, was the most dramatic of these efforts. Nonetheless, the world's population has continued to rise and according to UN projections is expected to reach 9.7 billion in 2050 and 11.2 billion in 2100.

People in Motion: Patterns of Migration

Growing numbers meant more people on the move. Transportation technology—steamships, trains, buses, cars, trucks, airplanes—has facilitated this vast circulation of people as well as goods. So has war, famine, climate change, poverty, industrialization, and urban growth. For millions of individuals, those decisions to move led to wrenching separations, exhilarating possibilities, immense disappointments, social conflicts, and new identities.

To the Cities: Global Urbanization

In the early twenty-first century, humankind reached a remarkable, though largely unnoticed, milestone. For the first time more people around the world lived in towns and cities than in the countryside. Although urban populations had been slowly increasing for centuries, it was massive **global urbanization**, the explosive growth of cities after 1900, that made the world an "urban place."[4] City-dwellers made up 15 percent of the world's population in 1900 and about 25 percent in 1950 before doubling again to 50 percent by 2007.

Mechanized farming and the Green Revolution had reduced the need for rural labor even as population was growing rapidly, pushing many to migrate to cities. Opportunities for employment in manufacturing, commerce, government, and the service industry drew such people to urban centers, where life expectancies were rising because of improving infrastructure and health care. "These shifts in population," wrote historian Michael Hunt, "stripped villages of healthy young men and young, unmarried women. Their departure tore the social fabric of villages, leaving wives, young children, and the elderly behind to struggle to preserve the tattered threads of economic and social life amidst a diminished circle of kin and compatriots."[5]

The timing of this movement to the cities varied. Europe and North America led the way, with about half their populations urbanized by 1950. Latin America, Africa, and Asia followed this general pattern in subsequent decades. And many of the urban centers to which they moved were unprecedentedly large **megacities** with populations of over 10 million. In 1950, only New York and Tokyo had reached megacity status, but by 2017 the world counted thirty-seven such cities on five continents.

This general trend of global urbanization hid a number of variations. The world wars and the Depression in the first half of the century slowed the growth of cities, especially in the industrialized world. World War II in particular damaged or destroyed innumerable cities in Western Europe, the Soviet Union, and East Asia. But some areas well away from conflict zones, such as Latin America, witnessed rapid urban growth. After 1945, the postwar economic boom led to the revival and growth of cities in Western Europe, parts of Asia, and North America. But in the communist world, where centralized command economies prevailed, migration to cities was sharply restricted. Passports and residency permits regulated migration in the Soviet Union, while in China the government created a household registration system in 1958 to limit movement of rural workers to cities. Communist governments, however, still embraced urban living, with over 1,000 new planned cities built in Eastern Europe and the Soviet Union in the aftermath of World War II.

From the 1970s, the decline in manufacturing in some regions of the developed world prompted many industrial cities to reinvent themselves as hubs for education, health care, logistics, information technology, and other services. And as industrialization took hold in the Global South after 1950, cities grew at around twice the rate of already industrialized regions. In the 1980s, the Chinese government loosened residency restrictions that had kept much of the population in the countryside, unleashing an unprecedented wave of urban migrants, so that by 2015, 56 percent of China's population lived in cities, dramatically up from 26 percent in 1990. Everywhere, cities attracted primarily young people from the countryside looking for better job prospects and educational, social, and cultural opportunities.

Even the most modern, well-managed cities had profound impacts on the environment, as large concentrations of people consumed huge amounts of food, energy, and water and in turn emitted enormous amounts of sewage, garbage, carbon dioxide, and toxic substances. Certainly, the poorly serviced slums and loosely regulated manufacturing enterprises of many cities across the planet created ecological disasters that destroyed the environment and damaged the health of residents, while elite neighborhoods boasted safe water, sewage systems, electricity, and fire and police services. On a per person basis, however, city living sometimes reduced electricity consumption and carbon emissions because public transportation, energy-efficient residences, and smaller families lessened the impact of humans on the environment.

Everywhere, wealth was concentrated in cities, but inequality was all the more apparent because the rich and poor often lived in close proximity, with luxury apartment buildings, office blocks, and malls overlooking slums and shantytowns. Improvements in public and private transport in the twentieth century allowed cities to spread out as never before. In the early twentieth century some cities, like Munich, Chicago, Sydney, and Cape Town, had large middle-class suburban communities composed of single-family houses, and after midcentury similar communities developed in cities across the globe where incomes and transportation networks allowed. In other cities, like Jakarta, Rio de Janeiro, Nairobi, and Lagos, rapid urban sprawl was driven primarily by recent arrivals who settled in slums on empty pieces of land with few public services, often at the edges of cities or in marginal spaces like steep hillsides or areas prone to flooding. In 2006, a visitor described the Kibera slum in Nairobi as "a squeezed square mile . . . home to nearly one million people. . . . Most of them live in one-room mud or wattle huts or in wooden or basic stone houses often windowless. . . . The Kenyan state provides the huge, illegal sprawl with nothing—no sanitation, no roads, no hospitals. It is a massive ditch of mud and filth, with a brown dribble of a stream running through it."[6] Clearly population growth and the rise of cities did not solve, and probably exacerbated in many places, the problem of urban poverty.

Moving Abroad: Long-Distance Migration

While most "people in motion" traveled to nearby cities, a growing number moved abroad. (See Map 23.1.) Older patterns of migration, from Europe to the Americas, for example, continued and even accelerated in the early twentieth century, but migration patterns changed as the century progressed. (For earlier patterns of migration, see "Europeans in Motion" in Chapter 17 and "Economies of Wage Labor: Migration for Work" in Chapter 18.) The number of migrants from Africa and Latin America grew significantly, while Europe, earlier a leading source of long-distance emigrants, instead became an important destination for immigrants. From the 1920s on, the percentage of female migrants steadily grew, and in 2016 women constituted nearly half of all international migrants.

During the twentieth century states increasingly sought to control the flow of migrants across their borders, requiring travelers to possess passports and creating numerous administrative categories to describe migrants—asylum seekers, guest workers, refugees, tourists, students, climate refugees, illegals, and undocumented persons. Since World War II, these efforts to regulate borders have helped create enormous increases in refugees as desperate individuals find routes for flight shut off, leaving many millions living in refugee camps, often for generations. The situation of Abdallah Hajji, a Somalian refugee in Kenya in 2016, was typical of displaced people around the world: "I arrived . . . in 1994, since then I never moved out of here. I can't return because it's not safe now."[7]

The twentieth century also witnessed new patterns of human migration driven by war, revolution, the end of empire, and the emergence of new nation-states—many of which proved less tolerant of ethnic minorities than the empires that they replaced.

Legal Migration and Major Routes, 1990–2000

1–3.5 million

500,000–1 million

300,000–500,000

Countries Experiencing Net Outward Migration, 2005

Countries with large-scale emigration (+15% of population living abroad)

Countries with significant emigration (5–15% of population living abroad)

Countries Experiencing Net Inward Migration, 2005

Countries with large-scale immigration (+15% of population born abroad)

Countries with significant immigration (5–15% of population born abroad)

PACIFIC OCEAN

INDIAN OCEAN

ATLANTIC OCEAN

PACIFIC OCEAN

Japan

East Asia

Southeast Asia

South Asia

Russia

Central and Eastern Europe

Turkey

Balkans

Western Europe

Gulf States

Africa

Australia

Caribbean

Mexico

North America

South America

The collapse of the Ottoman Empire following World War I prompted a large-scale exchange of populations as over a million Greek Orthodox Christians from Turkey relocated to Greece, while some 400,000 Turkish-speaking Muslims living in Greece moved in the other direction. Fleeing anti-Semitism, fascism, and the Holocaust, Jews immigrated to what is now Israel in large numbers, generating in the process a flow of Palestinian refugees to settlements in neighboring countries. Indian independence from Britain in 1947 resulted in the partition of the region along sectarian lines, forcing millions to migrate. In Rwanda, massacres by Hutus in July 1994 required over a million Tutsis to flee their homes, while the ultimate victory of the Tutsis sparked an even larger exodus of Hutus. Still other peoples moved as refugees fleeing violence or political oppression in places such as Vietnam, Cambodia, Sudan, Uganda, Cuba, Haiti, Iraq, Afghanistan, and Syria.

Perhaps the most significant pattern of global migration since the 1960s has featured a vast movement of people from the developing countries of Asia, Africa, and Latin America to the industrialized world of Europe and North America, with smaller flows to Australia and the oil-rich states of the Persian Gulf. Pakistanis, Indians, and West Indians moved to Great Britain; Algerians and West Africans to France; Turks and Kurds to Germany; Filipinos, Koreans, Cubans, Mexicans, and Haitians to the United States; and Egyptians, Pakistanis, Bangladeshis, and smaller numbers of highly skilled Westerners to the Persian Gulf states.

Much of this involved **labor migration**, as people moved, often illegally and with few skills, to escape poverty in their own lands, drawn by a belief that employment opportunities and a better future awaited them in the developed countries. Often their journeys have been dangerous, as migrants have confronted long treks through burning deserts in the American Southwest or braved dangerous crossings of the Mediterranean Sea to Europe in rickety and overcrowded vessels. Many depended on the expensive and sometimes unreliable human smugglers. Smaller numbers of highly skilled and university-trained people, such as doctors and computer scientists, came in search of professional opportunities less available in their own countries.

Everywhere migrants have struggled to find a place in their adopted communities. In some regions immigrant groups have for centuries assimilated into local societies without fully losing their distinct identities, a pattern that persisted into the twentieth century. Indians in East Africa, Chinese in Southeast Asia, and Japanese in Peru took advantage of their outsider status to become middlemen, forging links between existing groups in society as merchants, traders, or financiers. However, with the emergence or strengthening of national identities during the twentieth century, some of these minorities faced persecution. In Indonesia, huge numbers of ethnic Chinese who had lived in the region for generations were killed or driven from the country in 1965 by authorities suspicious that they held communist sympathies.

< MAP 23.1 Global Migration Patterns, 1990–2005
The late twentieth and early twenty-first centuries witnessed a large-scale movement of people, primarily from the Global South to the Global North. (Data from United Nations, World Bank, 2005; OEDC, 2001)

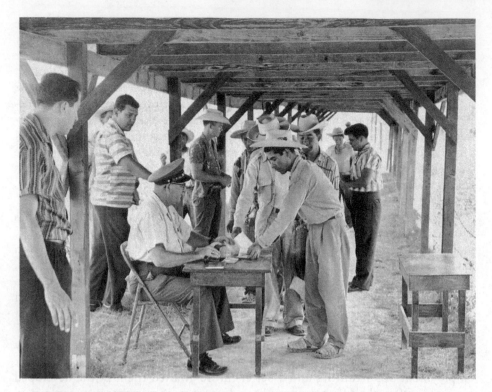

Mexican Migrant Workers Since the early twentieth century, U.S. growers had employed migrant Mexican workers. But the acute labor shortage associated with World War II prompted a formal agreement between the governments of the two countries. Known as the Bracero (migrant labor) program, it brought some 4.5 million agricultural workers to the United States between 1942 and 1964. This image shows some of these workers being processed at a labor center in Hidalgo, Texas, in 1959. (AP/REX/Shutterstock)

The most important countries of arrival for twentieth-century migrants — the United States, Canada, Australia, and, since the 1960s, Western Europe — all expected that immigrants would assimilate into their societies by adopting the language, political values, and cultural norms of the host society. Many migrants agreed, viewing assimilation as a pathway to better economic opportunities and social status even if it often took several generations for a migrant family to fully integrate into the host society. Despite this pressure toward assimilation, migrants also maintained aspects of their homelands' cultures, some of which were embraced by their new communities. Immigrants often opened eateries featuring dishes from their countries of origin, such as a Mexican tamale food truck in Los Angeles, an Indian curry house in London, or a Chinese noodle café in Sydney.

The expectation of migrant assimilation in the West also brought tensions and conflict, particularly over cultural integration. In France, for instance, the immigration of Muslims, mostly from North Africa, has sparked controversy over women's clothing. A French law in 2004 forbade the practice of wearing headscarves in public schools on the grounds that it compromised the secularism of French education and represented the repression of women. But many Muslim women strongly objected to the law, arguing that it undermined their freedom of religion and violated their cultural traditions. As one woman put it, "France is supposed to be a free country. Nowadays women have the right to take their clothes off but not put them on."[8] In the United States large-scale migration in recent decades from Latin America has led some to demand that English be designated the official language of the country. More recently, fears that immigrants openly hostile to Western values might bring terrorism to host societies have led to calls to limit or refuse admission to refugees from some Islamic countries. At the same time, other voices have advocated the benefits of multiculturalism for the globalized and knowledge-based societies and economies of the twenty-first century.

A final category of long-distance migrants has encompassed those engaged in short-term travel. International tourist arrivals grew from 25 million in 1950 to 988 million in 2011. Businesspeople in search of profits and students in search of education have crisscrossed the world in large numbers. These travelers have participated in "an unprecedented new era of transnational ties and mobility" that is only a few decades old.[9]

Microbes in Motion: Disease and Recent History

People in motion have carried not only their cultures but also their microbes. Everywhere growing populations, urban living, and unprecedented mobility created more efficient pathways for deadly diseases to mutate and spread across the globe. Even before the emergence of commercial air travel, the early twentieth century witnessed the worst pandemic in human history when three waves of an **influenza pandemic** swept across the globe in 1918 and 1919, carried by demobilized soldiers, refugees, and other dislocated people returning home from World War I. One American army doctor at a base just outside of Boston reported: "We used to go down to the morgue and look at the boys laid out in long rows. It beats any sight they ever had in France after a battle."[10] Between 50 and 100 million people died in the pandemic—five to ten times more than perished on the battlefields of World War I.

Another new pathogen, human immunodeficiency virus (HIV), which causes acquired immune deficiency syndrome (AIDS), sparked a second global pandemic beginning in the 1980s. Unlike the influenza virus of 1918, **HIV/AIDS** spread primarily through sexual contact, contaminated blood products, or the sharing of needles by intravenous drug users. Nonetheless, the disease has spread rapidly across the globe. In 2016 nearly 37 million people lived with HIV, while tens of millions have died since the 1980s of AIDS or its complications. In sub-Saharan Africa, where the disease first emerged—and where nearly 70 percent of those currently infected reside—the disease was spread in part by long-distance truck drivers and the commercial sex workers they frequented on their travels. However, the connected world that facilitated its spread also produced treatments, which have transformed this disease from a major killer into a serious but chronic and manageable disease for those with access to the latest medicines.

Modern communication meant that in the twentieth century reports of new diseases spread faster than ever before. Concerned communities and their governments took action to try to keep diseases out or limit their spread by ordering measures like border checks and quarantines. Recognizing the potentially destabilizing economic, social, and political effects of pandemics, governments created both national and international institutions, like the World Health Organization, to help coordinate efforts to combat disease within national borders and beyond. In the early twenty-first century, new threats—severe acute respiratory syndrome (SARS), the Ebola virus, and the Zika virus, among others—prompted large-scale international efforts to identify, track, and stop their spread. Thus, while the twentieth century saw humankind mobilize its resources as never before to combat deadly pandemics, the more connected and urbanized world of recent times has left us more vulnerable to such outbreaks than in the past.

Cultural Identity in an Entangled World

Large and impersonal global processes (industrialization, migration, and urbanization, for example) have had a profound and personal impact at the level of individual identity—how people define the communities to which they belong, the religions with which they affiliate, and even the food they eat, the clothes they wear, and the music they enjoy. Certainly older patterns of cultural identity have been challenged as individuals have come up against people and cultures quite different from their own. Secular ideas and values were often at odds with traditional religious outlooks; feminist ideas confronted patriarchal assumptions; socialist or communist thinking undermined the legitimacy of deeply rooted social hierarchies. Among the identities in question during the past century, those of political and religious loyalty loomed large.

Race, Nation, and Ethnicity

Nineteenth-century Europe gave rise to an elaborate ideology of "race" as a fundamental distinction among human communities based on allegedly permanent biological characteristics. (See "Industry and Empire" in Chapter 18.) But it was in the twentieth century that such ideas achieved their greatest prominence, shaping individual behavior, institutional practices, and government policies alike. Three societies in particular stand out as openly racist regimes: Nazi Germany, the southern United States from the 1890s to the 1950s, and apartheid-era South Africa. All of them officially sanctioned explicitly racist ideologies, prohibited marriage across racial lines, legislated extreme forms of social segregation, denied all political rights to Jews or blacks, and deliberately kept Jews or blacks in poverty.

In many other places, race was a pervasive reality, though perhaps racist thinking was less officially endorsed. Racial distinctions and white supremacy were prominent in European thinking and central features within all of the European colonies in Africa and Asia, generating in turn a new racial awareness among many colonized people. Aime Cesaire, a poet from the French island of Martinique in the Caribbean region, coined the term "negritude," which he defined in 1939 as "the simple recognition of the fact that one is black."[11] Black, Indian, and mixed-race people in Latin America clearly experienced discrimination and disadvantage in relationship to whites or Europeans, even in the absence of legal constraints.

During the second half of the twentieth century, race lost much of its public legitimacy as a social distinction, discredited in part by the horrors of the Nazi regime. As the American author Barbara Ehrenreich put it: "Hitler gave race a bad name." Furthermore, scholars thoroughly debunked the connection between biology and culture or behavior, which was so central to racial thinking. But perhaps most importantly, the sharp critique of white bigotry and discrimination that accompanied the surging independence movements across Asia and Africa made overt racism globally illegitimate. The 1948 UN Declaration of Human Rights inscribed this rejection of racism as a new global moral standard, even as it persisted in practice in many places.

Even more pervasive than race as a form of individual identity and political loyalty has been that of nationalism, and the two have sometimes overlapped. Loyalty to national states and their presumed interests drove the world wars of the past century and undermined empires around the globe. But if nation-states and national loyalties largely triumphed during the past century, they also faced challenges. Pan-African and pan-Arab aspirations beckoned to those seeking a larger identity and loyalty, though they never achieved an effective political expression. The European Union did give concrete political meaning to a broader European identity in the aftermath of two disastrous wars, though by the early twenty-first century the Union appeared shaky in the face of rising nationalist sentiments and the British decision to withdraw. Globalization too challenged national loyalties as visions of a world without borders and destructive national rivalries appealed to many. The League of Nations and the United Nations gave expression to such visions. The growth of international economic linkages as well as an increasing global awareness of problems common to all of humankind generated for some a sense of global citizenship, a cosmopolitan feeling of being at home in the world as a whole. Pictures of the earth viewed from the moon or outer space — a beautiful but solitary planet in an immense cosmos — came to symbolize this one-world sensibility. Any number of transnational organizations — the Red Cross, Amnesty International, sister-city projects, a vast array of international professional, charitable, and scientific groups — have also articulated a distinctly international outlook.

If globalization represented an external challenge to national loyalties and existing nation-states, a serious internal challenge took shape as ethnically based separatist movements. Most of the world's states, after all, contained several, and sometimes many, culturally distinct peoples. Such peoples readily adopted the rhetoric and logic of nationalism, arguing that they too deserved some separate political status such as greater autonomy or full independence. Under the pressure of such movements, a number of states have in fact disintegrated. British India dissolved immediately upon independence into a Muslim Pakistan and largely Hindu India. In the early 1990s, Czechoslovakia and Yugoslavia fragmented, the former peacefully and the latter amid great violence. In northeastern Africa, Eritrea seceded from Ethiopia in 1993, and in 2011 South Sudan claimed independence from the Republic of Sudan, both of them following decades of civil war. Even where a separate state was not achieved, ethnic separatist movements have threatened the integrity of existing nation-states. Scotland has sought to exit from the United Kingdom, Quebec from Canada, Tibet from China, the Basques from Spain, Igbo-speaking peoples from Nigeria, and the Moro people from the Philippines. Many Russians living in eastern Ukraine would prefer

Ethnic Cleansing in Vukovar, Croatia The disintegration of the multiethnic state of Yugoslavia in southeastern Europe during the 1990s gave rise to numerous violent conflicts among its various ethnic groups. This photograph shows Croatians making their way through the rubble of the city of Vukovar, from which some 20,000 of them had been expelled by Serbian troops. The city was almost completely destroyed and largely "cleansed" of its non-Serb population. (© Ron Haviv/VII/Redux)

annexation by Russia, and many Kurds living in Iraq, Iran, Syria, and Turkey aspire to an independent Kurdistan.

These various cultural identities—racial, national, ethnic, and global—have become politically and personally meaningful for much of the world's population even as they have mixed and mingled in many ways. German nationalism in the Nazi era found expression in racial terms. Some people found it possible to embrace both an ethnic heritage and loyalty to a larger nation with little contradiction, as many Irish, Italians, Hispanics, and African Americans have done in the United States. A sense of global citizenship, in the struggle against climate change, for example, remains compatible with loyalty to a particular country.

Popular Culture on the Move

Related to these cultural and political identities have been the many elements of popular culture that have increasingly permeated social life during the past century. They too have been on the move around the world in a process widely known as **cultural globalization**. It has been a many-sided phenomenon, with the heaviest currents moving from the West to the rest of the world. From the 1920s on, Hollywood films have been a major cultural export of the United States. Western music, including classical, jazz, rock and roll, and rap, has gained large audiences across the planet. By the late twentieth century, the United States accounted for roughly 75 percent of world TV programming exports. All of this has shaped patterns of taste globally. When American TV was introduced into Fiji in the 1990s, bulimia and anorexia among teenage girls soon increased substantially, as girls sought to acquire the slender body style of their TV favorites.

Beyond film, TV, and music, other elements of Western culture have gained widespread acceptance around the world. English has become a world language, with a billion or more people able to use it at some level, particularly within educated and elite circles. Western sports such as soccer, cricket, basketball, and baseball have an international presence. In 2015, more than 36,000 McDonald's restaurants in over 100 countries served 69 million people daily. And Western fashions — jeans, suits and ties, miniskirts, white wedding dresses — have become common in many places, sometimes losing their direct association with the West.

All of this has been driven by the dominance of the West in world affairs over the past several centuries and the impulse of many to imitate the ways of the powerful. But the assimilation of Western cultural forms has also come to symbolize modernity, inclusion in an emerging global culture, and sometimes liberation or rebellion, especially among the young. Such a sensibility informed Kemal Atatürk's desire for "civilized, international dress" for Turkish men when he sought to impose Western-style clothing on them during the 1920s and 1930s. The outlook was similar for liberated young women in Japan who imitated the dress style of Western "flappers" during the same time. They were *moga* or "modern girls" whose country was becoming a "province of the world."

The global spread of Western culture has raised fears in many places about cultural homogenization or cultural imperialism threatening local or national cultures, values, and traditions. Like other forms of globalization, the cultural variant of this larger process has witnessed not only enthusiastic embrace but also pushback, much of which has targeted the outsized American influence in the world. Communist Party officials in the Soviet Union, for example, were suspicious of the growing popularity of American jazz and later rock and roll. Associating these musical forms with Western individualistic values of spontaneity, open sexuality, and opposition to authority, they tried periodically to suppress them, though without much success.

In the Islamic world, pushback against cultural "contamination" from the West has been particularly prominent, especially in religiously fundamentalist circles. The Ayatollah Khomeini, architect of Iran's Islamic revolution, strongly expressed this outlook:

> Just what is the social life we are talking about? Is it those hotbeds of immorality called theatres, cinemas, dancing, and music? Is it the promiscuous presence in the streets of lusting young men and women with arms, chests, and thighs bared? Is it the ludicrous wearing of a hat like the Europeans or the imitation of their habit of wine drinking . . . [or] the disrobed women to be seen on the thoroughfares and in swimming pools? . . .[12]

Efforts to protect national languages have also prompted resistance to cultural globalization. The French Academy, for example, has long been on the lookout for English terms that have crept into general usage while urging their replacement by

French equivalents. Chinese authorities have sought to require foreign firms to use Chinese terms for their products, and in 2012 over 100 Chinese scholars urged the removal of English words from a prominent Chinese dictionary.

But the cultural flows of the past century have moved in many directions, not simply outward from the United States and Europe. In exchange for Big Macs, Americans and Europeans received Chinese, Indian, Thai, Mexican, and Ethiopian cuisine. Yoga, originally a mind-body practice of Indian origin, took hold widely in the West and elsewhere, losing much of its earlier association with spiritual practice and becoming a form of exercise or relaxation. India's huge film industry, known as Bollywood, had a major cultural impact in the Soviet Union, Western Europe, the United States, and Latin America. India-based Ayurvedic medicine and traditional Chinese medicine, including acupuncture, have become widely used "alternative" medical treatment in Europe and North America. Japanese and Chinese martial arts have attracted numerous participants in the West and have been featured in many highly popular films. Latin American telenovelas or "soap operas" have enthralled audiences around the world. Korean popular culture, including TV dramas, movies, and music, has taken hold widely in East and Southeast Asia. Congolese music, sometimes blended with Latin American dance rhythms, spread widely throughout Africa and by the 1980s attracted eager audiences in Europe as well. Jamaican-based reggae music has extended around the world, while its superstar Bob Marley became an international icon. In short, cultural traffic in the entangled world of the past century has moved in many directions.

Religion and Global Modernity

Among the various expressions of cultural identity during the past century, religion has often provoked perhaps the deepest personal response among individuals and has provided a potent source of identity in social and political life. Some of these responses were highly critical of religion, while others affirmed and sought to renew or revitalize religious belief and practice.

On the critical side, many of the most "advanced" thinkers of the past several hundred years—Enlightenment writers in the eighteenth century, Karl Marx in the nineteenth, and many academics and secular-minded intellectuals in the twentieth—believed that religion was headed for extinction in the face of modernity, science, communism, or globalization. In some respects, that prediction seemed to come true during the twentieth century and beyond. Soviet authorities, viewing religion as a backward-looking bulwark of an exploiting feudal or capitalist class, closed many churches and seminaries, promoted atheism in public education, prohibited any display of religion in public or the media, and denied believers access to better jobs and official positions. In several modernizing Islamic countries, the role of religion in public life was sharply restricted. Kemal Atatürk in Turkey sought to relegate Islam to the personal and private realm, arguing that "Islam will be elevated, if it will cease to be a political instrument."

Even without such state action, religious belief and practice during the past century declined sharply in the major European countries such as Britain, France, Italy, and the Netherlands. A recent poll found that in 2014 almost 23 percent of Americans defined themselves as religiously unaffiliated, while only 36 percent claimed to attend religious services every week.[13] Moreover, the spread of a scientific culture around the world persuaded small minorities everywhere, often among the most highly educated, that the only realities worth considering were those that could be measured with the techniques of science. To such people, all else was superstition, born of ignorance.

Nevertheless, the far more prominent trends of the last century have involved the further spread of major world religions, their resurgence in new forms, their opposition to elements of a secular and global modernity, and their political role as a source of community identity and conflict. Contrary to earlier expectations, religion has played an unexpectedly powerful role in this most recent century.

Buddhism, Christianity, and Islam had long functioned as transregional cultures and continued to do so in the twentieth century. Buddhist ideas and practices such as meditation found a warm reception in the West, and Buddhism has been reviving in China since the 1970s. Christianity of various kinds spread widely in non-Muslim Africa and South Korea, less extensively in parts of India, and after 1975 was growing even in China. By 2016 Christianity was no longer a primarily European or North American religion, as some 62 percent of its adherents lived in Asia, Africa, Oceania, and Latin America. Islam too continued its centuries-long spread in Asia and Africa, while migrants from the Islamic world have planted their religion solidly in the West, constructing over 2,000 mosques in the United States by 2010. Sufi mystical practices have attracted the attention of many in the West who have grown disillusioned with conventional religion.

Religious vitality in the twentieth century was expressed also in the vigorous response of those traditions to the modernizing and globalizing world. One such response has been widely called **religious fundamentalism** — a militant piety hostile to secularism and religious pluralism — that took shape to some extent in every major religious tradition. Many features of the modern world, after all, appeared threatening to established religion. The scientific and secular focus of global modernity challenged the core beliefs of religion, with its focus on an unseen realm of reality. Furthermore, the social upheavals connected with capitalism, industrialization, imperialism, and globalization thoroughly upset customary class, family, and gender relationships that had long been sanctified by religious tradition.

To such threats deriving from a globalized modern culture, fundamentalism represented a religious response, characterized by one scholar as "embattled forms of spirituality . . . experienced as a cosmic war between the forces of good and evil."[14] The term "fundamentalism" came from the United States, where religious conservatives in the early twentieth century were outraged and threatened by many recent developments: the growth of secularism; critical and "scientific" approaches to the Bible; Darwin's concept of evolution; liberal versions of Christianity that emphasized ethical behavior rather than personal salvation; the triumph of communism in the Soviet Union, which adopted atheism as its official doctrine; and postwar labor strikes that carried echoes of the Russian Revolution to many conservatives.

Feeling that Christianity itself was at stake, they called for a return to the "fundamentals" of the faith, which included a belief in the literal truthfulness of the scriptures, in the virgin birth and physical resurrection of Jesus, and in miracles. After World War II, American Protestant fundamentalists came to oppose political liberalism and "big government," the sexual revolution of the 1960s, homosexuality and abortion rights, and secular humanism generally. From the 1970s on, they entered the political arena as the "religious right," determined to return America to a "godly path."

In the very different setting of independent India, another fundamentalist movement—known as **Hindutva** (Hindu nationalism)—took shape during the 1980s. Like American fundamentalism, it represented a politicization of religion within a democratic context. To its advocates, India was, and always had been, an essentially Hindu land, even though it had been overwhelmed in recent centuries by Muslim invaders, then by the Christian British, and most recently by the secular state of the post-independence decades. The leaders of modern India, they argued, and particularly its first prime minister, Jawaharlal Nehru, were "the self-proclaimed secularists who . . . seek to remake India in the Western image," while repudiating its basically Hindu religious character. The Hindutva movement took political shape in an increasingly popular party called the Bharatiya Janata Party (BJP), promoting a distinctly Hindu identity in education, culture, and religion. Muslims in particular were sometimes defined as outsiders, potentially more loyal to a Muslim Pakistan than to India. The BJP's sweeping victory in national elections in 2014 raised questions about how its Hindu nationalism would fare in twenty-first-century India.

Nowhere were fundamentalist religious responses to political, social, and cultural change more intense or varied than within the Muslim world. Conquest and colonial rule; awareness of the huge technological and economic gap between Islamic and European civilizations; the disappearance of the Ottoman Empire, long the chief Islamic state; elite enchantment with Western culture; the retreat of Islam for many to the realm of private life—all of this had sapped the cultural self-confidence of many Muslims by the mid-twentieth century. Political independence for former colonies certainly represented a victory for Islamic societies, but it had given rise to major states—Egypt, Pakistan, Indonesia, Iraq, Algeria, and others—that pursued essentially Western and secular policies of nationalism, socialism, and economic development, often with only lip service to an Islamic identity.

Even worse, these policies were not very successful. Vastly overcrowded cities with few services, widespread unemployment, pervasive corruption, slow economic growth, a mounting gap between the rich and poor—all of this flew in the face of the great expectations that had accompanied the struggle against European domination. Despite formal independence, foreign intrusion still persisted. Israel, widely regarded as an outpost of the West, had been reestablished as a Jewish state in the very center of the Islamic world in 1948. In 1967, Israel inflicted a devastating defeat on Arab forces in the Six-Day War and seized various Arab territories, including the holy city of Jerusalem. Furthermore, broader signs of Western cultural penetration persisted—secular schools, alcohol, Barbie dolls, European and American movies, miniskirts, and more. Yet another example of Western-style modernity derived from the largely secular leader of independent Tunisia, Habib Bourguiba (president 1959–1987), who argued against the veil for women and polygamy for men and even discouraged his people from fasting during Ramadan.

To all of these failed policies and Western intrusions, many Muslims objected strongly. An emerging fundamentalist movement argued that it was the departure from Islamic principles that had led the Islamic world into its sorry state, and only a return to the "straight path of Islam" would ensure a revival of Muslim societies. To

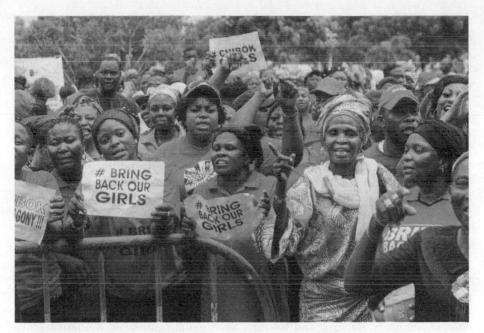

Confronting Islamic Radicalism The Nigerian Islamic radical group Boko Haram ("Western influence is a sacrilege") has waged a violent campaign of terror in support of a highly restrictive version of sharia law, killing thousands and displacing millions in northeastern Nigeria. In 2014 the group abducted over 200 schoolgirls, prompting this demonstration in Lagos to "bring back our girls." (Xinhua/Alamy)

politically militant Islamists, this meant the overthrow of those Muslim governments that had allowed these tragedies and their replacement by regimes that would purify Islamic practice while enforcing Islamic law and piety in public life. One of the leaders of an Egyptian Islamist group put the matter succinctly:

> We have to establish the Rule of God's Religion in our own country first, and to make the Word of God supreme. . . . There is no doubt that the first battlefield for jihad is the extermination of these infidel leaders and to replace them by a complete Islamic Order.[15]

Islamic fundamentalists won a significant victory in 1979 when the Iranian revolution chased out the country's long-reigning monarch, the shah of Iran. The leader of the revolution, the Ayatollah Khomeini, believed that the purpose of government was to apply the law of Allah as expressed in the *sharia*. Thus all judges now had to be competent in Islamic law, and those lacking that qualification were dismissed. The secular law codes under which the shah's government had operated were discarded in favor of those based solely on Islamic precedents. The new government soon closed some 200 universities and colleges for two years while textbooks, curricula, and faculty were "purified" of un-Islamic influences. Elementary and secondary schools, largely secular under the shah, now gave priority to religious instruction and the teaching of Arabic, even as about 40,000 teachers lost their jobs for lack of sufficient Islamic piety. Pre-Islamic Persian literature and history were now out of favor, while the history of Islam and Iran's revolution predominated in schools and the mass media. Sharp restriction of the lives of women represented a major element of this religious revolution.

A further expression of **Islamic radicalism** lay in violent attacks, largely against civilian targets, undertaken by radical groups such as al-Qaeda, the Taliban, Boko Haram, and the Islamic State. The most widely known of these attacks occurred on September 11, 2001, when the World Trade Center in New York and other targets were attacked. Subsequent assaults targeted various European and Russian cities, but this kind of terrorist violence was directed far more often and with far greater casualties against targets in the Islamic world itself, including Iraq, Pakistan, Afghanistan, Saudi Arabia, India, Indonesia, Yemen, Somalia, and Nigeria.

Violence, however, was not the only response of Islamic fundamentalists or radicals. All over the Muslim world, from North Africa to Indonesia, Islamic renewal movements spawned organizations that operated legally to provide social services—schools, clinics, youth centers, legal-aid societies, financial institutions, publishing houses—that the state offered inadequately or not at all. Islamic activists took leadership roles in unions and professional organizations of teachers, journalists, engineers, doctors, and lawyers. Such people embraced modern science and technology but sought to embed these elements of modernity within a more distinctly Islamic culture. Some served in official government positions or entered political life and contested elections where it was possible to do so. The Algerian Islamic Salvation Front was poised to win elections in 1992, when a frightened military government intervened to cancel them, an action that plunged the country into a decade of bitter civil war. Egypt's Muslim Brotherhood did come to power peacefully in 2012, but it was removed by the military a year later amid widespread protests against its policies.

Militant fundamentalism has certainly not been the only religious response to modernity and globalization within the Islamic world. Considerable debate among Muslims has raised questions about the proper role of the state; the difference between the eternal law of God (sharia) and the human interpretations of it; the rights of women; the possibility of democracy; and many other issues. In 1996, Anwar Ibrahim, a major political and intellectual figure in Malaysia, insisted:

> Southeast Asian Muslims . . . would rather strive to improve the welfare of the women and children in their midst than spend their days elaborately defining the nature and institutions of the ideal Islamic state. They do not believe it makes one less of a Muslim to promote economic growth, to master the information revolution, and to demand justice for women.[16]

In 2004 and 2005 scholars from all major schools of Islamic thought gathered in Amman, the capital of Jordan. They issued the "Amman Message," which called for Islamic unity, condemned terrorism, forbade Muslims from declaring one another as "apostate" or nonbelievers, and emphasized the commonalities shared by Muslims, Christians, and Jews.

Within other religious traditions as well, believers found various ways of responding to global modernity. A number of liberal and mainstream Christian groups spoke to the ethical issues arising from economic globalization and climate change. Many Christian organizations, for example, were active in agitating for debt relief for poor countries and the rights of immigrants. Adherents of "liberation theology," particularly in Latin America, sought a Christian basis for action in the areas of social justice, poverty, and human rights, while viewing Jesus as liberator as well as savior. In Asia, a growing movement known as socially engaged Buddhism addressed the needs of the poor through social reform, educational programs, health services, and peacemaking action during times of conflict and war. In short, religious responses to global modernity were articulated in many voices.

Humankind and the Environment: Entering the Anthropocene Era

The fossil fuel revolution and rapid technological innovation; industrialization and economic growth; urbanization and consumerism; population growth and migration; nationalism and global citizenship—all of these accelerating global processes of the past century connect with what is surely the most distinctive feature of that century: the human impact on the environment. As environmental historian J. R. McNeil put it: "This is the first time in human history that we have altered ecosystems with such intensity, on such a scale, and with such speed. . . . The human race, without intending anything of the sort, has undertaken a gigantic uncontrolled experiment on the earth."[17]

The Global Environment Transformed

By the early twenty-first century, that "experiment" had acquired a name: the **Anthropocene era** or the age of man. Many scientists and environmental historians now use this term to designate the contemporary era since the advent of the Industrial Revolution and more dramatically since 1950. It emphatically calls attention to the enduring impact of recent human activity on the planet. Species extinctions; mounting carbon dioxide emissions and climate change; the depletion of groundwater reserves; accumulating radioactive isotopes in the earth's surface; the enlargement of deserts; dead zones in the oceans; the prevalence of concrete and plastics—these and other environmental changes, all of them generated by human actions, will be apparent to archeologists many thousands of years in the future, should they be around to reflect on them. A prominent geologist recently declared: "We are the dominant geologic force shaping the planet. It's not so much river or ice or wind anymore. It's humans."[18]

As geologists reckon time, humankind has been living for the past 12,000 years in the **Holocene era**, a warmer and often a wetter period that began following the end of the last ice age. During this Holocene era, environmental conditions were uniquely favorable for human thriving. It was, according to prominent earth scientist Johan Rockstrom, a "Garden of Eden" era, providing "a stable equilibrium of forests, savannahs, coral reefs, grasslands, fish, mammals, bacteria, air quality, ice cover, temperatures, fresh water availability, and productive soils."[19] These conditions enabled the development of agriculture, significant population growth, and the creation of complex civilizations. Human activity during the Holocene era certainly transformed the environment in many ways, as plants and animals were domesticated, as native vegetation and forests gave way to agricultural fields and grazing land, as soils were eroded or became salty, as cities grew, and in many other ways. However, these environmental impacts were limited, local, and sometimes temporary.

That began to change as industrialization and population growth took hold first in Europe, North America, and Japan during the nineteenth century, in the Soviet Union during the 1930s, and then after 1950 in many other parts of the world. Everywhere, the idea of economic growth or "development" as something possible and desirable took hold, in capitalist, communist, and developing countries alike. Unlike in earlier times, human impact on the environment has become pervasive, global, and permanent, eroding the "Garden of Eden" conditions of the Holocene era.

Among the chief indicators of the emerging "age of man" were multiple transformations of the landscape.[20] The growing numbers of the poor and the growing consumption of the rich led to the doubling of cropland and pasturelands during the twentieth century. By 2015, some 40 percent of the world's land area was used to produce food for humans and their domesticated animals, whereas in 1750 that figure was only 4 percent.

As grasslands and swampland contracted, so too did the world's forests. Since the mid-1960s, about 20 percent of the Amazon rainforest has been cut down to make way for timbering and farming, more than had been lost since the beginning of European colonization over four centuries ago. The most dramatic deforestation took place in tropical regions of Latin America, Africa, and Southeast Asia, even as some reforestation took hold in Europe, North America, and Japan. Furthermore, huge urban complexes have transformed the landscape in many places into wholly artificial environments of concrete, asphalt, steel, and glass. China alone lost some 6.7 million hectares of farmland, over 5 percent of its available agricultural land, to urban growth between 1996 and 2003.[21]

These human incursions reduced the habitat available to wild plants and animals, leading to the extinction of numerous species and declining biodiversity. Extinction is of course a natural phenomenon, but by the early twenty-first century the pace of species extinction had spiked far beyond the natural or "background rate" because of human interventions in the form of agriculture, lumbering, and urban growth. Tropical rain forest habitats, home to a far richer diversity of species than more temperate environments, were particularly susceptible to human intrusion.

This loss of biodiversity extended to the seas of the world as well. Fishing with industrial-style equipment has led to the collapse or near collapse of fisheries around the world. The 1992 breakdown of the Grand Banks cod fishery off the coast of Newfoundland persuaded the Canadian government to place a moratorium on further fishing in that area. By the early 1960s, most whale species were on the verge of extinction, though many have begun to recover as restrictions on whaling have been put in place. "For the first time since the demise of the dinosaurs 65 million years ago," wrote the director of the World Wildlife Federation, "we face a global mass extinction of wildlife."[22]

The global spread of modern industry, heavily dependent on fossil fuels, generated dramatic changes in the air, water, soil, and atmosphere, with profound impacts on human life. China's spectacular economic growth since the 1980s, fueled largely

Urban Pollution in Beijing Deriving from auto exhausts, coal burning, and dust storms, the air pollution in China's capital city of Beijing has long been horrendous. In this photograph from early 2014, teenagers wear face masks to protect themselves from inhaling the noxious particles in the air. Many thousands of people across the globe die daily from the long-term effects of air pollution. (Rolex Dela Pana/EPA/REX/Shutterstock)

by coal, resulted in an equally spectacular pall of air pollution in its major cities. In 2004, the World Bank reported that 12 of the world's 20 most polluted cities were in China. Degradation of the world's rivers, seas, and oceans has also mounted, as pesticides, herbicides, chemical fertilizers, detergents, oil, sewage, industrial waste, and plastics have made their way from land to water. By the 1960s, Lake Erie in the United States was widely reported as "dead." The Great Pacific Garbage patch, an area of about 7 million square miles in the North Pacific, has trapped an enormous quantity of debris, mostly plastics, endangering oceanic food webs and proving deadly to creatures of the sea, which ingest or become entangled in this human garbage. Industrial pollution in the Soviet Union rendered about half of the country's rivers severely polluted by the late 1980s, while fully 20 percent of its population lived in regions defined as "ecological disasters." The release of chemicals known as chlorofluorocarbons thinned the ozone layer, which protects the earth from excessive ultraviolet radiation, before an international agreement put an end to the practice.

In other ways as well, human activity has left a lasting mark on the planet during the past century. Radioactive residue from the testing of nuclear weapons and from the storage of nuclear waste produced by power plants can remain detectable for tens or hundreds of thousands of years. Mining has also created a vast underground network of shafts and tunnels and above-ground scarring of open pit mines and quarries. As the demand for water to serve growing populations, industries, and irrigation needs increased by 900 percent during the twentieth century, many of the planet's aquifers have become substantially depleted. A number of large cities — Beijing, Mexico City, Bangkok, Tokyo, Houston, Jakarta, and Manila — have been measurably sinking over the past century due in part to groundwater depletion. All of these environmental changes deriving from human activity will be apparent to our descendants for a long time to come.

Changing the Climate

By the early twenty-first century, **climate change** had become the world's most pressing environmental issue. Since the Industrial Revolution took hold in Western Europe, higher concentrations of carbon dioxide and methane, generated by the burning of fossil fuels, as well as nitrous oxide derived largely from fertilizers, began to accumulate in the atmosphere, slowly at first and then much more rapidly after 1950. These so-called greenhouse gases act as a blanket around the world, limiting the escape of infrared energy from the earth's surface and so warming the planet. Carbon dioxide concentrations have increased by 43 percent since 1750, reaching 410 parts per million (ppm) by early 2017, a level well beyond the 350 ppm generally considered "safe" and greater than at any time during the over 200,000 years of human life on the planet. (See Figure 23.1 and Figure 23.2.) Average global temperature during this time increased by 1°C or more, and sixteen of the seventeen warmest years on record have all occurred since 2000. While this temperature increase may seem numerically small, its consequences have already

FIGURE 23.1   Carbon Dioxide Concentrations, 1750–2017
Rising concentrations of carbon dioxide in the atmosphere have been matched by a marked increase in global temperatures. (Scripps Institution of Oceanography at the University of California San Diego)

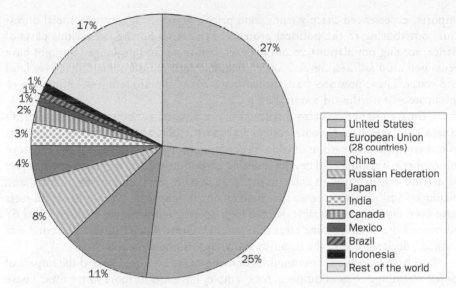

FIGURE 23.2   Distribution of Total World Carbon Dioxide Emissions, 1850–2011
The various regions or countries of the world have contributed very unevenly to carbon dioxide emissions over the past 160 years. By 2014, however, industrializing Asian economies had become major emitters, with China responsible for some 30 percent of global carbon dioxide discharges into the atmosphere in that year. (World Resources Institute)

been substantial, and projections into the near future of the twenty-first century are frightening.

Scientists have associated this warming of the planet with all manner of environmental changes. One of them involves the accelerating melting of glaciers and polar ice caps. Arctic temperatures, unprecedented in the past 44,000 years, have been melting glaciers and sea ice at record levels. Coupled with expanded sea volumes as the oceans warm, this rapid melting has raised sea levels by roughly 8.5 inches since 1850. Particularly threatened have been a number of small island nations in Occania—Tuvalu and Kiribati in particular. Coastal communities everywhere have become more vulnerable to storm surges. Low-lying regions of Bangladesh and the Philippines already flood almost every year and more catastrophically during particularly powerful storms, which seem to occur with increasing frequency and power as the planet warms. The first decade of the twenty-first century witnessed eight Category 5 hurricanes in the Atlantic Ocean, the most for any decade on record.

While global warming has exacerbated storms and rainfall in some regions, it has increased the prevalence and duration of droughts in others. Since the 1970s, droughts have been longer and more extreme in parts of Africa, the Middle East, southern Asia, and the western United States. In 2010 and 2011 extreme weather conditions characteristic of global warming— droughts, dust storms, fires, heavy rainfall—afflicted many grain-producing regions of the world, including Canada, Russia, China, Argentina, and Australia, causing a sharp spike in grain prices on the world market. The Middle East and North Africa, heavily dependent on grain imports, experienced sharply rising food prices, arguably aggravating social unrest and contributing to the political protests of the Arab Spring. In various parts of Africa, surging populations, record high temperatures, and prolonged drought have generated crop failures, devastation of livestock herds, and local conflicts over land and water. These pressures have turned many into "climate refugees," migrating to urban areas or northward toward Europe.

Climate change has also disrupted many aquatic ecosystems, as the world's oceans and lakes have become warmer and more acidic, absorbing some 25 percent of human-generated carbon dioxide. While this absorption has limited the extent of atmospheric warming to date, the resulting carbonic acid has damaged any number of marine organisms with calcium shells, such as oysters, clams, sea urchins, and plankton, and places entire aquatic food chains in jeopardy. The world's coral reefs have been especially vulnerable. Record high oceanic temperatures in 2016 killed 67 percent of the coral in some areas of Australia's Great Barrier Reef. "The coral was cooked," declared one of the scientists studying this phenomenon.[23]

Nor have land-based communities of living organisms been spared the impact of global warming. Drier conditions, for example, have meant more forest fires. Those in the western United States have increased fourfold since 1970, and the fire season has been extended by more than two months. Both plants and animals adapted to a particular temperature range were forced to migrate or die as temperatures increased. In Ethiopia, this has meant that mosquitos bearing malaria have migrated higher up the country's mountains, bringing the disease to people who never knew it before. Warmer temperatures in western North America have enabled bark beetles, which cause great damage as they feed on the bark and wood of trees, to survive the less intense winters and move to new environments. They have killed over 70,000 square miles worth of trees in recent decades. Polar bears have become an iconic image of the impact of global warming, as the sea ice on which they depend vanishes.

Clearly climate change as a marker of the Anthropocene era is in its early stages, with more, much more, to follow, if these emissions continue more or less unchecked. Projections to the year 2100, although subject to much dispute and controversy, paint a bleak picture: there will be carbon dioxide concentrations of 600 ppm and up, temperature increases of 1.8°C to 4°C, massive melting of glaciers and sea ice with sea level rise in the range of 2.5 to 6 feet; millions of homes and hundreds of cities at least partially under water, drought and falling food production in parts of Africa leading to mass migrations, widespread species extinction of up to half of earth's higher life forms by one estimate, and frequent international conflicts over dwindling fresh water supplies. Under these conditions, serious observers have begun to speak about the possibility of a major collapse of modern civilization. Widening awareness of both current conditions and future possibilities has energized the environmental movements of the twenty-first century.

Protecting the Planet: The Rise of Environmentalism

Long before climate change emerged as a global issue, a growing awareness of ecological damage and a desire to counteract it accompanied human entry into the Anthropocene era.[24] In the late eighteenth and early nineteenth centuries, Romantic English poets such as William Blake and William Wordsworth denounced the industrial era's "dark satanic mills," which threatened the "green and pleasant land" of an earlier England. In opposing the extension of railroads, the British writer John Ruskin declared in 1876 that "the frenzy of avarice is daily drowning our sailors, suffocating our miners, poisoning our children and blasting the cultivable surface of England into a treeless waste of ashes."[25] Another element in early environmentalism, especially prominent in the United States and Germany, derived from a concern with deforestation, drought, and desertification as pioneering settlers, lumbermen, miners, and the owners of colonial plantations inflicted terrible damage on the woodlands and pasturelands of the world. Articulated primarily by men of science often working in the colonial world, this approach sought to mobilize scientific expertise and state control to manage, contain, and tame modern assaults on the environment.

Protecting remaining wilderness areas was yet another piece of early environmentalism. The first international environmental conference, held in London in 1900, aimed at preserving African wildlife from voracious European hunters. In the United States it was the opening of the west to European settlers that threatened the natural order. "With no eye to the future," wrote naturalist John Muir in 1897, "these pious destroyers waged interminable forest wars . . . , spreading ruthless devastation ever wider and further. . . . Wilderness is a necessity . . . not only as fountains of timber and irrigating rivers, but as fountains of life."[26] This kind of sensibility found expression in the American national parks, the first of which, Yellowstone, was established in 1872.

These early examples of environmental awareness were distinctly limited, largely a product of literary figures, scientists, and some government officials. None of them attracted a mass following or elicited a global response. But "second wave environmentalism," beginning in the 1960s, certainly did. It began, arguably, with the publication in 1962 of Rachel Carson's *Silent Spring*, which exposed the chemical contamination of the environment with a particular emphasis on the use of pesticides. The book struck a chord with millions, triggering environmental movements on both sides of the Atlantic. Ten years later, the Club of Rome, a global think tank, issued a report called *Limits to Growth*, which warned of resource exhaustion and the collapse of industrial society in the face of unrelenting economic and population growth. Soon a mounting wave of environmental books, articles, treatises, and conferences emerged in Europe and North America, pushing back in various ways against the postwar emphasis on "development," consumerism, and unending economic growth. That sensibility was aptly captured in the title of a best-selling book by British economist E. F. Schumacher in 1973, *Small Is Beautiful.*

But what most clearly distinguished second-wave environmentalism was widespread grassroots involvement and activism. By the late 1990s, millions of people in North America, Europe, Japan, Australia, and New Zealand had joined one of the rapidly proliferating environmental organizations, many of them local. The issues addressed in these burgeoning movements were many and various: pollution, resource depletion, toxic waste, protecting wildlife habitats, nuclear power and nuclear testing, limiting development, and increasingly at the top of the agenda in the twenty-first century, climate change. Beyond particular issues, proponents of "deep ecology" argued that human beings should no longer be considered central but understood as occupying a place of equivalence with other species. Those supporting an "environmental justice" outlook were more concerned with the impact of environmental devastation on the poor, minorities, and developing countries. This social justice perspective informed Pope Francis's 2015 environmental encyclical, which commanded global attention, as the world's most prominent Christian leader called for humankind to "care for our common home."

The tactics of these movements were as varied as the issues they addressed. Much attention was given to public education and lobbying governments and corporations, often through professionally run organizations. In Germany, New Zealand, and Australia, environmentalists created Green parties, which contested elections and on occasion shared power. Teach-ins, demonstrations, street protests, and various local actions also played a role in the strategies of environmental activists.

In the communist world, environmentalism was constrained by highly authoritarian states that were committed to large-scale development. In the late 1980s, the Chinese government, for example, sharply repressed groups critical of the enormous Three Gorges Dam project across the Yangzi River. By the early twenty-first century, however, a grassroots environmental movement had taken root in China, expressed in hundreds of private groups and in state-sponsored organizations as well. Many of these sought to ground their activism in Buddhist or Daoist traditions that stressed the harmony of humankind and the natural order. In the Soviet Union during the 1970s and after, environmentalists were able to voice their concerns about the shrinking of the Aral Sea, pollution threats to Lake Baikal in Siberia, and poor air quality in many cities. After the nuclear disaster at Chernobyl in 1986, Gorbachev's policy of *glasnost* allowed greater freedom of expression as environmentalist concerns became part of a broader challenge to communism and Russian domination.

Quite quickly, during the 1970s and 1980s, environmentalism also took root in the Global South, where it frequently assumed a distinctive character compared to the more industrialized countries. There it was more locally based, with less connection to global issues or large national organizations than in the West; it involved more poor people in direct action rather than in political lobbying and corporate strategies; it was more concerned with issues of food security, health, and basic survival than with the rights of nature or wilderness protection; and it was more closely connected to movements for social justice. Thus, whereas Western environmentalists defended forests where few people lived, the Chikpo, or "tree-hugging," movement in India sought to protect the livelihood of farmers, artisans, and herders living in areas subject to extensive deforestation. A massive movement to prevent or limit the damming of India's Narmada River derived from the displacement of local people; similar anti-dam protests in the American Northwest were more concerned with protecting salmon runs.

In the Global South, this "environmentalism of the poor" took shape in various ways, often in opposition to the gigantic development projects of national governments. Residents of the Brazilian Amazon basin, facing the loss of their livelihood to lumbering interests, ranchers, and government road-building projects, joined hands and directly confronted workers sent to cut down trees with their chainsaws. When the Thai government sought to create huge eucalyptus plantations, largely to supply Japanese-owned paper mills, Buddhist teachers, known as "ecology monks," mobilized peasants to put their case to public officials. In the Philippines, coalitions of numerous local groups mobilized large-scale grassroots movements against foreign-owned mining companies. Kenya's Green Belt Movement organized groups of village women to plant millions of trees intended to forestall the growth of deserts and protect the soil.

By the early twenty-first century, environmentalism had become a matter of global concern and had prompted action at many levels. A growing market for solar and wind power helped drive its cost sharply lower, moving it closer to being competitive with conventional forms of electric generation like coal. Governments acted to curtail pollution and to foster the use of renewable energy sources, sometimes by putting a price on carbon-based fuels through "cap and trade" systems or a carbon tax. Germany, for example, increased the proportion of its electricity from renewable sources from 6.3 percent in 2000 to 32 percent in 2016. China has enacted a large body of environmental laws and regulations, has invested heavily in solar power, and in 2017 announced plans to close 100 coal-fired power plants. Brazil and Canada derive the bulk of their electricity from renewables, primarily hydropower. Some 6,000 national parks in over 100 countries served to protect wildlife and natural beauty. Many businesses found it commercially useful and therefore profitable to brand themselves as "green." Reforestation programs were under way in China, Honduras, Kenya, and elsewhere. International agreements have come close to eliminating the introduction of ozone-depleting substances into the atmosphere. And after extensive negotiations, the **Paris Climate Agreement** of 2015 committed some 195 countries, 700 cities, and many companies to reduce greenhouse gas emissions sufficiently to avoid a 2°C increase in global temperatures. Furthermore, millions of individuals altered their ways of life, agreeing to recycle, to install solar panels, to buy fuel-efficient cars, to shop in local markets, and to forgo the use of plastic bags.

But resistance has also surfaced, partly because moving toward a clean energy economy would require lifestyle adjustment for citizens in the Global North and for elites everywhere. Powerful and entrenched interests in fossil fuel industries likewise generate resistance. In 2017 the new Trump administration in the United States began to partially dismantle existing climate change regulations and stunned the world by announcing American withdrawal from the Paris agreement.

Furthermore, large-scale international agreement on global warming has come up against sharp conflicts between the Global North and South. Both activists and governments in the developing countries have often felt that Northern initiatives to address atmospheric pollution and global warming would curtail their industrial development, leaving the North/South gap intact. A Malaysian official put the dispute succinctly: "The developed countries don't want to give up their extravagant lifestyles, but plan to curtail our development."[27]

More than any other widespread movement, global environmentalism came to symbolize a focus on the common plight of humankind across the artificial boundaries of nation-states. It also marked a challenge to modernity itself, particularly its overriding commitment to endless growth and consumption. The ideas of sustainability and restraint, certainly not prominent in any list of modern values, entered global discourse and marked the beginnings of a new environmental ethic. This change in thinking, although limited, was perhaps the most significant achievement of global environmentalism.

Reflections: World History and the Making of Meaning

Among the most distinctive features of human life is our penchant for meaning. We seek to infuse almost every action and activity with some larger significance, and we are most apt to fall into despair when we are unable to do so. A large part of the historian's task involves identifying and describing the multiple meanings that individuals and societies have ascribed to their world and to their behavior in the past. For example, world historians notice and compare the various ways that humans have given meaning to the communities they create. Many small village-based societies have viewed themselves in terms of kinship, feeling themselves bonded by a relationship to a common ancestor. To distinguish themselves from neighboring "barbarians," Chinese thought of their country as the "middle kingdom," radiating "civilization" to their less fortunate neighbors. Americans have defined the United States as a "city set upon a hill," a melting pot, or the "land of the free." All such understandings are the product of human imagination, intended to provide some larger meaning to social and political life, even as those identities change over time.

But historians do more than record the meanings that have arisen in the course of the human journey. Historians themselves also create meaning as they give definition to the human past. World historians, for example, have sometimes pointed out a broad trend toward greater social complexity and more connectivity among regions and peoples during the course of our history. They give some meaning to human tragedies such as slavery, war, and genocide by explaining their origins and development. The notion of an "Anthropocene era," increasingly used by historians, provides a distinctive character to the past century or so.

In these ways historians seek to impose some shape and significance on the chaos of random events, ensuring that the human story becomes more than "one damned thing after another." Some might argue that any such "shape" is an illusion, an artificial product of human self-serving. Certainly historians' formulations are endlessly contested and debated. But we are apparently impelled to seek pattern or structure in the past. An infinite array of miscellaneous historical "facts" is neither satisfying nor useful.

The study of world history can also be helpful for each of us as we seek to make meaning in our own lives. As we witness the broad contours of the human journey and learn more about the wider world, we can more readily locate ourselves individually in the larger stream of that story. In short, world history provides context, which is so essential to the creation of meaning. If we base our understanding of the world only on what we personally experience in our own brief and limited lives, we render ourselves both impoverished and ineffective.

World history opens a marvelous window into the unfamiliar. It confronts us with the "ways of the world," the whole panorama of human achievement, tragedy, and sensibility. It allows us some modest entry into the lives of people far removed from us in time and place. And it offers us company for the journey of our own lives. Pondering the global past with a receptive heart and an open mind can assist us in enlarging and deepening our sense of self. In exposing us to the wider experience of "all under Heaven," as the Chinese put it, world history can aid us in constructing more meaningful lives. That is among the many gifts that the study of the global past offers to us all.

Second Thoughts

WHAT'S THE SIGNIFICANCE?

population explosion (p. 668)
Green Revolution (p. 668)
global urbanization (p. 669)
megacities (p. 670)
labor migration (p. 673)
influenza pandemic (p. 675)
HIV/AIDS (p. 675)
cultural globalization (p. 678)
religious fundamentalism (p. 681)

Hindutva (p. 682)
Islamic radicalism (p. 684)
Anthropocene era (p. 685)
Holocene era (p. 685)
climate change (p. 688)
second-wave environmentalism
   (p. 691)
Paris Climate Agreement (p. 693)

BIG PICTURE QUESTIONS

1. In what ways has population growth shaped the movement of people and the human impact on the environment?

2. How have cultural patterns evolved over the past century? What broader processes have contributed to those cultural changes?

3. To what extent do the changes described in these last two chapters justify considering the past century a new phase of world history?

4. Looking Back: How have the technological and economic changes explored in the previous chapter shaped the demographic, cultural, and environmental processes discussed in this chapter?

CHRONOLOGY

1948	• UN Universal Declaration of Human Rights
1949	• Apartheid begins in South Africa
1960	• Human population reaches 3 billion
1962	• Rachel Carson's *Silent Spring* launches modern environmentalism
ca. 1965	• Beginning of widespread deforestation in Amazon basin
1977	• Smallpox eradicated
1979	• Iranian revolution
ca. 1980	• Beginning of massive Chinese migration to coastal cities
ca. 1981	• Beginning of AIDS epidemic
1986	• Chernobyl nuclear disaster

1988	• Al-Qaeda established
ca. 1990	• Growing prominence of Indian Bollywood films
1992	• Collapse of Grand Banks cod fishery
2001	• Terrorist attack on World Trade Center
2004–2005	• Amman Message of a more tolerant Islam
2007	• 50 percent of human population in towns/cities
2014	• Rise of the Islamic State
2015	• Paris Climate Agreement
2018	• Human population reaches 7.6 billion
2017	• U.S. announces withdrawal from Paris Climate Agreement

Notes

Prologue

1. See David Christian, *Maps of Time* (Berkeley: University of California Press, 2004).

2. Voltaire, *Treatise on Toleration*, chap. 22.

3. See David Christian, "World History in Context," *Journal of World History* 14, no. 4 (December 2003): 437–58.

Chapter 12

1. Winona LaDuke, "We Are Still Here: The 500 Years Celebration," *Sojourners*, October 1991.

2. Jonathan Marcantoni, "Columbus Day . . . Is Complicated," October 9, 2015, http://www.latinorebels.com/2015/10/09/in-defense-of-columbus-day/.

3. Brian Fagan, *Ancient North America* (London: Thames and Hudson, 2005), 503.

4. Quoted in Charles C. Mann, *1491: New Revelations of the Americas before Columbus* (New York: Alfred A. Knopf, 2005), 334.

5. Louise Levanthes, *When China Ruled the Seas* (New York: Simon and Schuster, 1994), 175.

6. Christine de Pisan, *The Book of the City of Ladies*, translated by Rosalind Brown-Grant (New York: Penguin Books, 1999), pt. 1, p. 1.

7. Frank Viviano, "China's Great Armada," *National Geographic*, July 2005, 34.

8. Quoted in John J. Saunders, ed., *The Muslim World on the Eve of Europe's Expansion* (Englewood Cliffs, NJ: Prentice Hall, 1966), 41–43.

9. Leo Africanus, *History and Description of Africa* (London: Hakluyt Society, 1896), 824–25.

10. Quoted in Craig A. Lockhard, *Southeast Asia in World History* (Oxford: Oxford University Press, 2009), 67.

11. Quoted in Patricia Risso, *Merchants and Faith* (Boulder, CO: Westview Press, 1995), 49.

12. Quoted in Stuart B. Schwartz, ed., *Victors and Vanquished* (Boston: Bedford/St. Martin's, 2000), 8.

13. Quoted in Michael E. Smith, *The Aztecs* (London: Blackwell, 2003), 108.

14. Smith, *Aztecs*, 220.

15. Quoted in Miguel Leon-Portilla, *Aztec Thought and Culture*, translated from the Spanish by Jack Emory Davis (Norman: University of Oklahoma Press, 1963), 7.

16. For a summary of this practice among the Aztecs and Incas, see Karen Vieira Powers, *Women in the Crucible of Conquest* (Albuquerque: University of New Mexico Press, 2005), chap. 1.

17. Powers, *Women in the Crucible*, 25.

18. Louise Burkhart, "Mexica Women on the Home Front," in *Indian Women of Early Mexico*, edited by Susan Schroeder et al. (Norman: University of Oklahoma Press, 1997), 25–54.

19. The "web" metaphor is derived from J. R. McNeill and William H. McNeill, *The Human Web* (New York: W. W. Norton, 2003).

Chapter 13

1. See Kevin Meerschaert, "U.S. Sen. Nelson Says Putin Wants to Rebuild Russian Empire," *WJCT News*, March 17, 2014, http://news.wjct.org/post/us-sen-nelson-says-putin-wants-rebuild-russian-empire; and Asli Aydintasbas, "Rebuilding the Turkish Empire: Fantasy or Reality?" *The Caravan*, April 17, 2013, http://www.hoover.org/research/rebuilding-turkish-empire-fantasy-or-reality.

2. Quoted in Thomas E. Skidmore and Peter H. Smith, *Modern Latin America* (New York: Oxford University Press, 2001), 15.

3. George Raudzens, ed., *Technology, Disease, and Colonial Conquest* (Boston: Brill Academic, 2003), xiv.

4. Quoted in Noble David Cook, *Born to Die: Disease and the New World Conquest* (Cambridge: Cambridge University Press, 1998), 202.

5. Quoted in Cook, 206.

6. Quoted in Charles C. Mann, *1491: New Revelations of the Americas before Columbus* (New York: Alfred A. Knopf, 2005), 56.

7. Geoffrey Parker, *Global Crisis* (New Haven, CT: Yale University Press, 2013), chap. 15.

8. Quoted in Charles C. Mann, *1493: Uncovering the New World Columbus Created* (New York: Alfred A. Knopf, 2011), 165.

9. Felipe Fernandez-Armesto, "Empires in Their Global Context," in *The Atlantic in Global History*, edited by Jorge Canizares-Esguerra and Erik R. Seeman (Upper Saddle River, NJ: Prentice Hall, 2007), 105.

10. Quoted in Alejandro Lugo, *Fragmented Lives; Assembled Parts* (Austin: University of Texas Press, 2008), 53.

11. Quoted in Anthony Padgen, "Identity Formation in Spanish America," in *Colonial Identity in the Atlantic World, 1500–1800*, edited by Nicholas Canny and

Anthony Padgen (Princeton, NJ: Princeton University Press, 1987), 56.

12. Quoted in James Lockhart and Stuart B. Schwartz, *Early Latin America* (Cambridge: Cambridge University Press, 1983), 206.

13. Mary Prince, *The History of Mary Prince* (1831; Project Gutenberg, 2006), http://www.gutenberg.org/ebooks/17851.

14. Kevin Reilly et al., eds., *Racism: A Global Reader* (Armonk, NY: M. E. Sharpe, 2003), 136–37.

15. Benjamin Wadsworth, *The Well-Ordered Family* (1712), 39.

16. Willard Sutherland, *Taming the Wild Fields: Colonization and Empire on the Russian Steppe* (Ithaca, NY: Cornell University Press, 2004), 223–24.

17. Quoted in Michael Khodarkovsky, *Russia's Steppe Frontier* (Bloomington: Indiana University Press, 2002), 216.

18. Khodarkovsky, 222.

19. Geoffrey Hosking, "The Freudian Frontier," *Times Literary Supplement*, March 10, 1995, 27.

20. Peter Perdue, *China Marches West: The Qing Conquest of Central Eurasia* (Cambridge, MA: Harvard University Press, 2005), 10–11.

21. Quoted in P. Lewis, *Pirs, Shrines, and Pakistani Islam* (Rawalpindi, Pakistan: Christian Study Centre, 1985), 84.

22. Quoted in Stanley Wolpert, *A New History of India* (New York: Oxford University Press, 1993), 160.

23. Lewis Melville, *Lady Mary Wortley Montagu: Her Life and Letters* (Whitefish, MT: Kessinger, 2004), 88.

24. Jane I. Smith, "Islam and Christendom," in *The Oxford History of Islam*, edited by John Esposito (Oxford: Oxford University Press, 1999), 342.

25. Charles Thornton Forester and F. H. Blackburne Daniell, *The Life and Letters of Ogier Ghiselin de Busbecq* (London: C. Kegan Paul, 1881), 1:405–6.

26. Jean Bodin, "The Rise and Fall of Commonwealths," Chapter VII, Constitution Society, accessed February 21, 2012, http://www.constitution.org/bodin/bodin_4.htm.

Chapter 14

1. Jacob Wheeler, "From Slave Post to Museum," *Christian Science Monitor*, December 31, 2002.

2. M. N. Pearson, ed., *Spices in the Indian Ocean World* (Aldershot, UK: Valorium, 1996), xv.

3. Quoted in Paul Lunde, "The Coming of the Portuguese," *Saudi Aramco World*, July/August 2005, 56.

4. Quoted in Patricio N. Abinales and Donna J. Amoroso, *State and Society in the Philippines* (Lanham, MD: Rowman and Littlefield, 2005), 50.

5. Quoted in Craig A. Lockard, *Southeast Asia in World History* (Oxford: Oxford University Press, 2009), 85.

6. Anthony Reid, *Southeast Asia in the Age of Commerce, 1450–1680* (New Haven, CT: Yale University Press, 1993), 2:274, 290.

7. Anthony Reid, *Charting the Shape of Early Modern Southeast Asia* (Chiang Mai, Thailand: Silkworm Books, 1999), 227.

8. Quoted in Adam Clulow, "Like Lambs in Japan and Devils outside Their Land: Diplomacy, Violence, and Japanese Merchants in Southeast Asia," *Journal of World History* 24, no. 2 (2013): 343.

9. Kenneth Pomeranz and Steven Topik, *The World That Trade Created* (Armonk, NY: M. E. Sharpe, 2006), 28.

10. Makrand Mehta, *Indian Merchants and Entrepreneurs in Historical Perspective* (Delhi: Academic Foundation, 1991), 54–58.

11. Andre Gunder Frank, *ReOrient: Global Economy in the Asian Age* (Berkeley: University of California Press, 1998), 131.

12. Quoted in Richard von Glahn, "Myth and Reality of China's Seventeenth Century Monetary Crisis," *Journal of Economic History* 56, no. 2 (1996): 132.

13. Quoted in Kenneth Pomeranz and Steven Topik, *The World That Trade Created: Society, Culture and the World Economy, 1400 to the Present*, 3rd ed. (Armonk, NY: M. E. Sharpe, 2013), 165.

14. Quoted in John Hemming, *The Conquest of the Inca* (New York: Harcourt, 1970), 372.

15. Dennis O. Flynn and Arturo Giraldez, "Born with a 'Silver Spoon,'" *Journal of World History* 6, no. 2 (1995): 210.

16. Quoted in Mark Elvin, *The Retreat of the Elephants* (New Haven, CT: Yale University Press, 2004), 37.

17. Quoted in Robert Marks, *The Origins of the Modern World* (Lanham, MD: Rowman and Littlefield, 2002), 81.

18. See John Richards, *The Endless Frontier* (Berkeley: University of California Press, 2003), pt. 4. Much of this section is drawn from this source.

19. Quoted in Elspeth M. Veale, *The English Fur Trade in the Later Middle Ages* (Oxford: Clarendon Press, 1966), 141.

20. Quoted in Herbert Milton Sylvester, *Indian Wars of New England* (Cleveland, 1910), 1:386.

21. Quoted in Timothy Brook, *Vermeer's Hat: The Seventeenth Century and the Dawn of the Global World* (London: Bloomsbury, 2008), 44.

22. Quoted in Richards, *Endless Frontier*, 499.

23. Richards, *Endless Frontier*, 504.

24. Quoted in Jeff Crane, *The Environment in American History* (New York: Routledge, 2015), 68.

25. Pamela McVay, *Envisioning Women in World History* (New York: McGraw-Hill, 2009), 86.

26. These figures derive from the Trans-Atlantic Slave Trade Database, accessed December 26, 2017, http://www.slavevoyages.org/assessment/estimates.

27. Quoted in Charles E. Curran, *Change in Official Catholic Moral Teaching* (Mahwah, NJ: Paulist Press, 2003), 67.

28. David Brion Davis, *Challenging the Boundaries of Slavery* (Cambridge, MA: Harvard University Press, 2003), 13.

29. Quoted in Bernard Lewis, *Race and Slavery in the Middle East* (New York: Oxford University Press, 1990), 52–53.

30. Audrey Smedley, *Race in North America* (Boulder, CO: Westview Press, 1993), 57.

31. Kevin Reilly et al., eds., *Racism: A Global Reader* (Armonk, NY: M. E. Sharpe, 2003), 131.

32. Quoted in Donald R. Wright, *The World and a Very Small Place in Africa* (Armonk, NY: M. E. Sharpe, 1997), 109–10.

33. John Thornton, *Africa and Africans in the Making of the Atlantic World* (Cambridge: Cambridge University Press, 1998), 72.

34. Thomas Phillips, "A Journal of a Voyage Made in the Hannibal of London in 1694," in *Documents Illustrative of the History of the Slave Trade to America*, edited by Elizabeth Donnan (Washington, DC: Carnegie Institute, 1930), 399–410.

35. Erik Gilbert and Jonathan T. Reynolds, *Africa in World History* (Upper Saddle River, NJ: Pearson Educational, 2004), 160.

36. Anne Bailey, *African Voices in the Atlantic Slave Trade* (Boston: Beacon Press, 2005), 153–54.

Chapter 15

1. Andrew Rice, "Mission from Africa," *New York Times Magazine*, April 8, 2009; "African Missionaries Take Religion to the West," *Church Shift*, August 7, 2006, http://www.churchshift.org/in-the-press/70-african-missionaries-take-religion-to-the-west.

2. Quoted in Armin Siedlecki and Perry Brown, "Preachers and Printers," *Christian History*, Issue 118 (2016): 22.

3. Glenn J. Ames, *Vasco da Gama: Renaissance Crusader* (New York: Pearson/Longman, 2005), 50.

4. Quoted in Marysa Navarro et al., *Women in Latin America and the Caribbean* (Bloomington: Indiana University Press, 1999), 37.

5. Quoted in James Rinehart, *Apocalyptic Faith and Political Violence* (New York: Palgrave Macmillan, 2006), 42.

6. Quoted in Nicolas Griffiths, *The Cross and the Serpent* (Norman: University of Oklahoma Press, 1996), 263.

7. Richard M. Eaton, "Islamic History as Global History," in *Islamic and European Expansion*, edited

by Michael Adas (Philadelphia: Temple University Press, 1993), 25.

8. Patricia Buckley Ebrey, ed. and trans., *Chinese Civilization: A Sourcebook* (New York: Free Press, 1993), 257.

9. Robert Bly and Jane Hirshfield, trans., *Mirabai: Ecstatic Poems* (Boston: Beacon Press, 2004), ix–xi.

10. Quoted in Steven Shapin, *The Scientific Revolution* (Chicago: University of Chicago Press, 1996), 66.

11. This section draws heavily on Toby E. Huff, *The Rise of Early Modern Science* (Cambridge: Cambridge University Press, 2003), 48, 52, 76.

12. Huff, 339.

13. Huff, 76.

14. Jerome Cardano, *The Book of My Life*, translated by Jean Stoner (London: J. M. Dent, 1931), 189.

15. Quoted in Shapin, *Scientific Revolution*, 28.

16. Quoted in Shapin, 61.

17. Quoted in Shapin, 33.

18. Quoted in Shapin, 68.

19. David C. Lindberg and Ronald L. Numbers, "Beyond War and Peace: A Reappraisal of the Encounter between Christianity and Science," *Perspectives on Science and Christian Faith* 39, no. 3 (1987): 140–49.

20. H. S. Thayer, ed., *Newton's Philosophy of Nature: Selections from His Writings* (New York: Hafner Library of Classics, 1953), 42.

21. Immanuel Kant, "What Is Enlightenment?" translated by Peter Gay, in *Introduction to Contemporary Civilization in the West* (New York: Columbia University Press, 1954), 1071.

22. Voltaire, *Treatise on Tolerance* (1763), chap. 22, http://www.constitution.org/volt/tolerance.htm.

23. Quoted in Margaret C. Jacob, *The Enlightenment* (Boston: Bedford/St. Martin's, 2001), 103.

24. Quoted in Karen Offen, *European Feminisms, 1700–1950* (Stanford, CA: Stanford University Press, 2000), 39.

25. Quoted in Toby E. Huff, *Intellectual Curiosity and the Scientific Revolution* (Cambridge: Cambridge University Press, 2010), 48.

26. Joanna Waley-Cohen, *The Sextants of Beijing* (New York: W. W. Norton, 1999), 105–14.

27. Benjamin A. Elman, *On Their Own Terms: Science in China, 1550–1900* (Cambridge, MA: Harvard University Press, 2005).

28. Quoted in David R. Ringrose, *Expansion and Global Interaction, 1200–1700* (New York: Longman, 2001), 188.

Part 5

1. William H. McNeill, "*The Rise of the West* after 25 Years," *Journal of World History* 1, no. 1 (1990): 7.

Chapter 16

1. Quoted in Keith M. Baker, "A World Transformed," *Wilson Quarterly* (Summer 1989): 37.

2. Quoted in Thomas Benjamin et al., *The Atlantic World in the Age of Empire* (Boston: Houghton Mifflin, 2001), 205.

3. Quoted in Jack P. Greene, "The American Revolution," *American Historical Review* 105, no. 1 (2000): 96–97.

4. Quoted in Greene, 102.

5. Quoted in Susan Dunn, *Sister Revolutions* (New York: Faber and Faber, 1999), 11, 12.

6. Quoted in Dunn, 9.

7. Quoted in Lynn Hunt et al., *The Making of the West* (Boston: Bedford/St. Martin's, 2003), 625.

8. Quoted in Lynn Hunt, ed., *The French Revolution and Human Rights* (Boston: Bedford, 1996), 123.

9. Bonnie S. Anderson and Judith P. Zinsser, *A History of Their Own* (New York: Harper and Row, 1988), 283.

10. Hunt, *French Revolution*, 29.

11. From James Leith, "Music for Mass Persuasion during the Terror," copyright James A. Leith, Queen's University Kingston.

12. Franklin W. Knight, "The Haitian Revolution," *American Historical Review* 105, no. 1 (2000): 103.

13. Quoted in David P. Geggus, *Haitian Revolutionary Studies* (Bloomington: Indiana University Press, 2002), 27.

14. John Charles Chasteen, *Born in Blood and Fire* (New York: W. W. Norton, 2006), 103.

15. Peter Winn, *Americas: The Changing Face of Latin America and the Caribbean* (Berkeley: University of California Press, 2006), 83.

16. Quoted in Thomas E. Skidmore and Peter H. Smith, *Modern Latin America* (New York: Oxford University Press, 2001), 33.

17. Quoted in David Armitage and Sanjay Subrahmanyam, eds., *The Age of Revolutions in Global Context, c. 1760–1840* (New York: Palgrave Macmillan, 2010), xxiii.

18. James Walvin, "The Public Campaign in England against Slavery," in *The Abolition of the Atlantic Slave Trade*, edited by David Eltis and James Walvin (Madison: University of Wisconsin Press, 1981), 76.

19. Michael Craton, "Slave Revolts and the End of Slavery," in *The Atlantic Slave Trade*, edited by David Northrup (Boston: Houghton Mifflin, 2002), 200.

20. Joseph Dupuis, *Journal of a Residence in Ashantee* (London: Henry Colburn, 1824), 162–64.

21. Eric Foner, *Nothing but Freedom* (Baton Rouge: Louisiana State University Press, 1983).

22. Quoted in Daniel Moran and Arthur Waldron, eds., *The People in Arms: Military Myth and National Mobilization since the French Revolution* (Cambridge: Cambridge University Press, 2003), 14.

23. Barbara Winslow, "Feminist Movements: Gender and Sexual Equality," in *A Companion to Gender History*, edited by Teresa A. Meade and Merry E. Wiesner-Hanks (London: Blackwell, 2004), 186.

24. Quoted in Claire G. Moses, *French Feminism in the Nineteenth Century* (Albany: SUNY Press, 1984), 135.

Chapter 17

1. http://news.xinhuanet.com/english/2017-06/05/c_136342098.htm.

2. https://citifmonline.com/2017/06/07/webster-university-holds-public-lecture-on-africa-china-relations/.

3. Edmund Burke III and Kenneth Pomeranz, eds., *The Environment and World History* (Berkeley: University of California Press, 2009), 41.

4. Gregory T. Cushman, *Guano and the Opening of the Pacific World* (Cambridge: Cambridge University Press, 2013), chaps. 1–3.

5. Eric Hopkins, *Industrialization and Society* (London: Routledge, 2000), 2.

6. Joel Mokyr, *The Lever of Riches* (New York: Oxford University Press, 1990), 81.

7. Eric Hobsbawm, *Industry and Empire* (New York: New Press, 1999), 58. This section draws heavily on Hobsbawm's celebrated account of British industrialization.

8. Samuel Smiles, *Thrift* (London: John Murray, 1875), 30–40.

9. Quoted in Bonnie S. Anderson and Judith P. Zinsser, *A History of Their Own* (New York: Harper and Row, 1988), 2:131.

10. Hobsbawm, *Industry and Empire*, 65.

11. Peter Stearns and John H. Hinshaw, *Companion to the Industrial Revolution* (Santa Barbara, CA: ABC-CLIO, 1996), 150.

12. Quoted in Herbert Vere Evatt, *The Tolpuddle Martyrs* (Sydney: Sydney University Press, 2009), 49.

13. Hobsbawm, *Industry and Empire*, 171.

14. Dirk Hoeder, *Cultures in Contact* (Durham, NC: Duke University Press, 2002), 331–32.

15. Carl Guarneri, *America in the World* (Boston: McGraw-Hill, 2007), 180.

16. Quoted in Hoeder, *Cultures in Contact*, 318.

17. John Charles Chasteen, *Born in Blood and Fire* (New York: W. W. Norton, 2006), 181.

18. Peter Bakewell, *A History of Latin America* (Oxford: Blackwell, 1997), 425.

19. Ricardo Duchesne, *The Uniqueness of Western Civilization* (Leiden: Brill, 2011).

20. Eric Jones, *The European Miracle: Environments, Economics and Geopolitics in the History of Europe and Asia* (Cambridge: Cambridge University Press, 1981).

21. Kenneth Pomeranz, *The Great Divergence* (Princeton: Princeton University Press, 2000); Pier Vries, "Are Coal and Colonies Really Crucial?," *Journal of World History* 12 (2001): 411.

22. Peter Stearns, *The Industrial Revolution in World History*, 3rd ed. (Boulder, CO: Westview, 2007), 47.

23. Michael Adas, *Machines as the Measure of Men* (Ithaca, NY: Cornell University Press, 1990).

Chapter 18

1. Norimitsu Onishi, "A Colonial-Era Wound Opens in Namibia," *New York Times*, January 21, 2017, accessed July 30, 2017, https://www.nytimes.com/2017/01/21/world/africa/namibia-germany-colonial.html.

2. Quoted in Heinz Gollwitzer, *Europe in the Age of Imperialism* (London: Thames and Hudson, 1969), 136.

3. Quoted in Steven Roger Fischer, *A History of the Pacific Islands* (New York: Palgrave Macmillan, 2013), 112.

4. Charles Griffith, *The Present State and Prospects of the Port Phillips District . . .* (Dublin: William Curry and Company, 1845), 169.

5. Robert Knox, *Races of Man* (Philadelphia: Lea and Blanchard, 1850), v.

6. Quoted in Ralph Austen, ed., *Modern Imperialism* (Lexington, MA: D. C. Heath, 1969), 70–73.

7. Mike Davis, *Late Victorian Holocausts: El Niño Famines and the Making of the Third World* (New York: Verso, 2001), 12.

8. Quoted in John Iliffe, *Africans: The History of a Continent* (Cambridge: Cambridge University Press, 1995), 191.

9. Quoted in Nicholas Tarling, "The Establishment of Colonial Regimes," in *The Cambridge History of Southeast Asia*, edited by Nicholas Tarling (Cambridge: Cambridge University Press, 1992), 2:76.

10. R. Meinertzhagen, *Kenya Diary* (London: Oliver and Boyd, 1957), 51–52.

11. Mrinalini Sinha, *Colonial Masculinity* (Manchester: Manchester University Press, 1995), 35; Jane Burbank and Frederick Cooper, *Empires in World History* (Princeton, NJ: Princeton University Press, 2010), 308–9.

12. Nupur Chaudhuri, "Clash of Cultures," in *A Companion to Gender History*, edited by Teresa A. Meade and Merry E. Wiesner-Hanks (London: Blackwell, 2004), 437.

13. Quoted in Donald R. Wright, *The World and a Very Small Place in Africa* (Armonk, NY: M. E. Sharpe, 2004), 170.

14. Quoted in Scott B. Cook, *Colonial Encounters in the Age of High Imperialism* (New York: HarperCollins, 1996), 53.

15. D. R. SarDesai, *Southeast Asia: Past and Present* (Boulder, CO: Westview Press, 1997), 95–98.

16. Quoted in G. C. K. Gwassa and John Iliffe, *Records of the Maji Maji Rising* (Nairobi: East African, 1967), 1:4–5.

17. Quoted in Basil Davidson, *Modern Africa* (London: Longman, 1983), 79, 81.

18. This section draws heavily on Margaret Jean Hay and Sharon Stichter, eds., *African Women South of the Sahara* (London: Longman, 1984), especially chaps. 1–5.

19. Quoted in Robert A. Levine, "Sex Roles and Economic Change in Africa," in *Black Africa*, edited by John Middleton (London: Macmillan, 1970), 178.

20. Quoted in Davis, *Late Victorian Holocausts*, 37.

21. Josiah Kariuki, *Mau Mau Detainee* (London: Oxford University Press, 1963), 5.

22. Quoted in Harry Benda and John Larkin, *The World of Southeast Asia* (New York: Harper and Row, 1967), 182–85.

23. Quoted in William Theodore de Bary, *Sources of Indian Tradition* (New York: Columbia University Press, 1958), 619.

24. Quoted in Edward W. Smith, *Aggrey of Africa* (London: SCM Press, 1929).

25. Robert Strayer, *The Making of Mission Communities in East Africa* (London: Heinemann, 1978), 137.

26. Strayer, *The Making of Mission Communities*, 139.

27. C. A. Bayly, *The Birth of the Modern World* (Oxford: Blackwell, 2004), 343.

28. Nirad Chaudhuri, *Autobiography of an Unknown Indian* (London: John Farquharson, 1968), 229.

29. Edward Blyden, *Christianity, Islam, and the Negro Race* (Edinburgh: Edinburgh University Press, 1967), 124.

30. John Iliffe, *A Modern History of Tanganyika* (Cambridge: Cambridge University Press, 1979), 324.

Chapter 19

1. Xi Jinping, "Xi Jinping: UN Climate Deal 'Must Not Be Derailed,'" *Climate Home News*, January 19, 2017, http://www.climatechangenews.com/2017/01/19/xi-jinping-un-climate-deal-must-not-be-derailed/.

2. Dun J. Li, ed., *China in Transition, 1517–1911* (New York: Van Nostrand Reinhold, 1969), 112.

3. Quoted in Jonathan D. Spence, *The Search for Modern China* (New York: W. W. Norton, 1999), 169.

4. Quoted in Vincent Shih, *The Taiping Ideology: Its Sources, Interpretations, and Influences* (Seattle: University of Washington Press, 1967), 73.

5. Barbara Hodgson, *Opium: A Portrait of the Heavenly Demon* (San Francisco: Chronicle Books, 1999), 32.

6. Quoted in Teng Ssu and John K. Fairbanks, eds. and trans., *China's Response to the West* (New York: Atheneum, 1963), 69.

7. Quoted in Magali Morsy, *North Africa: 1800–1900* (London: Longman, 1984), 79.

8. Quoted in M. Sukru Hanioglu, *The Young Turks in Opposition* (New York: Oxford University Press, 1995), 17.

9. Marius B. Jansen, *The Making of Modern Japan* (Cambridge, MA: Harvard University Press, 2002), 33.

10. Quoted in Carol Gluck, "Themes in Japanese History," in *Asia in Western and World History*, edited by Ainslie T. Embree and Carol Gluck (Armonk, NY: M. E. Sharpe, 1997), 754.

11. Quoted in S. Hanley and K. Yamamura, *Economic and Demographic Change in Pre-Industrial Japan* (Princeton, NJ: Princeton University Press, 1977), 88–90.

12. Quoted in Harold Bolitho, "The Tempo Crisis," in *The Cambridge History of Japan*, vol. 5, *The Nineteenth Century*, edited by Marius B. Jansen (Cambridge: Cambridge University Press, 1989), 230.

13. Kenneth Henshall, *A History of Japan* (New York: Palgrave, 2004), 67.

14. Quoted in James L. McClain, *Japan: A Modern History* (New York: W. W. Norton, 2002), 177.

15. Kaoru Sugihara, "Global Industrialization: A Multipolar Perspective," in *The Cambridge World History* (Cambridge: Cambridge University Press, 2015), 7:117.

16. Quoted in Renée Worringer, *Ottomans Imagining Japan* (New York: Palgrave Macmillan, 2014), 59.

Part 6

1. David Christian et al., *Big History* (New York: McGraw-Hill, 2014), 283.

2. William McNeill, "*The Rise of the West* after 25 Years," *Journal of World History* 1, no. 1 (1990): 2.

Chapter 20

1. UN Secretary General, "Remarks to General Assembly . . . ," July 8, 2014, https://www.un.org/sg/en/content/sg/speeches/2014-07-08/remarks-general-assembly-commemoration-100th-anniversary-outbreak; meeting of the Valdai Discussion Club, October 19, 2017, http://en.kremlin.ru/events/president/news/55882.

2. Quoted in John Keegan, *The First World War* (New York: Vintage Books, 1998), 3.

3. Stanley Payne, *History of Fascism, 1914–1945* (Madison: University of Wisconsin Press, 1995), 208.

4. Quoted in Claudia Koonz, *Mothers in the Fatherland* (New York: St. Martin's Press, 1987), 75.

5. James L. McClain, *Japan: A Modern History* (New York: W. W. Norton, 2002), 414.

6. Quoted in Marius B. Jansen, *The Making of Modern Japan* (Cambridge, MA: Harvard University Press, 2000), 607.

7. Quoted in Jansen, 639.

8. Adam Gopnik, "The Big One: Historians Rethink the War to End All Wars," *New Yorker*, August 23, 2004, 78.

Chapter 21

1. Aaron Yakinyebi, "South Africa Celebrates . . . ," *International Business Times*, May 2, 2014, http://www.ibtimes.co.uk/south-africa-celebrates-20th-anniversary-since-end-apartheid-1446321.

2. NPR, "South Africa Celebrates . . . ," April 27, 2014, http://www.npr.org/sections/thetwo-way/2014/04/27/307427490/south-africa-marks-20-years-of-democracy.

3. Quoted in John L. Gaddis, *The Cold War: A New History* (New York: Penguin Press, 2005), 57.

4. Ronald Steel, *Pax Americana* (New York: Viking Press, 1970), 254.

5. Quoted in Craig A. Lockard, *Southeast Asia in World History* (Oxford: Oxford University Press, 2009), 138–39.

6. Quoted in Stanley Wolpert, *A New History of India* (Oxford: Oxford University Press, 1993), 331.

7. Quoted in J. D. Legge, *Sukarno: A Political Biography* (New York: Praeger, 1972), 341.

8. Deng Xiaoping, "The Necessity of Upholding the Four Cardinal Principles in the Drive for the Four Modernizations," in *Major Documents of the People's Republic of China* (Beijing: Foreign Language Press, 1991), 54.

9. Quoted in Abraham Brumberg, *Chronicle of a Revolution* (New York: Pantheon Books, 1990), 225–26.

Chapter 22

1. "Put Yourself in My Shoes," United Nations Office on Drugs and Crime, http://www.unodc.org/unodc/en/frontpage/2012/November/put-yourself-in-my-in-my-shoes-a-human-trafficking-victim-speaks-out.html.

2. Climate and Migration Coalition, "Moving Stories: Indonesia," September 26, 2013, http://climatemigration.org.uk/moving-stories-indonesia/.

3. http://www.gereports.com/post/77131235083/jet-engine-bracket-from-indonesia-wins-3d-printing/

4. International Energy Agency, "World Energy Outlook," 2015, http://www.worldenergyoutlook.org/resources/energydevelopment/energyaccess database/; The World Bank, "World Development Indicators," http://databank.worldbank.org/data/reports.aspx?source=2&series=EG.ELC.ACCS.ZS&country=.

5. Vaclav Smil, *Transforming the Twentieth Century* (New York: Oxford University Press, 2006), 2:266.

6. Douglas Brinkley, *Wheels for the World* (New York: Viking, 2003), 118.

7. Maja Adena et al., "Radio and the Rise of the Nazis in Pre-War Germany," *The Quarterly Journal of Economics* 130, no. 4 (2015): 2.

8. Jeffrey Frieden, *Global Capitalism* (New York: W. W. Norton, 2006), 476.

9. "Gross World Product, 1950–2009," in *World on the Edge*, by Lester R. Brown (New York: W. W. Norton, 2011).

10. Branko Milanovic, "Global Income Inequality: What It Is and Why It Matters," United Nations Department of Economic and Social Affairs, 2006, 9, www.un.org/esa/desa/papers/2006/wp26_2006.pdf.

11. Quoted in Frieden, *Global Capitalism*, 459.

12. Eric Hobsbawm, *The Age of Extremes: A History of the World, 1914–1991* (New York: Vintage, 1996), 289, 290, 292.

13. John Vidal, "Hi-Tech Agriculture Is Freeing the Farmer from His Fields," *The Guardian*, October 20, 2015, accessed February 4, 2017, https://www.theguardian.com/environment/2015/oct/20/hi-tech-agriculture-is-freeing-farmer-from-his-fields.

14. Amy Clark, "Is NAFTA Good for Mexico's Farmers?," CBS Evening News, July 1, 2006, accessed February 4, 2017, http://www.cbsnews.com/news/is-nafta-good-for-mexicos-farmers/.

15. Merry Wiesner-Hanks, *The Concise History of the World* (Cambridge: Cambridge University Press, 2015), 308.

16. Binyamin Appelbaum, "Perils of Globalization When Factories Close and Towns Struggle," *New York Times*, May 17, 2015, accessed February 8, 2017, https://www.nytimes.com/2015/05/18/business/a-decade-later-loss-of-maytag-factory-still-resonates.html?_r=0.

17. The Organisation for Economic Co-operation and Development (OECD) defined middle class as living in a household with a daily per capita income of between 10 and 100 U.S. dollars; Homi Kharas, *The Emerging Middle Class in Developing Countries*, Working Paper No. 285 (Paris: OECD, 2009), 6.

18. Studs Terkel, *The Great Divide: Second Thoughts on the American Dream* (New York: Pantheon, 1988), 175.

19. Norimitsu Onishi, "Nigeria Goes to the Mall," *New York Times*, January 5, 2016.

20. Chrystia Freeland, "The Rise of the New Global Elite," *The Atlantic*, January/February 2011, accessed February 4, 2017, https://www.theatlantic.com/magazine/archive/2011/01/the-rise-of-the-new-global-elite/308343/.

21. Quoted in Chrystia Freeland, *Plutocrats: The Rise of the New Global Super-Rich and the Fall of Everyone Else* (New York: Penguin, 2012), 59.

22. Tim Samuels, "Africa Goes Hardcore," *The Guardian*, August 30, 2009.

23. "Global Views on Premarital Sex 2013," Statista, https://www.statista.com/statistics/297288/global-views-on-premarital-sex/.

24. Quoted in Patrick B. Kinross, *Ataturk: A Biography of Mustafa Kemal* (New York: Morrow, 1965), 390.

25. Quoted in Sarah Shaver Hughes and Brady Hughes, *Women in World History* (Armonk, NY: M. E. Sharpe, 1997), 2:268.

26. Quoted in Wilhelmina Oduol and Wanjiku Mukabi Kabira, "The Mother of Warriors and Her Daughters: The Women's Movement in Kenya," in *Global Feminisms since 1945*, edited by Bonnie G. Smith (London: Routledge, 2000), 111.

27. Phyllis Schlafly, *The Power of the Christian Woman* (Cincinnati: Standard Publishers, 1981), 117.

28. Jason Hickel, "Global Inequality May Be Much Worse Than We Think," *The Guardian*, April 8, 2016.

29. The World Bank, "Life Expectancy at Birth," http://data.worldbank.org/indicator/SP.DYN.LE00.IN.

30. Charles Bright and Michael Geyer, "Benchmarks of Globalization," in *A Companion to World History*, edited by Douglas Northrup (New York: Wiley-Blackwell, 2012), 290.

Chapter 23

1. BBC, "Chad Urban Migrant's Story," http://news.bbc.co.uk/2/shared/spl/hi/picture_gallery/06/africa_chad_urban_migrant0s_story/html/2.stm.

2. J. R. McNeill, "Energy, Population and Environmental Change since 1750," in J. R. McNeill and Kenneth Pomeranz, *The Cambridge World History* (Cambridge: Cambridge University Press, 2015), vol. 7, part 1, pp. 63–67.

3. World Bank, "Death Rate, Crude," http://data.worldbank.org/indicator/SP.DYN.CDRT.IN.

4. David Clark, *Urban World/Global City* (London: Routledge, 1996), 1.

5. Michael H. Hunt, *The World Transformed: 1945 to the Present*, 2nd ed. (New York: Oxford University Press, 2016), 443.

6. Gareth McLean, "Where We're Headed," *The Guardian*, April 1, 2006.

7. https://kanere.org/2016/12/31/quotes-of-the -month-for-august-october-december-edition, accessed January 20, 2018.

8. Lizzy Davis, "The Young French Women Fighting to Defend the Full Face Veil," *The Guardian*, January 31, 2010.

9. Jose C. Moya and Adam McKeown, *World Migration in the Long Twentieth Century* (Washington, DC: American Historical Association, 2011), 39.

10. http://www.pbs.org/wgbh/americanexperience /features/primary-resources/influenza-letter/

11. Quoted in John J. Simon, "Aime F. Cesaire: The Clarity of Struggle," *Monthly Review* 60 (2008): 2.

12. *Sayings of Ayatollah Khomeini* (New York: Bantam Books, 1980), 4.

13. Pew Research Center, "America's Changing Religious Landscape," 2015, http://www.pewforum.org/2015 /05/12/americas-changing-religious-landscape/.

14. Karen Armstrong, *The Battle for God* (New York: Alfred A. Knopf, 2000), xi.

15. Quoted in John Esposito, *Unholy War* (Oxford: Oxford University Press, 2002), 63.

16. Quoted in John Esposito and John Voll, *Makers of Contemporary Islam* (New York: Oxford University Press, 2001), 193.

17. J. R. McNeill, *Something New under the Sun* (New York: W. W. Norton, 2001), 3–4.

18. Ker Than, "The Atomic Age Ushered In the Anthropocene, Scientists Say," *Smithsonian.com*, January 7, 2016, http://www.smithsonianmag .com/science-nature/scientists-anthropocene -officially-thing-180957742/.

19. Johan Rockstrom et al., *Big World, Small Planet* (New Haven, CT: Yale University Press, 2015), 33.

20. This section draws heavily on the work of John McNeill, a leading environmental historian. See McNeill, "Energy, Population," 72–77; and McNeill, *Something New.*

21. George J. Gilboy and Eric Heginbotham, "The Latin Americanization of China," *Current History*, September 2004, 258.

22. "Sixth Wildlife Mass Extinction May Happen in 2020, Experts Say," *Nature World News*, November 27, 2016, http://www.natureworldnews.com /articles/30805/20161027/year-2020-era-wildlife -mass-extinction.htm.

23. Hywel Griffith, "Great Barrier Reef Suffered Worst Bleaching on Record in 2016, Report Finds," *BBC News*, November 28, 2016, http://www.bbc.com /news/world-australia-38127320.

24. See Ramachandra Guha, *Environmentalism: A Global History* (New York: Longmans, 2000).

25. Quoted in Guha, *Environmentalism*, 14.

26. Quoted in Guha, 50, 53.

27. Quoted in Shiraz Sidhva, "Saving the Planet: Imperialism in a Green Garb," *UNESCO Courier*, April 2001, 41–43.

Acknowledgments

Excerpt beginning "Truly do we live on Earth" from *Aztec Thought and Culture: A Study of the Ancient Nahuatl Mind*, by Miguel Leon-Portilla. Reproduced with permission of the University of Oklahoma Press in the format Republish in a book via Copyright Clearance Center.

Excerpt beginning "Rarer, too, their timber grew" from Mark Elvin, *The Retreat of the Elephants*, (New Haven, CT: Yale University Press, 2004). Copyright © 2004 by Mark Elvin. Used by permission of Yale University Press.

Excerpt beginning "What I paid" from *Mirabai*, translated by Robert Bly and Jane Hirshfield. Copyright © 2004 by Robert Bly and Jane Hirshfield. Reprinted by permission of Beacon Press, Boston.

Glossary

Abd al-Hamid II: Ottoman sultan (r. 1876–1909) who accepted a reform constitution but then quickly suppressed it, ruling as a despotic monarch for the rest of his long reign.

abolitionist movement: An international movement that condemned slavery as morally repugnant and contributed much to ending slavery in the Western world during the nineteenth century; the movement was especially prominent in Britain and the United States beginning in the late eighteenth century.

African diaspora: The global spread of African peoples via the slave trade.

African identity: A new way of thinking about belonging that emerged by the end of the nineteenth century among well-educated Africans; it was influenced by the common experience of colonial oppression and European racism and was an effort to revive the cultural self-confidence of their people.

Africanization of Christianity: Process that occurred in non-Muslim Africa, where many who converted to Christianity sought to incorporate older traditions, values, and practices into their understanding of Christianity; often expressed in the creation of churches and schools that operated independently of the missionary and colonial establishment.

age of fossil fuels: Twentieth-century shift in energy production with increased use of coal and oil, resulting in the widespread availability of electricity and the internal combustion engine; a major source of the greenhouse gases that drive climate change.

Akbar: The most famous emperor of India's Mughal Empire (r. 1556–1605); his policies are noted for their efforts at religious tolerance and inclusion.

American Revolution: Successful rebellion against British rule conducted by the European settlers in the thirteen colonies of British North America, starting in 1776; a conservative revolution whose success preserved property rights and class distinctions but established republican government in place of monarchy.

Anthropocene era: A recently coined term denoting the "age of man," in general since the Industrial Revolution and more specifically since the mid-twentieth century. It refers to the unprecedented and enduring impact of human activity on the atmosphere, the geosphere, and the biosphere.

Asian Tigers: Nickname for the East Asian countries of South Korea, Taiwan, Singapore, and Hong Kong, which experienced remarkable export-driven economic growth in the late twentieth century.

Aurangzeb: Mughal emperor (r. 1658–1707) who reversed his predecessors' policies of religious tolerance and attempted to impose Islamic supremacy. (pron. ow-rang-ZEHB)

Aztec Empire: Major state that developed in what is now Mexico in the fourteenth and fifteenth centuries; dominated by the semi-nomadic Mexica, who had migrated into the region from northern Mexico.

Benin: West African kingdom (in what is now Nigeria) whose strong kings for a time sharply limited engagement with the slave trade.

Blyden, Edward (1832–1912): Prominent West African scholar and political leader who argued that each civilization, including that of Africa, has its own unique contribution to make to the world.

Boxer Uprising: Antiforeign movement (1898–1901) led by Chinese militia organizations, in which large numbers of Europeans and Chinese Christians were killed. It resulted in military intervention by Western powers and the imposition of a huge payment as punishment.

Bretton Woods system: Name for the agreements and institutions (including the World Bank and the International Monetary Fund) set up in 1944 to regulate commercial and financial dealings among the major capitalist countries.

British East India Company: Private trading company chartered by the English around 1600, mainly focused on India; it was given a monopoly on Indian Ocean trade, including the right to make war and to rule conquered peoples.

British textile industry: The site of the initial technological breakthroughs of the Industrial Revolution in eighteenth-century Britain, where multiple innovations transformed cotton textile production, resulting in an enormous increase in output.

cash-crop production: Agricultural production of crops for sale in the market rather than for consumption by the farmers themselves; operated at the level of both individual farmers and large-scale plantations.

caudillos: Military strongmen who seized control of a government in nineteenth-century Latin America and were frequently replaced. (pron. kow-DEE-yos)

Chinese revolution of 1911–1912: The collapse of China's imperial order, officially at the hands of organized revolutionaries but for the most part under the weight of the troubles that had overwhelmed the imperial government for the previous century.

Chinese Revolution of 1949: An event that marks the coming to power of the Chinese Communist Party under the leadership of Mao Zedong, following a decades-long struggle against both domestic opponents and Japanese imperialism.

civilizing mission: A European understanding of empire that emphasized Europeans' duty to "civilize inferior races" by bringing Christianity, good government, education, work discipline, and production for the market to colonized peoples, while suppressing "native customs," such as polygamy, that ran counter to Western ways of living.

climate change: The warming of the planet largely caused by higher concentrations of "greenhouse gases," generated by the burning of fossil fuels. It has become the most pressing environmental issue of the early twenty-first century.

cold war: Geopolitical and ideological conflict between communist regimes and capitalist powers after World War II, spreading from Eastern Europe through Asia; characterized by the avoidance of direct military conflict between the USSR and the United States and an arms race in nuclear weapons.

collectivization of agriculture: Communist policies that ended private ownership of land by incorporating peasants from small family farms into large-scale collective farms. Implemented forcibly in the Soviet Union (1928–1933), it led to a terrible famine and 5 million deaths; a similar process occurred much more peacefully in China during the 1950s.

Columbian exchange: The enormous network of transatlantic communication, migration, trade, and the transfer of diseases, plants, and animals that began in the period of European exploration and colonization of the Americas.

communication revolution: Modern transformation of communication technology, from the nineteenth-century telegraph to the present-day smart phone.

communism in Eastern Europe: Expansion of post–World War II communism to Poland, East Germany, Czechoslovakia, Hungary, Romania, and Bulgaria, imposed with Soviet pressure rather than growing out of domestic revolution.

Condorcet: The Marquis de Condorcet (1743–1794) was a French philosopher who argued that society was moving into an era of near-infinite improvability and could be perfected by human reason.

Congo Free State: A private colony ruled personally by Leopold II, king of Belgium; it was the site of widespread forced labor and killing to ensure the collection of wild rubber; by 1908 these abuses led to reforms that transferred control to the Belgian government.

consumerism: A culture of leisure and consumption that developed during the past century or so in tandem with global economic growth and an enlarged middle class; emerged first in the Western world and later elsewhere.

Copernicus, Nicolaus (1473–1543): Polish mathematician and astronomer who was the first to argue in 1543 for the existence of a sun-centered universe, helping to spark the Scientific Revolution.

Cortés, Hernán: Spanish conquistador who led the expedition that conquered the Aztec Empire in modern Mexico.

Counter-Reformation: An internal reform of the Catholic Church in the sixteenth century stimulated in part by the Protestant Reformation; at the Council of Trent (1545–1563), Catholic leaders clarified doctrine, corrected abuses and corruption, and put a new emphasis on education and accountability.

Cuban missile crisis: Major standoff between the United States and the Soviet Union in 1962 over Soviet deployment of nuclear missiles in Cuba; the confrontation ended in compromise, with the USSR removing its missiles in exchange for the United States agreeing not to invade Cuba.

cultivation system: System of forced labor used in the Netherlands East Indies in the nineteenth century; peasants were required to cultivate at least 20 percent of their land in cash crops, such as sugar or coffee, for sale at low and fixed prices to government contractors, who then earned enormous profits from resale of the crops.

cultural globalization: The global spread of elements of popular culture such as film, language, and music from various places of origin, especially the spread of Western cultural forms to the rest of the world; has come to symbolize modernity, inclusion in global culture, and liberation or rebellion. It has prompted pushback from those who feel that established cultural traditions have been threatened.

Cultural Revolution: China's Great Proletarian Cultural Revolution was a massive campaign launched by Mao Zedong in the mid-1960s to combat the capitalist tendencies that he believed reached into even the highest ranks of the Communist Party; the campaign threw China into chaos.

Dahomey: West African kingdom in which the slave trade became a major state-controlled industry. (pron. deh-HOH-mee)

Declaration of the Rights of Man and Citizen: Charter of political liberties, drawn up by the French National Assembly in 1789, that proclaimed the equal rights of all male citizens; the declaration gave expression to the essential outlook of the French Revolution and became the preamble to the French constitution completed in 1791.

decolonization: Process in which many African and Asian states won their independence from Western colonial rule, in most cases by negotiated settlement and in some cases through violent military confrontations.

Deng Xiaoping (1904–1997): Leader of China from 1976 to 1997 whose reforms dismantled many of the distinctly communist elements of the Chinese economy. (pron. dung shee-yao-ping)

dependent development: Term used to describe Latin America's economic growth in the nineteenth century, which was largely financed by foreign capital and dependent on European and North American prosperity and decisions; also viewed as a new form of colonialism.

devshirme: A term that means "collection or gathering"; it refers to the Ottoman Empire's practice of removing young boys from their Christian subjects and training them for service in the civil administration or in the elite Janissary infantry corps. (pron. devv-shirr-MEH)

Dream of the Red Chamber, The: Book written by Cao Xueqin that explores the life of an elite family with connections to the court; it was the most famous popular novel of mid-eighteenth-century China.

Dutch East India Company: Private trading company chartered by the Netherlands around 1600, mainly focused on Indonesia; it was given a monopoly on Indian Ocean trade, including the right to make war and to rule conquered peoples.

economic globalization: The deepening economic entanglement of the world's peoples, especially since 1950; accompanied by the spread of industrialization in the Global South and extraordinary economic growth following World War II; the process has also generated various forms of inequality and resistance as well as increasing living standards for many.

European Economic Community: An alliance formed in 1957 by six West European countries dedicated to developing common trade policies and reduced tariffs; it gradually developed into the larger European Union.

European Enlightenment: European intellectual movement of the eighteenth century that applied the principles of the Scientific Revolution to human affairs and was noted for its commitment to open-mindedness and inquiry and the belief that knowledge could transform human society.

European Renaissance: A "rebirth" of classical learning that is most often associated with the cultural blossoming of Italy in the period 1350–1500 and that included not just a rediscovery of Greek and Roman learning but also major developments in art, as well as growing secularism in society. It spread to Northern Europe after 1400.

export-processing zones (EPZs): Areas where international companies can operate with tax and other benefits, offered as an incentive to attract manufacturers.

fascism: Political ideology that considered the conflict of nations to be the driving force of history; marked by intense nationalism and an appeal to post–World War I discontent. Fascists praised violence against enemies as a renewing force in society, celebrated action rather than reflection, and placed their faith in a charismatic leader. Fascists also bitterly condemned individualism, liberalism, feminism, parliamentary democracy, and communism.

female circumcision: The excision of a pubescent girl's clitoris and adjacent genital tissue as part of initiation rites marking her coming-of-age; missionary efforts to end the practice sparked a widespread exodus from mission churches in colonial Kenya.

feminism in the Global South: Mobilization of women across Asia, Africa, and Latin America; distinct from Western feminism because of its focus on issues such as colonialism, racism, and poverty, rather than those exclusively related to gender.

French Revolution: Massive upheaval of French society (1789–1815) that overthrew the monarchy, ended the legal privileges of the nobility, and for a time outlawed the Catholic Church. The French Revolution proceeded in stages, becoming increasingly radical and violent until the period known as the Terror in 1793–1794, after which it became more conservative, especially under Napoleon Bonaparte (r. 1799–1815).

Fulbe: West Africa's largest pastoral society, whose members gradually adopted Islam and took on a religious leadership role that led to the creation of a number of new states in the nineteenth century. (pron. FULB)

fur trade: A global industry in which French, British, and Dutch traders exported fur from North America to Europe, using Native American labor and with great environmental cost to the Americas. A parallel commerce in furs operated under Russian control in Siberia.

Galileo (1564–1642): An Italian scientist who developed an improved telescope in 1609, with which he made many observations that undermined established understandings of the cosmos. (pron. gal-uh-LAY-oh)

Gandhi, Mohandas (1869–1948): Often known as "Mahatma" or "Great Soul," the political leader of the Indian drive for independence from Great Britain; rejected the goal of modern industrialization and advocated nonviolence.

General Crisis: The near-record cold winters experienced in much of China, Europe, and North America in the mid-seventeenth century, sparked by the Little Ice Age; extreme weather conditions led to famines, uprisings, and wars.

globalization of democracy: Late twentieth-century political shift that brought popular movements, multiparty elections, and new constitutions to countries around the world.

global urbanization: The explosive growth of cities after 1900, caused by the reduced need for rural labor and more opportunities for employment in manufacturing, commerce, government, and the service industry.

Gorbachev, Mikhail (1931–): Leader of the Soviet Union from 1985 to 1991 whose efforts to reform the USSR led to its collapse. (pron. GORE-beh-CHOF)

Great Depression: A worldwide economic contraction that began in 1929 with a stock market crash in the United States and continued in many areas until the outbreak of World War II.

Great Dying: Term used to describe the devastating demographic impact of European-borne epidemic diseases on the Americas; in many cases, up to 90 percent of the pre-Columbian population died.

Great Jamaica Revolt: Slave rebellion in the British West Indies (1831–1832) inspired by the Haitian Revolution, in which around 60,000 slaves attacked several hundred plantations; the discontent of the slaves and the brutality of the British response helped sway the British public to support the abolition of slavery.

Great Leap Forward: Communist push for collectivization that created "people's communes" and aimed to mobilize China's population for rapid development.

Green Revolution: Innovations in agriculture during the twentieth century, such as mechanical harvesters, chemical fertilizers, and the development of high-yielding crops, that enabled global food production to keep up with, and even exceed, growing human numbers.

Guomindang: The Chinese Nationalist Party led by Chiang Kai-shek that governed from 1928 until its overthrow by the communists in 1949. (pron. GWOH-mihn-dahng)

Haitian Revolution: The only fully successful slave rebellion in world history; the uprising in the French Caribbean colony of Saint Domingue (later renamed Haiti, which means "mountainous" or "rugged" in the native Taino language) was sparked by the French Revolution and led to the establishment of an independent state after a long and bloody war (1791–1804). Its first leader was Toussaint Louverture, a former slave.

Hidalgo-Morelos rebellion: Socially radical peasant rebellion in Mexico (1810) led by the priests Miguel Hidalgo and José Morelos.

Hinduism: A religion based on the many beliefs, practices, sects, rituals, and philosophies in India; in the thinking of nineteenth-century Indian reformers, it was expressed as a distinctive tradition, an Indian religion wholly equivalent to Christianity.

Hindutva: A Hindu nationalist movement that became politically important in India in the 1980s; advocated a distinct Hindu identity and decried government efforts to accommodate other faith communities, particularly Islamic.

Hitler, Adolf (1889–1945): Leader of the German Nazi Party and Germany's head of state from 1933 until his death.

HIV/AIDS: A pathogen that spreads primarily through sexual contact, contaminated blood products, or the sharing of needles; after sparking a global pandemic in the 1980s, it spread rapidly across the globe and caused tens of millions of deaths.

Ho Chi Minh (1890–1969): Leader of the Vietnamese communist movement that established control first in the north and then the whole of Vietnam after 1975.

Holocaust: Name commonly used for the Nazi genocide of Jews and other "undesirables" in German society.

Holocene era: A warmer and often a wetter period that began approximately 12,000 years ago following the end of the last ice age. These environmental conditions were uniquely favorable for human thriving and enabled the development of agriculture, significant population growth, and the creation of complex civilizations.

idea of "tribe": A new sense of clearly defined ethnic identities that emerged in twentieth-century Africa, often initiated by Europeans intent on showing the primitive nature of their colonial subjects, but widely adopted by Africans themselves as a way of responding to the upheavals of modern life.

ideology of domesticity: A set of ideas and values that defined the ideal role of middle-class women in nineteenth-century Europe, focusing their activity on homemaking, child rearing, charitable endeavors, and "refined" activities as the proper sphere for women.

Igbo: People whose lands were east of the Niger River in what is now southern Nigeria in West Africa. They built a complex society that rejected kingship and centralized statehood, while relying on other institutions to provide social coherence. (pron. EE-boh)

Inca Empire: The Western Hemisphere's largest imperial state in the fifteenth and early sixteenth centuries. Built by a relatively small community of Quechua-speaking people (the Incas), the empire stretched some 2,500 miles along the Andes Mountains, which run nearly the entire length of the west coast of South America, and contained perhaps 10 million subjects.

Indian National Congress: The political party led by Mahatma Gandhi that succeeded in bringing about Indian independence from Britain in 1947.

Indian Ocean commercial network: The massive, interconnected web of commerce in premodern times between the lands that bordered the Indian Ocean (including East Africa, India, and Southeast Asia); the network was transformed as Europeans entered it in the centuries following 1500.

Indian Rebellion of 1857–1858: Massive uprising of much of India against British rule caused by the introduction to the colony's military forces of a new cartridge smeared with animal fat from pigs and cows, which caused strife among Muslims, who regarded pigs as unclean, and Hindus, who venerated cows. It came to express a variety of grievances against the colonial order.

influenza pandemic: The worst pandemic in human history, caused by three waves of influenza that swept across the globe in 1918 and 1919, carried by demobilized soldiers, refugees, and other dislocated people returning home from World War I; between 50 million and 100 million people died in the pandemic.

informal economy: Also known as the "shadow" economy; refers to unofficial, unregulated, and untaxed economic activity.

informal empires: Term commonly used to describe areas that were dominated by Western powers in the nineteenth century but retained their own governments and a measure of independence (e.g., China).

Iranian revolution: Establishment of a radically Islamist government in Iran in 1979; helped trigger a war with Iraq in the 1980s.

Iroquois: Iroquois-speaking peoples in what is now New York State; around the fifteenth century they formed a loose alliance based on the Great Law of Peace, an agreement to settle disputes peacefully through a council of clan leaders.

Islamic radicalism: Movements that promote strict adherence to the Quran and the sharia, often in opposition to key elements of Western culture. Particularly prominent since the 1970s, such movements often present themselves as returning to an earlier expression of Islam. Examples include the Iranian revolution, Taliban, al-Qaeda, and Islamic State.

Israeli-Palestinian Conflict: Struggle between the Jewish state of Israel and the adjacent Palestinian Muslim territories that has generated periodic wars and upheavals since 1948.

Jesuits in China: Series of Jesuit missionaries from 1550 to 1800 who, inspired by the work of Matteo Ricci, sought to understand and become integrated into Chinese culture as part of their efforts to convert the Chinese elite, although with limited success.

kaozheng: Literally, "research based on evidence"; Chinese intellectual movement whose practitioners were critical of conventional Confucian philosophy and instead emphasized the importance of evidence and analysis, applied especially to historical documents.

laboring classes: The majority of Britain's nineteenth-century population, which included manual workers in the mines, ports, factories, construction sites, workshops, and farms of Britain's industrializing and urbanizing society; this class suffered the most and at least initially gained the least from the transformations of the Industrial Revolution.

labor migration: The movement of people, often illegally, into another country to escape poverty or violence and to seek opportunities for work that are less available in their own countries.

Labour Party: British working-class political party established in the 1890s and dedicated to reforms and a peaceful transition to socialism, in time providing a viable alternative to the revolutionary emphasis of Marxism.

Latin American export boom: Large-scale increase in Latin American exports (mostly raw materials and foodstuffs) to industrializing countries in the second half of the nineteenth century, made possible by major improvements in shipping; the boom mostly benefited the upper and middle classes.

Latin American revolutions: Series of risings in the Spanish and Portuguese colonies of Latin America (1808–1825) that established the independence of new states from European rule but that for the most part retained the privileges of the elites despite efforts at more radical social change by the lower classes.

Lenin (1870–1924): Born Vladimir Ilyich Ulyanov, leader of the Russian Bolshevik (later Communist) Party in 1917, when it seized power.

Lin Zexu, Commissioner: Royal official charged with ending the opium trade in China; his concerted efforts to seize and destroy opium imports provoked the Opium Wars. (pron. lin zuh-SHOO)

Little Ice Age: A period of unusually cool temperatures from the thirteenth to nineteenth centuries, most prominently in the Northern Hemisphere.

lower middle class: Social stratum that developed in Britain in the nineteenth century and that consisted of people employed in the service sector as clerks, salespeople, secretaries, police officers, and the like; by 1900, this group comprised about 20 percent of Britain's population.

Luther, Martin (1483–1546): German priest who issued the Ninety-Five Theses and began the Protestant Reformation with his public criticism of the Catholic Church's theology and practice.

Malacca: Muslim port city that came to prominence on the waterway between Sumatra and Malaya in the fifteenth century C.E.; it was the springboard for the spread of a syncretic form of Islam throughout the region.

Manila: The capital of the colonial Philippines, which by 1600 had become a flourishing and culturally diverse city; the site of violent clashes between the Spanish and Chinese.

Mao Zedong (1893–1976): Chairman of China's Communist Party and de facto ruler of China from 1949 until his death.

maroon societies / Palmares: Free communities of former slaves in remote regions of South America and the Caribbean; the largest such settlement was Palmares in Brazil, which housed 10,000 or more people for most of the seventeenth century.

Marshall Plan: Huge U.S. government initiative to aid in the post–World War II recovery of Western Europe that was put into effect in 1948.

Marx, Karl (1818–1883): The most influential proponent of socialism, Marx was a German expatriate in England who advocated working-class revolution as the key to creating an ideal communist future.

maternal feminism: Movement that claimed that women have value in society not because of an abstract notion of equality but because women have a distinctive and vital role as mothers; its exponents argued that women have the right to intervene in civil and political life because of their duty to watch over the future of their children.

megacities: Very large urban centers with populations of over 10 million; by 2017, there were thirty-seven such cities on five continents.

Meiji Restoration: The political takeover of Japan in 1868 by a group of young samurai from southern Japan. The samurai eliminated the shogun and claimed they were restoring to power the young emperor, Meiji. The new government was committed to saving Japan from foreign domination by drawing upon what the modern West had to offer to transform Japanese society. (pron. MAY-jee)

mercantilism: The economic theory that governments served their countries' economic interests best by encouraging exports and accumulating bullion (precious metals such as silver and gold); helped fuel European colonialism.

mestizo: A term used to describe the mixed-race population of Spanish colonial societies in the Americas, most prominently the product of unions between Spanish men and Native American women. (pron. mehs-TEE-zoh)

Mexican Revolution: Long and bloody war (1910–1920) in which Mexican reformers from the middle class joined with workers and peasants to overthrow the dictator Porfirio Díaz and create a new, much more democratic political order.

middle-class society: British social stratum developed in the nineteenth century, composed of small businessmen, doctors, lawyers, engineers, teachers, and other professionals required in an industrial society; politically liberal, they favored constitutional government, private property, free trade, and social reform within limits; had ideas of thrift, hard work, rigid morality, "respectability," and cleanliness.

Ming dynasty: Chinese dynasty (1368–1644) that succeeded the Yuan dynasty of the Mongols; noted for its return to traditional Chinese ways and restoration of the land after the destructiveness of the Mongols.

Mirabai (1498–1547): One of India's most beloved bhakti poets, she transgressed the barriers of caste and tradition.

Mughal Empire: A successful state founded by Muslim Turkic-speaking peoples who invaded India and provided a rare period of relative political unity (1526–1707); their rule was noted for efforts to create partnerships between Hindus and Muslims. (pron. MOO-guhl)

mulattoes: Term commonly used for people of mixed African and European blood.

Muslim League: Political group formed in response to the Indian National Congress in India's struggle for independence from Britain; the League's leader, Muhammad Ali Jinnah, argued that regions of India with a Muslim majority should form a separate state called Pakistan.

Mussolini, Benito (1883–1945): Charismatic leader of the Italian Fascist Party who came to power in 1922 and ruled until his death.

Napoleon Bonaparte: French head of state and general (r. 1799–1815); Napoleon preserved much of the French Revolution under a military dictatorship and was responsible for the spread of revolutionary ideals through his conquest of much of Europe.

nationalism: The focusing of citizens' loyalty on the notion that they are part of a "nation" with a unique culture, territory, and common experience, which merits an independent political life; first became a prominent element of political culture in nineteenth-century Europe and the Americas.

Nazi Party: German political party that established a fascist state dedicated to extreme nationalism, territorial expansion, and the purification of the German state.

Newton, Isaac (1642–1727): English scientist whose formulation of the laws of motion and mechanics is regarded as the culmination of the Scientific Revolution.

North American Free Trade Agreement (NAFTA): Free trade agreement between the United States, Mexico, and Canada, established in 1994.

North Atlantic Treaty Organization (NATO): A military alliance, created in 1949, between the United States and various European countries; largely aimed at defending against the threat of Soviet aggression during the cold war.

one-child family policy (China): Chinese policy of population control that lasted from 1980 to 2014; used financial incentives and penalties to promote birth control, sterilization, and abortions in an effort to limit most families to a single child.

Opium Wars: Two wars fought between Western powers and China (1840–1842 and 1856–1858) after China tried to restrict the importation of foreign goods, especially opium; China lost both wars and was forced to make major concessions.

Ottoman Empire: Major Islamic state centered on Anatolia that came to include the Balkans, parts of the Middle East, and much of North Africa; lasted in one form or another from the fourteenth to the early twentieth century.

Ottoman seizure of Constantinople: The city of Constantinople, the capital and almost the only outpost left of the Byzantine Empire, fell to the army of the Ottoman sultan Mehmed II "the Conqueror" in 1453, an event that marked the end of Christian Byzantium.

Paris Climate Agreement: An international agreement negotiated in 2015 among some 195 countries, 700 cities, and many companies to reduce greenhouse gas emissions sufficiently to avoid a 2°C increase in global temperatures. The United States withdrew from the agreement in 2017.

Philippines (Spanish): An archipelago of Pacific islands colonized by Spain in a relatively bloodless process that extended for the century or so after 1565, a process accompanied by a major effort at evangelization; the Spanish named them the Philippine Islands in honor of King Philip II of Spain.

piece of eight: The standard Spanish silver coin used by merchants in North America, Europe, India, Russia, West Africa, and China.

population explosion: An extraordinarily rapid growth in human population during the twentieth century that quadrupled human numbers in little more than a century. Experienced primarily in the Global South.

Potosí: City that developed high in the Andes (in present-day Bolivia) at the site of the world's largest silver mine and that became the largest city in the Americas, with a population of some 160,000 in the 1570s.

Progressives: Followers of an American political movement (progressivism) in the period around 1900 that advocated reform measures such as wages-and-hours legislation to correct the ills of industrialization.

Protestant Reformation: Massive schism within Christianity that had its formal beginning in 1517 with the German priest Martin Luther; the movement was radically innovative in its challenge to church authority and its endorsement of salvation by faith alone, and also came to express a variety of political, economic, and social tensions.

Qing expansion: The growth of Qing dynasty China during the seventeenth and eighteenth centuries into a central Asian empire that added a small but important minority of non-Chinese people to the empire's population and essentially created the borders of contemporary China.

religious fundamentalism: Occurring within all the major world religions, fundamentalism is a self-proclaimed return to the alleged "fundamentals" of a religion and is marked by a militant piety, exclusivism, and a sense of threat from the modern secular world.

Revolutionary Right (Japan): Also known as Radical Nationalism, this was a movement in Japanese political life during the Great Depression that was marked by extreme nationalism, a commitment to elite leadership focused around the emperor, and dedication to foreign expansion.

Robespierre, Maximilien (1758–1794): Leader of the French Revolution during the Terror; his Committee of Public Safety executed tens of thousands of enemies of the revolution until he was arrested and guillotined. (pron. ROHBS-pee-air)

Russian Empire: A Christian state centered on Moscow that emerged from centuries of Mongol rule in 1480; by 1800, it had expanded into northern Asia and westward into the Baltics and Eastern Europe.

Russian Revolution: Massive revolutionary upheaval in 1917 that overthrew the Romanov dynasty in Russia and ended with the seizure of power by communists under the leadership of Lenin.

Russian Revolution of 1905: Spontaneous rebellion that erupted in Russia after the country's defeat at the hands of Japan in 1905; the revolution was suppressed, but it forced the government to make substantial reforms.

Russo-Japanese War (1904–1905): Fought over rival ambitions in Korea and Manchuria, this conflict ended in a Japanese victory, establishing Japan as a formidable military competitor in East Asia. The war marked the first time that an Asian country defeated a European power in battle, and it precipitated the Russian Revolution of 1905.

Safavid Empire: Major Turkic empire established in Persia in the early sixteenth century and notable for its efforts to convert its people to Shia Islam. (pron. SAH-fah-vid)

scientific racism: A new kind of racism that emerged in the nineteenth century that increasingly used the prestige and apparatus of science to support European racial prejudices and preferences.

Scientific Revolution: The intellectual and cultural transformation that shaped a new conception of the material world between the mid-sixteenth and early eighteenth centuries in Europe; instead of relying on the authority of religion or tradition, its leading figures believed that knowledge was acquired through rational inquiry based on evidence, the product of human minds alone.

scramble for Africa: The process by which European countries partitioned the continent of Africa among themselves in the period 1875–1900.

second-wave environmentalism: A movement that began in the 1960s and triggered environmental movements in Europe and North America. It was characterized by widespread grassroots involvement focused on issues such as pollution, resource depletion, protection of wildlife habitats, and nuclear power.

second-wave feminism: Women's rights movement that revived in the 1960s with a different agenda than earlier women's suffrage movements; second-wave feminists demanded equal rights for women in employment and education, women's right to control their own bodies, and the end of patriarchal domination.

self-strengthening: China's program of internal reform in the 1860s and 1870s, based on vigorous application of traditional principles and limited borrowing from the West.

service sector: Industries like government, medicine, education, finance, and communication that have grown due to increasing consumerism, population, and communication technologies.

settler colonies: Imperial territories in which Europeans settled permanently in substantial numbers. Used in reference to the European empires in the Americas generally and particularly to the British colonies of North America.

"the sick man of Europe": Western Europe's description of the Ottoman Empire in the nineteenth and early twentieth centuries, based on the empire's economic and military weakness and its apparent inability to prevent the shrinking of its territory.

signares: The small number of African women who were able to exercise power and accumulate wealth through marriage to European traders.

Sikhism: Religious tradition of northern India founded by Guru Nanak (1469–1539); combines elements of Hinduism and Islam and proclaims the brotherhood of all humans and the equality of men and women.

"silver drain": Term often used to describe the siphoning of money from Europe to pay for the luxury products of the East, a process exacerbated by the fact that Europe had few trade goods that were desirable in Eastern markets; eventually, the bulk of the world's silver supply made its way to China.

social Darwinism: An outlook that suggested that European dominance inevitably led to the displacement or destruction of backward peoples or "unfit" races; this view made imperialism, war, and aggression seem both natural and progressive.

socialism in the United States: Fairly minor political movement in the United States; at its height in 1912, it gained 6 percent of the vote for its presidential candidate.

"soft gold": Nickname used in the early modern period for animal furs, highly valued for their warmth and as symbols of elite status.

Songhay Empire: Major Islamic state of West Africa that formed in the second half of the fifteenth century. (pron. song-GAH-ee)

Stalin, Joseph (1878–1953): Leader of the Soviet Union from the late 1920s until his death.

Stanton, Elizabeth Cady (1815–1902): Leading figure of the early women's rights movement in the United States. At the first Women's Rights Convention in Seneca Falls, New York, in 1848, she drafted a statement paraphrasing the Declaration of Independence, stating that men and women were created equal.

steam engine: The great breakthrough of the Industrial Revolution, the coal-fired steam engine provided an almost limitless source of power and could be used to drive any number of machines as well as locomotives and ships; the introduction of the steam engine allowed a hitherto unimagined increase in productivity and made the Industrial Revolution possible.

Syrian civil war: Conflict beginning in 2011 that generated over 12 million refugees and asylum seekers by mid-2016 and engaged both regional and world powers on various sides of the conflict.

Taiping Uprising: Massive Chinese rebellion against the ruling Qing dynasty that devastated much of the country between 1850 and 1864; it was based on the millenarian teachings of Hong Xiuquan.

Taki Onqoy: Literally, "dancing sickness"; a religious revival movement in central Peru in the 1560s whose members preached the imminent destruction of Christianity and of the Europeans and the restoration of an imagined Andean golden age.

Tanzimat: Important reform measures undertaken in the Ottoman Empire beginning in 1839; the term "Tanzimat" means "reorganization." (pron. tahn-zee-MAHT)

Thirty Years' War: Catholic-Protestant struggle (1618–1648) that was the culmination of European religious conflict, brought to an end by the Peace of Westphalia and an agreement that each state was sovereign, authorized to control religious affairs within its own territory.

Timbuktu: A major commercial city of West African civilization and a noted center of Islamic scholarship and education by the sixteenth century.

Timur: Turkic warrior, also known as Tamerlane, whose efforts to restore the Mongol Empire in the late fourteenth and early fifteenth centuries devastated parts of Persia, Russia, and India. His successors created a vibrant elite culture drawing on both Turkic and Persian elements, especially in the city of Samarkand. Timur's conquests represent the last major military success of Central Asian pastoral peoples.

Tokugawa Japan: A period of internal peace in Japan (1600–1850) that prevented civil war but did not fully unify the country; led by military rulers, or shoguns, from the Tokugawa family, who established a "closed door" policy toward European encroachments.

total war: War that requires each country involved to mobilize its entire population in the effort to defeat the enemy.

trading post empire: Form of imperial dominance based on control of trade through military power rather than on control of peoples or territories.

transatlantic slave system: Between 1500 and 1866, this trade in human beings took an estimated 12.5 million people from African societies, shipped them across the Atlantic in the Middle Passage, and deposited some 10.7 million of them in the Americas as slaves; approximately 1.8 million died during the transatlantic crossing.

transnational corporations: Global businesses that produce goods or deliver services simultaneously in many countries; growing in number since the 1960s, some have more assets and power than many countries.

Treaty of Versailles: The 1919 treaty that officially ended World War I; the immense penalties it placed on Germany are regarded as one of the causes of World War II.

Tupac Amaru: Leader of a Native American rebellion in Peru in the early 1780s, claiming the last Inca emperor as an ancestor.

unequal treaties: Series of nineteenth-century treaties in which China made major concessions to Western powers.

Vindication of the Rights of Woman: Written by Mary Wollstonecraft, this tract was one of the earliest expressions of feminist consciousness.

Vivekananda (1863–1902): Leading religious figure of nineteenth-century India; advocate of a revived Hinduism and its mission to reach out to the spiritually impoverished West.

Voltaire: The pen name of François-Marie Arouet (1694–1778), a French writer whose work is often taken as a model of the Enlightenment's outlook; noted for his deism and his criticism of traditional religion.

Wahhabi Islam: Major Islamic movement led by the Muslim theologian Muhammad Ibn Abd al-Wahhab (1703–1792) that advocated an austere lifestyle and strict adherence to the Islamic law; became an expansive state in central Arabia.

Wang Yangming: Influential Ming thinker (1472–1529) who argued that anyone could achieve a virtuous life by introspection and contemplation, without the extended education and study of traditional Confucianism.

Warsaw Pact: A military alliance between the Soviet Union and communist states in Eastern Europe, created in 1955 as a counterweight to NATO; expressed the tensions of the cold war in Europe.

Women's Department: A distinctive organization, known as Zhenotdel, within the Communist Party of the Soviet Union that worked to promote equality for women in the 1920s with conferences, publications, and education.

World Trade Organization (WTO): An international body representing 149 nations and charged with negotiating the rules for global commerce and promoting free trade; its meetings have been the site of major anti-globalization protests since 1999.

World War I: The "Great War" (1914–1918), in essence a European civil war with a global reach that was marked by massive casualties, trench warfare, and mobilization of entire populations. It triggered the Russian Revolution, led to widespread disillusionment among intellectuals, and rearranged the political map of Eastern Europe and the Middle East.

World War II in Asia: A struggle to halt Japanese imperial expansion in Asia, fought by the Japanese against primarily Chinese and American foes.

World War II in Europe: A struggle to halt German imperial expansion in Europe, fought by a coalition of allies that included Great Britain, the Soviet Union, and the United States.

yasak: Tribute that Russian rulers demanded from the native peoples of Siberia, most often in the form of furs.

Young Ottomans: Group of would-be reformers in the mid-nineteenth-century Ottoman Empire that included lower-level officials, military officers, and writers; they urged the extension of westernizing reforms to the political system.

Young Turks: Movement of Turkish military and civilian elites that advocated a militantly secular public life and a Turkish national identity; came to power through a coup in 1908.

Zheng He: Great Chinese admiral who commanded a huge fleet of ships in a series of voyages in the Indian Ocean that began in 1405. Intended to enroll distant peoples and states in the Chinese tribute system, those voyages ended abruptly in 1433 and led to no lasting Chinese imperial presence in the region. (pron. JUHNG-huh)

About the Authors

Jerry Burke

Robert W. Strayer (Ph.D., University of Wisconsin) brings wide experience in world history to the writing of *Ways of the World*. His teaching career began in Ethiopia, where he taught high school world history for two years as part of the Peace Corps. At the university level, he taught African, Soviet, and world history for many years at the College at Brockport: State University of New York, where he received the Chancellor's Awards for Excellence in Teaching and Excellence in Scholarship. In 1998 he was visiting professor of world and Soviet history at the University of Canterbury in Christchurch, New Zealand. Since moving to California in 2002, he has taught world history at the University of California, Santa Cruz; California State University, Monterey Bay; and Cabrillo College. He is a longtime member of the World History Association and served on its Executive Committee. He has also participated in various AP World History gatherings, including two years as a reader. His publications include *Kenya: Focus on Nationalism, The Making of Mission Communities in East Africa, The Making of the Modern World, Why Did the Soviet Union Collapse?,* and *The Communist Experiment*.

Jesse Scheve/Missouri State University

Eric W. Nelson (D.Phil., Oxford University) is a professor of history at Missouri State University. He is an experienced teacher who has won a number of awards, including the Missouri Governor's Award for Teaching Excellence in 2011 and the CASE and Carnegie Foundation for the Advancement of Teaching Professor of the Year Award for Missouri in 2012. His publications include *Layered Landscapes: Early Modern Religious Space across Faith and Cultures, The Legacy of Iconoclasm: Religious War and the Relic Landscape of Tours, Blois and Vendôme,* and *The Jesuits and the Monarchy: Catholic Reform and Political Authority in France*.